Care and Pandemic

Studies in Critical Social Sciences

VOLUME 291

The titles published in this series are listed at *brill.com/scss*

Care and Pandemic

A Transnational Perspective

Edited by

Nadya Araujo Guimarães
Heidi Gottfried
Helena Hirata
Javier A. Pineda D.

BRILL

LEIDEN | BOSTON

Cover illustration: "Caring" © Mustafa Hacalaki. Used with kind permission.

Library of Congress Cataloging-in-Publication Data

Names: Guimarães, Nadya Araujo, editor.
Title: Care and pandemic : a transnational perspective / edited by Nadya Araújo Guimarães, Heidi Gottfried, Helena Hirata, Javier A. Pineda D.
Description: Leiden ; Boston : Brill, [2025] | Series: Studies in critical social sciences, 1573-4234 ; volume 291 | Includes bibliographical references and index.
Identifiers: LCCN 2024026305 (print) | LCCN 2024026306 (ebook) | ISBN 9789004706996 (hardback ; alk. paper) | ISBN 9789004707009 (ebook)
Subjects: LCSH: Caregivers–Economic conditions. | Home care services. | Medical personnel. | Household employees. | Child care services. | COVID-19 Pandemic, 2020–Economic aspects.
Classification: LCC RA645.3 .C363 2025 (print) | LCC RA645.3 (ebook) | DDC 362.14–dc23/eng/20240731
LC record available at https://lccn.loc.gov/2024026305
LC ebook record available at https://lccn.loc.gov/2024026306

Typeface for the Latin, Greek, and Cyrillic scripts: "Brill". See and download: brill.com/brill-typeface.

ISSN 1573-4234
ISBN 978-90-04-70699-6 (hardback)
ISBN 978-90-04-70700-9 (e-book)
DOI 10.1163/9789004707009

For more information: info@brill.com

This book is printed on acid-free paper and produced in a sustainable manner.

Contents

Acknowledgements

This book is the result of an enormous collaborative effort across the international project *Who cares? Rebuilding care in a post-pandemic world.* This project, which arises from the call Recovering, Renewal and Resilience in a post-pandemic World (RRR) of the Transatlantic platform (T-AP), includes six countries and has allowed us to carry out the research presented in this book. Team members from four of the six countries participate in this book (Brazil, Colombia, France and USA). The research reported in these chapters is financed by the national partners of this international project, which we want to recognize: in Brazil, the *Fundação de Amparo à Pesquisa do Estado de São Paulo* (FAPESP), Grant 2021/07.888–3; the *Conselho Nacional de Desenvolvimento Científico e Tecnológico* (CNPq), Grant No. 421754/2021-4; and the Arymax Foundation; in Colombia, the *Fondo Nacional Financiamiento para la Ciencia, la Tecnología y la Innovación*, Francisco José de Caldas, Minciencias; in France, *Agence Nationale de la Recherche* (ANR); and, in USA, National Science Foundation (NSF) under Grant no. 2215780.

We also want to acknowledge the contribution of the external academic peer reviewers of each of the chapters, as follows: Bila Sorj, Lorena Poblete, Marcelo Medeiros, Maria Elena Valenzuela, Mignon Duffy, Miriam Wlosko, Monique Meron, Natacha Borgeaud Garciandia, and Rafael Grohmann. We thank all of them for providing concepts, which allowed us to substantially improve the manuscript.

Likewise, we would like to thank the following people for the professional work of data processing, the translation into English and the style correction of most of the texts: Paulo Henrique da Silva (data processing) in Chapter 2; Paulo Scarpa (translation into English) in Chapters 2 and 6; Sofía Rodríguez Nieto (data processing), María Camila Roldán Bernal (translation into English) and Cherie Pyne (style correction), in Chapter 4; Bárbara Castro (data processing), Kirsten Manson and Enterprise Essential Plus (style correction), in the Chapter 10; Dominic Higgins (style correction), in Chapters 8 and 9; Gabriela Alkmin (translation into English) in Chapter 11. We thank Jill Herring for her extensive copy-editing of all the chapters from Brazil and France: 2, 3, 6, 11 and 12 from Brazil, and 5, 7 and 10 from France.

Finally, we have a special thanks to: Cresppa/CNRS in Paris and especially to Helena Hirata and Aurélie Damamme for coordinating the event that led to the preparation and initial discussion of all the chapters found here; the universities to which we belong and to the entities and people that provided support to fund management and gave us the working conditions for the development of this research, especially Cebrap in Brazil; and Trans-Atlantic Platform consortium for its support for specialized research in the Humanities and Social Sciences, and for the sensitivity of a call about the impact of the pandemic at the time when we were still experiencing it in 2021.

Illustrations

Tables

Figures

Graphs

Annexes

Notes on Contributors

Gabriela Alkmin
is a PhD candidate in Law at Universidade Federal de Minas Gerais. She holds an LL.M. in Philosophy of Law and a Bachelor of Laws, both from Universidade Federal de Minas Gerais. She is a co-coordinator of Diverso UFMG – Legal Center of Sexual and Gender Diversity. Her research interests include: Gender Contentious Politics; Sexual and Reproductive Rights; Juridification and Democracy; Strategic Litigation and Supreme Courts.

Mariana Eugenio Almeida
is a PhD Candidate at the Department of Demography, Center for Regional Development and Planning (Cedeplar), Federal University of Minas Gerais (UFMG), Brazil. She is also a Social Policy Analyst at the Ministry of Labor and Employment, Brazil. Her main research interests include labor market, gender and race inequalities, care work and social policy.

Ana Carolina Andrada
holds a PhD in Sociology from the University of São Paulo in 2022. She is an associated researcher at the Brazilian Center of Analysis and Planning (Cebrap) and the Care, Rights and Inequalities Network (Rede CuiDDe – Cuidados, Direitos e Desigualdades). Among her research interests are the different types of matching processes, including those taking place in the labor market.

Eileen Boris
is Hull Professor and Distinguished Professor of Feminist Studies and Distinguished Professor of History, Black Studies and Global Studies, University of California, Santa Barbara. Advisory Board, UCSB Community Labor Project. President/President elect, Labor and Working Class History Association (LAWCHA), member of Health and Safety Committee of Hand-in-Hand, part of the California Domestic Worker Coalition, contributing editorial board member of *Women's History Review*, *Labor: Studies in Working Class History*, and *International Review of Social History*.

Ana Claudia Moreira Cardoso
holds a PhD in Sociology from the University of São Paulo and University of Paris 8 and post-doctorate from the Center de Recherche Sociologique et Politique de Paris – CRESPPA. She is a consultant at the National School of Public Health / Fiocruz and the Ministry of Women.

Suelen Castiblanco-Moreno
obtained a PhD in Interdisciplinary Studies on Development from Universidad de Los Andes, Colombia. Associate professor at the Faculty of Economics, Enterprises and Sustainable Development (FEEDS) at University of La Salle (Colombia). Associate researcher registered at the Colombian Ministry of Science, Technology and Innovation in topics related to women, labor and empowerment.

Daniella Castro-Barbudo
is a sociologist from Pontificia Universidad Javeriana (PUJ), Bogotá, Colombia. Master's program in Demography and Population Studies at the Universidad de La República (UdeLaR), Montevideo, Uruguay. Professor and researcher focused on health, women and quality of life studies, socio-demographic data analysis, social inequalities and feminist/ differential perspectives.

Aurélie Damamme
is a Lecturer in Sociology at the Université Paris 8 Vincennes-Saint-Denis, and a member of the CRESPPA-GTM laboratory. Her research focuses on domestic care work, the articulation between care theories and critical disability studies, and housing and disability issues from an intersectional perspective.

Guita Grin Debert
is a Full PhD Professor, Department of Anthropology, Institute of Philosophy and Human Sciences, Universidade Estadual de Campinas (UNICAMP) (State University of Campinas). Researcher at the Pagu Center for Gender Studies at UNICAMP, the Conselho Nacional de Desenvolvimento Científico e Tecnológico (CNPq) (National Council for Scientific and Technological Development) and the Fundação de Amparo à Pesquisa do Estado de São Paulo (FAPESP) (São Paulo Research Foundation). Research interests: aging, gender, care.

Jorge Felix
is Professor, Economy and Finance in Gerontology, School of Arts, Science and Humanities (EACH), Universidade de São Paulo (USP) (University of São Paulo). Researcher at the Pagu Center for Gender Studies at UNICAMP with sholarship by Fundação de Amparo à Pesquisa do Estado de São Paulo (FAPESP) (São Paulo Research Foundation). Research interests: aging population, public policies, silver economy, care economy.

Heidi Gottfried
is Associate Professor, Department of Sociology, Wayne State University, USA. PhD, 1987, University of Wisconsin-Madison, USA. Her recent publications include: *Global Labor Migration: New Directions* (University of Illinois Press, 2023) (with Eileen Boris, Julie Greene and Joo-Cheong Tham); *Care Work in Transition: Transnational Circuits of Gender, Migration and Care*, a special issue of *Critical Sociology* (with Jennifer Jihye Chun); *Gender, Work and Economy: Unpacking the Global Economy* (Polity Press, 2013) and *The Reproductive Bargain: Deciphering the Enigma of Japanese Capitalism* (Brill, 2015).

Nadya Araujo Guimarães
is Senior Professor at the University of São Paulo Department of Sociology, Researcher at CEBRAP (Brazilian Center of Analysis and Planning), and a regular member of the Brazilian Academy of Sciences. She received her Master's degree at the University of Brasilia (1974), her PhD at the Universidad Nacional Autónoma de México (1983) and did post-doctoral studies at the Massachusetts Institute of Technology (MIT) Special Program on Urban and Regional Studies for Developing Areas (1993–1994). She has been researching the Brazilian labor market focusing on economic change, unemployment and workers trajectories; labor market intermediaries; gender/race inequalities; care and care workers.

Amparo Hernández-Bello
holds a PhD in public health. Professor at the Institute of Public Health of the Pontificia Universidad Javeriana, Colombia. Activist for the right to health. Co-coordinator of the Care and Gender Working Group of Clacso. Member of the External Advisory Council of the National Care System. Research and teaching career on topics such as equity and social justice in health, social determinants of health and health, gender and care.

Helena Hirata
is Research Director Emerita at CNRS (National Center for Scientific Research), France and Associate Professor at the Sociology Department, University of Sao Paulo, Brazil. She is also a member of the editorial board of Cahiers du Genre, member of the Direction of the international and interdisciplinary network MAGE (Gender and Labour Market), and a member of the French team of the project *Who cares? Rebuilding care in a post-pandemic world*, from the Trans-Atlantic Platform.

Léa Lima
is Full Professor of Sociology at the Conservatoire national des arts et métiers and Researcher at the Laboratoire interdisciplinaire pour la sociologie économique and the Centre d'études de l'emploi et du travail. She has worked extensively on labor market intermediaries, both in Brazil and France, from a historical and sociological perspective that combines economic sociology and the sociology of work.

Pascale Molinier
is Professor of Social Psychology at Sorbonne Paris Nord University. Her research focuses on the relationship between work and the ethics of care, feminist epistemology, gender and sexuality. She is the author of numerous books and articles, including: Le travail du care, 2022 La Dispute, Le care monde, 2018, ENS Lyon, Les enjeux psychiques du travail, 2006, Payot.

Carolina Moreno
is a Lawyer and holds a PhD in Law from Los Andes University and Magister in Public Law from Universitat Pompeu Fabra. Currently, she is an Associate Professor and Head of Research at Los Andes University Law Faculty (Bogotá, Colombia). She is the Director of the Centre for Migration Studies and co-founder of the Legal Clinic for Migrants.

Renata Moreno
obtained a PhD in Sociology from the University of São Paulo in 2019. Associated researcher to the Care, Rights and Inequalities Network (Rede CuiDDe – Cuidados, Direitos e Desigualdades). Among her research interests are care, digital economy and feminist economics.

Pedro Augusto Gravatá Nicoli
holds a PhD in Law from the Universidade Federal de Minas Gerais (UFMG). Professor at the Faculty of Law of the Universidade Federal de Minas Gerais (UFMG). Visiting professor at the Gender, Sexuality and Feminist Studies department at Duke University, in the United States (2019–2020). Co-coordinator of Diverso UFMG – Legal Center of Sexual and Gender Diversity.

Maria Júlia Tavares Pereira
holds a Master in Social Sciences from Federal University of Juiz de Fora (UFJF) and is a Sociology PhD student at Universidade Estadual de Campinas (Unicamp). She develops research in the field of platformization of labor from a gendered standpoint, focusing on the experiences of women in platform

work and also on how platforms affect occupations typically undertaken by women in the labor market.

Javier A. Pineda D.
obtained his PhD from Durham University, UK. He is a full-time Associate Professor at the Interdisciplinary Center of Development Studies –CIDER, Universidad de los Andes. He currently is the Colombian IP for the project *Who cares? Rebuilding care in a post-pandemic world*, from the Trans-Atlantic Platform. Recent publications include: *La sociedad del cuidado y políticas de la vida* (Clacso, 2024) (with Karina Batthyány and Valentina Perrotta).

Luana Simões Pinheiro
holds a PhD in Sociology from the University of Brasilia, Brazil. She has been working as a planning and research specialist at the Institute for Applied Economic Research since 2004, where she conducted research on gender, race and inequality. She worked at the National Secretariat for Women's Policies, at the Presidency of Brazil between 2007 and 2011, and is currently heading the Department for Care Economy, at the Ministry of Development and Social Assistance, Family and Fight Against Hunger.

Jeanny Posso
holds a PhD in social anthropology from Universidad Autónoma de Madrid, Spain and is a Full-time professor at the Faculty of Social Sciences and Economics, Universidad del Valle. Researcher at the Social and Economics Sciences Research and Documentation Center, CIDSE. She currently is Coordinator of the Comprehensive Care Area for Violence and Discrimination based on Gender at de Universidad del Valle.

Marcelo Maciel Ramos
obtained a PhD in Law from the Universidade Federal de Minas Gerais (UFMG). Professor at the Faculty of Law of the Universidade Federal de Minas Gerais (UFMG). Visiting professor at the Gender, Sexuality and Feminist Studies department at Duke University, in the United States (2019–2020). Co-coordinator of Diverso UFMG – Legal Center of Sexual and Gender Diversity.

Michelle Redondo
is a post-doctoral student at the Centre de recherches sociologiques et politiques de Paris – Cresppa; member of the French team of the international project "Rebuilding Care in a post-pandemic world". PhD in Political Science from the Université Paris 8 Saint-Denis, France and in Social Sciences from the

State University of Campinas, Brazil. She has been studying care issues since her master's degree, also in these two countries, and has carried out qualitative research into the working conditions of care workers and how technology has changed labour relations in this field.

Maria Camila Vega-Salazar
is a Lawyer from Universidad Externado de Colombia and graduate student in Gender and Interdisciplinary Development Studies at the Interdisciplinary Center for Development Studies – CIDER, Universidad de los Andes.

Simone Wajnman
is a Professor and researcher at CEDEPLAR, Federal University of Minas Gerais (UFMG). PhD in Demography from CEDEPLAR/UFMG and completed a postdoctoral fellowship at the Office of Population Research at Princeton University. Her main research interests include family demography, economic demography, formal analysis of demographic dynamics and, more recently, care demography.

CHAPTER 1

Care and Pandemic: a Transnational Perspective

Heidi Gottfried and Eileen Boris

Care and Pandemic[1] captures an up-to-the-moment account of COVID-19 and its aftermath by scholars reporting from countries on both sides of the Atlantic. Like an emergency response team, the editors brought together experts in the field equipped to diagnose the problem and to advance an agenda for excavating the root causes of the devaluation of care and the underinvestment of the care infrastructure. Even before the pandemic swept across the world, the ILO's 2018 (ILO 2018) landmark publication sounded "an alarm" that current care systems would crack under the burdens of care and the growing care deficits unless nations took bold action (Duffy et al. 2023: 1). Then, the pandemic quickly spread globally, exacerbating a care crisis that became nearly catastrophic. Care systems were put to the test and were found woefully ill-equipped to respond.

In the wake of the crisis unleashed by COVID-19, a clearer picture of the underlying fault-lines of inequality emerges against the background of old fissures. The pandemic cleared the way for seeing social ruptures and economic dislocations that were already part of care systems. COVID-19 put in sharp relief the acute vulnerabilities among an already precarious workforce, particularly among the growing number of migrant workers and paid caregivers from poor, racialized communities. Disruptions due to COVID made visible the web of social relationships of care, exposed gaping holes in the infrastructure to protect older people and to deliver quality care, revealed the vulnerabilities of poor care recipients and paid caregivers, and uncovered systemic race, gender, sexual orientation, age, origin, and class disparities. Yet, insufficient attention to and lack of knowledge about the social infrastructure of care hampered countries' efforts to flatten the curve on virus transmission and to limit fatalities. As Burawoy has argued, "Institutions reveal much about themselves

1 This chapter is based on work supported by the National Science Foundation under Grant no. 2215780. Any opinions, findings, and conclusions or recommendations expressed in this material are those of the authors and do not necessarily reflect the views of the National Science Foundation. Special thanks to Ruth Milkman, Penelope Ciancanelli, and David Fasenfest whose comments are seamlessly woven into the fabric of this piece.

 | DOI:10.1163/9789004707009_002

under stress or in crisis, when they face the unexpected as well as the routine" (cited in Nathanson and Fairchild 2020). COVID was no exception.

This book presents findings from a larger, three-year collaborative project answering the call for proposals on Recovery, Renewal and Resilience in a Post Pandemic World, funded by the Transatlantic Platform (T-AP). The T-AP funded project, "Who Cares? Rebuilding Care in a Post-Pandemic World," was a unique opportunity to leverage expertise among an interdisciplinary network of scholars specializing in labor, health, and care from six countries transregionally: Latin America (Brazil and Colombia), North America (Canada and the US) and Europe (France and the UK) each with differing welfare regimes, level of inequalities, social organization of care, and health systems. It represents one of the few international collaborations designed around a common research agenda to study the care economy that utilizes in-depth case studies of care work in such a diverse constellation of countries across the global North and South, including private-public residual welfare states, skeletal public sectors, and state centered medical and social assistance regimes. The transnational, interdisciplinary and multi-method perspective adopted in this T-AP project decenter analyses based on developed countries that do not necessarily fit the realities of care systems in less developed countries with poorly structured formal labor markets for professionalized care services and welfare state regimes (Guimarães and Hirata 2021; Pineda 2021). A multi-scalar analytic shaped the agenda from the outset. By including countries from each of three transatlantic regions, the assemblage of country teams could analyze the unfolding care crisis and its aftermath both within countries and along a North/South axis and can help explain why countries in the same region and municipalities in the same country responded differently.

At the heart of this collection is a kind of "social autopsy," borrowing a phrase from Klinenberg (2024: 17), that uses the lens of the pandemic to uncover why care systems proved so inadequate for mitigating the contagion and why some countries fared better than others in bending the curve of infection and disruption. Each chapter highlights the complex processes that influence the social organization of care and the diverse set of actors and institutions in both devaluing and revaluing care as socially necessary for and integral to everyday life under capitalism. Case studies in this book sharpen our understanding of specific contexts and the meaning-making processes attached to care work. The book presents five main themes: (i) the conceptualization of paid care work and modalities of care provision to capture the socio-demographic dynamics of care labor markets; (ii) the importance of this conceptualization for gauging the impact of COVID-19 on care workers' employment and working conditions; (iii) the changing presence and consequences of online care platforms as matching mechanisms in the labor market; (iv) the resultant working conditions, experiences, and meanings of care and caring; and (v) the identification of caring strategies when the state fails, focusing instead on the different forms of community solidarity, and on emerging civil society associations and collective organizations, by identifying the largely invisible social practices of actors who have contributed to the daily provision of care. The following contributions examine care work across diverse national contexts and their implications for understanding new geometries of inequality.

1 Conceptualizing and Measuring Care

Paid care is amongst the fastest growing economic sectors, as commodification, financialization, and marketization increasingly extend to all dimensions of care and domestic work (Farris 2020; Himmelweit 2022; Dowling 2021; Fraser 2023; Gottfried 2023). The rise of paid care services has contributed to the transformation of the labor market in developed (Duffy 2020; Duffy and Armenia 2019) and developing countries alike (Guimarães 2021; Pineda 2021). Most research on care relies on existing data sources derived from national or international statistical and occupational categories that may be incommensurate and hampered by normative biases. This section on conceptualizing and measuring care lays out a shared vocabulary for understanding socio-demographic dynamics of care labor markets and a refined methodology for measuring the impact of the pandemic on types of care.

Broad categories of the service sector elide the specificity of care work as a social relation embodying affective, emotional, relational as well as physical labor activities (Gottfried 2013; Boris and Parrenas 2010, 1–12; Folbre et al. 2023; Soares 2012). Yet, as a social activity, care work tends to go unnoticed and become naturalized and inseparable from the person producing it. In general, tacit knowledge in care work, including emotional and affective competencies, remains invisible, unacknowledged, and devalued though critical to the care encounter (Gottfried 2022). Care – broadly understood as activities that contribute to human flourishing and public health – takes many forms. It can be organized by the family, the community, the state, or the market, and can occur in the household and/or in specialized institutions like hospitals, nursing homes, or day care centers (Anderson and Shutes 2014). Paid caring labor encompasses a wide spectrum of occupations from childcare, home health aides, personal care assistants, cooks, cleaners, nurses, doctors, teachers, and others (Folbre et al. 2023; England et al. 2002). Notably, waged forms of reproductive labor responsible for maintaining households and caring for dependents is devalued as unskilled, feminized, and servile from its associations with unpaid labor of wives, mothers, and unfree persons (Boris and Parrenas 2010).

Paid domestic work, as an occupational category, generally stands apart from other kinds of work for being ambiguously defined and often ignored in law and social policy—when not explicitly excluded from rights, rewards, and entitlements. Legacies of disparate treatment rooted in histories of domestic servitude inform the construction of operational definitions found in labor codes, legislation, national classification systems, and international datasets. The home location has emerged as a barrier to regulation of jobs located in spaces considered intimate, private, or familial, while emotional, bodily, and affective capacities and tacit skills have become seemingly unmeasurable and invisibilized as labor (Gottfried and Chun 2018). Definitions of care work were never "natural," but rather a product of struggle among employers and workers, governments, and scholars over naming and the very allocation of resources for reproductive labor and its regulation (Boris and Klein 2012).

The development of a robust conceptualization hinges on defining key dimensions of care that can encompass the complexity of social relations in care labor markets (Milkman 2023a), when arrayed together. A conceptual mapping is needed for measuring the heterogeneity and the occupational and status hierarchies across the care economy. Nadya Guimarães and Luana Pinheiro (in this volume) develop an innovative methodology to harmonize sociodemographic and administrative data on forms of care work. Their pioneering approach distinguishes between types of care according to three cross-cutting social dimensions: a) context, either domestic or non-domestic, b) nature of the interaction between the caregivers and beneficiaries, either direct or indirect, and c) recurrence of the relationship. In the resulting typology of a "halo," the institutional context of the domestic sphere marks a boundary condition determining a "nucleus" of care work. They postulate that caregiving is more intensive when care work is performed in direct, recurring interactions, within a home environment imbued by interpersonal and intimate relationships. Further differentiation within and across the circles of the halo denotes the extent to which society relies on different types of care work, which makes more visible the paid labor of social reproduction.

2 COVID Impacts on Domestic Workers' Employment

The pandemic heightened economic precarity and poverty rates, intensifying labor exploitation of domestic workers. In Latin America, domestic workers experienced an unprecedented wave of unemployment, while those who remained employed worked double shifts without financial compensation and/or were quarantined at their employers' homes against their will (Acciari et al. 2021; Posso and Pineda in this volume). Domestic workers provided essential services to households – though often they were not celebrated among health care workers deemed "essential" by governments and the media (Stevano and Jamieson 2021: 184). These domestic workers, however, were at high risk of experiencing reduction of working hours, losing their jobs as a result of their informal status and lack of employment protection, and sometimes as a consequence of strict confinement measures or travel bans (Acciari et al. 2021). COVID increased demand for tasks because of intensified cleaning and hygiene routines, emotional labor, and food preparation in private homes. Restrictions on mobility and intermingling of households left many in-home care workers as the primary point of emotional and physical contact for clients.

Domestic workers were the hardest hit yet the least protected. In the first phase of the pandemic, employment among domestic workers steeply declined, and hours were decreased, but the pattern spread unevenly across countries. Between the fourth quarter of 2019 and the second quarter of 2020, Brazil's domestic workforce saw a 26.6 decline as compared to a 12.3% decline for non-domestic workers. During the same period, the number of domestic workers leaving the labor market dramatically decreased by 50.6% as compared to 22.2% of the non-domestic workforce in Colombia (ILO, 2021, 233).[2] France saw a significant but less precipitous decline in domestic workers' job loss: Eurostat estimates that 16% in France domestic workers lost employment between Q2 2019 and Q2 2020 (Marchetti and Jokela, cited in Roskinka 2021a, b).

The impact of COVID-19 on care workers' lives and livelihoods comes into sharper focus through a temporal lens. Measuring workers' movement into and out of the labor market has been hampered by normative biases and static representations of labor market statuses. Mariana Almeida and Simone Wajnman (in this volume) problematize the notion of economic (in) activity. Using the halo to categorize care occupations and sectors, Almeida

2 In 2019, 40.1% of Colombian women working in the care sector were employed as informal employees, compared to 8% of men. The paid care sector accounted for 30% of women's total employment (2.8 million) and 6% of men's (776,000) in Colombia in 2019, just before the pandemic. By 2020, the overall care sector had the most significant absolute decrease in women's employment compared to the previous year, with 554,000 fewer jobs, which represents 39% of the total drop in female employment in Colombia (Pineda 2022; see Orozco et al. 2022; ILO 2020).

and Wajnman pinpoint the severity of the pandemic for each occupational grouping. Inactivity statistics reported over the course of the pandemic likely misrepresented the actual exodus of informal in-home workers from the paid labor force. Some informal workers who appeared to exit from the labor market had taken on unreported, intermittent work (Guimarães et al. 2023).

Data from Brazil and Colombia suggest that fluidity between statuses may be more widespread in less regulated markets where informal labor relations prevail when combined with weak unemployment protection (Almeida and Wajnman; and Hernandez-Bello et al. in this volume). France offers a glimpse into the lower volatility among care workers who had access to job retention benefits during the lockdown, though fragmented policies left some of the most vulnerable, precarious workers without adequate protection (Eydoux 2023; Damamme et al. in this volume). The impacts noted in these case studies are contingent on prior characteristics, in particular the combined result of labor market structure (such as the size of the informal market) and social protection systems in place prior to the crisis.

3 Intermediation, Labor Markets and Care Platforms

The pandemic demonstrated the importance of public infrastructure, and yet care provisioning and social reproduction returned to the home, intensifying the burdens on both paid and unpaid caregivers (Mezzadri 2022). Already under way, but hastened during the pandemic, a reorganization of care was resituating the household as a central arena of wage labor and as a hub in the broader care economy, increasingly through digital platforms managed by on-line labor market intermediaries (Ticona 2022), but also through political reforms refamilializing care. Private for-profit companies have seized digital tools to develop personal service platforms: some platforms resemble traditional labor market intermediaries serving as the employer of care workers, responsible for wages and working conditions (including paying into the social security system), while others such as Care.com function as an online matching service or job board. From the employer's perspective, the platform offers a search engine to find care workers. Despite increasing platformization of reproductive labor, these sites have received less attention than Uber, even though a larger number of workers used Care.com (5.3 million) as compared to 160,000 Uber drivers in the US (Ticona and Mateescu 2018: 4400). Both Uber and care work platforms are part of the larger shift to a new form of governance over economic transactions (Vallas and Schor 2020: 282). Ride-hailing, in contrast to most care work, does not rely on continuity of service or performance of intimate labor, which is neither expected nor central to their interactive service encounter even if drivers facilitate social reproduction through transport activities (Hua and Ray 2021).

Comparative case studies of labor market intermediaries in Brazil, Colombia, and France ground analysis in the histories of specific places, dislodging theories from their moorings anchored in the global North (see Ness 2023). They contrast with the overview of the literature by Vallas and Schor (2020) whose typology of platform workers and work fails to consider the uneven effects within and across world regions, and which inadequately theorizes the relationship between global, local, and sectoral forces. Their tight focus on platforms as a distinctive form of economic activity differing from the logic of traditional economic sectors and corporations magnifies only one side of digital intermediaries' economic activities: that of capturing markets. This focus leaves out the other side of market-making and market shaping by platforms and by the state. Recentering the analytic on the care sector in different national contexts highlights the state's active role in privatizing previously socialized care provision, including through platforms, thereby creating what Apitzsch and Shire (2021) call a "welfare" market for personal services. Care platforms themselves have engaged in the alchemical transformation of labor into a marketable commodity. To their point, platforms can and do influence their institutional environment (Vallas and Schor 2020: 281), but we must also account for the impact of specific institutional frameworks on forms of care platforms and their outcomes.

A wider survey of countries in the global South also points to the platform model developing along different temporalities (Pun et al. 2022; Ness 2023). Thus, even under similar levels of care commodification, countries such as Brazil and Colombia vary significantly on the relevance of intermediation platforms operating in the care labor market. In Brazil their presence is visible, and platforms are increasingly used as matching mechanisms as the internationalization of intermediation markets grows, while a smaller sector of care platforms operate in Colombia. Different modalities of intermediation also come to light when examining the landscape of care platforms in countries across the global North and South. These country-specific case studies show how the institutional framework produces specific forms of care work platforms.[3]

Lea Lima (in this volume) foregrounds the French state as a central actor engaging in both market making and market shaping of care provision. More

3 Worker coops can improve the conditions for lower "wage workers in occupations such as care work where agencies capture rents for reputation assurances" (Vallas and Schor 2020: 287).

generally, European countries have adopted regulatory reforms fueling marketization and resulting in re-familialization of care through a neoliberal toolbox of state-based tax codes and social security reforms that encourage households to purchase private in-home personal services (ILO 2021: 10; van Hooren 2018: 98; Ledoux et al. 2021: 40; Hobson et al. 2015; Jany-Catrice 2015). French public policy in the home care sector favors and encourages salaried employment, whether directly (through an employment contract binding the employee to the individual employer) or indirectly (the employment contract signed between the organization providing the labor and the employee working in the home), as indicated by Lima. Industrial as well as social policies uniquely steer the French organization of platformization in keeping with the nation's history of trying to create winning companies. Platforms developed as part of the fostering of a "French" tech sector – privileging French firms' market share and crowding out foreign multinational companies like Care.com. State provided monetary transfers, thus, subsidize the outsourcing of care and domestic services to private-for-profit care providers (see Farris 2020: 4).[4]

Privatized solutions to the care crisis include digital intermediaries earning profits by paying low wages and offering precarious work. Care platforms extract "rents" from both workers and customers, lack transparency in part due to algorithmic labor control, and are based on asymmetry between employers and workers using these sites. Ana Andrada, Nadya Guimarães, and Renata Moreno (in this volume) mined new data sources (online complaints) in combination with worker interviews to understand how management disciplined workers during the pandemic in Brazil. Platforms foster new labor regimes enlisting customers in labor control. Clients rate workers using Olympic-type medals from bronze to gold. These customer ratings enter the calculus of employers' choices and function as disciplinary practices in the absence of direct management by the platform intermediary (see Gottfried, 1991). Workers strive for a good rating, building a portfolio of job performance and reputational capital, that customers use when faced with multiple choices searching for service providers on a platform. Many care workers, like prototypical gig workers, assume responsibility for operating costs (cleaners may bring their own equipment), bear risks and conform to the temporal rhythms of customer demand which can reduce autonomy and heightened uncertainty

4 In Belgium, by contrast to France, vouchers are sold at a discounted price, and participating households receive an income tax deduction. The Belgian service voucher scheme, with its considerable wage and matching subsidies reduced informal employment in the activities covered by the scheme, so that by 2015 the voucher scheme employed 153,301 workers (Adriaenssens et al. 2023).

(Vallas and Schor 2020). Platforms not only rely on calculative mechanisms of control that metrics afford, but also utilize normative mechanisms in the form of symbolic awards and other inducements that seek to foster loyalty (Vallas and Schor 2020: 279).

Digital platforms entered the care labor market relatively recently, growing exponentially before and after the pandemic. The number of apps surged during intertwined COVID-19 and economic crises in Brazil and elsewhere, fueled by customers seeking convenient, low-cost options for care services and private digital companies seeking new profitable avenues for the extraction of rents. Care platforms in Brazil and Colombia, like paid domestic work more generally, cater to affluent families. Labor market intermediaries have a long history embedded in the institution of domestic servitude and the management of colonial labor systems.

Regulatory changes aimed at liberalizing the labor market, on the one hand, and weak regulation of this sector, on the other hand, drove marketization of care work but also shaped different modalities of care provision. In the context of neoliberal reforms, the French state's labor activation and industrial policies promoted digitalization and marketization of care services in the home with some platforms formalizing employment relations. New markets delivering care in France reduced expenditures by the state and shifted costs and risks onto families and individuals. At the other end of the spectrum, largely unregulated intermediaries long have shaped the Brazilian household labor market. There are no specific regulations governing the recruitment process and fees charged by private employment agencies that serve as digital intermediaries in recruiting and placing domestic workers in Brazil. As a result, care workers hired through digital intermediaries face uncertain and fluctuating jobs, precarious, informal employment, and new forms of algorithmic labor control. A focus on regulations highlights the embeddedness of economic forms. However, emphasizing institutional contingencies that shape platform technology runs the risk of neglecting the common features that platforms do exhibit, especially in a globalizing world (Vallas and Schor 2020: 281).

4 Working Conditions, Experiences, and Meanings

The question, "Who cares?" is particularly poignant when it comes to the issue of working conditions focusing on the experiences and meanings of those who provide care, on the public authorities who set the policy frameworks for workers, on institutions both private as well as public, and on other stakeholders in the structures designated or authorized for such labors. Care workers often find themselves in a matrix of relationships: worker-employer-family of patient/client/receiver-client/patient—at least a four-fold relationship with the state as a silent partner. The massive failure of governments to plan and respond to the pandemic comes through—the shutdowns instituted brought hardships to the most precarious and to care workers in hospitals, households and senior facilities deemed for the most part as "essential."

The chapters on Brazil, France, and Colombia (with their focus on Bogota, Cali, southwest Indigenous lands, and Afro-Colombian rural settlement) underscore what we have already recognized: care work consists of many kinds of workers; there are hierarchies among care occupations and jobs based on skill, gender, race/citizenship status, and education. Added to that are the factors of unionization, national industrial relations and social welfare policies that also vary. Pascale Molinier (in this volume) sketches the functioning of service contracts and deregulation of social rights that has divided contract employees, such as nurses from care assistants who can undercut them. Yet, striking similarities crosscut occupational categories and spaces before vaccines became available, when protective gear was nonexistent or in short supply, and prior to understanding the nature of the virus and the mechanisms for its spreading. While the reproductive work required to sustain households and society at large has dramatically increased, the conditions of the workers remunerated to perform these services have been severely degraded, threatening their capacity not only to provide care but also to survive. The pandemic crisis has revealed and worsened entrenched pre-existing inequalities, leaving the most precarious, yet "essential" workers to choose between health and income.

The pandemic intensified the amount of work for nurses, others laboring in facilitates and in homes, and some visiting caregivers who either had sicker patients or took up the slack from absent co-workers who were themselves sick or taking forms of paid leave, such as the "right of withdrawal" in France. The physical preparation of caring itself required additional labor: putting on protective gear when available, or finding such protection, making masks, and suiting up. The reorganization of facilities called for increased work as well, not only for hands-on workers but also their administrators. During lockdowns, new forms of caring labor emerged as workers improvised communication with families of seniors in residence via the use of tablets. However, unspecified numbers of families told in-home care workers and domestics to stay away—with workers losing necessary income, as evidenced by the mushrooming unemployment and inactivity rates as documented by Almeida and Wajnman (in this volume).

In addition, loss of income hit the most marginalized, not only those who entered homes, who were seen as potential virus carriers, but also those impacted by the lockdowns who earned their living on the streets, especially migrants who were deported, as seen in Carolina Moreno Velasquez and Maira Camila Veja Salazar's study in this volume. To get sick meant not working and losing pay, though some workers turned to intermittent, unreported informal work to make ends meet. The occupational health and safety conditions faced by domestic workers in Cali resemble those of domestic workers, mostly immigrant women of color and African Americans and Mexican Americans, in the US—health hazards, "humiliation," and lack of contracts, social security and other worker rights.

Despite different contexts, the pandemic evoked emotional cadences shared by care workers, whether in-home care workers (*aide à domicile*), assistant nurses (*aide soignantes*) or caregivers (*auxiliaires de vie*) in homes and facilities, but also nurses, domestic workers, and women within their own households, as well as refugees and migrants. Anxiety and fear gripped workers who reported feeling "paranoid" as they faced people without masks on public transportation during journeys to and from work, while uniformed nurses generated terror that they would contaminate other riders. Directors and supervisors spoke of "guilt." The mental burdens of rearranging daily life intensified as a form of labor accompanying the emotional life of the pandemic where care sector workers faced death and dying with little recourse. In this collection, Pascale Molinier explores for France the divides expressed by the discourse of exhausted nurses and exaltation of love among others who were more protective, and the divide between self-sacrifice among teachers in nursing schools and the politicized experts focused on professionalism.

Molinier's emphasis on nurses' self-care and belief "we are skin" offers tools for further analysis of the meanings that care workers gave in general and to their specific experiences, including their idealization of care as service. Black feminists in the US have cautioned against universalizing the ethic of care for its white-centric focus, even as they have promoted self-care and Black joy as race affirming among Black mothers and other Black women care workers (Nadasen 2023). The nurse, according to Molinier, stands as the model of bourgeois femininity and whiteness infused with Christian compassion and other virtues. By justifying love as the product of the work some nurses depoliticize their care in an effort at self-protection amid so much morbidity.

What policies relieved stress or made it worse? The ability to stay at home, even with the absence of childcare, was available in France, but not in Brazil or Colombia. Lack of safety nets for most workers who were contract, precarious, informal, and/or irregular amplified fear of contamination. COVID-19 policies in France provided relief to help many caregivers, yet inadequate and insufficient support for safety equipment by the French state left caregivers at risk, as vividly shown by Aurélie Damamme, Helena Hirata and Michelle Redondo (in this volume).

However, to assess policies, a review of pre-pandemic conditions is necessary. The contours differ considerably among the case studies, reflecting variation even within states, as Jeanny Posso and Javier Pineda's comparison (in this volume) of Indigenous regions with Cali underscores. Neoliberal reforms in Colombia led to privatization and poorly regulated growth of precarious contracts before COVID hit, as Amparo Hernandez-Bello, Daniella Castro-Barbudo, and Suelen Castiblanco-Moreno document (in this volume, also see Franzoni and Siddharth 2023). The afterlife of colonialism and racialized subservience may have intensified COVID harms. Compliance with labor standards varied before and after the pandemic for domestic workers and the undocumented, refugees, and migrants. Uneven coverage of emergency measures in Colombia denied the most vulnerable of aid. Even specific decrees assumed formality of employment and social security contributions, such as the Decree 676 of May 2020 that recognized COVID as an occupational disease of health workers and thus covered costs of illness and testing and paid for personal protective equipment (PPE). The requirement of formal employment effectively deprived the majority of paid domestic workers benefits and protections.

Prior citizenship status in the polity and at work through collective bargaining and state benefits also mattered. The case before the Colombian Constitutional Court on blocked access to the Ingreso Solidario Program, which made it impossible to receive pandemic benefits for migrants, questions administrative convenience, raising the issues of who brought the case and who was leading the fight back. In a time of great need, many states excluded the non-registered and the irregularly employed. To its credit, California, among a few other US states, offered relief to immigrants regardless of their status (Gottfried and Boris 2024). But this was the exception. That there are organizations pushing for better conditions and rights is heartening; that they have won so little suggests how difficult the battle—and how worse off low-waged care workers and domestic workers would be without such avenues for redress and protest (Acciari 2024). Creative responses ranged from taxi transport, safe resting houses, making one's own masks, to designating buildings to house the sick, note Damamme et. al. (in this volume). But then there was also burnout and the presence of individual solutions when powerlessness hampered workforces.

5 Toward a Caring Economy: Rebuilding Care in a Post-pandemic World

Transnational case studies of COVID-19's impact on the care economy occasioned conceptual and methodological innovations pushing the frontiers of social scientific research on socio-economic processes. New ways of measuring economic (in)activity challenged conventional ways of representing transitions between employment statuses. By accelerating economic transitions, the pandemic exposed both normative gender biases and bases of categorical labor demarcations, which became more evident when considering trends among countries with large informal labor markets. Transnational comparisons focusing on the pandemic and care more readily uncovered connections between the economy, civil society, the polity, and their variations. Case studies of developments within states called attention to the importance of theorizing civil society and the polity not simply as national unities but also as relatively autonomous from the national.

Crises are opportunities for political interventions that can nourish forms of collective association that can steer society in new directions. The pandemic seemed to offer just such an opportunity to redesign failing care and health systems on a more egalitarian basis, understanding mistakes and preventing them, and in this case, saving lives. Now, in its wake, COVID-19 laid bare a fragile care infrastructure and entrenched care deficits unaddressed by national governments. In moments of broad social, economic, and political change, disarticulation of former economic arrangements and social structures cultivate a fertile terrain for new cycles of organizing activity, the emergence of new organizational forms, and new repertoires of collective action. Indeed, during the pandemic, alternative forms of care provision based on networks of solidarity energized civil society engagements (Debert and Felix in this volume) and forged new "repertoires of care-resistance" (Acciari 2024; Damamme et al. in this volume).

Deeper inequalities and more extreme poverty exacerbated during the pandemic created a vacuum of unmet needs filled by alternative forms of care provision based on networks of solidarity. Nevertheless, vulnerability does not just stem from poverty and material deprivation. Inequalities in access to care also come from stigmatization and discrimination processes based on other intersecting dimensions, such as race/ethnicity, sexual orientation, or cultural/religious background. Circuits rooted in interpersonal "help" relationships supported care provision when resources to purchase care were scarce, and public policies and care infrastructures were ineffective (Guimarães 2021). Neglected by the national state, LGBTQIA+ communities relied on interpersonal circuits of care, as shown by Marcelo Ramos, Pedro Nicoli, and Gabriela Alkmin's chapter on Brazil (in this volume). In response to the national rollback of the rights of older persons by Brazil's Bolsonaro government, local governments in cooperation with civil society organizations came together to shore up the rights of older people (see Debert and Felix in this volume). Prior to the pandemic, a rich tapestry of participatory forms of local governance in Brazil laid the ground for new rounds of civil societal engagements in response to COVID-19. Examples throughout this book showcase solidaristic networks of family, friends, and neighbors—along with community organizations and domestic workers' associations—raising funds, distributing emergency food and other supplies to sustain those in need and substituting mutual aid for state inaction.

The interplay between civil societal actors (strategic alliances and associations) and local state institutions prompted the resurgence of local spaces for pursuing progressive political agendas against the regressive/repressive national polity. These local and mutualistic arrangements of caring and cooperation emphasized the basic right of "everyone to be cared for, and to care for others, i.e., a re-valuation of caring in the context of intimate relations and 'the mutual dependence and interconnectedness of people and developing visions of decentralized care at the local level'" (Lenz 2018: 23–24, cited in Shire 2023: 4). Caring labor embracing the principle of mutuality is a potential source of "alternative epistemologies and ontologies" (Weeks 2011: 236–7). Economic deprivations and unfair labor conditions prompted domestic workers to mobilize, framing rights in a new grammar enunciated around "the right to care and be cared for in times of crisis" (Acciari 2024: 322). Plumbing the experiences of domestic workers, domestic workers' associations articulated an alternative vision of society that was inclusive and based on love and solidarity (Acciari 2024).

Rebuilding care in a post-pandemic world begins with the recognition of care as labor deserving decent wage compensation, social protection, and associated rights, but also as a practice and as an ethic orienting social relations in our most intimate settings and relationships (Tronto 2015, Molinier, 2013). An alternative vision based on caring for others and receiving care within an ethic of shared responsibility can orient action toward interdependence and mutual recognition, and it can offer a critique of the marketization of care and point to the lack of responsibility for social provisioning. Care constitutes the social reproduction activities that sustain society, but can also uphold inequalities grounded in race, gender, and citizenship if tethered to top-down and undemocratic structures (Nadasen 2023). Thus, it is necessary to inject concepts of global justice with an understanding of care as a practice, as a responsibility, as an ethic in people's everyday lives, and as integral to citizenship (Fraser, cited in Williams 2014: 27).

To rebuild a robust and more resilient care organization requires a comprehensive understanding of why systems failed in order to build capacity to absorb and adapt to external shocks and structural changes before, during and after disasters. We gain a better understanding of vulnerabilities and capacities for responding to care crises from cross-national, transregional comparative research. Taken together, the chapters serve as a postmortem to assess the disruptions by the pandemic in diverse transatlantic countries. The transnational, transregional comparisons found in this book yield new insights theoretically, methodologically, and empirically. They reveal similar tendencies toward marketization against the backdrop of specific actors and institutional actions shaping these processes and structuration of the care economy at multiple scales. They point to economic-political development patterns that do not neatly align with the global North/South divide. They can disentangle the social forces behind the correlation between societal inequality and the prevalence of domestic labor (Milkman 2023b). Though COVID has been downgraded from a pandemic to an endemic, the impacts wrought by the pandemic on caregivers' working conditions continue to reverberate. Future results from this larger T-AP project will contribute to the vital project of recognizing who bears responsibility to care for those in need, and for creating the conditions under which such care should be equitably provided.

References

Acciari, L. (2024) Caring is Resisting: Lessons from Domestic Workers' Mobilizations during COVID-19 in Latin America. *Gender, Work and Organization* 31(1): 319–336.

Acciari, L., Juana del Carmen Britez, & Andrea del Carmen Morales (2021) Right to Health, Right to Live: Domestic Workers Facing the COVID-19 Crisis in Latin America. *Gender & Development* 29(1): 11–33.

Adriaenssens, Stef, Theys, T., Verhaest, D. & Deschacht, N. (2023) Subsidized Household Services and Informal Employment: The Belgian Service Voucher Policy. *Journal of Social Policy* 52(1): 85–106.

Anderson, B. & Shutes, I. (2014) *Migration and Care Labour*. Basingstokes: Palgrave-Macmillan.

Apitzsch, B. & Shire, K. (2021) Informalisation of Work, and Workers' Voice in Welfare markets for In-Home Domestic/Care Services in Germany. In: C. Ledoux, K. Shire and F. van Hooren (eds) *The Dynamics of Welfare Markets: Private Pensions and Domestic/Care Services in Europe*. London: Palgrave Macmillan, 347–371.

Boris E. & Klein, J. (2012) *Caring for America: Home Health Workers in the Shadow of the Welfare State*. New York: Oxford University Press.

Boris, E. & Parrenas, R., eds. (2010) *Intimate Labors: Cultures, Technologies, and the Politics of Care*. New York: Routledge.

Dowling, E. (2021) *The Care Crisis: What Caused It and What Can End It?* London: Verso.

Duffy, M. (2020) Driven by Inequalities: Exploring the Resurgence of Domestic Work in U.S. Cities. *Sociological Forum* 35(3): 608–627.

Duffy, M., Armenia, A. & Price-Glynn, K. (2023) Introduction. In: Duffy, M., Armenia, A. and Price-Glynn, K (eds) *From Crisis to Catastrophe: Care, COVID and Pathways to Change*. New Brunswick: Rutgers University Press, 1–5.

Duffy, M. & Armenia, A. (2019) Paid Care Work around the Globe: A Comparative Analysis of 47 Countries Prepared for UN Women. LIS, No. 758.

England, P., Budig, M. & Folbre, N. (2002) Wages of Virtue: The Relative Pay of Care Work. *Social Problems* 49 (4): 455–473.

Eydoux, A. (2023) Care Workers and Care Employment During the Pandemic Iin France; Segmented Policies and Regulations in a Fragmented Landscape. Unpublished paper presented at the Who Cares? Colloquium, May 25, 2023, CRESPA, Paris.

Farris, S. (2020) The Business of Care: Private Placement Agencies and Female Migrant Workers in London. *Gender, Work, and Organization* 27(6): 1450–1467.

Folbre, N., Fremstad, S., Gonalons-Pons, P. & Coan, V. (2023) Measuring Care Provision in the United States Resources, Shortfalls, and Possible Improvements. Working Paper, University of Massachusetts, Center for Economic and Policy Research, June 7.

Franzoni, J. M. & Siddharth, V. (2023) Latin America's Response to COVID-19: The Risk of Sealing an Unequal Care Regime. In: Duffy, M., Armenia, A. and Price-Glynn, K (eds) *From Crisis to Catastrophe: Care, COVID And Pathways to Change*, New Brunswick: Rutgers University Press, 19–26.

Fraser, N. (2023) *Cannibal Capitalism: How Our System Is Devouring Democracy, Care, and the Planet and What We Can Do about It*. London: Verso Press.

Gottfried, H. (2023) Multi-Scalar Geographies of Inequalities: Trajectories of Gender Regimes in a World Regional Perspective. *Women's Studies International Forum* 99.

Gottfried, Heidi (2022) Tacit Knowledge in Low-Status Care Work. *AMA Journal of Ethics* 24 (9): 883–889.

Gottfried, H. (2013) *Gender, Work and Economy: Unpacking the Global Economy*. Cambridge: Polity Press.

Gottfried, H. (1991) Mechanisms of Control in the Temporary Service Industry. *Sociological Forum* 6(4): 699–713.

Gottfried, H. & Boris, E. (2024) Care beyond Crisis? Rebuilding Just Social Policies and Effective Regulations in a Post-Pandemic World: Pre-Pandemic and Emergency Measures in the US. T-AP Working Paper 7.

Gottfried, H. & Chun, J. J. (2018) Care Work in Transition: Transnational Circuits of Migration, Gender, and Care. *Critical Sociology* 44 (7–8): 997–1012.

Guimarães, N. (2021) The Circuits of Care. Reflections from the Brazilian Case. In: Guimarães, N. and Hirata, H. (eds) *Care and Care Workers: A Latin American Perspective*. Cham, Switzerland: Springer, 1–24.

Guimarães, N., Pineda, J., Wajnman, S. & Castiblanco, S. (2023) Pandemic, Labor Market, and Gender in Brazil and Colombia, Unpublished paper presented at the International Sociological Association World Congress, June 26, Melbourne.

Himmelweit, S. (2022) COVID-19 and the Financialisation of Social Care, Feb. 22. Webinar, SOAS.

Hobson, B., Hellgren, Z. & Bede, L. (2015) How Institutional Contexts Matter: Migration and Domestic Care Services and the Capabilities of Migrants in Spain and Sweden. Families and Societies, Working Paper 46.

Hua, J. & Ray, K. (2021). *Spent behind the Wheel: Drivers' Labor in the Uber Economy*. Minneapolis: University of Minnesota Press.

International Labor Organization (2021) *Making Decent Work a Reality for Domestic Workers*.Geneva: ILO.

International Labor Organization (2020) *Domestic Workers in Latin America and the Caribbean during the COVID-19 Crisis*. Geneva: ILO.

International Labor Organization (2018) *Care Work and Care Jobs for the Future of Decent Work*. Geneva: ILO.

Jany-Catrice, F. (2015) The Academic Legitimacy of a Political Project. The Case of the Creation of a 'Personal Services' Sector. *L'Homme et la Societe* 197 (3): 105–129.

Klinenberg, E. (2024) 2020: *One City, Seven People, and the Year Everything Changed*. New York: Alfred Knopf.

Ledoux, C., K. Shire and F. van Hooren (eds) *The Dynamics of Welfare Markets: Private Pensions and Domestic/Care Services in Europe*. London: Palgrave Macmillan.

Mezzadri, A. (2022) Social Reproduction and Pandemic Neoliberalism: Planetary Crises and the Reorganisation of Life, Work and Death. *Organization* 29 (3): 379–400.

Milkman, R. (2023a) Stratification among In-Home Care Workers in the United States. *Critical Sociology* 49 (1): 11–22.

Milkman, R. (2023b) How Exceptional Is the U.S. Case? Immigration, Inequality, and Stratification among In-Home Care Workers. International Sociological Association World Congress, June 26, 2023.

Molinier, P. (2013) *Le travail du care*. Paris: la Dispute.

Nadasen, P. (2023) *Care: The Highest Stage of Capitalism*. Chicago: Haymarket.

Nathanson, C. & Fairchild, A.L. (2020) Condemned to Repeat It: The US Response to COVID-19. *Footnotes* 48, 3: 19–20.

Ness, I. (ed) (2023) *The Routledge Handbook of the Gig Economy*. London: Routledge.

Orozco, M., Franco, J., Marchant, M. & Valdivia, R. (2022) The Role of Care and the Local Economy in Women's Labour Force Participation: Evidence from Mexico and Colombia in the Pandemic Era. *Gender & Development* 30 (1–2): 145–175.

Pineda, J. (2021) Care Work: Professionalization and Valuation of Nurses and Nursing Assistants in Health and Old Age in Colombia. In: Guimarães, N. and Hirata, H. (eds) *Care and Care Workers: A Latin American Perspective*. Cham, Switzerland: Springer, 125–148.

Pineda, J. & Castiblanco, S. (2022) Labor Markets, Inactivity, Care and the COVID-19 Pandemic. El Congreso 2022 de la Asociación Latinoamericana de Estudios del Trabajo (ALAST), July 22, Chile (online).

Pun, N., Kaxton S. & Gottfried, H. (2022) Global Capitalism and Labour in the Age of Monopoly: Hong Kong and Mainland China. *Critical Sociology* 48 (7–8): 1115–1122.

Rosińska, A.M. (2021a) Damned If You Do, Damned If You Don't (Work). Domestic Workers in the COVID-19 Pandemic Double Bind. A report based on an online survey in the United States. Center of Migration Research Newsletter.

Rosińska, A.M. (2021b) Comparative activism and policy in the US and in Italy report, Ca' Foscari University of Venice, MAJORdom project.

Shire, K. (2023) Social Democratic Imaginaries of Transformation in Conservative Gender Regimes. *Women's Studies International Forum*.

Stevano, S., Rosimina, A. & Jamieson, M. (2021) Essential for What? A Global Social Reproduction View on the Re-Organisation of Work during the COVID-19 Pandemic. *Canadian Journal of Development Studies / Revue canadienne d'études du développement* 42 (1–2): 178–199.

Ticona, J. (2022) *Left to Our Own Devices*. Oxford: Oxford University Press.

Ticona, J. & Mateescu, A. (2018) Trusted Strangers: Care Work Platforms' Cultural Entrepreneurship in the On-demand Economy. *New Media & Society* 20 (1): 4384–4404.

Tronto, J. (2015). *Who Cares? How to Shape a Democratic Politics*. Ithaca: Cornell University Press.

Vallas, S. & Schor, J. (2020) What Do Platforms Do? Understanding the Gig Economy. *Annual Review of Sociology* 46: 273–294.

van Hooren, F. (2018) Intersecting Social Divisions and the Politics of Differentiation: Understanding Exclusionary Domestic Policy in the Netherlands. *Social Politics* 25 (1): 92–117.

Weeks, K. (2011) *The Problem with Work: Feminism, Marxism, Anti-work Politics, and Post-work Imaginaries*. Durham: Duke University Press.

Williams, F. (2014). Across the Transnational Political Economy of Care. In *Migration and Care Labour*, edited by Bridget Anderson and Isabel Shutes, 11–30. Basingstokes: Palgrave-Macmillan.

CHAPTER 2

The Halo of Care: Paid Care Work in Brazil (2012–2022)

Nadya Araujo Guimarães and Luana Simões Pinheiro

> Care work is not just a cornerstone of our economy – it is a rock-bottom foundation.
>
> ALBELDA, DUFFY & FOLBRE, 2009

1 Introduction[1]

Shortly before the outbreak of the COVID-19pandemic, the International Labor Organization released an extensive report on carework (ILO 2018). The numbers were unambiguous regarding the importance of this sector in generating employment. Circa 381 million people performed some form of this activity, representing almost 12% of global employment. Of these, no less than 249 million were women who accounted for 65% of paid work in the care sector, which represented 11.5% of total employment and 19.3% of female employment on a global scale. Moreover, while on average women made up two-thirds of the care workforce, they represented three-quarters of the care workforce in the Americas, Europe, and Central Asia.

The impressive numbers presented by the ILO report affirmed a set of priorities that academic literature has long underscored. As early as 1990, Abel and Nelson (1990) emphasized the need for a more thorough understanding of paid care providers, advocating a change of approach to what was largely focused on the needs of those receiving care. The authors stressed the complex

1 We acknowledge the support received from Fapesp/Trans-Atlantic Platform (grant #2021/07888-3), CNPq (grant #421754/2021-4), and Arymax Foundation (Donnation Contract Arymax/Cebrap July 2022). We are also grateful to Paulo Henrique da Silva for his support on data processing, and to Marcelo Medeiros, Bila Sorj, Simone Wajnman, Monique Meron, Heidi Gottfried, and Mignon Duffy for their comments and suggestions.

 | DOI:10.1163/9789004707009_003

and multifaceted nature of this activity, comprising instrumental duties and skills as well as affectional relationships. According to Folbre (1995), this occupation usually entails a continual, in-person service based on recurring face-to-face contact that is motivated, to a greater or lesser extent, by the intention of providing beneficiaries with well-being. Therefore, it is not coincidental that the interpersonal relationships underpinning this kind of work suggest that, in Gardiner's words (1997), these occupations seem to resist "complete commodification," a term that Folbre and Wright (2012) propose should be eliminated.

Thus, in the early 2000s not only was there a significant increase in research on the importance of unpaid care work (England, 2005), which had long been a priority in feminist economic theory (Benería & Stimpson, 1987; Folbre, 1995; Bruschini, 2006; Razavi, 2007), but also research devoted to the multiple forms of paid care work. At the same time, attempts to categorize this growing roster of employment modalities made strides that brought about further refinements (Duffy, 2005, 2011; Albelda, Duffy & Folbre, 2009; Folbre, 2012; Duffy, Albelda & Hammonds, 2013).

Since then, Brazilian scholarly literature has also sought to articulate similar lines of research, such as studies on domestic employment, unpaid domestic work, older adults' access to institutional care, as well as analyses regarding younger children and access to daycare centers (Guimarães, Hirata & Posthuma, 2020). The increased presence of women in the labor market, and the convergence of a fast decline in fertility rates and the aging of the Brazilian population (Arretche, 2019) went side by side with the longstanding prevalence of domestic employment and the surge in the number of female caregivers employed in Brazilian households. This challenged researchers to evaluate the breadth of the care labor market in the country.[2] Another clue to the importance of the care economy in job creation in Brazil is the growing relevance of labor market intermediaries in the sector; both physical and virtual employment agencies have become key mediators in the supply and demand of care services (Araujo, 2015). Moreover, platform companies have gained increasing visibility and offer multiple care services (Moreno, 2022; Cardoso & Pereira, 2023; Andrada et al., 2023).

2 In fact, ILO's comparative study on care work revealed that Brazil had the highest number of women domestic workers among the countries included in this report, concentrating no less than 7 of the 52 million domestic workers. This led the authors to conclude that Brazil's care regime was heavily reliant on the employment of paid domestic workers (ILO, 2018, p. XI). Just as remarkable was the expansion of home care workers at a pace that remained high even amid economic recessions, signaling its pivotal role in the daily lives of Brazilian families, or at least for those with the financial means to hire them (Guimarães & Hirata, 2020).

In short, researchers were confronted with the challenge of gauging the size of this thriving job market and systematizing the heterogeneous forms of care services circulating therein. Thus, two important aspects must be addressed, which we do in sections 2 and 3.

Previous attempts in international literature to measure the care labor market needed to be considered, but without losing sight of the specificities of the Brazilian case, where the provision of care has been strongly anchored to multiple forms of paid work carried out in homes. In other words, the commodification of care did not mean externalizing or defamiliarizing its provision. The occupational structure and the inequalities of the Brazilian care labor market strongly reflect this feature. Thus, Section 2 will address the complexity of defining the boundaries of this care labor market, which we call the "halo."[3] This requires systematizing the different dimensions deemed necessary to comprehend this scope, to grasp its magnitude without compromising the ability to discern the heterogeneous forms of care work therein. To this end, we have devised a typology of care occupations grounded in the specificities of Brazil. Section 2 will explore the capacity of this typology to identify the profile and working conditions of those within it based on information obtained from the Continuous National Household Sample Survey (PNAD-C). The reference year to assess the importance of care occupations prior to the pandemic is 2019.

In section 3, another important aspect is addressed, questioning the duration of the halo configuration for care occupations. Data from 2012, the first year made available by PNAD-C, is mobilized to explore the degree of continuity in the features observed in section 2 as a sign of its consolidation in scope, heterogeneity, and inequality patterns. However, a last dialogue between literature and data needs to be considered. Several studies have demonstrated the significant impact of the COVID-19 pandemic on the labor market structure (ILO, 2020a and 2020b; Weller, Contreras, Caballero & Tropa, 2020; Gentilini et al., 2021; Verick, Schmidt-Klau & Lee, 2021). Care occupations were not immune to this impact since the health crisis and the implementation of social

---

3 We use the metaphor of "halo" to refer to the limits or the sometimes imprecise contours that demarcate a phenomenon. Just like in Astronomy, where this word is used to name the spherical region that surrounds spiral galaxies; or in Medicine, to name the pink circle around a nipple; or in photography, to allude to the dark halo that forms around a bright image when a photo is taken against the light. Obviously, we are not adopting the positive and vulgar religious sense of a light ring around the head of a holy person, which inspired Thorndike (1920) to coin as "halo effect" the psychological process of producing a necessarily favorable cognitive bias. No positive bias is assumed here as inherent to care social relations.

distancing measures had deep effects on the dynamics of this market and on care workers transitioning between employment, unemployment, and inactivity (Almeida & Wajnman, 2023). How lasting were these impacts in Brazil? Have they changed the structure of the care labor market from what it was before the health crisis? The third section will also address this issue based on information from PNAD-C for 2022.

In the fourth and final section we discuss our research findings from both a methodological and a substantive angle, emphasizing the relevant role of paid care work in the broader dynamics of the Brazilian social organization of care and, in this sense, in the reproduction of a highly unequal society.

2 The Brazilian Care Labor Market: Addressing Measurement Challenges

2.1 *Circumscribing the Multifaceted Domain of Paid CareWork in Brazil*

Assuming that "paid care" is a broad field, we approach it as a domain of work performed in the market of paid personal services. Thus, three points of convergence encompass the various forms it can take:

(i) It is a form of *work*.
(ii) It is work performed as *a service provided to people*.
(iii) It is a commercial service *that requires financial compensation*.

To outline the boundaries of this market we assume that professional occupations in care services share a common trait: they seek to restore the well-being or to develop the capacities (physical, social, or emotional/self-esteem) of care workbeneficiaries. It means that, even though the concrete forms of work in the sector vary, the paid occupations it encompasses should have a common objective: to maximize the well-being of others, either by restoring or developing their capacities.[4]

But social relationships in paid care work take on various forms, with myriads of occupations devoted to restoring the well-being of others.[5] Therefore,

4 This formulation finds a point of convergence with the conceptualization proposed by Fisher and Tronto (1990) and also enables us to draw on a definition in tandem with Folbre (1995).

5 We must bear in mind that once we adopt the government statistics definition for "occupations", we become immersed in a web of societal conventions of what is officially recognized as such, and therefore, identified, classified, and measured (Desrosières, 1993). This discretionary role of state conventions can render invisible some forms of care work. In a significant case, it was not until 2002, following a revision of the Brazilian Classification of Occupations,

once the common zone circumscribing the halo of care is established, the next challenge is to organize the diversity within this halo. As such, and in light of the literature, we postulate that there are some key dimensions for organizing this highly diverse occupational environment.

The first dimension concerns the *context* in which work relations come about: either within a home setting through domestic employment, or outside it without a domestic employment relationship. Differentiating this dimension is particularly relevant for the Brazilian case because of the longstanding, enduring weight of paid domestic work, which is one of the main occupational alternatives for women, especially black women (Pinheiro, Tokarski & Posthuma, 2021), or because of the specific characteristics of managing and controlling the work performed in private spheres, where relationships and hierarchies are permeated by interpersonal relationships (Kofes, 2001) that are always performed within more intimate settings (Brites, 2000; Zelizer, 2005, 2010).

The second dimension concerns the *nature of the interaction* established between care workers and beneficiaries. This interaction may be direct – for example, in the form of care provided by babysitters (to younger children) or caregivers (to older people or people in some situation of dependency), or indirect – in the form of care provided by domestic servants (cooks, cleaners, and others). This same logical assertion sometimes appears in the literature under the terms "interactive care" versus "support care" (Folbre & Wright, 2012) or embedded in the notion of "nurturant care" versus "non-nurturant care" (Duffy, 2011).

The third dimension refers to the *recurrence* of the care relationship. Recurrence increases or decreases according to the level of dependence. In situations of very low autonomy, recurrence is imperative since any discontinuation may compromise the quality of care and well-being of the beneficiaries, as well as their very lives. Conversely, the greater the autonomy, the greater the chance that the beneficiary can safely experience interludes in the required care service. In this sense, the third dimension refers to the importance of continuity in the care relationship based on the need of the care recipient.[6]

When combined, these three dimensions form clusters of care occupations that not only have diverse profiles, but also vary in nature. We postulate that

---

that the paid work of "caregivers for children, young people, and older adults" was officially recognized as an "occupation" in Brazil. (Guimarães & Hirata, 2020; Groisman, 2015)

6 We are grateful to Mignon Duffy for showing us the need to differentiate between situations where recurrence means primarily continuity over time and situations where it means the frequency of interaction.

caregiving is more intensive when performed in direct, recurring interactions within a home environment imbued by interpersonal and intimate relationships. At the opposite end we find care occupations where the care work takes place in non-recurring, indirect relationships, outside the domestic environment. To better express this gradient, we will employ the metaphor "circles of care" as coined by Emily Abel and Margaret Nelson (1990), in the opening chapter of their famous book. The authors identified three "circles" associated with three different contexts: domestic, where family members (or friends) provide care on an informal and unpaid basis; formal institutions, where paid workers provide qualified care services on a regular basis protected by the contractual rules of the market; and "unaffiliated" workers, who provide paid care services, although deprived of rights.[7] The metaphor of "circles" will be used here with somewhat different content to further explore the characteristics of the social relationship underlying the work of care.

Furthermore, we will argue that these circles can be thought of as concentric insofar as the intensity of care (according to personality, intimacy, and recurrence) decreases as we move away from the first and most central circle. In this sense, the occupations that comprise the central nucleus of paid care work are those performed in a home environment through direct relationships with dependent persons. Hence, these occupations involve intense interaction, greater recurrence of care (often of imperative continuity), and in a private setting that allows for closer interpersonal relationships and intimacy, since the work typically involves direct contact with the beneficiary's body. In this nucleus we find the occupations of child caregivers (nannies) and a whole range of personal caregivers (for older adults, for people with disabilities, for patients in situations of dependence). In Brazil, these two occupational categories account for 50% of this circle at the core of the care sector.

The second circle also encompasses paid care services performed in a home setting, but differs from the first in that the care relationship is generally indirect, being conducted under a domestic employment agreement. In Brazil, this group comprises domestic workers (cleaners, cooks, etc.), who account for 94%

7 Abel and Nelson (1990, p.26) also refer to these three as "arenas" (1990, p.26), in a classification that certainly draws on the USA reality that inspired the authors. It is true, as they recognize, that this way of classifying is not intended to be exhaustive, since other modalities of providing care can transversely cut these "arenas" such as, for example, unpaid voluntary work provided in formal institutions, or wage earners recruited by formal organizations but working in private spaces on a daily basis. Here, we will restrict the focus to the work performed under wage relations, observing activities that, by their nature, can be classified as care work and are officially recognized as occupations in the labor market.

of the jobs in this circle. However, the line dividing this group from the previous one – based on the predominance of direct carein the first and indirect care in the second – is quite flexible. This is because the boundaries between hired and performed work are often fluid, particularly in cases where families engage individuals to provide services in their homes. Qualitative studies have provided a wealth of evidence that workers hired as housekeepers routinely become responsible for the care of children, older adults, or other dependents who need assistance. Neither is it unusual for workers hired as babysitters or to care for an old person or to oversee the cooking and housekeeping for the rest of the family. In this sense, we can infer that there is an important intersectional area between circles 1 and 2.[8]

In contrast, all the other circles are concentric and do not intersect, denoting groups to be mutually exclusive, as they move away from the nucleus of the halo of care. Thus, the third circle comprises occupations that are also performed directly and recurrently, but occur in public or impersonal settings, as opposed to the common hierarchical and authoritative environment of care provided in the home under domestic employment relationships. In the Brazilian case, the largest occupational category in this group is nursing technicians and assistants, who account for one third of the jobs. If we include nurses, we find that the broad set of workers in the nursing field represents close to half of the almost three million jobs in Circle 3. Equally important are early childhood educators working in institutions such as daycare centers and nursery schools, and who occupy one in every four jobs.

Moving further away from the core of the care sector, we identified a cluster of occupations we grouped into Circle 4. Here, caregivers and beneficiaries still have a direct relationship, but the care does not take place in a domestic setting and discontinuity is manageable since recurrence is not imperative. In Brazil, these occupations are more heterogeneous, ranging from beauty professionals (31% of the total, including hair stylists, aestheticians, and others) to elementary school teachers (20%). The circle also includes health professionals (26%) such as physicians, physiotherapists, dentists, speech therapists, nutritionists, and others with a higher education degree, as well as some occupations that require only a high school diploma.

The last circle of care encompasses occupations where service provision is indirect, with infrequent recurrence, and outside the home. In Brazil, Circle 5

8 Effectively, this intersection could widen the boundary between the first two circles, either towards the first (direct domestic care) or the second (indirect domestic care). However, we cannot quantify this intersection since our sources are limited to descriptions of occupation classifications and data derived from self-classifications.

is comprised by a combination of food professionals (52%) and cleaning professionals (34%).

Table 2.1 provides a summary of the entire analytical course of this section. In it we specify the five major circles of care occupations. It shows how each group results from the convergence of the three variables that organize the internal diversity of this broad segment of the labor market, namely the nature of the care relationship (direct versus indirect), the context where it takes place (whether in a domestic employment setting – thus more personal and intimate – or outside the home), and the recurrence of this relationship. With the Brazilian case in mind, we also specify the typical occupations that stand out for their relative weight in each of the five groups. Table 2.1 provides an overview of what we understand to be the halo that surrounds the care sector in Brazil, while also presenting its internal differentiations, as systematized in our typology. Thus, the halo of care comprises almost 70 occupations, listed in the annex to this chapter.

A word of caution is appropriate here. In line with scholarly literature (ILO, 2018; Folbre, 2012; Duffy, 2011), we acknowledge that the division of labor in care provision also encompasses a range of professional activities that, while not strictly care work, are necessary to support care activities. Examples of this include managerial and administrative occupations in care settings. These occupations undoubtedly form an integral part of the "care economy" insofar as they constitute a job market that develops *around* the activity of care, fueled by the demand for care services. However, to accurately measure the workforce *of care*, we chose to exclude the outermost circle of care from the halo, since its main purpose is restricted to providing support to other activities that are (indeed) care.

Figure 2.1 portrays how we envision the halo of and the five circles that represent its internal heterogeneity.[9]

Lastly, we emphasize that this representation serves a specific analytical purpose, namely demarcating the occupations encompassed within the "care-sector" of Brazil's particular social reality. Doing so meant tackling some methodological challenges carefully discussed in a previous paper (Guimarães; Pinheiro, 2023) and briefly presented in the following subsection.

9 We would like to express our gratitude to Simone Wajnman for suggesting the graph presented here. In Wajnman (2022) the author explored our argument to address in greater detail the links between paid and unpaid home-based work.

TABLE 2.1 Grouping care occupations

Recurrency of interaction	**Context and nature of interaction**			
	Domestic work – ***more*** **intimate**		**Outside domestic work** – ***less*** **intimate**	
	Direct – ***more*** **interaction**	**Indirect**–***less*** **interaction**	**Direct** – ***more*** **interaction**	**Indirect** – ***less*** **interaction**
Demands *more* recurrence and dependency in the care relationship	50% child caregivers 50% personal caregivers (1)	94% general domestic workers (2)	33% mid-level nursing 23% preschool teachers 14% higher level nursing 13% child caregivers – non-domestic (3)	
Demands *less* recurrence and dependency in the care relationship			26% health professionals 20% elementary school teachers 16% hair stylists 15% beauty treatment specialists (4)	33% cleaning workers 18% cooks 11% doormen and janitors (5)

SOURCE: PREPARED BY THE AUTHORS

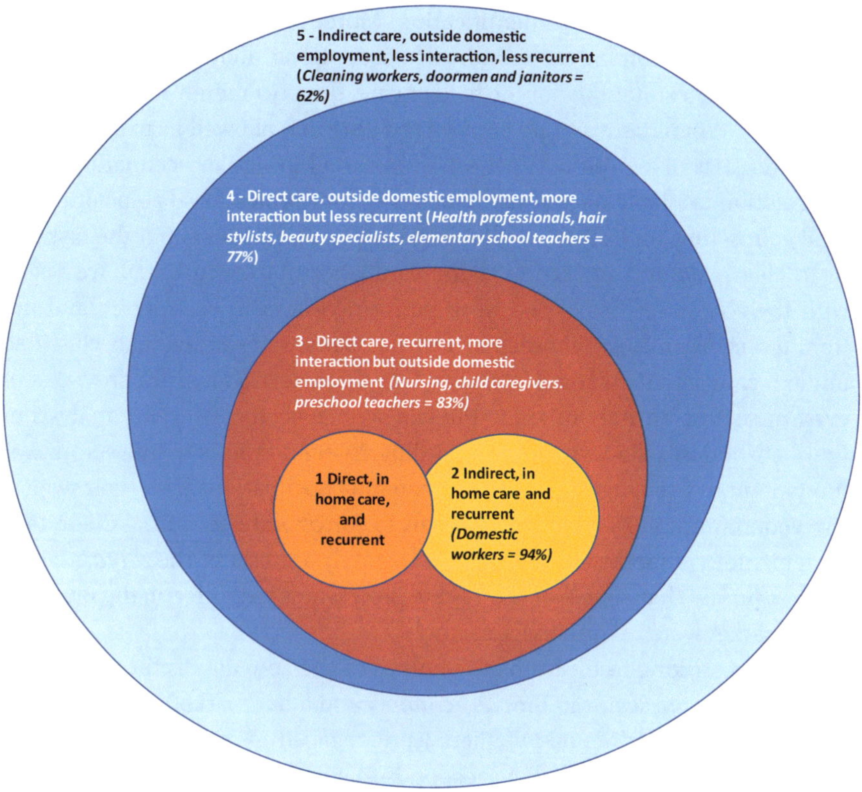

FIGURE 2.1 The halo of care, its five circles and main occupations
SOURCE: PREPARED BY THE AUTHORS

2.2 *The Structure of the Care Labor Market in Pre-pandemic Brazil: Exploring Heterogeneity and Identifying Inequalities*

Classification always poses challenges, even if grounded in valid theoretical arguments. The nature of available data significantly constricts the classifier's scope of freedom – and existing information does not always provide the ideal basis for deciding whether to include one specific occupation into a sector or to exclude another. Thus, we begin by briefly presenting the available databases and the limitations of the information we can extract from them.

To explore the typology presented above in considering the Brazilian case, we used the Continuous National Household Sample Survey (PNAD-C). This survey uses a specific tool for classifying occupations called Classification of Occupations for Household Research (COD – Portuguese acronym). While derived from the Brazilian Classification of Occupations (CBO – Portuguese acronym), the COD is a leaner classification and not all CBO occupations have a corresponding COD identification. Moreover, while the CBO provides detailed information on each family of occupations, allowing for a coherent analysis of their suitability for the field of care, the COD merely lists these same categories. When there was no entry in the CBO that allowed us to analyze the characteristics of a given occupation, we resorted to similar occupations or to information available on various websites – from professional associations or legal counseling, for example – that provided further detail about the tasks.

To clearly delimit the scope of the care labor market in Brazil, we began with the characteristics of the work performed in each occupation and not from the economic activity sector. However, sometimes individuals classified under a care activity worked in sectors not characterized by care provision or even in sectors entirely unrelated to the service sector. Thus, an analysis of the distribution of occupations according to economic activity sectors was fundamental. The diligent process of matching occupations with their respective economic activity sectors allowed us to corroborate our initial theoretical understanding that the domain of care is largely a subset of the service sector. In 2019, no less than 95.5% of the 70 care professions identified in the Brazilian labor market were in the service sector.[10]

The first striking result from our analysis of the 2019 data is the sheer magnitude of the care sector in Brazil's economy and labor market. In 2019, almost 24 million male and female workers were engaged in activities classified as part of the care sector, which corresponds to circa 25% of the total employed population in the country. The care sector is second only to the rest of the service subsectors, which all together account for 27.3% of employed persons, followed by commerce in a distant third place (18.6%). These results are in line with the findings of preceding studies that sought to measure care as a profession in other countries. Duffy's (2005) pioneering study in the United States during the 2000s found that the care sector, in that year, employed nearly 20% of the total workforce in the country, most of them within what the author defined as "nurturant care," i.e., the provision of care that relies on a strong interpersonal relationship, and thus presumes a substantial relational dimension. Roughly speaking, "nurturant care" would correspond to groups 1, 3 and 4 in our classification, which involve direct interaction between care providers and beneficiaries.

According to the ILO's (2018) effort to estimate the global paid workforce in the care sector, the care labor market comprises circa 381 million people

10 Annex 2.1 provides a list of those occupations, classified by circle and identified by its code number in the Brazilian Classification of Occupations.

or 11.5% of total jobs available, a proportion that varies between 20% in the Americas, Europe and Central Asia, and 8% in Africa and the Asia-Pacific, where unpaid care within families was proportionately more expressive. Thus, the magnitude of the care sector regarding job generation is significant, and as Duffy, Albelda, and Hammond (2013) showed in the US, has had growing relevance over the years. Between 1990 and 2000 alone, the US care sector grew 15%, underscoring the rising trend in the commodification of care in modern economies throughout the 20th century (Duffy; Armenia; Stacey, 2015).

Returning to the Brazilian case, the pivotal role of the care sector in the overall number of occupations suggests that, as in other societies, we cannot discuss the country's labor market as a whole or the income generated by care occupations without considering the characteristics and weight of the sector. Paid care is, and will remain in the foreseeable future, a major source of employment, particularly for women, while also operating as a driving force in national economies. It is therefore imperative for governments to devise political and policymaking strategies that consider this type of work so that efforts to create quality employment and income can accommodate the specific characteristics of the sector.

When we divided the 70 care occupations into the five concentric circles, we found relevant differences in size that clarify the way commodified care has been configured in Brazilian society (Table 2.2). Thus, almost two-thirds of people engaged in providing care (62.5%) are in circles where care relationships are less recurring and probably less intense. In turn, the two circles closest to the nucleus account for a quarter (25.4%) of the sector, while the middle circle comprised just over 12% of the care workforce.

TABLE 2.2 Population employed in the care sector by circles. Brazil, 2019

Circles of care	Freq.	%
Circle 1 – recurring, direct, domestic	1,184,624	5.0
Circle 2 – recurring, indirect, domestic	4,877,358	20.4
Circle 3 – recurring, direct, non-domestic	2,926,411	12.2
Circle 4 – less recurring, direct, non-domestic	7342,647	30.7
Circle 5 – less recurring, indirect, non-domestic	7,616,478	31.8
Total	23,947,518	100.0

SOURCE: IBGE. PNAD-C. 2019 – 1ST INTERVIEW

Adding this wide range of activities to the framework of care allows expanding the demarcation line to incorporate workers with broader backgrounds and experiences. In Brazil, it means including over 7.6 million workers who perform their activities in circle 5, and over 280,000 in circle 2. The affinity between these circles and the care work force also reflects in their specific profile: of the total of these "additional" workers, 60% are black people and 37.5% are black women. Duffy (2005) and Glenn (1992) made the same effort by including activities only contemporarily recognized as "indirect care," such as cleaning, cooking, and laundering; in these occupations the relational dimension expresses itself in different modalities and densities. Thus, by opting to include indirect occupations of care, we expanded our field to include workers and work experiences that are, as expressed by Glenn (1992), in the "backroom", that is, performed in the "backstage" without compulsory and recurring contact with the public and/or care consumer. By positioning this notion at the center of the debate, Glenn sought to demonstrate that, in addition to the gender division of care work, there is also a noticeable racial division. Hence the concentration of white women in activities that demand intense interactions with care beneficiaries – therefore more socially and economically valued – while black women are proportionally more present in activities performed "behind the counters", as we will document below.

2.2.1 The Gender and Racial Divisions of Labor

An expressive share of the studies on care in Brazil and elsewhere stems from the assumption that this is an activity historically associated with the female universe, largely performed by women in the private environment without monetary compensation as a sign of the acceptability of conventional gender-based divisions of labor. The transformation of care into a commodity has perpetuated this inequality, entrusting most of the care offered through the labor market to women. Our analysis corroborates such findings, as women occupy 75.3% of the nearly 24 million jobs in the sector (Table 2.3). While female overrepresentation progressively declines as we move away from the innermost circle of care, women never cease to form the majority in each subsector. Thus, when we consider Circle 1 – where the intensity of care is at maximum – 98% of the workforce is comprised of women. This declines as we shift towards outer circles, reaching 59% when we focus on occupations such as cleaning, restaurant, and laundry workers, and other professional activities that do not require personal interaction.[11]

11 By way of comparison, commerce is the second most female sector in the Brazilian economy, in which women account for only 42% of occupations. The care sector, therefore, is

TABLE 2.3 Population employed in the care sector by circles, gender, and race/color. Brazil, 2019

in %

Circles of care	Gender			Race/Color		
	Male	Female	Total	White	Black	Total
Circle 1 – recurring, direct, domestic	2.2%	97.8%	100.0%	36.3%	63.7%	100.0%
Circle 2 – recurring, indirect, domestic	9.5%	90.5%	100.0%	32.3%	67.7%	100.0%
Circle 3 – recurring, direct, non-domestic	11.8%	88.2%	100.0%	46.7%	53.3%	100.0%
Circle 4 – less recurring, direct, non-domestic	26.6%	73.4%	100.0%	50.5%	49.5%	100.0%
Circle 5 – less recurring, indirect, non-domestic	40.9%	59.1%	100.0%	36.2%	63.8%	100.0%
Total	24.7%	75.3%	100.0%	41.1%	58.9%	100.0%

SOURCE: IBGE. PNAD-C. 2019 – 1ST INTERVIEW

Significantly, a quarter of the occupations in the care sector are in domestic work (represented by the sum of circles 1 and 2), with women being particularly prominent in these occupations. In Brazil, domestic employment continues to be one of the main pathways for women into the labor market, especially for Black women with low income and education levels. For every 100 employed women in Brazil, approximately 14 were domestic workers in 2019, performing activities as diverse as childcare or care for older adults (circle 1 in our classification) or working as cooks, cleaners, or housekeepers (classified in circle 2).

We must also draw attention to the racial division of care work. While black people form the majority of care workers (occupying 59 out of every 100 available jobs), their participation varies in the different circles of care. Some doors are more open to black people while others remain only slightly ajar, leading to a segmentation in the field that is closely connected to skill requirements

not only a female domain, but the most female economic sector of all, at a considerable distance from the rest.

and the nature of occupations, albeit not exclusively. Thus, we find a scenario in which black men and (above all) black women have a higher proportional representation at the two extremes of our diagram of concentric circles. Black people account for 64% of the sum of circles 1 and 2, which encompasses both direct and indirect domestic work and where we expect the intensity of care to be highest, and account for 68% of the occupations in circle 5, where we find the lowest intensity of care. How do we make sense of this scenario? Our hypothesis is that these two circles share a common trait, in that they include occupations usually deemed as "basic," do not require higher education, and have low social and economic recognition. These seemingly disparate circles, the innermost and outermost circles in the diagram, share precariousness, low wages, and lack of social protection.

The only circle in which black people are not the majority is Circle 4, precisely the one that has occupations with higher entry requirements, like doctors, teachers, and social workers, even though it also includes occupations without such barriers, such as beauty professionals and health technicians. This bipolarity is the probable reason for the fact that Circle 4 presents a more even distribution of black and white people among the available occupations. Thus, if we only focus on occupations that demand higher education, white people make up the majority (59%), whereas the opposite is true for occupations without such requirements, and where black people comprise most of the workforce (58%).

By intersecting race and gender, we find that the provision of paid care in Brazil is not only female but constitutes space par excellence for black women. In 2019, they occupied close to 45% of all care employment in Brazil. This proportion increases to two thirds of the occupations in domestic employment, whether in Circle 1 or 2 (see Graph 2.1). Significantly, black women are less present in Circle 4, but are still dominant in 36% of the occupations. It is worth noting that they accounted for just 29% of the country's population (aged 15 or over) in 2019. This leads us to conclude that, even in circles where Black women are not the majority, they are still overrepresented vis-à-vis their participation in the population. White women, who accounted for 31% of care occupations and 23% of the country's population, were overrepresented in almost all subsectors, apart from the one furthest from the nucleus of care. Conversely, men, whether white or black, were always underrepresented in paid care, regardless of the circle.

The gender and racial divisions of care work are not merely a separation of menand women or black and white people across different occupations in the sector. It entails a divide that grants certain groups occupations of greater prestige, higher wages, and greater social protection, while others are relegated

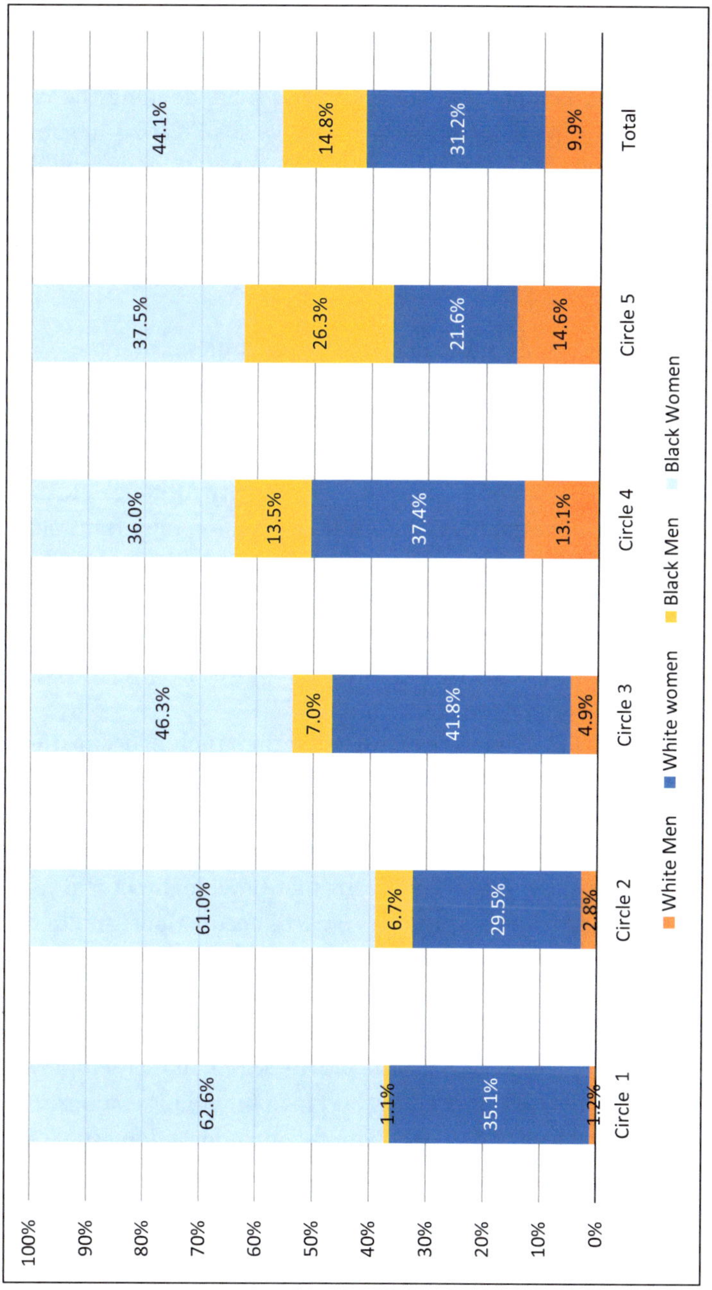

GRAPH 2.1 Distribution of the population employed in the care sector by gender and race/color, by circles. Brazil, 2019
SOURCE: IBGE. PNAD-C 2019 – 1ST INTERVIEW

to occupations with lower social recognition, inferior financial returns, and lower protection from the State. That configuration reproduces what Bruschini and Lombardi (2000) coined as the "bipolarity" of the female labor market in Brazil. Given the profound inequalities found in the paid care sector we could transpose Bruschini and Lombardi's concept to this field, defining the care labor market as a bipolar market. However, and as we shall discuss in subsequent sections, this bipolarity becomes increasingly complex as inequalities and hierarchies are reproduced among women (in terms of race, and even among women in the lowest level of the hierarchy, a trend also observed in other countries (MILKMAN, 2022).

2.2.2 State, Market, Family: Providing Job Opportunities … and Inequalities

Understanding the contexts of care provision allows us to recognize the different circuits through which job opportunities run – public, private, and domestic – but also how they shape different patterns of inequality. Although PNAD-C data does not allow detailed analysis, it does provide some important clues and warning signs, once we explore the variable "position in the occupation," which informs how workers engage in the labor market.[12] Table 2.4 presents the different ways people participate in the Brazilian care sector, four of which stand out: private sector employee (34%), family employee (25.3%), business employee (22.7) and self-employed (14.9).

The private sector is indeed largely responsible for the supply of occupations in the fifth circle, which do not entail intense personal interaction, recurrence, or intimate bonds, and account for almost 70% of all workers. However, as we move towards the nucleus of the care sector, the State's presence grows and has a significant role in recruiting for job positions that provide direct and non-domestic care. In the fourth circle, it reaches 40% of occupations, and in the third circle 50%. The State carries significant weight in the areas of education, health, and social assistance and ensures greater democratization in accessing those services. Therefore, as we move away from the nucleus of care, the State ceases to be the protagonist, leaving the private sector and self-employed workers to provide services such as cleaning and food in public locations. The first two circles, or the nucleus of care occupations, encompass domestic work activities in which families act as the contractors.

12 For further details on categories and definitions of the variable "position in the occupation" see IBGE (2016)

TABLE 2.4 Distribution of the population employed in the care sector, by position in occupation and circles. Brazil, 2019

	Circle 1 – recurring, direct, domestic	Circle 2 – recurring, indirect, domestic	Circle 3 – recurring, direct, non-domestic	Circle 4 – less recurring, direct, non-domestic	Circle 5 – less recurring, indirect, non-domestic	Total
Private sector	0.0	0.0	45.5	24.0	69.0	34.9
Domestic work	100.0	100.0	0.0	0.0	0.0	25.3
Public sector	0.0	0.0	50.0	39.3	14.3	22.7
Employer	0.0	0.0	0.1	4.1	1.2	1.6
Self-employed	0.0	0.0	3.6	32.4	13.2	14.6
Assisting family worker	0.0	0.0	0.9	0.2	2.3	0.9
Total	100.0	100.0	100.0	100.0	100.0	100.0

SOURCE: IBGE, PNAD-C 2019 – 1ST INTERVIEW

The private market is the primary employer of male workers in the care sector, encompassing more than half of male-held occupations– with or without a formal work contract. In turn, domestic work remains the main entry point for women, with the State playing a proportionately more prominent role in their engagement than in men's. The large supply of public care in the areas of assistance, health, and education, all of which are traditionally regarded as female, combined with public hiring processes, may explain an important part of this difference.

2.2.3 Work and Social Protection

Under a contributory system like Brazil's, workers are required to pay for social security to be eligible to receive State assistance in the event of temporary inability to work (maternity or illness) or permanent inability (age or disability). Social protection can be attained either via formal employment contracts, where the employer signs work papers (*carteira de trabalho*), or by making individual payments as an independent contributor or an individual micro-entrepreneur (open modality for some occupational categories) to social security. To measure the social protection of careworkers, we used the variable "contribution to social security." Therefore, we considered both male and female workers with a formal employment relationship that grants them labor rights such as paid holidays and a 13th salary (an end-of-year extra salary), and those who contribute independently with no employer counterpart, thus having social security rights but no labor rights.

In general, close to two out of three professionals in the caresector had social security protection (63.7%), a rate that practically mirrored the Brazilian labor market in 2019. The care sector has the third highest coverage rate after the general service sector (excluding care services) and industry, with 73% and 74%, respectively. Social protection varies, however, depending on the circle of care, as shown in Table 2.5. While almost 90% of professionals in the intermediate circle contributed to social security, less than half of those employed in domestic employment (both circles 1 and 2) were in the same situation. In other words, social protectionin some care categories is standard, whereas lack of protection is the norm in others.

In the case of domestic work, extremely low social protection is the rule. Furthermore, social security coverage has been declining since 2016 for domestic workers that work on a monthly or daily basis throughout all regions of the country and across different racial groups. This occupation is undoubtedly one of the most precarious in the Brazilian economy (Pinheiro et al., 2016) and, not coincidentally, an occupation largely performed by Black and low-income women. These workers face much harder challenges in making social security payments, not only because they lack employer contributions, but as the most vulnerable and lowest income group, the necessary trade-off between present and future income is not always feasible in everyday life. Furthermore, precarious working conditions mean more irregular social security contributions, which tend to be suspended in the event of financial hardships or difficulties in performing paid work (such as illness), thereby making it more difficult to reach the minimum contribution period required to retrieve social security benefits.[13]

13 As such, for many of these female workers, the State becomes visible and acknowledged via social welfare and benefit programs such as the BPC (Continuous Cash Benefit Program, which stands for *Benefício de Prestação Continuada* in Portuguese).

TABLE 2.5 Proportion of people employed in the care sector who contribute to social security, by circles, gender, and race/color. Brazil, 2019

Circles of care	Gender		Race/color		Total
	Male	Female	White	Black	
Circle 1 – recurring, direct, domestic	37.4	32.8	36.7	30.7	32.9
Circle 2 – recurring, indirect, domestic	47.1	38.9	45.0	37.1	39.7
Circle 3 – recurring, direct, non-domestic	89.0	86.5	89.5	84.5	86.8
Circle 4 – less recurring, direct, non-domestic	68.7	69.8	74.6	64.3	69.5
Circle 5 – less recurring, indirect, non-domestic	69.4	69.3	71.7	68.0	69.4
Total	68.5	62.1	69.5	59.7	63.7

SOURCE: IBGE, PNAD-C 2019 – 1ST INTERVIEW

Table 2.5 reveals a similar level of social protection for female and male workers in the care sector, except for those in Circle 2 (domestic employees providing indirect care), in which the protection of men, while still low, is almost 10% higher when compared to women. Two points merit mention. First, while this disparity is noteworthy in Circle 1 (paid home caregivers for dependent persons), it is decidedly lower than in Circle 2, revealing the intricacies of the inequality matrix and the multifaceted bipolar pattern being reproduced at the bottom of the hierarchy. Second, in a subsector where women hold more than 90% of the jobs, the greatest social coverage is allocated to the group with the lowest population weight. In fact, as shown in other studies, men and women have vastly different experiences in domestic work, whether regarding the type of work or the quality of the occupations (Fontoura; Marcolino, 2021; Pinheiro et al., 2021). Undoubtedly, domestic employment incorporates gendered divisions of labor that not only separates men and women by activities performed, but also tends to reserve higher-quality jobs for men.

The scenario changes when we compare black and white workers insofar as the latter will always, regardless of their care occupation, contribute the most to Social Security. This distance is, on average, 10 percentage points. In an intersectional analysis, social security coverage rates are typically lowest among black women, while the most secured varies between white men and white women, depending on the circle. Race therefore seems to be particularly relevant when considering protection against unpredictable adversities. But, once again, the gap in Circle 1 is smaller than in Circle 2, demonstrating the complexity of the inequality patterns.

2.2.4 How Much Is Paid Care Work Worth?

Lastly, when we take note of the fact that women in families provide most of the care work without any compensation, we must ask the important question: what is paid care work worth?

Studies have revealed that there is a wage penalty in care services, which ultimately places this sector at the bottom of the income pyramid, despite the significant number of professionals with higher education backgrounds employed in this field. This penalty is substantiated by the fact that care sector employees tend to receive lower wages than would be expected, given the nature of the work and the qualifications of the individuals who perform it (England, Budig & Folbre, 2002). In a study conducted in the USA, Duffy, Albelda, and Hammond (2013) identified that this penalty persists even when controlling for variables such as gender, because the care workforce is disproportionately female when compared to other sectors. The authors outline multiple factors to explain this phenomenon, of which we highlight three. First, care is a public good that benefits not just the individual recipient. This means that its market price does not precisely reflect its utility, since many of the indirect beneficiaries of the service do not pay for it. Second, increasing work productivity per worker without significant quality loss is difficult. Third, the fact that care is associated to "the feminine," to skills understood as innately female, to unpaid labor performed in the home, to motherhood, and to other socially devalued elements, all serve to influence the social and economic recognition of care work when conducted as a professional activity. (England, Budig & Folbre, 2002; Duffy, Albelda & Hammond, 2013).

While our goal is not to quantify the extent of this wage penalty in Brazil, the evidence demonstrates that, compared to the other economic sectors, the R$1,820 per month received by care sector workers was lower in 2019 than the average wage on the Brazilian labor market (R$2,213), and in particular to the wage earned by other service workers (R$3,118). Comparatively, it has one of the highest gender wage gaps, with women earning 72% of men's wages, second only to industry where the ratio is 64%. Regarding race, the inequalities observed are not vastly different from other sectors: in 2019, black workers received only 60% of what white workers earned, a figure marginally greater when compared to the overall labor market (57.5%).

When we examine the internal situation of the care sector, income inequalities between the circles of care reflect inequalities in worker profiles and in the quality of jobs offered. It is not surprising that workers engaged in domesticemployment – whether in direct or indirect care – earn the lowest incomes among all care categories, even lower than the minimum wage of R$998, as per 2019 values (see Table 2.6). As shown above, these occupations, like those in the group farthest away from the nucleus of care, have the most basic qualification requirements. But they are also very similar activities, essentially differing in that the former is performed within a domestic employment relationship, while the latter is tied to the private sector. In addition to low education, the inferior socio-economic status of these activities has a similar impact on both groups. However, we should note that work outside a domestic employment relationship means a 36% increase in the average monthly income.

The subgroup with the highest income, as expected, consists of workers in the fourth circle of care, since these occupations require higher levels of education. They earned on average R$3,000, which is over three times the monthly wage of domestic workers and is 40% higher than the average income of Brazilian workers in 2019. While this sector includes some of the most socially and economically valued professionals such as physicians, it also includes workers at the opposite end of the pyramid, with no minimum education requirements, thus forming a highly polarized circle.

However, when we consider the characteristics of care workers, especially their gender and racial background, the picture changes. Table 2.7 presents the

TABLE 2.6 Average regular income from the main job of those employed in the care sector, by circles, gender, and race/color. Brazil, 2019

			(in R$)
Circles of care	**Men**	**Women**	**Total**
Circle 1 – recurring, direct, domestic	1,011.5	872.9	875.9
Circle 2 – recurring, indirect, domestic	1,102.9	876.6	897.7
Circle 3 – recurring, direct, non-domestic	2,440.2	2,070.9	2,114.3
Circle 4 – less recurring, direct, non-domestic	4,106.5	2,721.5	3,089.6
Circle 5 – less recurring, indirect, non-domestic	1,337.0	1,124.5	1,211.6
Total	2,307.5	1,661.9	1,820.3

SOURCE: IBGE. PNAD-C 2019 – 1ST INTERVIEW

income ratios for each circle of care, comparing the salaries of women and men, black and white people, and black women and white men, the latter representing the two extremities of Brazil's unequal income structure.

The first revealing evidence is that in any circle, women earn less than men, black individuals earn even less than white individuals, and black women much less than white men. In 2019, these ratios were 72%, 59.8%, and 42.3% respectively. Even when we consider the effects of women's shorter working hours, there is a substantial gender inequality that pervades the care sector, which in fact does not stray far from the country's general labor market. When comparing the hourly income of men and women, the ratio rises to 81.6%, thus narrowing the gender pay gap, albeit still with almost 20 percentage points between them. In the same direction, we find an increase in the hourly income of black women when compared to white men, corresponding to 48.4% of their income. As the working hours of black and white people are not vastly different, the ratio of monthly income and hourly income between these two groups shows no substantial disparity.

TABLE 2.7 Ratio of regular monthly income from the main job of those employed in the care sector, by subsector. Brazil, 2019

			(in %)
Circles of care	**Women/ men**	**Black/ white**	**Black women / white men**
Circle 1 – recurring, direct, domestic	86.3%	83.7%	89.9%
Circle 2 – recurring, indirect, domestic	79.5%	86.8%	71.6%
Circle 3 – recurring, direct, non-domestic	84.9%	79.0%	65.2%
Circle 4 – less recurring, direct, non-domestic	66.3%	57.7%	37.6%
Circle 5 – less recurring, indirect, non-domestic	84.1%	85.0%	71.2%
Total	72.0%	59.8%	42.3%

SOURCE: IBGE. PNAD-C 2019 – 1ST INTERVIEW

Another revealing fact in Table 2.7 is that the circle with the highest income, greatest social protection, and highest level of education is also where gender and race disparities are most pronounced. Thus, when we look at care work in the fourth circle, we find a scenario in which women earn around two-thirds of what men earn, black people earn less than 60% of what white people earn, and black women earn only a startling 37.6% of what white men earn. Inequalities are particularly intense in this circle when compared to the other circles, undoubtedly indicating that not everyone can reap the "benefits" of the social and economic recognition of this circle. On the other hand, in the most precarious circles (informal and lowest income) inequalities are less pronounced: in domestic employment, for example, black women received 73% of what white men earned, roughly the same as in the fifth circle, which also includes "more basic" occupations. Here, by contrast, precariousness and low wages appear to be more evenly distributed.

Lastly, the disparate economic value of the different types of care work relates to the kind of employers that prevail in each circle, whether a business, the State, or a family member. According to PNAD-C data for 2019, public sector care workers earned 50% higher wages than workers in the private sector (or those who entered the market independently, such as self-employed workers). At the bottom of this hierarchy, we find those paid by families, with incomes equivalent to 33% of the public care circuit. As we move towards publicly supplied care services, we not only find a more democratic offer of goods and services, but also a space in which male and female workers seem to be more protected and whose jobs tend to be less precarious than in the other circuits.

3 How Lasting Are the Care Circles and How Durable Are the Inequalities in the Brazilian Care Sector (2012–2022)?

How solid is the occupational structure of the Brazilian care sector and how recurrent is its pattern of inequalities? The empirical evidence to answer this question will be gathered in a two-way strategy that is retrospective and prospective. However, as we will see, regardless of the strategy, the results are the same: a consolidated occupational structure in terms of the circles that organize its internal heterogeneity and its pattern of inequalities, which is anchored in intersecting differences between gender and race groups that reinforce disparities in income and in worker protection.

Focusing on the same features outlined in the previous section from a retrospective outlook, we went back to 2012, when we first had PNAD-C information. We found that the same structure described for 2019 was also prevalent in the beginning of the 2010s. In other words, the important factors that marked Brazilian society between 2012 and 2019 did not change the characteristics of its care labor market. The weight of care occupations compared to other segments of the labor market, the internal structure of the care halo with its different circles, as well as the inequalities that characterize them remained immune to events such as the decline in economic activity between 2014–2017, the introduction of normative regulations that expanded the rights of important segments of domestic workers in 2015, and the changes brought about by the 2017 labor legislation reform.

On the other hand, COVID-19 had strong cyclical effects in Brazil, that affected economic and occupational dynamics mainly in 2020 (Almeida & Wajnman, 2023). However, when they are assessed in the pandemic's more extended results, no impact is visible on the occupational configuration of the care sector either. As we will see, the post-pandemic trends, captured by the 2022 PNAD-C had already been underway since the beginning of the previous decade, particularly with the decline in the share of domestic services (a light but persistent shrinking of Circle 2, comprising indirect home care). Unfortunately, the PNAD-C does not capture home care employment generated through platforms, which has been expanding rapidly in the sector (Andrada et al., 2023). This new movement increases the number of hourly workers, notably as providers of indirect home care services (mainly as cleaners) now working under an unknown employment relation in Brazil.

TABLE 2.8 Employment composition by economic sectors. Brazil, 2012, 2019 and 2022 (%)

Economic sectors	2012		2019		2022	
	N	%	N	%	N	%
Care	20,697,506	23.08	23,947,518	25.22	24,125,228	24.88
Other services	22,205,653	24.76	25,895,147	27.28	27,216,060	28.07
Agriculture/livestock	10,140,472	11.31	8,535,763	8.99	8,435,805	8.7
Manufacturing	12,486,002	13.92	11,948,565	12.59	11,852,739	12.22
Construction	7,550,613	8.42	6,901,533	7.27	7,188,621	7.41
Commerce	16,570,175	18.47	17,679,678	18.62	18,123,985	18.69
Others (imprecise definition)	44,470	0.05	31,287	0.03	32,360	0.03
Total	89,694,891	100	94,939,491	100	96,974,798	100

SOURCE: IBGE. PNAD-C 2019 – 1ST INTERVIEW

When observing each of these aspects in more detail, we first detected the share of care occupations in the sectoral composition of employment in the Brazilian labor market, which remained the same. As we see in Table 2.8, care occupations continue to represent a quarter of the country's stock of employed people (23.1% in 2012, 25.2% in 2019 and 24.9% in 2022).

A second important aspect that we observed previously for the year 2019 was the internal composition of the care halo in Brazil. That composition remained constant between 2012 and 2022. In other words, the same pattern of internal heterogeneity that we found for the pre-pandemic period is replicated after it, as can be seen in Table 2.9. The novelty was the contraction in the weight of indirect home care workers (cooks, cleaners, ironers, and others). Even though they are still largely dominant in households, domestic] workers dropped by eight percentage points in care employment in Brazil (from 26% in 2012, to 20.4% in 2019 and 18.6% in 2022). But this, as the numbers show, is a trend that had already begun before the pandemic.

TABLE 2.9 Population in the care sector by circles. Brazil, 2012, 2019 and 2022

Circles of care	2012		2019		2022	
	Freq.	%	Freq.	%	Freq.	%
Circle 1 – recurring, direct, domestic	710,222	3.43	1,184,624	4.95	1,223,540	5.07
Circle 2 – recurring, indirect, domestic	5,382,591	26.01	4,877,358	20.37	4,488,787	18.61
Circle 3 – recurring, direct, non-domestic	2,154,797	10.41	2,926,411	12.22	3,119,471	12.93
Circle 4 – less recurring, direct, non-domestic	6,039,528	29.18	7,342,647	30.66	7,899,532	32.74
Circle 5 – less recurring, indirect, non-domestic	6,410,368	30.97	7,616,478	31.8	7,393,898	30.65
Total	20,697,506	100	23,947,518	100	24,125,228	100

SOURCE: IBGE.PNAD-C 2012, 2019, 2022 – 1ST INTERVIEW

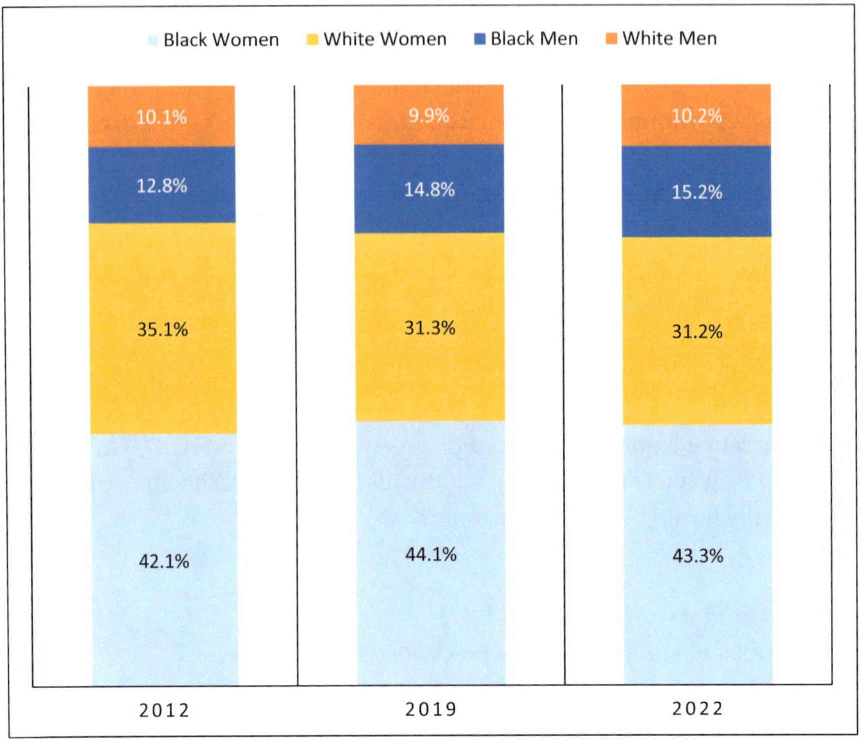

GRAPH 2.2 Distribution of the population employed in the care sector by gender and race/color. Brazil, 2012, 2019 and 2022

SOURCE: IBGE.PNAD-C 2012, 2019, 2022 – 1ST INTERVIEW

Finally, while care provision in Brazil is anchored in female work, its weight has always been borne by black women. This has not changed in the period of time considered here, before and after the pandemic (Graph 2.2).

A curious observation is a slight expansion in the relative weight of male work in the care labor force (Graph 2.3), which increased by two percentage points in these ten years.

In short, the persistence of gender/race inequality reproduced, in both 2012 and 2022, the same patterns of income inequality and precarity in employmentrelations with lower earnings and less worker protection the closer we get to the inner circles of the Brazilian halo of care. This correlates with the significant differences between the circuits of State, business, and family employment relations.

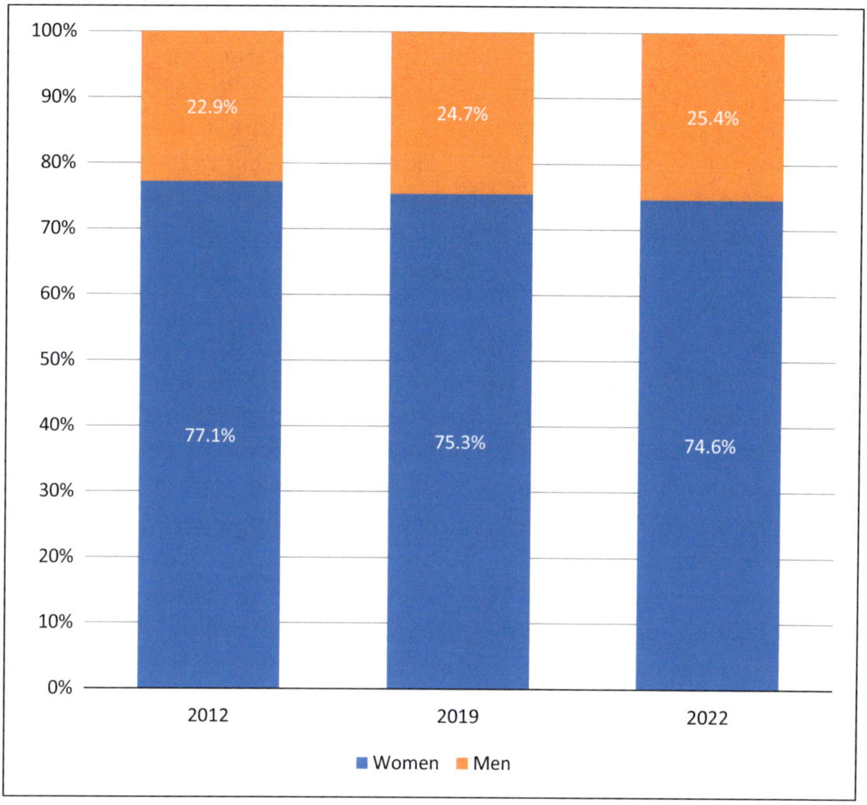

GRAPH 2.3 Distribution of the population employed in the care sector by gender. Brazil, 2012, 2019 and 2022

SOURCE: IBGE.PNAD-C 2012, 2019, 2022 – 1ST INTERVIEW

4 Final Remarks

We have centered this chapter around the challenge of how to measure and systematize the internal heterogeneity of an economic sector whose recent expansion has been remarkable for its fast pace, systematic development, and wide range. In fact, shortly before the outbreak of the COVID-19 pandemic a study by the International Labor Organization on care work (ILO, 2018) left no room for doubt that care work is a crucial segment for developing employment opportunities in the world, accounting for nearly 12% of global employment and circa 20% of female employment, the latter of which, in a universe close to 250 million workers, represented no less than 65% of the paid care workforce.

While international literature has devoted efforts to delineate the boundaries of this sector more precisely by using comparable statistics, in Brazil we have trod fruitful and almost parallel research paths, yet circumscribed to studies on domestic work unpaid housework, aging and care for older adults in institutions, and analyses of early childhood education and access to day care centers. This comes as no surprise, seeing as our limitations hindered our capacity to include a large portion of the paid care work force, such as caregivers for older, disabled, or bedridden people, who were only included in statistical records after 2002. This is why we have only just begun to make attempts to quantify the range of care occupations in our labor market (Melo & Morandi, 2020) and increase academic production in this field (Guimarães, Hirata & Posthuma, 2020).

Encouraged by this challenge, we embarked upon a theoretical-methodological effort in this chapter to measure precisely and reliably, with technical accuracy and robust analytical proficiency, the size of this burgeoning labor market by systematizing the heterogenous form of care services that circulate within it, and to corroborate our endeavors with data on the Brazilian reality. It was a challenging task to account for the complexities involved in this attempt to circumscribe what we call "the halo of the care labor market." This is because the breadth and categorization of the occupations encompassed by this halo largely hinge on the theoretical concept of care. But they also depended on the careful and critical management of databases and an immersion in Brazilian occupational classifications. Thus, we began by systematizing the multiple facets of the concept to comprehend its magnitude and, at the same time, differentiate the heterogeneous forms of care work that are part of this great halo. In view of this, we devised a typology of paid care occupations based on a meticulous review of the job descriptions for each occupation, as documented in the multiple occupational classifications in effect in Brazil This typology sought to factor in two intertwining dimensions. The first dealt with the nature of the care relationship, focused on the closeness between provider and recipient (whether in a direct or indirect relationship) as well as the environment in which the care was delivered (whether in a domesticemployment relationship, thus within the private and more intimate confines of the home, or outside it). The second dimension sought to account for the recurrence of this relationship.

Our broad halo of care encompassed no less than 70 occupations. This roster of occupations is not fixed or definite, but rather can (and should) change as analytical interests vary and, above all, react to the ever evolving and flourishing labor world classified by the State in an equally mutable fashion, according to its own guidelines. In this sense, our proposal here serves as a starting point. However, it is also the result of an effort to delineate a wide range of activities whose internal subdivisions can be constructed and reconfigured according to the different interests of researchers, managers, activists, students, and others. The five circles proposed here serve our purpose of trying to build a demarcation line for this sector, whose central variable was the intensity of care present in each occupation. We operationalized this intensity, as detailed above, through the notions of recurrence in the relationship, the prevailing interpersonal/intimate bond in the care setting, and the nature of the interaction between the care actors (direct/indirect). Other purposes in other studies may be on the agenda and lead to a reorganization of this set of 70 occupations based on interests such as, for example, the role of the State in providing care – a situation in which internal divisions may be more related to the bond of workers or the settings where care is delivered. In short, flexibility is an essential part of our suggested methodology.

Lastly, let us share some final reflections about our experiment to measure the capacity to accurately describe the scope of care in Brazil using occupations as a starting point. Much like in other parts of the world, these occupations are notably present in Brazil's labor market. In 2019, the care sector alone employed almost 24 million workers, equivalent to circa 25% of the total employed population in the country. Only slightly larger than the care sector are the remaining service subsectors, which account for 27.3% of the employed population. Our measurement effort has shed light on vital aspects of the social organization of care within our society. Notably, two major considerations emerge.

First, despite the centrality of paid care services and its importance for women's employment, care service providers face immense and persistent inequalities. Disparities among women providing care are widened by multiple, intersectional inequalities depending on the setting in which they operate – whether working for a family in a domestic setting, in privately owned entities that operate in the public sector, or in State institutions. Moreover, the racialization of labor relations is especially prominent in this domain, segregating a significant portion of women caregivers to domestic work. These women endure greater disparities in income, working conditions, access to rights, and social protection. It is significant that this happens precisely in Circles 1 and 2, which comprise the epicenter of the care halo. Nonetheless, while more pronounced, inequalities are not exclusive to these spaces. In circles more distant from the central nucleus (such as circle 4), where care relationships take place in institutions, in the public sphere, and are usually less recurring, the dichotomy between good and bad jobs is equally perceptible and correlated with gender and racial identifiers.

Second, in a context such as Brazil, where the commodification of care has not advanced in unison with externalization and defamiliarization, we must not overlook the crucial role of protective policies for care workers. The

State's deficient presence, whether through a public system with integrated and transversal care policies, or through the regulation of the private offer of this service, renders this a pressing issue. Again, this is especially felt in the epicenter of paid care occupations, whether expressed by the 2019 presidential decree that denied recognition to the profession of caregiver, or the tenuous rights granted to hourly domestic workers who are increasingly present in this market, or the lack of adequate regulation of the working conditions for nurses, who are presently calling for a minimum wage law for their sector.

We hope the effort put into this chapter will contribute to the construction of this epistemic field, which, in Brazil as elsewhere, has been gaining significant ground in recent years.

ANNEX 2.1 The halo of care: Care occupations in Brazilian labor market (with codes)

Recurrence of the interaction	**Context and nature of the interaction**			
	Direct – more interaction		**Indirect – less interaction**	
	In domestic work – more intimate	**Outside domestic work – less intimate**	**In domestic work – more intimate**	**Outside domestic work – less intimate**
Demands *more* recurrence and dependency in the care relationship	Child caregivers (v4010=5311 & pos ocup=2) Personal care workers at home and companion care (v4010= 5322+5162 & pos ocup=2)	Preschool teachers (2342) Special education teachers(2352) Nursing professionals (2221) Mid-level nursing professionals (3221)	Housekeepers and domestic butlers (v4010=5152 & pos ocup=2) General domestic service workers (v4010=9111 & pos ocup=2) Kitchen chefs (v4010=3434 & pos ocup=2) Cooks (v4010= 5120 & pos ocup=2)	

ANNEX 2.1 The halo of care: Care occupations in Brazilian labor market (with codes) (*cont.*)

Recurrence of the interaction	Context and nature of the interaction			
	Direct – more interaction		Indirect – less interaction	
	In domestic work – more intimate	Outside domestic work – less intimate	In domestic work – more intimate	Outside domestic work – less intimate
		Personal care workers at home and companion care (5322 + 5162 & pos ocup!=2) Personal care workers in health services not classified above (5329) Personal care workers in institutions (5321) Child caregivers (v4010=5311 & pos ocup!= 2) Teaching assistants (5312)	Kitchen assistants (v4010=9412 & pos ocup=2) Security guards (v4010=5414 & pos ocup=2) Skilled farmers and workers in vegetable gardens, arboretum, and general gardens and basic gardening and horticultural workers (v4010=6112 + 9214 & pos ocup=2) Motor vehicle operators (v4010=8322 & pos ocup=2) Other cleaning workers (v4010=9129 & pos ocup=2)	

ANNEX 2.1 The halo of care: Care occupations in Brazilian labor market (with codes) (*cont.*)

Recurrence of the interaction	Context and nature of the interaction			
	Direct – more interaction		Indirect – less interaction	
	In domestic work – more intimate	Outside domestic work – less intimate	In domestic work – more intimate	Outside domestic work – less intimate
Demands *less* recurrence and dependency in the care relationship		General physicians (2211) Specialist physicians (2212) Childbirth professionals (2222) Traditional and alternative medicine professionals (2230) Dentists (2261) Dieticians and nutritionists (2265) Physiotherapists (2264) Speech therapists and logopedicians (2266) Psychologists (2634) Paramedics (2240)		Kitchen chefs (v4010=3434 & pos ocup!=2) Cooks (v4010= 5120 & pos ocup!=2) Kitchen assistants (9412 & pos ocup!=2) Street food service vendors (5212) Food service clerks (5246) Fast-food cooks (9411) Waiters (5131) Bartenders (5132) Doormen and janitors (5153) Interior cleaning workers for buildings, offices, hotels, and other venues (9112)

ANNEX 2.1 The halo of care: Care occupations in Brazilian labor market (with codes) (*cont.*)

Recurrence of the interaction	Context and nature of the interaction			
	Direct – more interaction		Indirect – less interaction	
	In domestic work – more intimate	Outside domestic work – less intimate	In domestic work – more intimate	Outside domestic work – less intimate
		Occupational and environmental health and hygiene professionals (2263) Health professionals not classified above (2269) Elementary school teachers (2341) Secondary school teachers (2330) Specialist in pedagogical methods (2351) Social workers (2635) Ministers of religious cults, missionaries and similar (2636) Medical assistants (3256)		Laundry washers and ironers (9121) Window cleaners (9123) Other cleaning workers (v4010= 9129 & pos ocup!=2) Garbage and recyclable material collectors (9611)

ANNEX 2.1 The halo of care: Care occupations in Brazilian labor market (with codes) (*cont.*)

Recurrence of the interaction	Context and nature of the interaction			
	Direct – more interaction		Indirect – less interaction	
	In domestic work – more intimate	Outside domestic work – less intimate	In domestic work – more intimate	Outside domestic work – less intimate
		Mid-level childbirth professionals (3222) Mid-level traditional and alternative medicine professionals (3230) Dentistry assistants and helpers (3251) Optometrists (2267) Physical therapist technicians and assistants (3255) Community healthcare workers (3253) Ambulance assistant (3258) Mid-level healthcare professionals not classified above		

ANNEX 2.1 The halo of care: Care occupations in Brazilian labor market (with codes) (*cont.*)

Recurrence of the interaction	Context and nature of the interaction			
	Direct – more interaction		Indirect – less interaction	
	In domestic work – more intimate	Outside domestic work – less intimate	In domestic work – more intimate	Outside domestic work – less intimate
		Physical education and recreational activities instructors (3423) Sex workers (5168) Middle-level social workers and assistants (3412) Lay religious assistants (3413) Hair stylists (5141) Beauty treatment specialists and similar workers (5142)		

SOURCE: PREPARED BY THE AUTHORS

References

Abel, E., & Nelson, M. (1990). Circles of Care: An Introductory Essay. In E. Abel & M. Nelson (Eds.), *Circles of Care: Work and Identities in Women's Lives* (pp. 4–34). Albany: State University of New York Press.

Albelda, R., Duffy, M., & Folbre, N. (2009). *Counting on Care Work: Human Infrastructure in Massachusetts*. Center for Social Policy Publications, Paper 33. Retrieved from http://scholarworks.umb.edu/csp_pubs/33.

Almeida, M., Wajnman, S. (2023). Occupational transitions of paid care workers during the COVID-19 pandemic in Brazil. Coleção Documentos de Trabalho. São Paulo: Centro Brasileiro de Análise e Planejamento, n. 3. https://cuidado.cebrap.org.br/wp-content/uploads/2023/11/WhoCares_DT03.pdf.

Andrada, A. C., Cardoso, A. C., Guimarães, N. A., Moreno, R., & Pinheiro, M. J. (2023). Plataformas digitais de cuidado no Brasil: acesso e controle do trabalho no entrecruzamento de múltiplas crises. *Tempo Social*, 35(3), 5–32. https://www.revistas.usp.br/ts/article/view/218376.

Araujo, A. B. (2015). *Gênero, profissionalização e autonomia: o agenciamento do trabalho de cuidadoras de idosos por empresas* [Master's thesis, Universidade Federal do Rio de Janeiro].

Arretche, M. (Ed.). (2019). *Paths of Inequality in Brazil: A Half-Century of Changes*. Cham: Springer.

Benería, L., & Stimpson, C. (1987). *Women, Households and the Economy*. New Brunswick, NJ: Rutgers University Press.

Brites, J. (2000). *Afeto, desigualdade e rebeldia: bastidores do serviço doméstico* [Doctoral dissertation, Universidade Federal do Rio Grande do Sul].

Bruschini, C., & Lombardi, M. R. (2000). A bipolaridade do trabalho feminino no Brasil contemporâneo. *Cadernos de Pesquisa*, 110, 67–104.

Bruschini, C. (2006). Trabalho doméstico: inatividade econômica ou trabalho não-remunerado. *Revista Brasileira de Estudos de População*, 23(2), 331–353.

Cardoso, A. C. M., & Pereira, M. J. T. (2023). A plataformização do trabalho no Brasil e o subsetor dos cuidados: uma revisão de achados bibliográficos. Coleção Documentos de Trabalho. São Paulo: Centro Brasileiro de Análise e Planejamento. http://cuidado.cebrap.org.br/2023/02/15/a-plataformizacao-do-trabalho-no-brasil-e-o-subsetor-dos-cuidados-uma-revisao-de-achados-bibliograficos/.

Desrosières, A. (1993). *La Politique des Grands Nombres: Histoire de la Raison Statistique*. Paris: La Découverte.

Duffy, M. (2005). Reproducing Labor Inequalities: Challenges for Feminists Conceptualizing Care at the Intersections of Gender, Race and Class. *Gender & Society*, 19(1), 66–82.

Duffy, M. (2011). *Making Care Count: A Century of Gender, Race and Paid Care Work*. New Jersey: Rutgers University Press.

Duffy, M., Albelda, R., & Hammond, C. (2013). Counting Care Work: The Empirical and Policy Applications of Care Theory. *Social Problems*, 60(2), 145–167.

Duffy, M., Armenia, A., & Stacey, C. (2015). *Caring on the Clock: The Complexities and Contradictions of Paid Care Work*. New Jersey: Rutgers University Press.

England, P. (2005). Emerging theories of care work. *Annual Review of Sociology*, 31, 381–399.

England, P., Budig, M. J., & Folbre, N. (2002). Wages of virtue: the relative pay of care word. *Social Problems*, 49, 455–473.

Fisher, B., & Tronto, J. (1990). Toward a Feminist Theory of Caring. In E. Abel & M. Nelson (Eds.), *Circles of Care: Work and Identity in Women 's Lives* (pp. 36–54). Albany, NY: Suny Press.

Folbre, N. (1995). "Holding hands at midnight": the paradox of caring labor. *Feminist Economics*, 1(1), 73–92.

Folbre, N. (2012). (Ed.). *For Love and Money: Care Provision in the U.S.* New York: Russell Sage Foundation.

Folbre, N., & Wright, E. (2012). Defining Care. In N. Folbre (Ed.), *For Love and Money: Care Provision in the U.S.* (pp. 1–20). New York: Russell Sage Foundation.

Fontoura, N., & Marcolino, A. (2021). A heterogeneidade do trabalho doméstico no Brasil. In L. Pinheiro, C. Tokarski, & A. C. Posthuma (Eds.), *Entre relações de cuidado e vivências de vulnerabilidade: dilemas e desafios para o trabalho doméstico e de cuidados remunerado no Brasil* (pp. 105–124). Brasília: Ipea e OIT.

Gardiner, J. (1997). *Gender, Care, and Economics*. Basingstoke, UK: Macmillan.

Gentilini, U. et al. (2021). Social Protection and Jobs Responses to COVID-19: A Real-Time Review of Country Measures. World Bank. Retrieved from: https://documents1.worldbank.org/curated/en/281531621024684216/pdf/Social-Protection-and-Jobs-Responses-to-COVID-19-A-Real-Time-Review-of-Country-Measures-May-14-2021.pdf.

Glenn, E. N. (1992). From Servitude to Service Work: Historical Continuities in the Racial Division of Paid Reproductive Labor. *Signs*, 18(1), 1–43.

Groisman, D. (2015). *O cuidado enquanto trabalho. Envelhecimento, dependência e política para o bem-estar no Brasil* [Doctoral dissertation, Universidade Federal do Rio de Janeiro].

Guimarães, N. A., & Hirata, H. (2020). *O Gênero do Cuidado. Desigualdades, Identidades, Significações*. Cotia – SP: Ateliê Editorial.

Guimarães, N. A., Hirata, H., & Posthuma, A. C. (2020). El cuidado: sus formas, relaciones y actores. Reflexiones a partir del caso de Brasil. In N. A. Guimarães & H. Hirata (Eds.), *El cuidado en América Latina: mirando a los casos de Argentina, Brasil, Chile, Colombia y Uruguay* (pp. 27–74). Buenos Aires: Fundación Medifé Edita.

Guimarães, N. A., & Pinheiro, L. (2023). O halo do cuidado. Desafios para medir o trabalho remunerado de cuidado no Brasil. In A. A. Camarano & L. Pinheiro (Eds.), *Cuidar, Verbo Transitivo. Caminhos para a provisão de cuidados no Brasil* (pp. 443–486). Brasília: Instituto de Pesquisa Econômica Aplicada (Ipea).

Instituto Brasileiro de Geografia e Estatística (IBGE). (2016). Pesquisa Nacional por Amostra de Domicílios Contínua: manual básico da entrevista. Rio de Janeiro: IBGE. Retrieved from https://biblioteca.ibge.gov.br/visualizacao/instrumentos_de_coleta/doc5361.pdf.

International Labor Organization (ILO). (2018). *Care Works and Care Jobs: For the FUTURE of Decent Work*. Geneva: ILO.

International Labor Organization (ILO. (2020a). COVID-19 and the world of work: Impact and policy responses. *ILO Monitor*, 1st edition. Geneva: ILO. Retrieved from: https://www.ilo.org/wcmsp5/groups/public/---dgreports/---dcomm/documents/briefingnote/wcms_738753.pdf.

International Labor Organization (ILO. (2020b) COVID-19 and the world of work: Impact and policy responses. *ILO Monitor*, 7th edition. Geneva: ILO. Retrieved from: https://www.ilo.org/wcmsp5/groups/public/---dgreports/---dcomm/documents/briefingnote/wcms_767028.pdf.

Kofes, S. (2001). *Mulher, Mulheres, a Relação entre Patroas e Empregadas domésticas. A Identidade nas Armadilhas da Diferença e da Desigualdade*. Campinas: Editora da Unicamp.

Melo, H., & Morandi, L. (2020). *Cuidados no Brasil. Conquistas, legislação e políticas públicas*. São Paulo: Friedrich-Ebert-Stiftung – FES Brasil. Retrieved from https://economistaspelademocracia.org.br/2022/02/25/cuidados-no-brasil-conquistas-legislacao-e-politicas-publicas/.

Milkman, R. (2022). Stratification among In-Home Care Workers in the United States. *Critical Sociology*, 49(1), 11–22. https://doi.org/10.1177/08969205221123034.

Moreno, R. (2022). Implicações da digitalização para o cuidado. As plataformas digitais de trabalho e os caminhos da "inteligência artificial". São Paulo: Instituto Lula, Front-D. Retrieved from https://www.institutolula.org/implicacoes-da-digitalizacao-para-o-cuidado.

Pinheiro, L., Lima Junior, A., Fontoura, N. de O., & Silva, R. da. (2016). Mulheres e trabalho: breve análise do período 2004–2014. Brasília: Ipea. (Nota técnica, n. 26).

Pinheiro, L., Goes, F., Rezende, M., & Fontoura, N. (2021). Os desafios do passado no trabalho doméstico do século XXI: reflexões para o caso brasileiro a partir dos dados da PNAD Contínua. In L. Pinheiro, C. Tokarski, & A. C. Posthuma (Eds.), *Entre relações de cuidado e vivências de vulnerabilidade: dilemas e desafios para o trabalho doméstico e de cuidados remunerado no Brasil*. Brasília: Ipea; OIT.

Pinheiro, L., Tokarski, C., & Posthuma, A. C. (Eds.). (2021). *Entre relações de cuidado e vivências de vulnerabilidade: dilemas e desafios para o trabalho doméstico e de cuidados remunerado no Brasil*. Brasília: Ipea; OIT.

Razavi, S. (2007). *The Political and Social Economy of Care in a Development Context: Conceptual Issues, Research Questions and Policy Options*. Geneva: UNRISD.

Thorndike, E. L. (1920). A constant error in psychological ratings. *Journal of Applied Psychology*, 4(1), 25.

Verick, S., Schmidt-Klau, D., & Lee, S (2021). Is this time "really" different? How the impact of the COVID-19 crisis on labour markets contrasts to the global financial crisis of 2008–9. *International Labour Review* 161(1): 125–148.

Wajnman, S. (2022). Desafios da mensuração da economia dos cuidados no Brasil. Plenária 2: Los desafios del cuidado en America Latina y Caribe ante los cambios demográficos. In CONGRESO ASOCIACIÓN LATINOAMERICANA DE POBLACIÓN (Alap), 10, Valparaíso, Santiago. Anais ... Valparaíso: Alap.

Weller, J., Contreras, M., Caballero, A., & Tropa, R. (2020) *El impacto de la crisis sanitaria del COVID-19 en los mercados laborales latinoamericanos*. Santiago: Comisión Económica para América Latina y el Caribe (CEPAL).

Zelizer, V. (2005). *The Purchase of Intimacy*. Princeton, NJ: Princeton University Press.

Zelizer, V. (2010). *Economic Lives: How Culture Shapes the Economy*. Princeton, NJ: Princeton University Press.

CHAPTER 3

Occupational Transitions of Paid Care Workers during the COVID-19 Pandemic in Brazil

Mariana Eugenio Almeida and Simone Wajnman

1 Introduction[1]

The COVID-19 pandemic significantly exacerbated pre-existing inequalities in the world of work, affecting vulnerable workers in various ways. Those engaged in informal work without social protection or job security and whose occupations require physical proximity to the public have been hit the hardest and were often the first to lose their jobs. Women have been disproportionately affected both in the productive sphere, as seen in a significant retraction of female participation in the labor force in many countries, and in the reproductive sphere, as their domestic workload has multiplied with the increased presence of family members at home.

The provision of care is, therefore, a central issue in understanding the impacts of the crisis on people's lives. The pandemic created the conditions for a new crisis of social reproduction that has strong long-term effects on women and families (Acciari, Britez and Pérez, 2021). According to the International Labor Organization (ILO, 2018), 381 million people are employed in the care economy, which represents almost 12% of global employment. Women are responsible for 65% of paid care work worldwide. These big numbers hide, however, the heterogeneity of paid care occupations, which can be characterized according to different dimensions, such as the context of the labor relation (domestic or non-domestic); the nature of the interaction between the care worker and the beneficiary (direct or indirect), and the recurrence of the care relationship (Guimarães and Pinheiro, 2023). These characteristics can be

1 We are grateful for the support received from: *Fundação de Amparo à Pesquisa do Estado de São Paulo* (Fapesp) and Trans-Atlantic Platform (T-AP) Internacional Call "Recovery, Renewal and Resilience in a Post-Pandemic World/2021," proc. Fapesp 2021/07888-3; Conselho Nacional de Desenvolvimento Científico e Tecnológico (CNPq) – Call CNPq/Min. Ciência, Tecnologia e Inovações/FNDCT no. 18/2021 – Universal. Proc. 421754/2021-4; and Fundação Arymax. The authors are grateful for the contributions made by Nadya Araujo Guimarães, Anna Bárbara Araújo, and Maria Laura Miranda in previous versions of this Chapter.

 DOI:10.1163/9789004707009_004

decisive in how a society attributes value to care work and are therefore fundamental to understanding how these workers are affected in times of crisis.

The pandemic drew sharp attention to the disparities between two main groups of paid care workers. The first is healthcare professionals, who experienced dramatically higher work demands during the pandemic, leaving them with little time for the care demands of their own families. The second is workers in less urgent care sectors like domestic work, food services, beauty services, and transportation, who experienced significant income losses due to prolonged periods without clients.

In Brazil, a background of inequality exposes pre-existing vulnerabilities that contributed to deepening gender, race, and occupational inequalities in the labor market. Historically, female participation rates in the labor market have been inferior to male rates. Despite the significant increase of women's engagement in economic activities, inequalities remain visible in several aspects, such as the gender pay gap, maternity penalties, and the concentration of women in occupations with less access to social protection (Macedo and Pinheiro, 2022).

Another particularity must be highlighted since Brazil is in the cluster of countries where paid domestic work represents a high percentage of total female employment (ILO, 2018). In 2018, 14.6% of women in Brazil employed in the labor market were domestic workers, which is the second largest occupational group of women in the country, just behind the trade sector (Pinheiro *et al.*, 2019). Furthermore, 63% of all domestic workers are Black women (Pinheiro *et al.*, 2019). In 2018, only 28.6% of the category were registered employees (Pinheiro *et al.*, 2019), making informality a relevant characteristic of this sector.

Thus, in this context of multiple inequalities, the economic crisis triggered by the COVID-19 pandemic led to a significant retraction of female participation in the Brazilian labor force, mirroring trends occurring worldwide. In Brazil, however, women experienced specific impacts related to the structural aspects that characterize its female labor force. Female domestic workers were one of the groups that had the greatest loss of employment (Pinheiro, Tokarski and Vasconcelos, 2020), although we lack evidence on how the pandemic affected them and different groups of paid care workers.

Thus, this chapter aims to analyze the heterogeneous effects of the COVID-19 pandemic on paid care work in Brazil from a gender and race perspective. The chapter is organized in five sections, including the introduction. Section two establishes the theoretical basis and describes our object of analysis, namely paid care work. We assume paid care work is not homogeneous and identify essential occupational differences to understand the impact of the pandemic on these workers. In section three, we present data and research methods, and in section four we proceed to an analysis of employment evolution in occupational paid care sub-groups during the pandemic period. Finally, section five contains our final considerations. Based on descriptive and longitudinal data analysis, this chapter brings reflections on long-term effects and the need for specific actions and public policies.

2 Theoretical Focus

2.1 *Gender and Care: an Unequal Background*

The increasing participation of women in the workforce is a global phenomenon, which occurs at different rates and under varying conditions. In Brazil, the process is marked by the rapid engagement of women in economic activity, which began accelerating in the 1970s and consolidated in the 1980s and 1990s (Paiva, 1986; Guimarães, Brito and Barone, 2016). The increase ran parallel with demographic transformations that reflected structural changes and are the conditions for other transformations in the private sphere (Paiva, 1986; Bruschini, 1998; Lavinas, 1997; Oliveira, Vieira, and Marcondes, 2015). Dropping fertility rates in Brazil had begun before the 1930s (Horta, Carvalho and Frias, 2000; Rios Neto, 2005), but intensified in the 1970s with the introduction of contraceptive pills (Carvalho, Paiva and Sawyer, 1981). By the 1980s a pattern of restrictive fertility was consolidated in Brazil, reaching rates below two children per woman in the first decade of the 21st century, which is below the population replacement level (Oliveira, Vieira and Marcondes, 2015). Parallel to the decline in fertility rates, Brazil experienced a process of urbanization that profoundly changed the dynamics of people's lives. For women, urbanization extended their work beyond the family in a process of individualizing women as workers (Oliveira, 1984). Their activities became central to care work in areas such as education and health, while at the same time, the services sector became dominant in the labor market (Bruschini, 1994; Wajnman, 1998).

However, traces of "bipolarity" remain within female employment in Brazil: one pole is characterized by lower income levels, rates of formalization, and social protection, and the other pole has "good occupations" with higher wages, formal work relations and guaranteed social protection (Bruschini and Lombardi, 2000). According to the authors, ironically, what unites these two poles is domestic work, where the professionals in the "good occupations" rely on the work of domestic servants (on the other pole) to dedicate themselves to their careers. This scenario is also found in the paid care work sector as it encompasses both general domestic workers, positioned at the bottom of the wage hierarchy among employed women, and specialized caregivers that are primarily employed by the public sector, meaning they are safeguarded by legislation that emphasizes job stability and labor rights.

Although women have entered the labor market, there have been no significant changes regarding the sexual division of unpaid domestic work carried out within the family. Women continue to be solely or primarily responsible for household chores and care activities. The unequal distribution of unpaid domestic work and the difficulties of reconciling work and family can be considered the two most important factors in the so-called "incomplete revolution" of gender relations in Brazil (Wajnman, 2016). Therefore, care and domestic work play a central role in female employment in Brazil, but heterogeneities persist in the field. While there is growing institutionalization and recognition of care as an occupation, that is, an approach that sees the field as professional work, there is still a focus on private, domestic, and family life (Guimarães, Hirata and Sugita, 2011).

Within this context, paid domestic work supports the social reproduction of the richest families in Brazil. In 2009, 17.5% of Brazilian households had at least one domestic worker. Among the highest-income households, this number reached 51.7% (Sorj and Fontes, 2012). High income is the most important factor that explains hiring domestic workers (Guerra, 2017). This highlights the country's significant income inequality, as employers often pay for such services using a portion of their own salaries. This situation results from the lack of effective and comprehensive care policies, which drives families to outsource some of their care demands and is compounded by a context of low male participation in such activities. This dependence also reveals significant intra-gender inequality, as women from higher classes guarantee their professional success by transferring part of their household's domestic and care activities to poor, uneducated, mostly Black women.

In recent decades, there have been significant changes in paid care work, both domestic and non-domestic. Domestic workers, who in the past usually resided in the homes in which they worked, often providing unrestricted services in exchange for room and board, today have better contracts, albeit predominantly informal, that define working hours and duties (Guerra, 2017). The relative professionalization of care work also better differentiates domestic care work, thus introducing caregivers for older adults, nurses, physiotherapists, speech therapists, etc. The non-domestic care labor market has also diversified, with greater coverage for social services such as education, health, and social assistance, as well as the unprecedented expansion of personal care services in general, and beauty in particular.

The heterogeneity that paid care work assumes in Brazil, therefore, poses challenges for its own definition. The social and institutional construction of care is a more recent phenomenon than the rise of the term "caregiver/s" (Guimarães, Hirata and Sugita, 2011). The growing institutionalization and recognition of care as an occupation has implied the growth of care professions. At the same time, we can observe the persistence and expansion of paid domestic care work controlled by hierarchical and unequal relations established within the family (Guimarães, Hirata and Sugita, 2011).

An important debate on care refers to the line between studies on professional regulation and "care work." On one hand, "caregiver" was only socially recognized as an occupation in 2002, when it was included in the Brazilian Occupational Classification (CBO). This made it possible to visualize the various facets of care as an occupation in the labor market. On the other hand, there is a need to deepen the understanding of plurality in forms of care that are not even recognized as care work (Guimarães, Hirata and Posthuma, 2020). This scenario is reflected in the lack of a systematic effort to measure the scope of care occupations in the Brazilian labor market.

2.2 *Defining Paid Care Work*

According to the International Labor Organization (ILO), the "care economy" is the sum of all forms of care work, including both for-profit or paid care workers that provides health services and education, and domestic workers who provide care services in the home. This chapter is based on a comprehensive approach to care work, which includes care activities and social reproduction related activities. In this sense, there are two kinds of care activities. One is *direct*, meaning face-to-face, personal care activities, and the other is *indirect*, but destined to support the living conditions and the well-being of its recipients (ILO, 2018). Care can be performed in paid or unpaid forms of work relations.

In this chapter, paid care work is considered a type of service provided to people and paid for on a monetary basis (Guimarães and Pinheiro, 2023). We also use the concept of "occupations" in the labor market according to the occupational classification defined by the Brazilian Institute of Geography and Statistics. We assume that the occupations within the care sector share a common goal of rebuilding well-being or developing skills (physical, social, or emotional/self-esteem) for the beneficiaries (Guimarães and Pinheiro, 2023).

Guimarães and Pinheiro (2023), circumscribed the so-called "halo of the care labor market" and proposed a typology of care occupations that will be used in our empiric analysis. The authors divide care occupations into different subgroups considering three dimensions. The first dimension refers to the context in which the labor relation is established (domestic, with a domestic employment relation, or non-domestic). The second refers to the nature of the interaction between the care worker and the beneficiary (direct or indirect). Finally, the third dimension considers the recurrence of the care relationship, which can vary according to the degree of beneficiary dependence.

Based on this typology, paid care work can be represented by concentric circles, as shown in Figure 3.1 (Wajnman, 2022). The density of care work is greater when it occurs in a domestic context where the nature of the interaction is direct and recurrent. At the opposite extreme, we have care occupations outside the domestic environment carried out in indirect and non-recurrent relationships (Guimarães and Pinheiro, 2023).

Four subgroups of care occupations will be analyzed: 1) Domestic, direct and recurrent; 2) Domestic, indirect and recurrent; 3) Non-domestic, direct and recurrent; 4) Non-domestic, direct and less recurrent. It is important to note that a fifth subgroup, proposed by Guimarães and Pinheiro (2023), of paid care work that is non-domestic, indirect, and less recurrent has not been included. This is justified by the importance of specifying the very diverse impacts of COVID-19, and therefore this chapter does not present a complete perspective of the so-called care sector.

Table 3.1 summarizes the typology of care occupations adopted in this chapter and shows the most representative occupations in each subgroup. The detailed typology by occupation and respective frequency can be found in Annex 3.1.

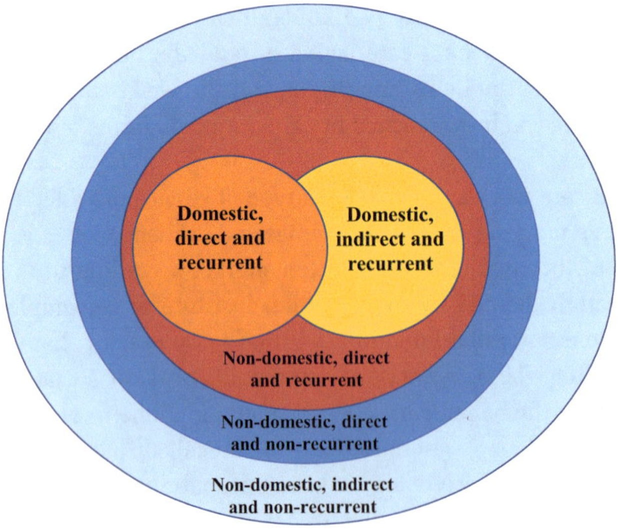

FIGURE 3.1 Graphic representation of paid care typology
SOURCE: WAJNMAN, 2022

TABLE 3.1 Total of employed by occupation and subgroup of care. Brazil – 2nd quarter of 2019

Subgroup	Occupation	Frequency	Relative distribution within subgroup (%)
1. Domestic, direct and recurrent	Personal caregivers in household	572.207	50.15
	Child caregivers	568.725	49.85
2. Domestic, indirect and recurrent	Domestic service workers in general	4,615,737	93.56
3. Non-domestic, direct and recurrent	Mid-level nursing professionals	925.287	32.12
	Preschool teachers	625.861	21.73
	Child caregivers	435.579	15.12
	Nursing professionals	384.46	13.35
4. Non-domestic, direct and less recurrent	Health professionals	2,045,720	27.78
	Elementary school teachers	1,484,672	20.16
	Hairdressers	1,184,991	16.09
	Specialists in beauty treatment	1,116,278	15.16

SOURCE: IBGE. PNAD CONTÍNUA. SELF-ELABORATION

Considering these four subgroups of care occupations, Table 3.2 shows that there are approximately 16.3 million paid care workers in Brazil, or 17.3% of total employment. While 33.4% of employed women work in care occupations, this percentage is only 5.2% for men.

Table 3.3 shows the frequency and proportional distributions of men and women among the care subgroups we observe in this chapter. We can see that men who work in the care sector are concentrated in subgroup 4, which includes occupations with non-domestic employment, direct employment, and less recurrent interactions.

TABLE 3.2 Employed in general and in care. Brazil – 2nd quarter of 2019

	Men	Women	Total
Employed in general	53,650,044	40,508,913	94,158,957
Employed in care	2,773,217	13,546,911	16,320,127
% employed in care	5.2%	33.4%	17.3%

SOURCE: IBGE. PNAD CONTÍNUA. SELF-ELABORATION

TABLE 3.3 Employed by care subgroups and gender. Brazil – 2nd quarter of 2019

Subgroups	Men		Women		Total	
	Freq.	%	Freq.	%	Freq.	%
1. Domestic, direct and recurrent	32.053	1.2	1,108,879	8.2	1,140,931	7.0
2. Domestic, indirect and recurrent	458.731	16.5	4,474,860	33.0	4,933,591	30.2
3. Non-domestic, direct and recurrent	324.896	11.7	2,555,900	18.9	2,880,796	17.7
4. Non-domestic, direct and less recurrent	1,957,536	70.6	5,407,272	39.9	7,364,808	45.1
Total	2,773,217	100.0	3,546,911	100.0	16,320,127	100.0

SOURCE: IBGE. PNAD CONTÍNUA. SELF-ELABORATION

Within paid care, women are the majority at 83% of total paid care (Table 3.4). When we look at the care subgroups, we can see that women are overrepresented especially in domestic work (subgroups 1 and 2). Regarding race, 56.6% of total paid care workers are non-white and are also overrepresented in domestic work. Finally, 26.6% of paid care workers are employed as public servants, which guarantees them stability at work and social protection. This type of job matters especially for subgroups 3 and 4, which include many workers in education and health.

TABLE 3.4 Proportional distribution of paid care workers by gender, race and type of job. Brazil – 2nd quarter of 2019 (%)

Subgroup	Sex		Race		Type of job	
	Men	Women	White	Non-white	Public	Non-public
1. Domestic, direct and recurrent	2.8	97.2	36.3	63.7	0.0	100.0
2. Domestic, indirect and recurrent	9.3	90.7	32.2	67.8	0.0	100.0
3. Non-domestic, direct and recurrent	11.3	88.7	46.7	53.3	48.9	51.1
4. Non-domestic, direct and less recurrent	26.6	73.4	50.7	49.3	39.8	60.2
Total	17.0	83.0	43.4	56.6	26.6	73.4

SOURCE: IBGE. PNAD CONTÍNUA. SELF-ELABORATION

3 Data and Research Methods

Data was gathered from the Continuous National Household Sample Survey (PNAD *Contínua*) produced by the Brazilian Institute of Geography and Statistics (IBGE). The survey provides labor force data, and quarterly microdata allow longitudinal studies. We use data for the entire country, from 2019 to 2021, covering the period before, during, and after the pandemic crisis for the working-age population in Brazil, which includes individuals aged 14 or older, according to definitions adopted by IBGE for this survey.

Data analysis is divided into two stages. First, we explore descriptive data to understand the short-term effects on the Brazilian labor market from a gender and race perspective. Second, we analyze occupational status transitions in consecutive quarters for each year, using longitudinal data from PNAD *Contínua*. In the labor force survey, a person is either in or out of the workforce. Being in the workforce means being employed or unemployed. Within the labor market dynamics, individuals can shift between employment and unemployment several times over the lifecourse. Leaving the workforce can occur through unemployment, which means that a person would move from employment to unemployment and, after long-term unsuccessful job searching, end up in inactivity. But it can also mean moving directly from employment to inactivity, usually the result of retirement. An unexpected increase in the latter, however, can indicate a significant change in the labor market dynamics, usually caused by a crisis or a shock.

This chapter aims to characterize how paid care workers experienced the following transitions: 1) employment to unemployment and; 2) employment to inactivity. In this sense, we want to understand how the crisis caused by the COVID-19 pandemic affected the Brazilian labor market dynamics, specifically for paid care workers.

4 Results

4.1 *Brief Description of the Effects of COVID-19 on the Brazilian Labor Market*

The COVID-19 pandemic had a significant effect on the Brazilian labor market in that it contributed to deepening inequalities, especially those related to gender and race. Tables 3.5 and 3.6 summarize the total number of people by occupational status and the main labor market indicators in 2019 and 2020, considering gender and race.

In general, the immediate effect of the pandemic crisis decreased the Brazilian workforce (-9.2%), especially the female workforce (-12,1%) (Table 3.5). It reduced the participation rate by 6.5 percentual points and increased the unemployment rate by 1.5 percentual points.

The impact on the workforce in terms of gender and race (Table 3.6) was stronger for women in general, but especially for non-white women (-14.5%). It also caused a sharper decrease in their participation rate (-7.6 p.p.).

A deeper look into female employment, considering only paid care workers (Graph 3.1) shows the relative variation in number of employees between consecutive quarters by subgroups of care occupations. There was a bigger drop for the two subgroups of domestic workers during the first months of lockdown. Of these two subgroups, direct care, which includes caregivers for children and older adults, was more affected initially but seemingly recuperated in the following quarters.

TABLE 3.5 Total of people by occupational status (by thousand) and main labor market indicators by gender. Brazil – 2nd quarter of 2019 and 2020

	2019			2020			Relative interannual variation (%)		
Occupational status	**Men**	**Women**	**Total**	**Men**	**Women**	**Total**	**Men**	**Women**	**Total**
Workforce	59.813	47.357	107.17	55.642	41.637	97.279	-7.0	-12.1	-9.2
Employed	53.65	40.509	94.159	48.87	35.181	84.051	-8.9	-13.2	-10.7
Unemployed	6.163	6.848	13.011	6.772	6.456	13.228	9.9	-5.7	1.7
Out of workforce	21.486	39.472	60.958	26.481	46.092	72.573	23.2	16.8	19.1
	2019			**2020**			**Interannual variation (p.p)**		
Indicator	**Men**	**Women**	**Total**	**Men**	**Women**	**Total**	**Men**	**Women**	**Total**
Participation rate (%)	73.6	54.5	63.7	67.8	47.5	57.3	-5.8	-7.1	-6.5
Occupational level (%)	66.0	46.7	56.0	59.5	40.1	49.5	-6.5	-6.6	-6.5
Unemployment rate (%)	10.3	14.5	12.1	12.2	15.5	13.6	1.9	1.0	1.5

SOURCE: IBGE. PNAD CONTÍNUA. SELF-ELABORATION

TABLE 3.6 Total of people by occupational status (by thousand) and main labor market indicators by gender and race. Brazil – 2nd quarter of 2019 and 2020

	2019				2020				Relative interannual variation (%)			
Occupational status	**White man**	**Non-white man**	**White women**	**Non-white women**	**White man**	**Non-white man**	**White women**	**Non-white women**	**White man**	**Non-white man**	**White women**	**Non-white women**
Workforce	25.328	34.483	21.286	26.07	24.252	31.363	19.321	22.3	-4.2	-9.0	-9.2	-14.5
Employed	23.251	30.398	18.886	21.621	21.891	26.963	17.069	18.096	-5.8	-11.3	-9.6	-16.3
Unemployed	2.077	4.085	2.4	4.448	2.361	4.4	2.253	4.203	13.7	7.7	-6.1	-5.5
Out of workforce	8.686	12.797	16.605	22.863	10.712	15.766	19.55	26.529	23.3	23.2	17.7	16.0
	2019				**2020**				**Interannual variation (p.p)**			
Indicator	**White man**	**Non-white man**	**White women**	**Non-white women**	**White man**	**Non-white man**	**White women**	**Non-white women**	**White man**	**Non-white man**	**White women**	**Non-white women**
Participation rate (%)	74.5	72.9	56.2	53.3	69.4	66.5	49.7	45.7	-5.1	-6.4	-6.5	-7.6
Occupational level (%)	68.4	64.3	49.8	44.2	62.6	57.2	43.9	37.1	-5.7	-7.1	-5.9	-7.1
Unemployment rate (%)	8.2	11.8	11.3	17.1	9.7	14.0	11.7	18.8	1.5	2.2	0.4	1.8

SOURCE: IBGE. PNAD CONTÍNUA. SELF-ELABORATION

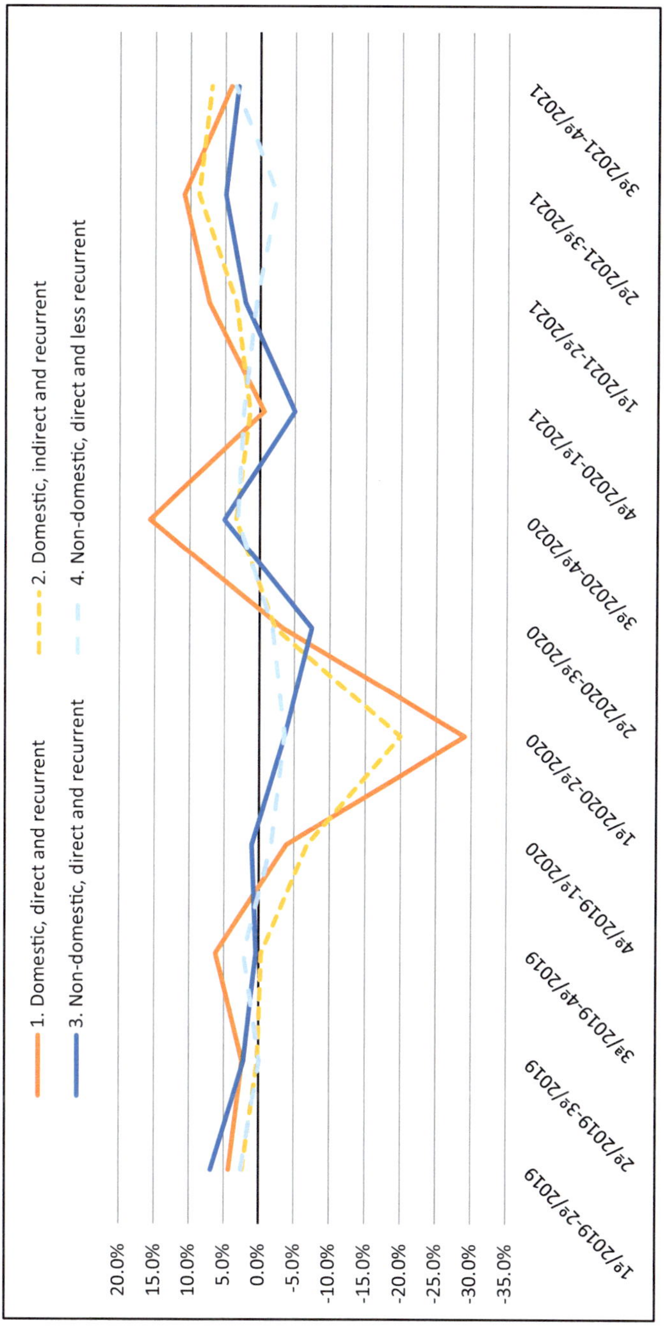

GRAPH 3.1 Variation in the number of employees between consecutive quarters, by subgroups of care. Brazil – 2019–2021 (%)
SOURCE: IBGE. PNAD CONTÍNUA. SELF-ELABORATION

4.2 *Going Further towards a Transition Perspective*

Descriptive data identifies different labor market effects when compared to previous crises with employment being seriously affected by almost 10 million people leaving the workforce. Analysis of occupational status based on longitudinal data shows the percentage of employed people who experienced a transition in two consecutive quarters.

4.2.1 Employment → Unemployment

Graphs 3.2 to 3.5 show the percentage of people who moved from employment to unemployment over two consecutive quarters by gender, race, and subgroups of care occupations. The analysis includes the comparison of the indicators in the same period of different years to minimize any possible seasonal effects.

Regarding gender, Graph 3.2 shows that from the first to the second quarter of 2020, 3.8% of employed people became unemployed for both men and women. In 2021, the difference between men and women grew larger, with women having a higher percentage.

Graphs 3.3 and 3.4 show the differentials by race and gender. When it comes to race, there is a significant gap between white and non-whites, which already existed in 2019 but that widened in 2020. While 2.9% of white employed people became unemployed in the second quarter of 2020, this percentage was

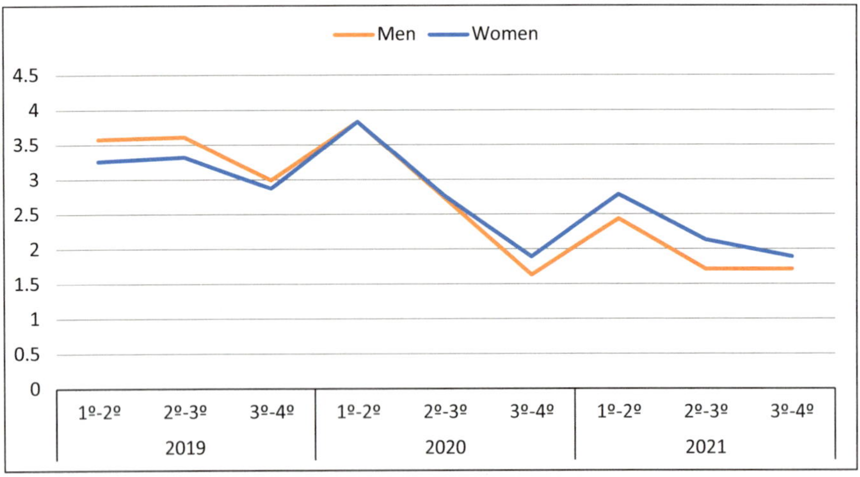

GRAPH 3.2 Transition from employment to unemployment over two consecutive quarters, by gender. Brazil – 2019–2021 (%)
SOURCE: IBGE. PNAD CONTÍNUA. SELF-ELABORATION

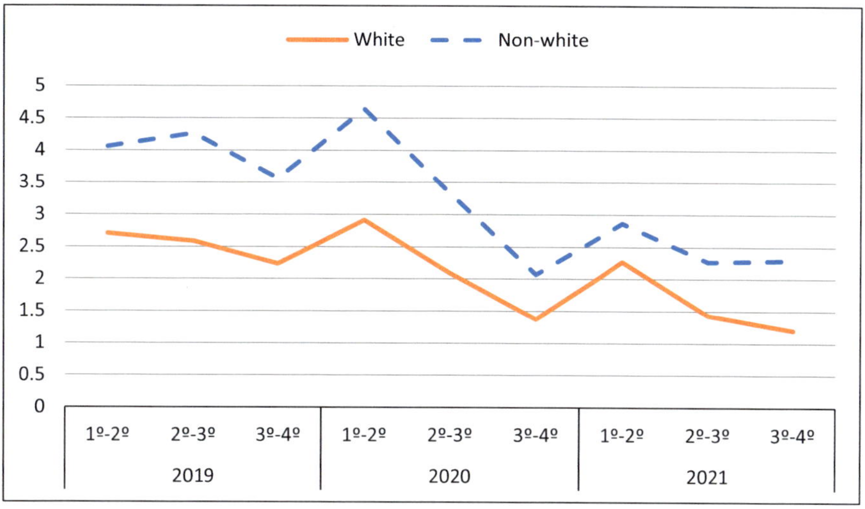

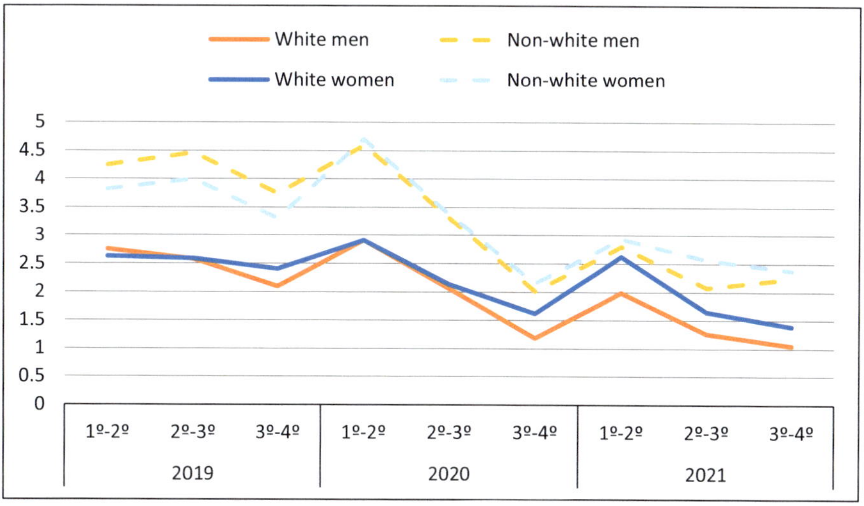

GRAPHS 3.3–3.4 Transition from employment to unemployment over two consecutive quarters by race and gender. Brazil – 2019–2021 (%)
SOURCE: IBGE. PNAD CONTÍNUA. SELF-ELABORATION

4.6% for non-white people. Non-white people had higher percentages in this transition independent of gender over the entire analysis period.

The analysis by subgroups of care occupations indicates two different poles (Graph 3.5). One side contains subgroups 3 and 4, which include occupations within the health and education sectors. These workers were in high demand during the pandemic and were primarily women from the public sector, which

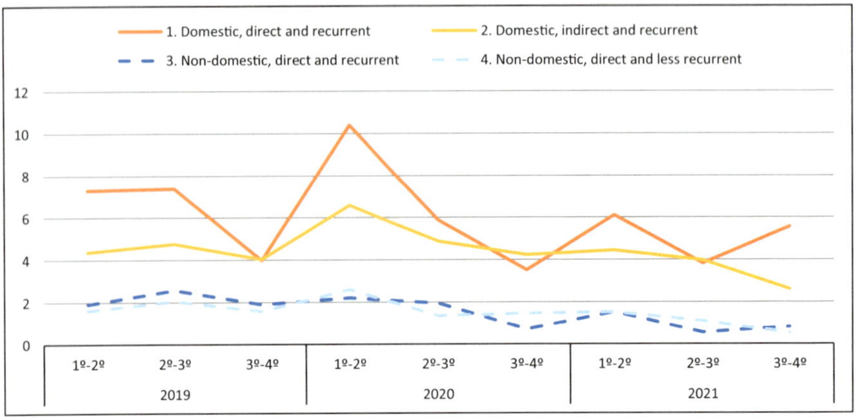

GRAPH 3.5 Transition from employment to unemployment over two consecutive quarters, by subgroups of care occupations, women. Brazil – 2019–2021 (%)
SOURCE: IBGE. PNAD CONTÍNUA. SELF-ELABORATION

is characterized by job security. The other contains subgroups 1 and 2, which include all domestic workers like cleaners, caregivers, cooks, gardeners, etc.

4.2.2 Employment → Inactivity

Graphs 3.6 to 3.9 present the percentage of people who moved from employment to inactivity over two consecutive quarters, according to gender, race, and subgroups of care occupations.

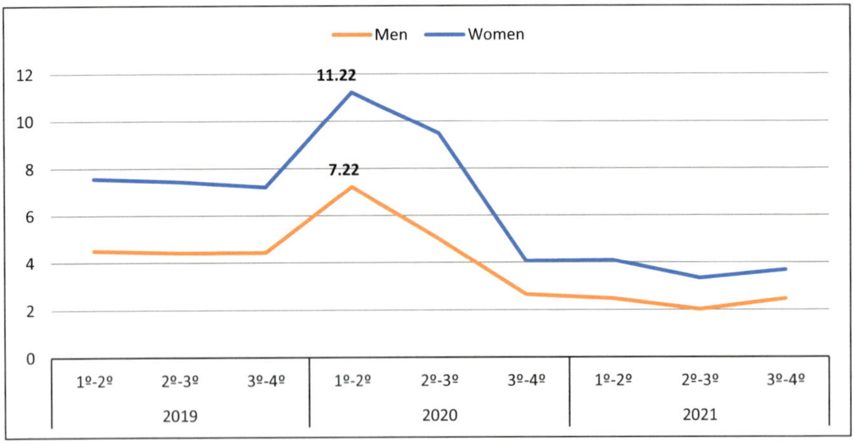

GRAPH 3.6 Transition from employment to inactivity over two consecutive quarters, by gender. Brazil – 2019–2021 (%)
SOURCE: IBGE. PNAD CONTÍNUA. SELF-ELABORATION

Unlike the previous transition, the analysis of the flow from employment to inactivity reveals greater inequality between men and women, which widened in 2020 during the pandemic (Graph 3.6). From the first to the second quarter of 2020, 11.2% of employed women became inactive or left the workforce, while this percentage was 7.2% for men.

Regarding race, we also see the inequality between white and non-white workers (Graphs 3.7 and 3.8). When considering race and gender, women seem to tend toward inactivity, regardless of their race.

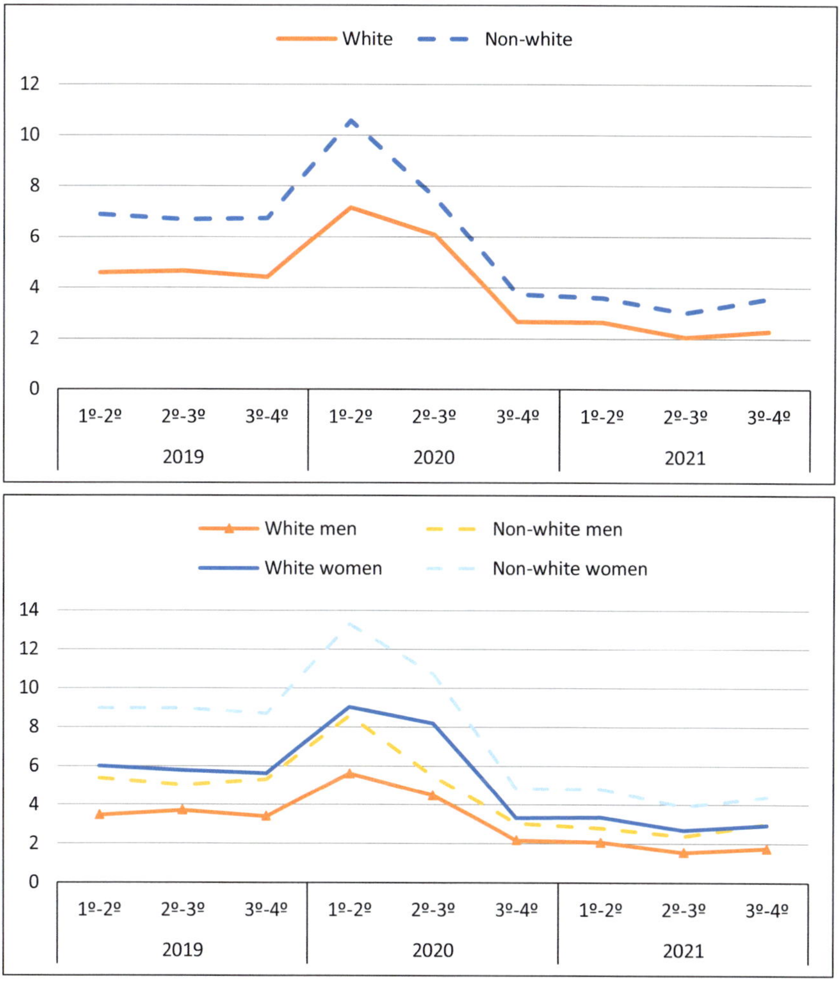

GRAPHS 3.7–3.8 Transition from employment to inactivity over two consecutive quarters, by race gender. Brazil – 2019–2021 (%)
SOURCE: IBGE. PNAD CONTÍNUA. SELF-ELABORATION

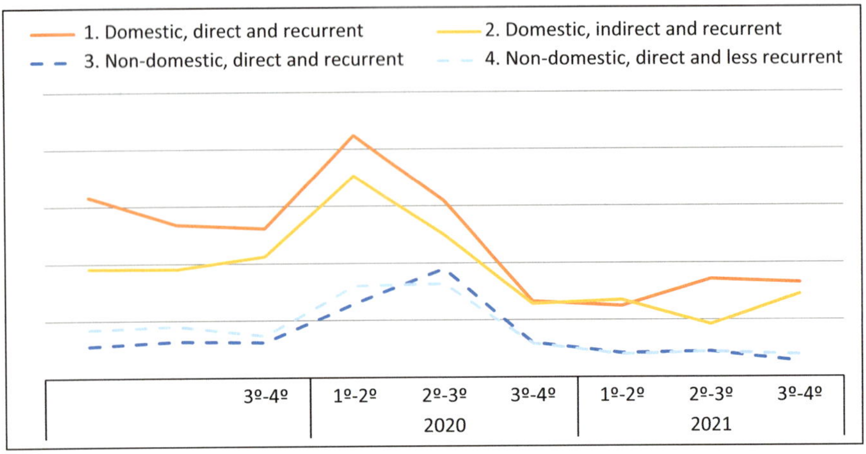

GRAPH 3.9 Transition from employment to inactivity over two consecutive quarters, by subgroups of care occupations, women. Brazil – 2019–2021 (%)
SOURCE: IBGE. PNAD CONTÍNUA. SELF-ELABORATION

Finally, the analysis by subgroup of care occupations reveals significant inequality within female employment. While for women in general the percentage transitioning from employment to inactivity was 11.2% (Graph 3.9), for domestic workers this percentage reached 17.6% (subgroup 2) and 21.2% (subgroup 1). These two subgroups include cleaners, caregivers for children and older adults, cooks, gardeners and so on. Subgroups 3 and 4 experienced much less significant increases in this indicator in 2020. It is important to note that these differences already existed in 2019, before the crisis.

5 Final Considerations

The impact of the COVID-19 pandemic on the Brazilian labor market was characterized by an intense transition of workers to both visible and invisible economic inactivity with stronger effects on female employment. The analysis of paid care work in Brazil shows that not only did the inequality between men and women deepen, but also the inequality within female employment, largely due to the negative impacts on domestic work. In this context, the interdependence of gender, race, and class domination relations is a fundamental aspect in the field of care (Kergoat, 2010), especially in a country marked by structural and historical inequalities like Brazil. The diversity and heterogeneity of paid care workers stand in contrast with the fact that such occupations in Brazil receive lower wages and are socially less valued (Hirata, 2014). Both paid and unpaid care work is predominantly performed by women and both housekeepers and caregivers are mostly Black (Guimarães, Hirata and Posthuma, 2020).

One of the factors that joins the dimensions of gender and class in the labor market in Brazil is the organization of care and domestic work. The effects of the pandemic on these workers, however, are heterogeneous. While the demand for paid care work increased significantly, vulnerabilities remained, considering the lack of regulations for these occupations. This is even more relevant for domestic caregivers. Furthermore, care penalties were observed in some countries, meaning that workers in care service jobs earn less than other essential workers (Folbre, Gautham and Smith, 2021).

The results suggest that there are two very distinct poles of paid care work in Brazil, with essential care and health and education occupations that are primarily public jobs with more social protection (subgroups 3 and 4) on one side, and domestic work occupations like cleaners, caregivers, cooks, gardeners, etc. (subgroups 1 and 2) on the other side. Even amongst domestic workers, we found important differences that show direct domestic workers (subgroup 1) as being in more unstable situations and more exposed to transitions when compared to indirect domestic workers (subgroup 2). This result may be explained by the circumstances of the sanitary crisis, which forced the population to avoid having direct contact.

The attempt to define and classify paid care work in different subgroups revealed a dichotomy in the female labor force in Brazil. While the sector increasingly demands specialized work that is formal and protected, paid care still relies on work characterized by informality and insecurity, such as domestic work. Furthermore, even within domestic work, we see a movement of polarization that reflects the values that care work has in Brazilian society.

The lack of social protection for domestic workers in Brazil raises important concerns about the impacts of the COVID-19 crisis on the lives of women and families. During the pandemic, the Brazilian government created an emergency income transfer program to provide economic relief, especially for the poorer and informal shares of the population (Cardoso *et al.*, 2021). However, uncertainties remain regarding the long-term effects of COVID-19 on female employment. The results presented in this Chapter show that the transitions from employment to unemployment and from employment to inactivity in 2021 are lower compared to 2020. But this apparent "improvement" can be misunderstood if we do not consider the number of people, especially women, who left the workforce in 2020 and did not go back. In this sense, further studies are needed to more fully understand the characteristics of paid care workers who lost their jobs during the pandemic and to better analyze the conditions in which recovery is taking place.

ANNEX 3.1 Typology of paid care occupations

Frequency of workers and relative distribution by care occupation, Brazil – 2º quarter of 2019

1. Domestic, direct and recurrent

Occupation	Frequency	Distribution (%)
Personal caregivers in household	572.207	50.15
Child caregivers	568.725	49.85
Total	1,140,931	100.00

2. Domestic, indirect and recurrent

Occupation	Frequency	Distribution (%)
Domestic service workers in general	4,615,737	93.56
Cooks	122.587	2.48
Farmers and skilled workers in the cultivation of vegetable gardens, nurseries and gardens	120.891	2.45
Car, taxi and truck drivers	38.777	0.79
Housekeepers and house butlers	21.208	0.43
Cook's helpers	5.701	0.12
Animal caretakers	4.307	0.09
Security guards	2.34	0.05
Other cleaning workers	1.148	0.02
Chefs	894	0.02
Total	4,933,591	100.00

3. Non-domestic, direct and recurrent

Occupation	Frequency	Distribution (%)
Mid-level nursing professionals	925.287	32.12
Preschool teachers	625.861	21.73
Child caregivers	435.579	15.12
Nursing professionals	384.46	13.35
Teacher's assistants	323.975	11.25
Personal caregivers in institutions	65.737	2.28
Personal caregivers in health services not previously classified	55.226	1.92
Personal caregivers in household	40.995	1.42
Special Needs Educators	21.454	0.74
Private companions	2.224	0.08
Total	2,880,796	100.00

ANNEX 3.1 Typology of paid care occupations (*cont.*)

4. Non-domestic, direct and less recurrent		
Occupation	**Frequency**	**Distribution (%)**
Elementary school teachers	1,484,672	20.16
Hairdressers	1,184,991	16.09
Specialists in beauty treatment	1,116,278	15.16
High school teachers	679.074	9.22
Community health workers	441.413	5.99
Specialists in teaching methods	326.376	4.43
Specialist doctors	299.371	4.06
Dentists	296.315	4.02
Physical education and recreational activities instructors	240.117	3.26
Psychologists	221.509	3.01
Physiotherapists	181.123	2.46
Ministers of religious services, missionaries and the like	128.28	1.74
General Doctors	112.781	1.53
Social workers	111.605	1.52
Dietitians and Nutritionists	97.433	1.32
Middle-level social workers	95.511	1.30
Dentist assistants	93.926	1.28
Physiotherapists assistants	57.265	0.78
Health professionals not previously classified	39.756	0.54
Medical assistants	35.278	0.48
Speech therapists and logopedists	30.474	0.41
Middle-level health professionals not previously classified	25.944	0.35
Ambulance helpers	22.234	0.30
Middle-level professionals in traditional and alternative medicine	15.772	0.21
Lay assistants of religion	11.18	0.15
Mid-level childbirth professionals	5.873	0.08
Health, occupational and environmental hygiene professionals	5.386	0.07
Traditional and alternative medicine professionals	2.814	0.04
Optometrists	1.868	0.03
Optometry and opticians technicians	191	0.00

ANNEX 3.1 Typology of paid care occupations (*cont.*)

Childbirth professionals	-	-
Paramedics	-	-
Total	7,364,808	100.00

SOURCE: IBGE. PNAD CONTÍNUA. SELF-ELABORATION

ANNEX 3.2 Summary of transitions results

Transition 1: Employment--> Unemployment (%)

Variable	**2019**			**2020**			**2021**		
	1º-2º	2º-3º	3º-4º	1º-2º	2º-3º	3º-4º	1º-2º	2º-3º	3º-4º
Total	3.44	3.49	2.94	3.83	2.74	1.73	2.58	1.88	1.78
Sex									
Men	3.58	3.61	2.99	3.83	2.73	1.63	2.43	1.71	1.71
Women	3.26	3.32	2.87	3.83	2.76	1.89	2.78	2.13	1.89
Race									
White	2.7	2.58	2.23	2.91	2.09	1.37	2.27	1.43	1.2
Non-white	4.06	4.26	3.56	4.64	3.33	2.07	2.86	2.27	2.29
Sex X Race									
White men	2.75	2.58	2.09	2.91	2.05	1.18	1.99	1.26	1.05
Non-white men	4.24	4.46	3.74	4.59	3.3	2.01	2.8	2.07	2.24
White women	2.63	2.59	2.4	2.91	2.13	1.62	2.63	1.65	1.39
Non-white women	3.82	3.99	3.3	4.7	3.37	2.15	2.94	2.57	2.37
Subgroups of care occupations – only women									
1. Domestic, direct and recurrent	7.3	7.38	3.98	10.39	5.88	3.51	6.11	3.82	5.56
2. Domestic, indirect and recurrent	4.37	4.76	4.04	6.58	4.87	4.22	4.44	3.97	2.6
3. Non-domestic, direct and recurrent	1.92	2.57	1.9	2.2	1.95	0.7	1.53	0.54	0.82
4. Non-domestic, direct and less recurrent	1.6	2.05	1.58	2.6	1.34	1.46	1.52	1.09	0.52

ANNEX 3.2 Summary of transitions results (*cont.*)

Transition 2: Employment--> Inactivity (%)									
Variable	**2019**			**2020**			**2021**		
	1º-2º	**2º-3º**	**3º-4º**	**1º-2º**	**2º-3º**	**3º-4º**	**1º-2º**	**2º-3º**	**3º-4º**
Total	5.83	5.74	5.65	8.97	6.88	3.23	3.15	2.57	2.97
Sex									
Men	4.52	4.43	4.44	7.22	5.00	2.65	2.47	2.01	2.45
Women	7.57	7.44	7.21	11.22	9.47	4.07	4.09	3.33	3.68
Race									
White	4.58	4.64	4.4	7.15	6.08	2.66	2.64	2.05	2.28
Non-white	6.88	6.68	6.74	10.56	7.58	3.75	3.6	3.01	3.58
Sex X Race									
White men	3.45	3.71	3.39	5.6	4.47	2.18	2.07	1.55	1.75
Non-white men	5.37	5.02	5.31	8.57	5.45	3.05	2.8	2.38	3.02
White women	5.98	5.78	5.61	9.02	8.17	3.31	3.36	2.69	2.94
Non-white women	8.98	8.97	8.69	13.3	10.71	4.83	4.8	3.92	4.39
Subgroups of care occupations – only women									
1. Domestic, direct and recurrent	15.79	13.39	13.06	21.19	15.46	6.64	6.22	8.55	8.24
2. Domestic, indirect and recurrent	9.55	9.52	10.59	17.63	12.47	6.42	6.74	4.57	7.23
3. Non-domestic, direct and recurrent	2.78	3.17	3.08	6.45	9.49	3.01	2.08	2.22	1.34
4. Non-domestic, direct and less recurrent	4.21	4.49	3.64	8.01	8.18	2.93	1.98	2.19	1.93

SOURCE: IBGE. PNAD CONTÍNUA. SELF-ELABORATION

References

Acciari, Louisa; Britez, Juana Del Carmen; Pérez, Andrea del Carmen Morales. (2021) Right to health, right to live: domestic workers facing the COVID-19 crisis in Latin America. *Gender & Development*, 29:1, 11–33.

Bruschini, Cristina. (1994) O trabalho da mulher brasilera nas décadas recentes. *Estudos Feministas*, v.2, n.3, p.179–199.

Bruschini, Cristina. (1998) *Gênero e trabalho feminino no Brasil*: novas conquistas ou persistência da discriminação? Brasil, 1985 a 1995. Comunicação apresentada no seminário Trabalho e gênero: mudanças, persistências e desafios, Abep/Nepo, Campinas, 14–15 abr.

Bruschini, Cristina.; Lombardi, Maria Rosa. (2000) A bipolaridade do trabalho feminino no Brasil contemporâneo. *Cadernos de Pesquisa* [online]. n. 110, p.67–104.

Cardoso, Débora Freire; Domingues, Edson; Magalhães, Aline; Simonato, Thiago; Miyajima, Diego. (2021) Pandemia de COVID-19 e Famílias: impactos da crise e da renda básica emergencial. *Políticas Sociais*: acompanhamento e análise, n. 23. Brasília: Ipea.

Carvalho, José Alberto.; Paiva, Paulo De T. Almeida.; Sawyer, Donald. R. (1981) The recent sharp decline in fertility in Brazil: economic boom, social inequality and baby bust. México: Population Council/Latin America and Caribbean Regional Office, Working Papers, n. 8.

Folbre, Nancy; Gautham, Leila; Smith, Kristin. (2021) Essential Workers and Care Penalties in the United States. *Feminist Economics*, v. 27, n. 1–2, p. 173–187.

Guerra, Maria de Fátima Lage. (2017) *Trabalhadoras domésticas no Brasil*: coortes, formas de contratação e famílias contratantes. Tese (Doutorado) – Programa de Pós-Graduação em Demografia da Universidade Federal de Minas Gerais, Belo Horizonte.

Guimarães, Nadya Araujo; Brito, Murillo Marschner Alves De; Barone, Leonardo Sangali. (2016) Mercantilização no Feminino: a visibilidade do trabalho das mulheres no Brasil. *Revista Brasileira de Ciências Sociais* [online]. v. 31, n. 90, p.17–38.

Guimarães, Nadya Araujo;; Hirata, Helena Sumiko; Sugita, Kurumi. (2011) Cuidado e Cuidadoras: o trabalho de *care* no Brasil, França e Japão. *Sociol. Antropol.* [online], v. 1, n. 1, p. 151–180.

Guimarães, Nadya Araujo; Hirata, Helena Sumiko; Posthuma, Anne. (2020) El cuidado: sus formas, relaciones y actores. Reflexiones a partir del caso de Brasil. *In*: Guimarães, Nadya Araujo; Hirata, Helena Sumiko (comp.). *El Cuidado en América Latina*. Ciudad Autónoma de Buenos Aires: Fundación Medifé Edita, p. 75–117.

Guimarães, Nadya Araujo; Pinheiro, Luana. (2023) O halo do cuidado. Desafios para medir o trabalho remunerado de cuidado no Brasil. *In*: Camarano, Ana Amélia;

Pinheiro, Luana. (orgs.). *Cuidar, Verbo Transitivo. Caminhos para a provisão de cuidados no Brasil*. Brasília: Ipea, Cap. 10, p. 443–486.

Hirata, Helena Sumiko. (2014) Gênero, classe e raça Interseccionalidade e consubstancialidade das relações sociais. *Tempo Social*, v. 26, n. 1, p. 61–74, jan.-jun.

Horta, Cláudia Júlia Guimarães; Carvalho, José Alberto; Frias, L. A. (2000) Recomposição da fecundidade por geração para Brasil e Regiões: atualização e revisão. In: ENCONTRO NACIONAL DE ESTUDOS POPULACIONAIS, 12, Caxambu. Anais ... Belo Horizonte: Abep.

ILO. International Labor Organization. (2018) *Care Work and Care Jobs for the Future of Decent Work*. International Labor Office – Geneva: ILO.

Kergoat, Danièle. (2010) Dinâmica e consubstancialidade das relações sociais. *Revista Novos Estudos*, n. 86, p. 93–103, mar.

Lavinas, Lena. (1997) Emprego feminino: o que há de novo e o que se repete. *Dados*, v. 40, n. 1, p. 41–67.

Macedo, Natália Guerra Da Rocha; Pinheiro, Luana Simões. (2022) Determinantes da participação das mulheres brasileiras na força de trabalho durante a pandemia da COVID-19. *Boletim de Mercado de Trabalho*: conjuntura e análise. Brasília: Ipea, ano 28, n. 73, abr.

Oliveira, Maria Coleta. A individualização da força de trabalho e o trabalho feminino familiar: um estudo de caso de Pederneiras, SP. In: Aguiar, Newma. (Org.). *Mulheres na Força de Trabalho na América Latina: Análises Qualitativas*. 1ed. Rio de Janeiro: Vozes, 1984, v. , p. 99–122.

Oliveira, Maria Coleta; Vieira, Joice Melo; Marcondes, Glaucia dos Santos. (2015) Cinquenta anos de relações de gênero e geração no Brasil: mudanças e permanências. In: Arretche, Marta (Ed.). *Trajetórias das desigualdades: como o Brasil mudou nos últimos cinquenta anos*. São Paulo: Editora Unesp; Centro de Estudos da Metrópole.

Paiva, Paulo de Tarso A. (1986) Cinquenta anos de crescimento populacional e absorçao da mao de obra no Brasil: de 1950 a 2000. *Revista Brasileira de Estudos Populacionais*, Campinas v.3, n.1, p. 63–86, jan/jun.

Pinheiro, Luana; Lira, Fernanda; Rezende, Marcela; Fontoura, Natália. (2019) *Os desafios do passado no trabalho doméstico do século XXI*: reflexões para o caso brasileiro a partir dos dados da PNAD contínua. Brasília: Ipea, Textos para discussão, n. 2528.

Pinheiro, Luana; Tokarski, Carolina; Vasconcelos, Márcia. (2020) *Vulnerabilidade das trabalhadoras domésticas no contexto da pandemia de COVID-19 no Brasil*. Brasília: Ipea, Nota técnica n. 75.

Rios Neto, Eduardo Luiz Gonçalves. (2005) Questões emergentes da análise demográfica. Revista Brasileira de Estudos de População, v. 22, n. 2, p. 371–408.

Sorj, Bila; Fontes, Adriana. (2012). O *care* como um regime estratificado: implicações de gênero e classe social. *In*: Hirata, Helena Sumiko; Guimarães, Nadya Araujo (org.). *Cuidados e cuidadoras: as várias faces do trabalho do care*. São Paulo: Atlas.

Wajnman, Simone. (1998) O crescimento da atividade feminina nos anos noventa no Brasil. In: ENCONTRO NACIONAL DE ESTUDOS POPULACIONAIS, 10, Caxambu. Anais ... Caxambu: Abep.

Wajnman, Simone. (2016) "Quantidade" e "qualidade" da participação das mulheres na força de trabalho brasileira. *In*: Itaborai, Nathalie Reis; Ricoldi, Arlene Martinez. *Até onde caminhou a revolução de gênero no Brasil?*. Belo Horizonte: Abep.

Wajnman, Simone. (2022) Desafios da mensuração da economia dos cuidados no Brasil. *In*: Congreso Asociación Latinoamericana de Población (ALAP), 10, 2022, Plenária 2: Los desafios del cuidado en America Latina y Caribe ante los cambios demográficos. Valparaiso, 6 a 9 dez.

CHAPTER 4

Pandemic, Precariousness, and Gender Inequalities in Health Care Jobs: the Case of Colombia

Amparo Hernández-Bello, Daniella Castro-Barbudo and Suelen Castiblanco-Moreno

> The pandemic has revealed four crises that highlight gender inequalities and their implications for women and society at large: the health crisis, the care crisis, the economic crisis, and the crisis of masculinity and gender violence. These crises have significant implications for women and society as a whole.
>
> ROSA CAÑETE, 2020, our translation

1 Introduction[1]

The COVID-19 pandemic caused unprecedented transformations in social, economic, political, and cultural relationships and deepened existing inequalities. Its impact is undeniable. The pandemic has highlighted the criticality of the health system in promoting the welfare of individuals, families, and communities, as well as ensuring economic stability. However, it has also exposed the deficiencies of health systems that are unable to effectively deal with health emergencies due to fragmented health infrastructure, underfunding, and inadequate investment in healthcare workers, which, in turn, have resulted in a lack of universal access and coverage (OPS, 2012; Naciones Unidas, 2020; CEPAL-OPS, 2020; CEPAL, 2021).

1 This chapter is a product of the research project *Who cares? Rebuilding care in a post-pandemic world*, financed with resources from the Fondo Nacional de Financiamiento para la Ciencia, la Tecnología y la Innovación Francisco José de Caldas, Minciencias, Colombia. The authors would like to thank Sofia Rodríguez Nieto for her invaluable support in processing the household survey data and María Camila Roldán Bernal for her collaboration in translating and editing the first version of the text into English.

 DOI:10.1163/9789004707009_005

Several investigations in Latin America have uncovered the challenging circumstances facing healthcare workers and their connections to trends such as reducing the State's role, privatization, and commodification of social reforms implemented since the 1990s. Evidence supports a process of precariousness and deregulation in labor relations that has led to instability, income loss, and lack of protection, leading to the implementation of reforms (Brito, 2000). Although measures have been taken to increase healthcare efficiency through flexible mechanisms, the inadequate distribution of human resources remains an issue (Carpio & Santiago Bench, 2015; Lucio-García, Recaman, & Arredondo, 2017).

During the first year of the COVID-19 pandemic, the health workforce experienced significant impacts, particularly in the frontline sectors of hospitals, ambulatory care, home health, and community healthcare. This increase in patient volume, combined with a decrease in personnel due to illness or death, resulted in an overwhelming burden. Many healthcare workers suffered from job instability and were unprotected against increased contagion risks due to the lack of biosecurity measures and equipment (OECD, 2021; OIT, 2021; Downey et al., 2023; Caldichoury et al., 2023).

However, among health workers, women were the most affected. Gender discrepancies in the impact were observed to be linked to the sector's highly feminized nature with notable gender segregation. Women make up more than 70% of the workforce, yet they often enter the labor market in a disadvantaged position due to lower status and pay. This position can be attributed to the horizontal gender division of labor, which distinguishes between professions and activities typically associated with men and women, as well as the vertical gender division of labor, where women tend to occupy the lowest levels in terms of remuneration, recognition, and decision-making (Messing & Ostlin, 2006; WHO Gender Equity Hub, 2019). Despite this, the health system constitutes a primary source of female employment (CEPAL, 2021; OIT, 2017).

Various studies and reports have highlighted the pandemic's more significant impact on women workers due to their overrepresentation in the healthcare sector. The wage gap between men and women also expanded during this period (Downey et al., 2023). Women had higher exposure to infection or suspected COVID-19 owing to direct contact with infected patients. In addition, they bore the brunt of reduced job opportunities and changes in working conditions, such as longer working hours, alterations in work schedules, and job loss. As such, juggling household and care responsibilities became even more difficult (OPS, 2021; 2022).

In respect to work-related stress, women experienced the most significant impact on their mental health (Amnesty International, 2020; OPS, 2022).

Furthermore, due to their position within the lowest hierarchical levels, they were provided with less personal protection for their job; for instance, they encountered difficulties managing menstruation, which was not adequately considered in biosecurity regulations and predictions (OIT, 2021; OPS, 2022; WHO-ILO, 2022).

The health system in Colombia is gender segregated, with a predominantly female workforce. Research conducted in the country primarily focuses on mental health effects such as stress, anxiety, depression, and burnout syndrome among health personnel because of the pandemic (Instituto Nacional de Salud, 2021; OPS, 2022). However, research on the impact of gender on employment conditions of health workers is scarce. Based on existing research, three general conclusions can be drawn. First, female health workers experience more significant job loss, and second, the gender wage gap deepens (Florián, De la Hoz, & Lara, 2022; Herrera-Idárraga et al., 2020). Finally, there has been a significant increase in the burden of unpaid domestic and care work, making it difficult for health workers to manage these demands alongside their paid work (Tribín-Uribe, Mojica-Urueña, Díaz-Pardo, & DANE, 2021).

Further investigation into the impact of COVID-19 must take a comprehensive gender equity perspective into account. Therefore, this chapter analyzes transformations in employment conditions in the Colombian health sector and the pandemic's contribution to maintaining and deepening gender inequalities.

Based on the characterization of the sector workforce available in the country and its segregation by gender, we describe the working conditions and the effects of the COVID-19 pandemic on the job stability, work organization, salaries, social protection, and perceptions of working conditions. It concludes that the feminization of the sector contributes to the gender inequities that the pandemic made visible and, in some areas, exacerbated.

2 Contextual Framework

2.1 *Gendered Division of Labor in the Healthcare Sector*

The gendered division of labor has long been a focal point for feminist analyses of the relationships between labor, gender, and capitalism. Within the healthcare industry, this division of labor manifests through the assignment of men to positions within the public sphere of production. At the same time, women are primarily relegated to the private sphere of reproduction. This social division of labor is an integral component of the capitalist mode of production. This distinction is not a natural fact but a cultural and social construct arising from patriarchal traditions embedded in capitalism. This construct assigns more significant value to the production of goods and services for the market than to tasks related to the social output of human beings (Borderías & Carrasco, 1994; Molyneux, 1994).

An essential contribution of feminist theorists in reconceptualizing and broadening the concept of work has been overcoming the artificial contradictions between productive and reproductive work, the professional and domestic spheres, salaried work, and family responsibilities. Additionally, feminist theorists helped to incorporate social relations of sex and domestic, non-professional, non-salaried, and unpaid work (Hirata, 1997). These perspectives challenge the assumption that reproductive responsibilities are secondary to market production and emphasize their interdependence at an equal hierarchical level. It is also crucial to recognize the impact of unpaid domestic and care work on paid employment and the injustice when women's waged work, due to its association with women's "natural" abilities, results in lower pay and status for these positions (Himmelweit, 2011; Molyneux, 1994; Picchio, 1994).

As noted by Kergoat (2003), the sexual division of labor is guided by the principles of separation and hierarchy, where jobs are categorized as either men's or women's work, and men's roles are assigned greater value. It should be noted that the increased participation of women in wage labor does not render the labor market neutral or egalitarian; instead, it exposes the interconnectedness between class relations (exploitation in wage labor) and gender relations (gender-based oppression).

The healthcare sector represents a significant source of paid employment for women, employing an estimated 3.4% of the global workforce. Notably, female participation in this sector surpasses their involvement in the overall labor market (OIT, 2017; OECD, 2021). Currently, 70% of the industry's workforce comprises women across various professions and occupations beyond direct caregiving, including service administration and maintenance. This composition represents a highly feminized sector that highlights workforce gender segregation, with women overrepresented in lower occupational positions, working fewer hours, and, consequently, receiving lower wages (Durán, 2000; WHO-ILO, 2022). A study conducted in 2019 analyzing 104 countries found that women comprise most nurses, midwives, and care assistants, while men predominate among physicians, dentists, and pharmacists. In addition, female workers tend to have more part-time contracts, earn an average of 28% less than their male counterparts, and are the primary resource in rural and remote regions (Boniol et al., 2019).

Not only do women in traditionally female-dominated professions face lower pay and social status due to the stereotypes surrounding their occupations

(Molinier, 2011; Wlosko & Ros, 2018), but they also hold the lowest leadership positions and lack decision-making power. Despite being a sector predominantly composed of women, it is led by men (WHO Gender Equity Hub, 2019).

Although the healthcare sector is a comparatively steady employer, recent health reforms designed to enhance efficiency and address shortages in healthcare personnel have transformed hiring practices and work organization. Consequently, there has been a proliferation of temporary, intermediary part-time jobs and flexible scheduling arrangements that extend working hours, impeding work-life balance, with women being particularly impacted by this situation (Carpio & Santiago Bench, 2015; OIT, 2017).

Evidence indicates a decline in job quality that facilitates the implementation of reforms (Brito, 2000), disproportionately affecting women through wage discrimination, vertical gender segregation, undervaluation of jobs that support paid care, and even exclusion from the labor market due to concentration in highly skilled jobs. Therefore, the WHO's 2030 human resources strategy proposes addressing gender-based discrimination by incorporating a gender perspective into organizational and recruitment models in health services, education, and personnel training (OPS-OMS, 2017; WHO, 2016b).

2.2 *Labor in the Health System in Colombia*

Due to the neoliberal social reforms promoted in Colombia in recent decades, the country's health sector has experienced significant changes with adverse impacts on the employment conditions of health workers. In this situation, the privatization and commodification of education, labor, and healthcare converge.

Education sector reforms have led to growth in training for health professions and new occupations. However, this has been poorly regulated and not absorbed by the labor market. Despite the growth of the health insurance system and subsequent demand for services, human resources are insufficient to meet the healthcare sector's demand (Minsalud, 2018; Ruiz et al., 2009).

As a result of labor reforms, employment in the sector has become tenuous due to the development of non-traditional hiring methods such as partial, fixed term, and intermediary contracts, lack of workplace safety protections, deregulated working hours, flexible wages, and diversified forms of compensation and dismissal. These factors have all contributed to the individualization of labor relations, enabling companies to reduce hiring costs and the social benefits system for workers (Briceño-Ayala, 2000). In other words, policies support private firms to enhance their productivity and competitiveness in the global market, often at the expense of workers' rights (Pineda & Rodríguez, 2021).

Health insurance organizations have implemented these measures to manage the human resources required for their operations effectively. Conceived as an insurance system grounded in market relations and featuring a new regulatory role for the State, the 1993 social health insurance law facilitated private sector participation in both the administration and provision of services, prioritizing efficiency and cost control as primary operational objectives (Cardona, Hernández, & Yepes, 2005; Hernández & Vega, 2001). Within this framework, various forms of contracting have been expanded, the flexibility of working hours and salaries has increased, and social protection has been curtailed to reduce labor costs.

Concerning changes in the contracting model, the health system has identified three primary types: direct contracts, service provision contracts, and contracts through intermediary entities. The direct contract is considered the standard and a decent, stable, and secure option. Nevertheless, increasing contracts within the sector are fixed-term agreements, offering legal benefits and protections without ensuring continuity. The service contract assumes that the worker is providing services autonomously and thus responsible for paying their social benefits. This contractual modality is widely used in professional relationships, reducing companies' labor costs. Lastly, labor intermediation contracts involve associated work cooperatives, temporary service companies, or union agreements. In this approach, workers do not have direct labor relations with the companies where their services are offered; instead, they work with third parties that manage the human resources required by the organizations. This model places the responsibility for social benefits and job security on the workers (Flórez, Atehortúa, & Arenas, 2009; Pineda & Rodríguez, 2021; Torres-Tovar, 2021).

The paradox lies in the significant shortage of personnel in the country, unequal distribution, and productivity and performance issues that impede the fulfillment of health system requirements (Ruiz et al., 2009). Reforms have further deteriorated the situation through outsourcing, moonlighting, instability, reduced incomes, widened salary gaps, and increased informality. These changes have benefited institutions within the sector but have made working conditions more precarious for employees and weakened the unionization and wage bargaining power of workers (Flórez, Atehortúa, & Arenas, 2009; Molina-Marín et al., 2016; Vargas, 2014).

Due to gender segregation in the sector, the reforms have disproportionately and adversely impacted women's employment in several ways. There is a lack of representation of women in managerial positions and an overrepresentation in unskilled occupations. Women are paid less than men for jobs of equal value, have less job security, and women who are paid to provide health care receive minimal recognition of their professions and occupations. Furthermore, unemployed female workers face more significant challenges in recovering employment. These effects result from a lack of gender-inclusive approaches in healthcare that consider gender segregation in the industry and the burden of unpaid work disproportionately borne by women (Florián, De la Hoz, & Lara, 2022; García-Roa & Tapias-Torrado, 2013; Pineda & Rodríguez, 2021).

3 Methods

We conducted a descriptive study based on secondary sources from official administrative records. Our data sources include the *Registro Único de Talento Humano en Salud* (ReTHUS)[2] and the Great Integrated Household Survey (GEIH). ReTHUS, part of the Observatory for Human Talent in Health under the Ministry of Health and Social Protection,[3] has kept records on health professionals based on demographic, educational, and income factors since 2011. Meanwhile, the GEIH, conducted by the National Administrative Department of Statistics (DANE),[4] is a probabilistic sample survey that captures labor market information using a geostatistical framework from the 2018 Population and Housing Census. For our analysis of the COVID-19 pandemic's impacts, we utilized data from 2019 to 2022.[5] This timeframe covers the pre-pandemic period and concludes with the end of the public health crisis in Colombia in June 2022.[6]

---

2 Unified Registry of Human Talent in Health

3 https://www.minsalud.gov.co/salud/PO/Paginas/registro-unico-nacional-del-talento-humano-en-salud-rethus.aspx.

4 https://www.dane.gov.co/index.php?option=com_content&view=article&id=2921&catid=178.

5 It should be noted that in 2020 and 2021, the Great Integrated Household Survey -GEIH- underwent a series of changes to adapt it to the new census framework. A methodological exercise showed differences in comparing data obtained before and after 2021. The original datasets -without the comparison correction- were used because of difficulties with the available information at the time of the analysis displayed in this manuscript. This methodological choice could affect the sample sizes and the response rates in some questions, especially in 2021.

6 The Colombian national government declared the end of the emergency in the country in June 2021, although the ending of the COVID-19 pandemic as an international public health emergency was declared by WHO only until May 2023. See Statement on the fifteenth meeting

The study universes were constructed using the population employed[7] in health service provision, which includes hospitals, clinics, medical and dental offices, diagnostic centers, and therapeutic support centers that correspond to Section Q, Division 85 (2019) and 86 (2020–2022) of the International Standard Industrial Classification of Activities, ISIC (DANE, 2020). The annual data was processed using Stata v.14 and Excel v.1808.

The labor market analysis adheres to the International Labor Organization's principles of decent work. It measures the quality of employment, distinguishing between stable employment (with open-ended contractual relationships, access to social security and benefits) and precarious employment (with flexible contracts, schedules, and salaries and a lack of social protection) (Benach et al., 2013; Eurofound & ILO, 2019). For this purpose, we used the categories and variables of labor scholars in Colombia that include the characterization of income, job stability, protection, and work organization disaggregated by sex, educational level, occupational profile, and geographic area, including aspects such as subsidies, overtime pay, affiliation to labor risks, affiliation to occupational risks and job satisfaction (Farné, 2003; Pineda & Acosta, 2011), and the examination of gender gaps to characterize segregation, discrimination, and exclusion of female health workers (DANE-CPEM-UN Women, 2020; Florián, De la Hoz, & Lara, 2022; García-Roa & Tapias-Torrado, 2013; Herrera-Idárraga, et al., 2020).

4 The COVID-19 Pandemic and Its Impact on Health Sector Employment Conditions in Colombia, 2019–2022

Following an overview of human resources in the healthcare sector, our study delves into employment conditions by gender. We explore the quality of employment by assessing job stability, work organization, salaries, and social protection. Furthermore, we investigate perceptions about work, shifts in employment patterns during the pandemic, and gender inequalities.

---

of the IHR (2005). Emergency Committee on the COVID-19 pandemic. https://www.who.int/news/item/05-05-2023-statement-on-the-fifteenth-meeting-of-the-international-health-regulations-(2005)-emergency-committee-regarding-the-coronavirus-disease-(covid-19)-pandemic 5-May-2023.

7 According to the DANE, the employed population corresponds to people over 15 years of age who worked at least one hour during the last week, didn't work but held a job, or worked at least one hour without pay (DANE, 2023).

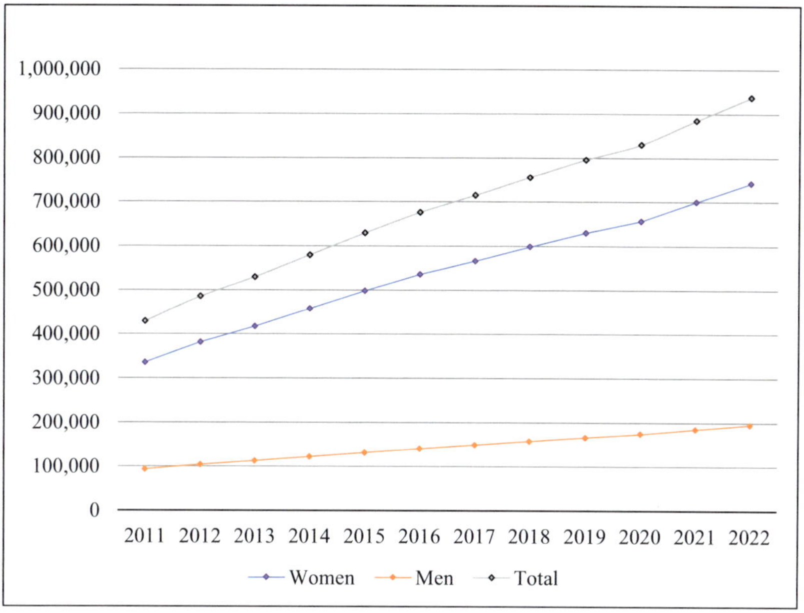

GRAPH 4.1 Human resources for health. Colombia 2011–2022
SOURCE: AUTHORS' ESTIMATES BASED ON SISPRO-RETHUS DATA SET, MARCH-APRIL 2023

4.1 *Socio-demographic Characteristics of Health and Care Workforce: a Female and Feminized Sector*

According to data from ReTHUS, Human Resources for Health (HRH) has steadily increased over the past twelve years (see Graph 4.1). In 2022, 936,981 individuals were qualified to work in healthcare, more than double the 428,411 registered in 2011. This growth can be attributed to the increased availability of health-related educational programs (Minsalud, 2018). However, of these individuals, only 483,035 (51.6%) reported working in inpatient, outpatient, or home care settings.

The data show the unequal gender composition of the sector. Women make up the highest proportion of the available human resources, and during the period analyzed, the gap between women and men has widened.

Despite sustained growth, the country fails to meet international density standards of 44.5 physicians and nurses per 10,000 inhabitants (OPS-OMS, 2017; WHO, 2016a) and faces issues with geographic distribution. The national average for physicians and nurses was 34.4 per 10,000 in 2019 and increased to 36.8 in 2022, but significant differences exist across regions, with 24 of the country's 33 regions reporting low ratios. Thus, in Bogotá, the density was 66.2

per 10,000, whereas in impoverished and rural departments with a higher racialized population, it did not exceed 20 per 10,000.

Human resources in the health sector are characterized by gender segregation (Table 4.1). This female-dominated sector historically deals with the care of bodies, a role instituted for women in both the private and public spheres.

As shown in Graph 4.1 and Table 4.1, there are sex-based horizontal and education/salary-based vertical segregation. Women constitute most of the available human resources in the period analyzed (79%), have lower levels of education -with around 50% having auxiliary education- and only 43% holding a college degree.[8] In contrast, more men have university and specialist degrees, with a 10–20 percentage point difference.

Gender disparities in professional demographics highlight that women with university degrees outnumber men in non-medical professions. However, men dominate medical professions and specialist roles. In medical specialties, the gender division is also visible, with most men working in surgical fields and a majority of females in care-oriented roles like pediatrics, psychiatry, and family health.

As a result of their belonging to the lower levels of education and greater participation in non-medical professions and specialties, women have lower incomes than men. In this period, more than 70% of women and 50–55% of men earned two minimum wages or less. In contrast, at the highest wage levels, men earned significantly more than women, with the proportion of men earning more than ten minimum wages being four times higher.

Based on ReTHUS data, this overview outlines registered individuals with the potential to work in the sector. However, it cannot accurately reflect the labor force due to non-registration and lack of updates among those with technical or professional health training. To consider sociodemographic and occupational characteristics, we rely on GEIH data (Table 4.2), showing that over 70% of employed individuals in the health system are women. Before the pandemic, the total working individuals numbered 658,216, increasing to 784,470 by 2022. The majority are of working age[9] and mainly employed as salaried workers.

---

8 The ReTHUS distinguishes human resources in health according to their level of education into two main groups: higher education and job training. The first group includes those with a professional, technical professional, or technologist health degree, and the second workers with a certificate from training institutions for work and human development. See: https://www.minsalud.gov.co/salud/PO/Paginas/talento-humano-salud.aspx.

9 According to the 19th International Conference of Labor Statisticians, the working-age population comprises people 15 years old or older.

TABLE 4.1 Human resources for health. Distribution by sex and level of education, professional profile, and salary range. Colombia, 2019–2022

	2019		2020		2021		2022	
	Women	Men	Women	Men	Women	Men	Women	Men
	(n=172.056)	(n=53.592)	(n=185.882)	(n=58.441)	(n=208.597)	(n=63.835)	(n=220.837)	(n=67.037)
Educational level								
Auxiliary (non-university)	47.3%	21.8%	47.2%	22.7%	48.5%	28.4%	50.6%	28.7%
Technical/ Technological	6.4%	6.8%	6.0%	6.5%	5.9%	7.7%	6.0%	7.8%
University	42.5%	54.4%	43.0%	54.5%	42.1%	64.6%	44.3%	64.3%
Specialization	4.8%	17.8%	4.6%	17.0%	4.4%	19.7%	4.6%	19.5%
Professional profile (university degree)								
Medicine	27.2%	69.2%	27.8%	68.6%	28.1%	67.9%	28.2%	67.8%
Nursing and other non-medical	72.8%	30.6%	72.2%	31.4%	79.9%	32.1%	71.8%	32.2%
Specialization								
Medical	83.7%	95.0%	83.4%	95.0%	84.4%	95.0%	85.0%	95.2%
Non-medical	16.3%	5.0%	16.6%	5.0%	15.6%	5.0%	15.0%	4.8%
Some medical specialties								
General surgery	16.2%	83.8%	16.6%	83.4%	18.3%	81.7%	18.7%	81.3%

TABLE 4.1 Human resources for health. Distribution by sex and level of education, professional profile, and salary range. Colombia, 2019–2022 (*cont.*)

	2019		2020		2021		2022	
	Women	**Men**	**Women**	**Men**	**Women**	**Men**	**Women**	**Men**
	(n=172.056)	(n=53.592)	(n=185.882)	(n=58.441)	(n=208.597)	(n=63.835)	(n=220.837)	(n=67.037)
Obstetrics and gynecology	44.2%	55.8%	45.5%	54.5%	46.8%	53.2%	48.3%	51.7%
Critical care	23.2%	76.8%	23.0%	77.0%	23.8%	76.2%	23.6%	76.4%
Cardiology	15.9%	84.1%	16.5%	83.5%	17.6%	82.4%	17.6%	82.4%
Dermatology	69.0%	31.0%	67.2%	32.8%	69.7%	30.3%	70.3%	29.7%
Pediatrics	61.3%	38.7%	61.4%	38.6%	62.3%	37.7%	64.0%	36.0%
Psychiatry services	54.2%	45.8%	53.2%	46.8%	55.1%	44.9%	55.0%	45.0%
Family and community health	54.5%	45.5%	61.0%	39.0%	63.5%	36.5%	62.8%	37.2%
Salary ranges according to BPR[(a)]								
< 1 LMMW[(b)]	31.2%	22.4%	31.7%	22.8%	32.9%	24.3%	33.5%	25.2%
1–2 LMMW	38.0%	29.7%	36.6%	29.7%	37.0%	30.0%	37.5%	30.4%
2–4 LMMW	20.3%	23.7%	20.7%	23.8%	20.0%	23.6%	19.6%	23.3%
4–10 LMMW	9.3%	18.2%	9.6%	17.9%	9.0%	16.9%	8.4%	16.2%
≥ 10 LMMW	1.3%	6.0%	1.3%	5.8%	1.1%	5.1%	1.1%	5.0%

Notes: [(a)] Base payment rate (BPR). [(b)] Legal minimum monthly wage. The monthly salary for the year 2023 is equivalent to US $251 at the representative market rate (October 2023) COP 4,219.16/USD.

SOURCE: AUTHORS' ESTIMATES BASED ON THE SISPRO-RETHUS DATA SET, MARCH-APRIL 2023

TABLE 4.2 Health workers by socio-demographic characteristics, by sex. Colombia, 2019–2022

	2019		2020[a]		2021		2022	
	Women	Men	Women	Men	Women	Men	Women	Men
	(n=478,435)	(n=179,781)	(n=237,175)	(n=38,567)	(n=543,574)	(n=222,349)	(n=563,640)	(n=220,830)
Age (years)								
< 20	2.9%	2.6%	2.4%	2.3%	1.7%	1.0%	1.5%	0.9%
20–49	86.0%	75.4%	84.2%	78.9%	84.3%	76.8%	83.8%	74.7%
50–69	11.2%	20.6%	13.2%	17.9%	13.9%	22.2%	14.5%	22.5%
≥ 70	0.1%	1.1%	0.2%	1.0%	0.1%	1.0%	0.2%	1.9%
Educational level								
Bachelor's degree	23.4%	27.8%	22.9%	28.0%	14.9%	19.8%	15.4%	20.4%
Technician/ Technologist	36.0%	20.7%	36.8%	22.6%	40.7%	24.5%	38.0%	21.4%
University degree	26.6%	29.0%	25.2%	26.7%	32.6%	34.6%	32.5%	34.3%
Postgraduate	10.7%	17.1%	11.5%	17.2%	9.3%	18.3%	11.3%	19.8%
Don't know	2.9%	5.4%	3.5%	5.3%	2.2%	2.8%	2.6%	3.9%
Occupational position[b]								
Salaried	74.0%	71.0%	74.6%	68.1%	82.1%	77.6%	76.2%	69.6%
Independent	26.2%	29.0%	26.2%	31.7%	18.2%	22.3%	23.8%	30.4%

Notes: [a] In 2020, the GEIH was conducted by telephone, and the non-response rate for socio-demographic variables was 30% for both sexes. [b] The salaried category includes workers or employees of a private company and workers or employees of the government, and the independent category includes self-employed workers and employers.

SOURCE: AUTHORS' ESTIMATES BASED ON GEIH 2019–2022, DANE

ReTHUS data reveals a noticeable gender gap in education levels among the working population. Women typically have lower educational attainment, particularly in fundamental, technical, and technological fields, whereas men are more likely to hold university and postgraduate degrees.

The interplay of these variables suggests that women workers tend to be younger, have lower education levels, and are predominantly employed as salaried workers. In contrast, men tend to be older, have higher education levels, and are mainly self-employed.

4.2 *COVID-19 and Employment Conditions in the Health Care Sector: Precariousness and Gender Inequalities*

According to GEIH survey data, individuals employed in the healthcare industry constituted 3.1% of the total employed population in 2019. This proportion increased during the pandemic, reaching 4.6% in 2020, despite job losses in other sectors (Graph 4.2). Nevertheless, there was a significant decrease in healthcare jobs, with a 28.9% decline between 2019 and 2020, resulting in a loss of 190,363 jobs. The sector rebounded swiftly, experiencing a growth rate of 63.7% in 2021. Consequently, the balance between 2019 and 2021 reflects a growth of over 16%.

Graph 4.3 shows that the pattern of loss and recovery did not affect men and women equally. In 2020, 139,957 women's jobs were eliminated (-29.3%) and 50,406 men's (-28%).

The pandemic's impact on unemployment and decreased income is evident, as indicated by responses to the question introduced by the GEIH in 2020 regarding its effects on people's lives (Table 4.3).

In 2022, a substantial number of workers contracted the virus, and a notable percentage faced income reduction due to economic activity reduction or job loss/suspension without pay.

The impacts of the pandemic on employment quality in terms of stability, organization, compensation, social protection, and work perceptions, as well as gender differences in urban and rural contexts, are examined in the following sections.

4.2.1 Changes in Job Stability

The job stability of the health sector working class, defined by the contractual relationship between companies and workers, is a cause for concern, as indicated by the data in Table 4.4.

In urban areas, 75% of workers were salaried, with the remainder being self-employed. The proportion of salaried workers was even lower in rural areas. While most workers had an employment agreement, more men worked without one. A notable issue for job stability is that, despite having a written contract, the contract duration was predetermined in approximately 40% of cases. Not all contracts were direct, especially in rural areas. Between 10–18% of urban workers had contracts through intermediaries, with temporary companies constituting over 50% of these arrangements. In rural areas, the proportion of indirect hiring was significantly higher.

Since 2020, there has been an increase in the proportion of individuals with secure contracts (permanent and direct contracts), particularly in rural regions. The surge in formal employment in 2021 may be attributed to mass vaccination efforts, demanding substantial human resources in urban and rural areas.

4.2.2 Effects on the Organization of Work

Work organization encompasses timetables, hours, and tasks. However, the GEIH overlooks the healthcare industry's reality, where services, especially hospitals, operate 24/7 with 8–12 hours shifts, including weekends, while other services, like public health, occur mainly during the day and are predominantly extra-mural. Working the legal 48-hour week is not equivalent in the daytime versus at night, on weekdays vs. weekends, or at the health service main office vs. in communities. The survey's limitations in reporting specific activities hindered the differentiation of more complex care workplace characteristics and professional profiles (see Table 4.5).

Table 4.5 reveals significant gender disparity. On average, 25% of individuals worked less than 48 hours per week, while 15–20% worked more than 48 hours. Women worked fewer hours, especially those in rural areas, while men tended to work longer. Notably, only a tiny percentage reported receiving additional overtime compensation, indicating that some individuals worked extended hours for the same pay.

Ten percent of individuals usually work less than 40 hours per week, with many choosing this schedule for its suitability. However, a notable portion of women have yet to access any other option but to work such hours. Furthermore, a small percentage worked less than 30 hours in the week leading up to the survey, with women comprising the majority, and this percentage was higher in 2019 than in subsequent years.

During the pandemic, while the standard workday generally increased in length and fewer individuals worked reduced hours, gender disparities persisted. In 2020, the percentage of urban and rural women forced to work less than 40 hours per week rose due to limited other options. A concerning trend emerged where many people worked less than 30 hours per week due to

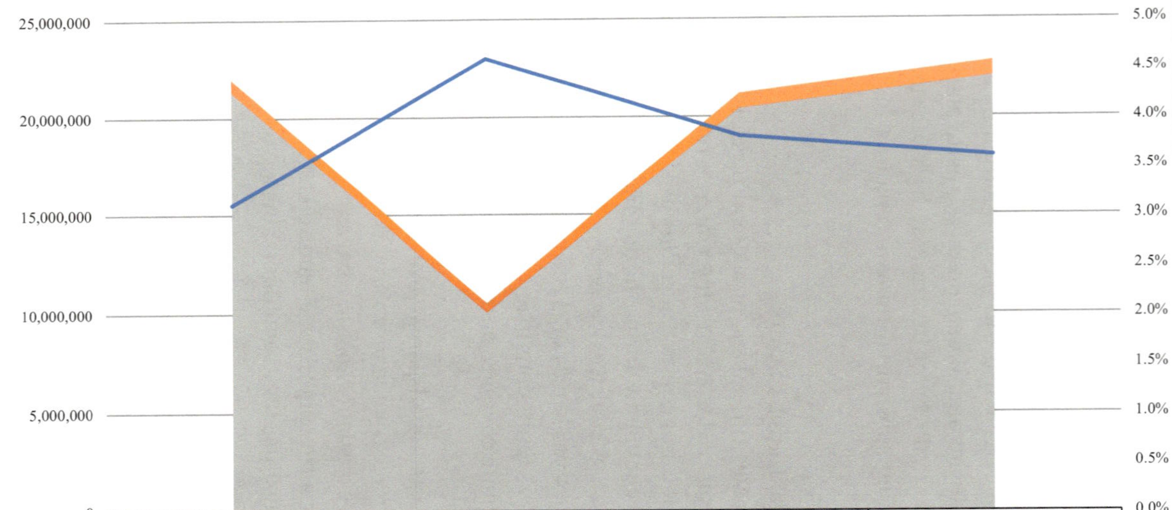

	2019	2020	2021	2022
Health care sector employed	658,216	467,853	765,923	784,470
National employed population	21,309,813	10,064,128	20,391,742	22,032,180
Health/national	3.1%	4.6%	3.8%	3.6%

GRAPH 4.2 Employed population, national and healthcare sector. Colombia 2019–2022
SOURCE: AUTHORS' ESTIMATES BASED ON GEIH 2019–2022, DANE

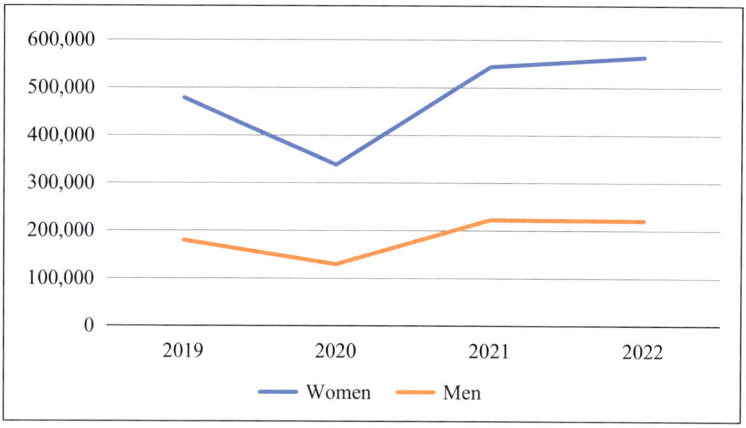

GRAPH 4.3 Population employed in health sector by gender. Colombia 2019–2022
SOURCE: AUTHORS' ESTIMATES BASED ON GEIH 2019–2022, DANE

suspended contracts or reduced hours, impacting many rural women. Working fewer hours was accompanied by a reduction in earnings.

4.2.3 Impact on Wages

Contracting forms, working hours, activities, and qualifications influence remuneration. According to Table 4.6 data, wages in the sector are generally low, with over 80% of women and 75% of men in urban areas and over 90% of workers in rural areas earning less than three minimum monthly wages. On average, more urban men make above that range.

A notable change for both men and women during the first year of the pandemic was a decrease in the percentage of individuals earning less than the minimum wage and an increase in those earning between one and three minimum monthly wages. In general, there was a change in the distribution of wage ranges, explained by the loss of jobs at the extremes of the wage distribution (less than one and more than seven minimum wage) of more than 65% on average in both ranges.

In 2021, in absolute terms, there was an increase of almost 200% in the amount of health workers who earned less than a minimum wage. A possible explanation for this shift is the massive vaccination campaign that demanded health workers without professional qualifications (For instance, auxiliary workers). In 2022, with the ending of the vaccination campaign, the behavior

TABLE 4.3 Health workers according to perceived impacts of the COVID-19 pandemic, by sex. Colombia, 2020–2022

Difficulties during the COVID-19 pandemic	2020		2021		2022	
	Women	Men	Women	Men	Women	Men
	(n=338,478)	(n=129,375)	(n=543,574)	(n=222,349)	(n=563,640)	(n=220,830)
Is/was sick with the virus	3.7%	4.1%	3.3%	3.2%	36.2%	36.8%
↓ Economic activity/income	10.3%	13.9%	3.8%	3.1%	33.8%	34.5%
Suspension from work without pay	1.4%	0.7%	0.5%	0.6%	3.5%	3.2%
Loss of job/source of income	2.3%	3.5%	0.8%	0.9%	10.0%	8.1%
Other hardship[a]	26.1%	26.8%	7.5%	4.3%	63.6%	58.3%
No hardship	19.5%	20.0%	3.8%	4.8%	31.7%	32.7%

a Includes difficulties in obtaining food, paying bills and debts, performing, or looking for work, or attending classes.

SOURCE: AUTHORS' ESTIMATES BASED ON GEIH 2019–2022, DANE

TABLE 4.4 Employment conditions of the population employed in the health sector, by sex and area of residence. Colombia, 2019–2022

Employed population	**2019**		**2020**		**2021**		**2022**	
	Women	**Men**	**Women**	**Men**	**Women**	**Men**	**Women**	**Men**
	(n=478,435)	(n=179,781)	(n=338,478)	(n=129,375)	(n=543,574)	(n=222,439)	(n=563,640)	(n=220,830)
Occupational position[(a)]								
Urban	(n=456,534)	(n=174,151)	(n=227,884)	(n=86,626)	(n=513,788)	(n=209,392)	(n=539,501)	(n=210,756)
Salaried employee	74.0%	71.0%	74.6%	68.1%	82.1%	77.6%	76.2%	69.9%
Self-employed	25.8%	28.9%	25.4%	31.8%	17.7%	22.1%	23.7%	30.0%
Rural	(n=20,586)	(n=5,605)	(n=9,205)	(n=4,080)	(n=28,513)	(n=12,091)	(n=23,723)	(n=9,932)
Salaried employee	66.1%	67.9%	53.9%	71.5%	72.5%	74.1%	74.5%	61.6%
Self-employed	33.9%	30.0%	46.2%	28.5%	27.2%	25.9%	25.5%	38.4%
Has a contract								
Urban	91.8%	89.2%	91.3%	90.9%	91.2%	88.6%	89.7%	86.8%
Rural	95.2%	97.9%	91.3%	81.8%	92.1%	91.8%	93.0%	84.0%
Written contract								
Urban	96.0%	95.9%	96.3%	98.6%	95.5%	97.8%	95.6%	97.3%
Open-ended	*58.2%*	*57.4%*	*57.5%*	*57.4%*	*64.6%*	*63.0%*	*61.6%*	*60.6%*
Fixed term	*41.8%*	*42.2%*	*42.2%*	*42.6%*	*34.1%*	*36.0%*	*38.2%*	*39.3%*
Rural	92.6%	87.6%	99.9%	100.0%	92.7%	89.7%	94.3%	95.9%
Open-ended	*33.4%*	*32.8%*	*60.5%*	*49.1%*	*44.7%*	*58.7%*	*51.8%*	*43.7%*
Fixed term	66.6%	*67.2%*	*39.5%*	*50.9%*	*55.3%*	*41.3%*	*48.2%*	*56.3%*
Direct contract								

TABLE 4.4 Employment conditions of the population employed in the health sector, by sex and area of residence. Colombia, 2019–2022 (*cont.*)

Employed population	**2019**		**2020**		**2021**		**2022**	
	Women	**Men**	**Women**	**Men**	**Women**	**Men**	**Women**	**Men**
	(n=478,435)	(n=179,781)	(n=338,478)	(n=129,375)	(n=543,574)	(n=222,439)	(n=563,640)	(n=220,830)
Urban	84.1%	80.5%	83.5%	81.4%	92.2%	91.5%	89.0%	87.2%
Rural	69.7%	79.2%	77.2%	90.7%	87.7%	80.9%	82.0%	72.4%
Indirect contract								
Urban	15.9%	19.4%	17.2%	18.9%	8.0%	8.3%	11.5%	13.1%
Temporary services company	*56.0%*	*42.7%*	*59.1%*	*37.6%*	*57.7%*	*47.8%*	*55.0%*	*45.4%*
Associated work cooperative	*8.3%*	*7.0%*	*10.6%*	*10.4%*	*20.6%*	*20.8%*	*15.3%*	*16.5%*
Associated company	*3.3%*	*2.6%*	*3.2%*	*7.5%*	*9.0%*	*4.8%*	*7.9%*	*10.6%*
Other	*32.4%*	*47.6%*	*27.0%*	*44.5%*	*12.7%*	*26.6%*	*21.8%*	*27.5%*
Rural	30.3%	20.8%	22.8%	9.3%	12.0%	19.1%	18.0%	27.6%
Temporary services company	*64.4%*	*78.2%*	*18.9%*	*32.7%*	*38.5%*	*41.6%*	*58.1%*	*47.3%*
Associated work cooperative	*6.2%*	*21.8%*	*25.9%*	*0.0%*	*32.9%*	*11.3%*	*13.4%*	*4.8%*
Associated company	*0.7%*	*0.0%*	*0.0%*	*0.0%*	*4.3%*	*35.1%*	*8.0%*	*1.8%*
Other	*28.7%*	*0.0%*	*55.2%*	*67.3%*	*24.2%*	*12.0%*	*20.5%*	*46.1%*

SOURCE: AUTHORS' ESTIMATES BASED ON THE GEIH 2019–2022, DANE

TABLE 4.5 Work organization of the population employed in the health sector, by sex and area of residence. Colombia, 2019–2022

	2019		2020		2021		2022	
	Women	**Men**	**Women**	**Men**	**Women**	**Men**	**Women**	**Men**
Weekly working hours								
Urban	(n=457,849)	(n=174,176)	(n=227,970)	(n=86,728)	(n=515,061)	(n=210,258)	(n=539,917)	(n=210,898)
< 48 hours	32.1%	28.8%	28.4%	24.7%	23.3%	20.9%	24.5%	23.2%
48 hours	52.8%	48.7%	55.7%	53.1%	61.4%	58.2%	59.4%	55.6%
> 48 hours	15.1%	22.5%	15.9%	22.2%	15.4%	21.0%	16.1%	21.2%
Rural	(n=20,586)	(n=5,605)	(n=9,205)	(n=4,080)	(n=28,513)	(n=12,091)	(n=23,723)	(n=9,932)
< 48 hours	43.5%	24.7%	42.7%	24.3%	28.3%	16.5%	30.7%	29.0%
48 hours	46.7%	39.3%	37.0%	60.1%	56.7%	63.3%	60.8%	52.0%
> 48 hours	9.7%	36.0%	20.3%	15.6%	15.0%	20.2%	8.5%	19.0%
Reasons <40 h regularly	(n=49,121)	(n=14,552)	(n=24,688)	(n=6,400)	(n=50,623)	(n=15,547)	(n=53,036)	(n=15,402)
Urban	10.7%	8.4%	10.8%	7.4%	9.8%	7.4%	9.8%	7.3%
It is the only thing they've reached	*35.4%*	*25.6%*	*40.1%*	*28.6%*	*32.3%*	*28.1%*	*28.2%*	*16.4%*
Fits your needs	*55.8%*	*55.4%*	*50.6%*	*57.6%*	*61.4%*	*69.3%*	*69.4%*	*78.6%*
Other reason	*8.7%*	*19.0%*	*9.3%*	*13.8%*	*6.3%*	*2.6%*	*2.4%*	*5.0%*
	(n=2,519)	(n=119)	(n=1,695)	(n=128)	(n=2,643)	(n=402)	(n=2,337)	(n=296)

TABLE 4.5 Work organization of the population employed in the health sector, by sex and area of residence. Colombia, 2019–2022 (*cont.*)

	2019		2020		2021		2022	
	Women	**Men**	**Women**	**Men**	**Women**	**Men**	**Women**	**Men**
Rural	12.2%	2.1%	18.4%	3.1%	9.3%	3.3%	9.9%	3.0%
It is the only thing they've reached	40.6%	0.0%	77.3%	0.0%	35.9%	29.7%	42.9%	0.0%
Fits your needs	55.5%	100.0%	22.7%	100.0%	63.3%	70.3%	57.1%	100.0%
Other reason	3.9%	0.0%	0.0%	0.0%	0.7%	0.0%	0.0%	0.0%
Reasons <30 h. prior week								
	(n=78,004)	(n=24,367)	(n=31,922)	(n=1,024)	(n=20,790)	(n=8,018)	(n=35,530)	(n=9,037)
Urban	17.0%	14.0%	14.0%	12.7%	4.0%	3.8%	6.6%	4.3%
Illness, license or leave of absence	18.8%	12.6%	28.0%	11.7%	21.7%	11.1%	24.0%	15.9%
Suspension/termination of employment	0.9%	0.2%	3.5%	1.0%	0.4%	0.0%	0.9%	0.2%
Reduction of economic activity	6.7%	8.1%	18.2%	26.6%	24.9%	22.5%	12.1%	7.6%
Other[a]	73.7%	79.1%	50.3%	60.8%	53.0%	66.3%	62.9%	76.2%
	(n=1,169)	(n=328)	(n=1,158)	(n=223)	(n=651)	(n=0)	(n=1,078)	(n=261)
Rural	5.8%	5.7%	12.6%	5.5%	2.3%	0.0%	4.5%	2.6%
Illness, license or leave of absence	12.4%	0.0%	0.0%	0.0%	18.7%	0.0%	42.8%	16.8%

TABLE 4.5 Work organization of the population employed in the health sector, by sex and area of residence. Colombia, 2019–2022 (*cont.*)

	2019		2020		2021		2022	
	Women	**Men**	**Women**	**Men**	**Women**	**Men**	**Women**	**Men**
Suspension/termination of employment	*0.0%*	*0.0%*	*0.0%*	*0.0%*	*0.0%*	*0.0%*	*14.0%*	*0.0%*
Reduction of economic activity	*0.0%*	*0.0%*	*71.0%*	*0.0%*	*31.0%*	*0.0%*	*0.0%*	*0.0%*
Other	*87.6%*	*100.0%*	*29.0%*	*100.0%*	*50.2%*	*0.0%*	*43.2%*	*83.2%*
Worked overtime	(n=14,396)	(n=6,276)	(n=7,271)	(n=2,873)	(n=12,930)	(n=6,582)	(n=12,061)	(n=5,070)
Urban	3.1%	3.6%	3.2%	3.3%	2.5%	3.1%	2.2%	2.4%
Rural	0.3%	0.8%	0.0%	0.4%	0.5%	0.0%	2.9%	3.0%

Note. Includes working fewer hours due to vacations, holidays, training, and other opportunities.
SOURCE: AUTHORS' ESTIMATES BASED ON GEIH 2019–2022, DANE

TABLE 4.6 Salary range of the health workers, by sex and area of residence. Colombia, 2019–2022

Salary range (LMMW)[a]	2019		2020		2021		2022	
	Women	Men	Women	Men	Women	Men	Women	Men
Urban	(n= 438,855)	(n= 163,467)	(n= 214,428)	(n= 80,632)	(n= 442,923)	(n= 171,563)	(n= 520,810)	(n= 198,316)
<1	23.9%	18.7%	15.2%	9.9%	21.9%	17.2%	8.3%	4.9%
1–3	59.6%	52.1%	70.1%	63.9%	62.3%	52.9%	73.1%	58.8%
3–5	11.5%	14.5%	10.2%	11.8%	10.5%	16.1%	12.4%	15.9%
5–7	2.4%	5.5%	2.9%	7.4%	2.8%	5.4%	3.5%	7.8%
>7	2.6%	9.2%	1.6%	7.0%	2.5%	8.4%	2.7%	12.6%
Rural	(n= 20,541)	(n= 5,368)	(n= 8,945)	(n= 3,686)	(n= 26,170)	(n= 20,750)	(n= 23,199)	(n= 9,723)
<1	39.9%	43.7%	27.6%	39.4%	35.1%	63.1%	14.8%	9.8%
1–3	55.6%	51.7%	69.5%	52.9%	59.8%	23.6%	80.5%	80.5%
3–5	3.6%	2.8%	2.9%	7.7%	4.2%	6.1%	3.5%	3.4%
5–7	0.7%	1.7%	0.0%	0.0%	0.3%	5.0%	0.3%	3.5%
>7	0.2%	0.0%	0.0%	0.0%	0.6%	2.2%	0.8%	2.7%

a The monthly salary for the year 2023 is equivalent to US $251 by the representative market rate (October 2023) COP 4,219.16/USD.

SOURCE: AUTHORS' ESTIMATES BASED ON GEIH 2019–2022, DANE

of the health labor force returned to its previous trend; this is, almost half of the workers earned between 1–3 minimum legal monthly salaries.[10]

Substantial wage gaps persist between men and women, with urban areas exhibiting more considerable disparities than rural areas. Graph 4.4 illustrates urban-rural gaps that contribute to gender differences. In urban areas, men's wages increased by COP 976,678, compared to only COP 442,741 for women. In rural areas, the increase in men's salaries surpassed that of urban women, at COP 593,072, although rural workers experienced the lowest overall increase, at just COP 311,933.

10 Due to the low representation of rural health workers among the national total (less than 10%), it is impossible to guarantee this data's statistical representation. Therefore, the data presented are indicative and require careful consideration.

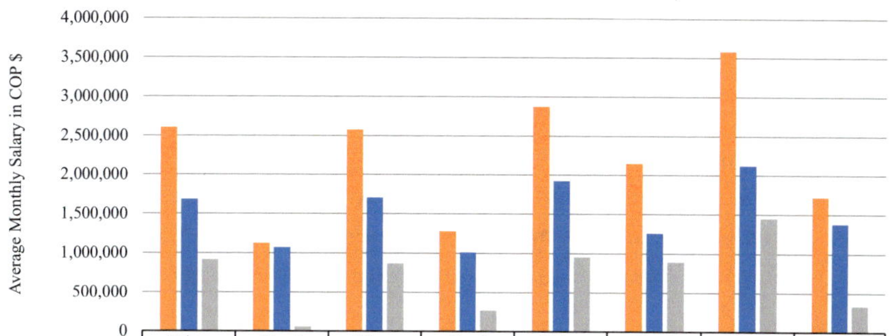

	2019		2020		2021		2022	
	Urban	Rural	Urban	Rural	Urban	Rural	Urban	Rural
Men	2,601,198	1,125,493	2,572,998	1,275,413	2,873,487	219,355	3,577,876	1,718,565
Women	1,682,115	1,070,285	1,703,853	1,010,560	1,921,589	1,258,222	2,124,856	1,382,218
Wage gap M-W	919,083	55,208	869,145	264,853	951,898	891,133	1,453,020	336,347

Men Women Wage gap M-W

GRAPH 4.4 Differences in the average monthly salary of the employed population in the health sector, by sex and area of residence. Colombia, 2019–2022
SOURCE: AUTHORS' ESTIMATES BASED ON GEIH 2019–2022, DANE

Next we address the question of whether the wage gap between men and women persists despite equal levels of education or equivalent occupations.

TABLE 4.7 Gender wage gap by education level and occupational category. Colombia, 2019–2022

	2019	2020	2021	2022
Educational level				
High school diploma	5.6%	7.2%	5.4%	9.1%
Technician/Technologist	9.1%	9.1%	8.3%	0.0%
University level	18.2%	10.0%	20.0%	23.1%
Postgraduate	40.7%	44.1%	40.0%	41.2%
Occupational category				
Private worker/employee	9.1%	8.3%	14.3%	14.3%
Government worker/employee	15.0%	10.0%	20.0%	14.3%
Self-employed	31.6%	35.0%	30.6%	28.6%
Employer/Employee	25.0%	0.0%	2.9%	37.5%

SOURCE: AUTHORS' ESTIMATES BASED ON GEIH 2019–2022, DANE

Wage disparities cannot be solely attributed to women being generally less educated and occupying lower positions. Table 4.7 reveals that women earned less than men even with the same educational and occupational background. Furthermore, the wage gap widens as women's academic qualifications increase. Women earn 90% of what men earn at the lowest education levels but only 60% at the graduate level. Salaried women earn between 80–90% of men's wages, whereas self-employed women earn only 60–70%. These wage gaps underscore the gender segregation present in the sector.

4.2.4 Social Protection

Table 4.8 indicates that most of the population is affiliated with healthcare regarding social security,[11] with no significant gender or location differences. However, it is essential to note that not all health workers contribute to pensions and occupational risks.

In urban areas, pension contributors fall nearly ten percentage points lower than healthcare contributors, are primarily affiliated with private funds, and around 10% lack coverage for occupational risks. In rural areas in 2020, there was decreased occupational risk coverage for both genders. It is concerning that individuals lacked protection against occupational risks during the pandemic.

This disparity in social security protection is likely among those with the least formal employment arrangements, as contributions to these three systems are compulsory for workers with direct contracts. Even with these differences, health and pension contributions remained stable during the period, which can be explained by the regulations enacted by the national government to maintain affiliation and services considering the social, economic, and ecological emergency caused by the pandemic.[12]

---

11 In Colombia, employees must contribute 12.5% of their salary to the health system and 16% to the pension system. Of these percentages, the employer must contribute 8.5% for health and 12% for pension; Independent workers must contribute the entire contribution. The unemployed and people outside the labor force can access the health-subsidized system or as contributor beneficiaries. Consequently, health affiliation coverage in the country is close to 90%. In the case of the pension, affiliation rates are much lower since the country does not have a subsidized pension system, so one person can only access the pension system via direct contribution to public or private companies.

12 See Ministry of Health and Social Protection. Decree 538 of 2020, which adopted measures to guarantee the provision of health services during the pandemic; Decree 558 of 2020, which implemented measures to temporarily reduce contributions to the General Pension System; and Decree 800 of 2020, which established measures to maintain the affiliation of those who have lost the ability to pay.

TABLE 4.8 Social protection coverage of the health workers by sex and area of residence. Colombia, 2019–2022

Social protection	2019		2020		2021		2022	
	Women	Men	Women	Men	Women	Men	Women	Men
	(n=478,435)	(n=179,781)	(n=338,478)	(n=129,375)	(n=543,574)	(n=222,349)	(n=563,640)	(n=220,830)
Affiliation to the health system								
Urban	99.0%	97.3%	97.6%	97.5%	99.2%	98.8%	99.0%	98.7%
Rural	97.1%	100.0%	100.0%	100.0%	98.9%	99.9%	99.4%	100.0%
Pension fund contribution								
Urban	88.4%	87.3%	88.2%	91.6%	89.5%	90.6%	89.1%	89.5%
Rural	81.9%	82.9%	86.0%	56.5%	84.5%	89.7%	87.7%	81.9%
Professional risk affiliation								
Urban	89.0%	88.4%	89.6%	91.9%	88.6%	89.6%	89.1%	89.0%
Rural	85.1%	78.1%	81.8%	72.0%	83.2%	88.4%	85.5%	79.3%

SOURCE: AUTHORS' ESTIMATES BASED ON GEIH 2019–2022, DANE

TABLE 4.9 Employment perceptions of the health workers by sex and area of residence. Colombia, 2019–2022

	2019		2020		2021		2022	
	Women	Men	Women	Men	Women	Men	Women	Men
	(n=478,435)	(n=179,781)	(n=338,478)	(n=129,375)	(n=543,574)	(n=222,349)	(n=563,640)	(n=220,830)
Contract satisfaction								
Urban	82.7%	82,0%	82.0%	84.2%	86.9%	83.3%	84.1%	84.3%
Rural	76.5%	77,2%	72.2%	86.9%	72.2%	86.9%	76.9%	73.7%
Job stability perception								
Urban	78.2%	79,7%	77.7%	80.3%	78.7%	78.9%	80.1%	81.0%
Rural	57.0%	45,2%	56.1%	50.5%	62.9%	76.3%	75.7%	62.6%
Union/ trade union membership								
Urban	5.1%	7,7%	5.0%	7.6%	6.0%	7.9%	5.1%	7.7%
Rural	2.4%	5,8%	5.8%	7.9%	4.1%	5.5%	6.4%	4.3%
Compatibility of paid and unpaid work								
Urban	89.7%	89.2%	88.8%	91.8%	87.6%	87.8%	87.1%	90.0%
Rural	92.7%	70.9%	94.1%	91.9%	87.8%	89.6%	86.9%	87.6%

SOURCE: AUTHORS' ESTIMATES BASED ON GEIH 2019–2022, DANE

TABLE 4.10 Unpaid domestic and care work of the health workers, by sex. Colombia, 2019–2022

	2019		2020	
	Women	Men	Women	Men
	(n= 478,435)	(n= 179,781)	(n= 338,478)	(n= 129,375)
Participation (%)				
Household occupations	88.6%	59.5%	88.8%	67.5%
Work in other homes/ institutions	1.0%	1.0%	0.9%	1.3%
Childcare	35.9%	17.7%	32.9%	19.2%
Care of the elderly	2.5%	1.8%	2.5%	1.9%
Participation in community activities	1.4%	1.5%	1.0%	0.7%
Dedication (hours/week)				
Household occupations	13.76	7.16	14.42	8.02
Work in other homes/ institutions	5.25	5.75	4.82	8.03
Childcare	19.06	13.23	20.21	12.83
Care of the elderly	14.33	13.62	17.30	11.85
Participation in community activities	4.54	5.05	5.52	7.21

SOURCE: AUTHORS' ESTIMATES BASED ON GEIH 2019–2022, DANE

4.2.5 Perceptions about the Employment of Male and Female Workers

A final aspect concerns workers' perception of their employment conditions (Table 4.9). In urban areas, the contract satisfaction rate was high, with over 80% of individuals reporting that they were content with their work conditions despite the reduction in job openings and unstable contracts in 2020. However, satisfaction tended to be lower in rural areas, particularly among women, due to a more significant proportion of individuals working without a written, fixed term, or indirect contracting, a potential explanation of the perception of low job stability in rural areas.

Satisfaction was significantly related to contract quality. Individuals who possessed fixed-term contracts expressed a greater degree of satisfaction (60–70%). Conversely, in contrast to other sectors, less educated employees, who constitute most salaried workers, exhibited higher satisfaction levels. One encouraging finding was that beginning in 2021, there was an improvement in the perception of job stability in rural areas due to an increase in open-ended contracts, a decrease in work through intermediaries, and possibly because keeping a job during difficult times is seen as an achievement. While having more significant union participation would enable workers to negotiate their working conditions, the proportion of union members remains very low.

Finally, it is noteworthy that a substantial proportion of individuals perceived their work schedule to be compatible with family responsibilities, as evidenced by the high percentage observed in Table 4.10, even though the unpaid workload rose in 2020.

Table 4.10 shows an increase in men‘s participation in unpaid care activities. It is noticeable that women‘s involvement in unpaid care activities remained steady, which can be explained by the rise in women's participation in the labor market. However, there was a surge in the hours devoted to some care activities, such as household occupations (for men and women), work in other homes or institutions (for men), and children and elderly care (for women). Nonetheless, these growing men's participation in care activities hasn't improved the unpaid care work gaps.

5 Final Considerations

This analysis highlights critical features of the labor market in the health system. Employment in this sector often lacks high quality due to precarious and flexible labor relations. Feminization of the sector contributes to gender inequalities intersecting with other social stratification variables like education and residential location (urban or rural). These variables reveal disparities between and within genders, with women in health professions facing disadvantages.

Being female, having lower education levels, engaging in lower-status trades, and residing in rural areas result in lower income, less autonomy, and limited recognition, placing individuals in vulnerable positions in normal circumstances, especially collective crises. Women who serve in the healthcare sector face numerous disadvantages. Female healthcare workers who live in rural areas, have less education, or work in lower-status positions are at risk of experiencing low income, limited autonomy, and inadequate recognition. This situation leaves them vulnerable in times of crisis and ordinary circumstances. The COVID-19 pandemic exposed and exacerbated gender inequalities and disparities among women.

Various studies have cautioned about the impact of the pandemic on the labor market, paid and unpaid work, and the decline of socioeconomic indicators. Farné and Sanín (2021) emphasized that the most severe impact of the pandemic in 2020 was the surge in unemployment, which disproportionately affected women due to substantial job losses. Particularly in service sectors, women faced significant challenges with reduced labor market participation and income due to pandemic containment measures. Even among employed women, wage gaps persisted and worsened. Concerningly, women faced slower reintegration into the workforce (DANE-CPEM-UN Women, 2022). Additionally, employed and unemployed women experienced an increased burden of unpaid work, widening the time gap between men and women (Tribín-Uribe et al., 2021).

Significant job losses occurred in the direct-paid care sector, including health care and care services for the elderly, disability, and early childhood. Herrera et al. (2020) reported a 32% decrease in women's employment between the first half of 2019 and 2020, twice that of men. In the same train of thought, our findings show that the overall loss in the sector in the same period was 29%, with women's job losses being 2.6 times higher than men's (absolute numbers). This loss was considerable during times of great need, although Rodríguez (2021) notes that the health system's employment decline was less severe than in other fields. Our findings corroborate this. In the period studied, the workforce increased from 3.1% of the total employed in 2019 to 4.6% in 2020, which is explainable by the strategic nature of the health sector for pandemic care. Even so, the health sector is one of the sectors with the highest loss of employment among paid care activities (Herrera, Hernández & Gélvez, 2021).

The most important finding is the increase in the wage gap after 2020, a trend that seems contrary to studies on the labor market that point to its reduction due to the loss of employment for both men and women and the fall in income (Isaza, 2021). However, these data require further discussion in the light of new research that evaluates the health workers' situation.

The pandemic impacted the health system beyond unemployment, affecting the employment and working conditions of those still working. During 2020, various unions representing healthcare professionals conducted surveys and follow-ups to demonstrate the precarious working conditions, including high rates of unstable and outsourced contracts, limited social security protection and employment benefits, and inadequate wages (Mesa de Monitoreo Crítico, 2020). These conditions were further exacerbated by the demands of the pandemic and decisions related to the health emergency. There have been changes to working hours and schedules, increased workloads due to changes or increased responsibilities, postponed breaks and vacations, delayed payment of fees and salaries (FMC-CMC, 2020), and even reduced working hours and wages resulting from postponed procedures and the closure of outpatient services (CGR, 2020). Additionally, employees have experienced workplace harassment, discrimination, and violence from the community.

However, the primary demand of these stakeholders was that of biosafety. They denounced the non-compliance with regulations on biomedical equipment and physical conditions for the care of patients with COVID-19, the shortage and poor distribution of personal protective equipment to reduce the risk of infection of patients and staff, and the non-recognition of COVID-19 as an occupational hazard. Consequently, the risk of infection was higher in frontline workers, and it was contradictory to attend to the population's health during the pandemic and to threaten the health and employment rights of personnel.

It seems that the many pronouncements and studies during the first months of 2020, together with the increased cases of infection and deaths of health personnel, pressured the national government to introduce measures to protect working conditions, provide training and personal protection elements, and recognize COVID-19 as an occupational hazard; which took for granted the formality of employment, ignoring the historical precariousness and flexibilization, and did not address the structural problem of human resources for health and their gender segregation.

The COVID-19 pandemic did not alter and even deepen the precarious employment situation in the sector, but the changes were not gender-neutral. In the first place, it is contradictory that jobs were lost just when more human resources were required to deal with the emergency in 2020. This loss was critical for women since the health system is crucial to their position in the labor market. Second, given their lower qualifications, women are inserted at the lowest levels of the sector's structure, and in the face of very little unionization, they were less able to negotiate layoffs, suspensions, and reduced working hours. Third, wage gaps, the predominance of women in the lower wage brackets, and unequal remuneration as compared to men affect women's autonomy and economic independence. Fourth, domestic and care work increased in the first year of the pandemic, making the overall workload for women high and unequal. This demonstrates that women's paid work does not transform the gender division of unpaid work.

Despite the importance of HRH in confronting the pandemic, government regulations and policies did not improve working conditions. Hiring and work organization arrangements involving increased workloads and changing working hours were not gender sensitive. Many seemingly neutral decisions concealed the gender segregation of the sector and the differential effects, ignored women's increased involvement in unpaid domestic and care work with the consequent increase in overall workload, and failed to consider women's concerns for their health and that of their families in the face of biosafety failures to protect against risks.

However, these findings are subject to some considerations. First, the analysis was based on the GEIH. This survey is not fully adequate to capture the specificities of the health labor market. For instance, it does not provide information about auxiliary workers or physicians with medical specialties. On the other hand, because of data availability at the time of carrying on these analyses, it was not possible to use the information corrected to guarantee the comparability between the four years considered; therefore, data obtained for 2021 is not fully comparable with 2019 and 2020. Finally, the scarcity of health workers in rural areas implies that they represent less than 10% of the national employed population; consequently, information for rural workers is indicative.

In the future, a better understanding of the effects of the pandemic on women's health work must be incorporated into the analysis of other axes of social stratification from an intersectional perspective to deepen the study of inequities. More importantly, it must articulate the voices, demands, and proposals to guide decision-making in the sector and contribute to women's struggles for workplace equity.

References

Amnistía Internacional (2020) *Expuesto, acallado y atacado. Deficiencias en la protección del personal sanitario y que realiza labores esenciales durante la pandemia.* London: Amnesty International.

Benach, J., Muntaner, C., Santana, V., Solar, O., Quinlan, M., & Employment Conditions Network (2013) *Employment, Work and Health Inequalities: A Global Perspective.* España: Icaria editorial.

Boniol, M., McIsaac, M., Xu, L., Wuliji, T., Diallo, K., & Campbell, J. (2019) *Gender Equity in the Health Worforce: Analysis of 104 Countries.* Geneva: World Health Organization.

Borderías, C., & Carrasco, C. (1994) Introducción. En C. Borderías, C. Carrasco, & C. Alemany (eds.) *Las mujeres y el trabajo: aproximaciones históricas, sociológicas y económicas.* Barcelona: Icaria editorial, 17–109.

Briceño-Ayala, R. (2000) Impacto de la globalización sobre la salud de los trabajadores colombianos. *Nómadas* (12): 142–151.

Brito, P. (2000) Impacto de las reformas del sector de la salud sobre los recursos humanos y la gestión laboral. *Revista Panamericana de Salud Pública* 8(1/2): 43–54.

Caldichoury, N., García-Roncallo, P., Saldías, C., Zurita, B., Castellanos, C., Herrera-Pino, J., et al. (2023) Impacto psicológico del COVID-19 en los trabajadores sanitarios durante el segundo año de pandemia en Latinoamérica: estudio de encuesta transversal. *Revista Colombiana de Psiquiatría* (abril).

Cañete, R. (2020) Las desigualdades de género en el centro de la solución a la pandemia de la COVID-19 y sus crisis en América Latina y el Caribe. *Análisis Carolina* (20).

Cardona, J., Hernández, A., & Yepes, F. (2005) La reforma a la seguridad social en salud en Colombia. ¿Avances reales? *Gerencia y Políticas de Salud* 4(9): 81–99.

Carpio, C. & Santiago Bench, N. (2015) *The Health Workforce in Latin America and the Caribbean. An Analysis of Colombia, Costa Rica, Jamaica, Panama, Peru, and Uruguay*. The World Bank.

Contraloría General de la República -CGR- (2020) Encuesta de la Contraloría a personal de la salud confirma falta de implementos de seguridad y desventajosas condiciones laborales. *Comunicados de prensa* 87, 5, julio. Available (consulted 3 January, 2023) at https://www.contraloria.gov.co/es/w/encuesta-de-la-contralor%C3%ADa-a-personal-de-la-salud-confirma-falta-de-implementos-de-seguridad-y-desventajosas-condiciones-laborales?p_l_back_url=%2Fes%2Fsearch%3Fq%3Dpersonal%2Bde%2Bsalud.

Departamento Administrativo Nacional de Estadísticas -DANE- (2020) *Clasificación Industrial Internacional Uniforme de todas las actividades económicas. Revisión 4 adaptada para Colombia. CIIU. Rev. 4 A.C.* Bogotá: DANE.

Departamento Administrativo Nacional de Estadísticas -DANE- (2023) *Principales indicadores del mercado laboral. Boletín técnico* (*septiembre*). Bogotá: DANE.

Departamento Administrativo Nacional de Estadísticas -DANE-CPEM-ONU Mujeres (2022) *Mujeres y hombres: brechas de género en Colombia* (2 ed.). Bogotá: DANE.

Downey, E., Shan, H. & Catton, H. (2023) *What the COVID-19 Pandemic Has Exposed: The Findings of Five Global Health Workforce Professions*. World Health Organization.

Durán, M. (2000) La nueva división del trabajo en el cuidado de la salud. *Política y Sociedad* 35: 9–30.

Comisión Económica para América Latina y El Caribe – CEPAL – (2021) La autonomía económica de las mujeres en la recuperación sostenible y con igualdad. *Informe especial COVID-19* (9). Santiago de Chile: CEPAL.

Comisión Económica para América Latina y el Caribe -CEPAL- & Organización Panamericana de la Salud -OPS- (2020) *Salud y economía: una convergencia necesaria para enfrentar el COVID-19 y retomar la senda hacia el desarrollo sostenible en América Latina y el Caribe* (julio). CEPAL, OPS.

Eurofound & International Labor Organization -ILO- (2019) *Working Conditions in a Global Perspective.* Geneva: Publications Office of the European Union, Luxembourg, and International Labour Organization.

Farné, S. (2003) *Estudio sobre la calidad del empleo en Colombia.* Lima: International Labour Office / Oficina Subregional para los Países Andinos.

Farné, S., & Sanín, C. (2021) *Impacto de la COVID-19 sobre el mercado de trabajo colombiano y recomendaciones para la reactivación.* Bogotá: OIT / Oficina de la OIT para los Países Andinos.

Federación Médica Colombiana -FMC- & -Colegio Médico Colombiano -CMC- (2020) *Condiciones de Bioseguridad y ruta de atención de pandemia SARS COV2-COVID19. Resultados de encuesta, Federación Médica Colombiana y Colegio Médico Colombiano* (abril). Bogotá: FMC-CMC.

Flórez, J., Atehortúa, S., & Arenas, A. (2009) Las condiciones laborales de los profesionales de la salud a partir de la Ley 100 de 1993: evolución y un estudio de caso para Medellín. *Gerencia y Políticas de Salud,* 8(16): 107–131.

Florián, I., De la Hoz, M.C., & Lara, M.A. (2022) *Mujeres trabajadoras en el sector de la salud en Colombia.* PNUD-MPODERA.

García-Roa, E., & Tapias-Torrado, L. (2013) Discriminación y exclusión de las mujeres trabajadoras del sector salud en Colombia. Empleo, un tema pendiente para avanzar en la equidad de género en salud. *Gerencia y Políticas de Salud,* 12(24): 226–248.

Hernández, A., & Vega, R. (2001) El sistema colombiano de seguridad social en salud: desigualdad y exclusión. *Gerencia y Políticas de Salud,* 1(1): 48–73.

Herrera-Idárraga, P., Hernández-Bonilla, H., Gélvez, T., Ramírez-Bustamante, N., Tribín, A.M., & Garzón, T. (2020) *Informe sobre cifras de empleo y brechas de género. Cambios en el empleo en actividades de cuidado remunerado a raíz del COVID-19.* Bogotá: Departamento Administrativo Nacional de Estadística.

Herrera, P., Hernández, H., Gélvez, T (2021) *Recomendaciones de política. Cuidado en Colombia: contexto y perspectivas.* Bogotá: Fescol, Pontificia Universidad Javeriana-Género y Economía.

Himmelweit, S. (2011) El descubrimiento del trabajo no remunerado. En C. Carrasco, C. Borderías, & T. Torns (eds.) *El trabajo de cuidado. Historia, teoría y políticas.* Catarata editorial, 199–224.

Hirata, H. (1997) División sexual e internacional del trabajo. En: H. Hirata, D. Kergoat, & M.-H. Zylberberg-Hocquard. *La división sexual del trabajo. Permanencia y cambio.* Buenos Aires: Asociación Trabajo y Sociedad, 41–53.

Instituto Nacional de Salud -INS- & Observatorio Nacional de Salud -ONS-(2021) *COVID-19: progreso de la pandemia y sus desigualdades en Colombia.* Décimo tercero Informe Técnico. Bogotá: INS-ONS.

Isaza, J.G. (2021) *El impacto de la COVID-19 en las mujeres trabajadoras de Colombia.* Colombia: OIT / Oficina de la OIT para los Países Andinos.

Kergoat, D. (2003) De la relación social de sexo al sujeto sexuado. *Revista Mexicana de Sociología* 65(4): 841–861.

Lucio-García, C., Recaman, A. & Arredondo, A. (2017). Evidencias sobre la inequidad en la distribución de recursos humanos en salud. *Horizonte Sanitario,* 17(1): 77–82.

Mesa de Monitoreo Crítico. (2020) Boletín de monitoreo crítico de las condiciones de bioseguridad. *Boletín 003,* 18, agosto. Available (consulted 2 February, 2023) at https://www.oceinfo.org.co/component/jdownloads/?task=download.send&id=200&catid=10&m=0&Itemid=101.

Messing, K. & Ostlin, P. (2006) *Gender Equality, Work and Health: A Review of the Evidence*. Geneva: World Health Organization.

Ministerio de Salud y Protección Social -MSPS- (2018) *Política Nacional de Talento Humano en Salud. Ministerio de Salud y Protección Social.* Bogotá: MSPS.

Molina-Marín, G., Oquendo-Lozano, T., Rodríguez-Garzón, S., et al. (2016) Gestión del talento humano en salud pública. Un análisis en cinco ciudades colombianas, 2014. *Revista Gerencia y Políticas de Salud* 15(30): 108–125.

Molinier, P. (2011) Antes que todo, el cuidado es un trabajo. En P. Molinier, & L. Arango (eds.) *El trabajo y la ética del cuidado*. Bogotá: La Carreta Editores/Universidad Nacional de Colombia, 45–64.

Molyneux, M. (1994) Mas allá del debate sobre el trabajo doméstico. En C. Borderías, C. Carrasco, & C. Alemany (eds.) *Las mujeres y el trabajo: aproximaciones históricas, sociológicas y económicas*. Barcelona: Icaria, 111–149.

Naciones Unidas (2020) *La COVID-19 y la cobertura sanitaria universal*. Geneva: Naciones Unidas.

Organization for Economic Cooperation and Development -OECD- (2021) *Health at a Glance 2021: OECD Indicators*. Paris: OECD Publishing.

Organización Internacional del Trabajo -OIT- (2017) *Mejora del empleo y las condiciones de trabajo en el ámbito de los servicios de salud. Informe para la discusión en la Reunión tripartita sobre la mejora del empleo y las condiciones de trabajo en el ámbito de los servicios de salud* (abril). Ginebra: Oficina Internacional del Trabajo.

Organización Internacional del Trabajo -OIT- (2021) *Las desigualdades y el mundo del trabajo*. Conferencia Internacional del Trabajo, 109.ª reunión. Ginebra: Oficina Internacional del Trabajo.

Organización Panamericana de la Salud -OPS- (2012) *Estudio comparativo de las condiciones de trabajo y salud de los trabajadores de la salud en Argentina, Brasil, Costa Rica y Perú*. Washington: OPS.

Organización Panamericana de la Salud -OPS- (2021) *Análisis de género y salud: COVID-19 en las Américas*. Washington: OPS.

Organización Panamericana de la Salud -OPS- (2022) *The COVID-19. Health Care Workers Study* (HEROES). *Informe Regional de las Américas*. Washington: OPS.

Organización Panamericana de la Salud -OPS- y Organización Mundial de la Salud -OMS- (2017) *Estrategia de recursos humanos para el acceso universal a la salud y la cobertura universal.* 29a. Conferencia Sanitaria Panamericana. 69a. sesión del comité regional de la OMS para las Américas (julio). Washington.

Picchio, A. (1994) El trabajo de reproducción, tema central en el análisis del mercado laboral. En C. Borderías, C. Carrasco, & C. Alemany (eds.), *Las mujeres y el trabajo. Rupturas conceptuales.* Barcelona: Icaria, 451–490.

Pineda, J., & Acosta, C. (2011) Calidad del trabajo: aproximaciones teóricas y estimación de un índice compuesto. *Ensayos sobre Política Económica*, 29(65): 62–105.

Pineda, J. & Rodríguez, O. (2021) Trabajadoras del cuidado en la salud: crecimiento sin reconocimiento. En L. Porras-Santillana, & N. Ramírez-Bustamante (eds.), *Mucho camello, poco empleo. Por qué el trabajo de las mujeres en Colombia es escaso, desvalorado y mal remunerado.* Bogotá: Ediciones Uniandes, 145–168.

Rodríguez, L. (2021) *Impacto de la pandemia por COVID-19 en los trabajadores de la salud en Colombia.* [Tesis de maestría, Pontificia Universidad Javeriana]. https://repository.javeriana.edu.co/bitstream/handle/10554/57859/ths-covid%2019%20versi%c3%b3n%20final.pdf?sequence=2&isAllowed=y.

Ruiz, F., Matallana, M., Amaya, J., Vásquez, M., Parada, L., & Piña, M. (2009) *Recurso humano de la salud en Colombia. Balance, competencias y prospectiva.* Ministerio de la Protección Social, Pontificia Universidad Javeriana-Cendex. Bogotá.

Torres-Tovar, M. (2021) COVID-19: pandemia y precariedad laboral en el sector salud y su impacto en la salud de las y los trabajadores. En C. Tetelboin Henrión, D. Iturrieta Henríquez, & C. Schor-Landman (coords.) *América Latina. Sociedad, política y salud en tiempos de pandemia.* Ciudad Autónoma de Buenos Aires: CLACSO; Xochimilco: Universidad Autónoma Metropolitana; Xalapa: Universidad Veracruzana; Cochabamba: Universidad Mayor de San Simón; Valparaíso: Universidad de Valparaíso, 291–308.

Tribín-Uribe, A., Mojica-Urueña, T., Díaz-Pardo, G., & DANE (2021) *El tiempo de cuidado durante la pandemia de COVID-19: ¿cuánto han cambiado las brechas de género?* Bogotá: DANE.

Vargas, A.M. (2014) *Reforma sanitaria y condiciones de empleo de los trabajadores del sector salud en Colombia.* [Tesis de maestría, Universidad El Bosque]. Reforma sanitaria y condiciones de empleo de los trabajadores del sector salud en Colombia (unbosque.edu.co).

Wlosko, M., & Ros, C. (2018) La profesión enfermera y el trabajo de cuidado. Puntuaciones de investigación a la luz de la psicodinamia del trabajo y la teoría del care. En N. Borgeaud-Garciandía (ed.) *El trabajo de cuidado.* Buenos Aires: Fundación Medifé Edita, 161–184.

World Health Organization Gender Equity Hub. (2019) *Delivered by Women, Led by Men: A Gender and Equity Analysis of the Global Health and Social Workforce.* Geneva: World Health Organization.

World Health Organization -WHO- (2016a) *Health Workforce Requirements for Universal Health Coverage and the Sustainable Development Goals.* Geneva: WHO.

World Health Organization -WHO- (2016b) *Global Strategy on Human Resources for Health: Worforce 2030.* Geneva: WHO.

World Health Organization -WHO- & International Labor Organization -ILO- (2022) *The Gender Pay Gap in the Health and Care Sector: A Global Analysis in the Time of COVID-19.* Geneva: WHO-ILO.

CHAPTER 5

Embedded Home Care Platforms: Pre- and Post-pandemic Trajectories of Digital Home Care Intermediaries in France

Léa Lima

A number of comparative studies on home care services have highlighted the specific features of the French model (Ledoux, Shire, and Van Hooren 2021; Devetter, Jany-Catrice, and Ribault 2015), and underscored the precociousness of French collective actors in creating what Apitzsch and Shire (Apitzsch and Shire 2021) call a welfare market. In Europe, France is "a front-runner in including domestic workers in its formal workforce" and in the collective regulation of employment relationships (van Hooren et al. 2021). Since at least the beginning of the 1990s, home care and domestic services have been the object of intense public interventions with many different objectives (Guiraudon and Ledoux 2015). In addition to the concern of meeting the needs of vulnerable people wanting to stay at home, public authorities wanted to stimulate formal employment in the home service sector.

This assessment of the French specificity gives little attention to the development of domestic service platforms on the national care market. In France, the uberization of domestic and care work, which links digital contact between customers and service providers and the informalization of work, is more a matter of political rhetoric espoused by a few interest groups than of objective, empirically supported observations. Furthermore, analyses of the platformization of the French economy tend to rely on other sectors such as passenger transport and delivery as examples and case studies, thus feeding the homogenizing hypothesis of the atomization and liberalization of the labor market (Flichy 2017; Abdelnour and Meda 2019; Bernard 2023; Rosenblat 2018; Manriquez 2019).

Can we speak of the uberization of care work in France in the same way it is happening in the United States (Ticona, Mateescu 2018; Glaser 2021), Germany (van Doorn 2020), Brazil (Andrada et al. 2023), or Spain (Rodríguez-Modroño, Agenjo-Calderón, López-Igual 2022)? We argue that the economic trajectories of work and employment platforms in the home care sector are embedded in an institutional framework shaped by public policies that involve home services, personal care for vulnerable people, and the digital economy.

 | DOI:10.1163/9789004707009_006

In particular, public policy specifically for the home care sector favors and encourages salaried employment either directly (through an employment contract that binds the employee to the individual employer) or indirectly (the employment contract is between the organization providing the labor and the employee working in the home).

Our findings are based on administrative data regarding home services employment produced by Dares (Ministry of Labor statistics service) and the Urssaf[1] until 2018. Labor statistics on home services after 2018 are not yet available, making it impossible to measure the effects of the pandemic on this type of work at this time. By applying criteria based on the type of services offered (housekeeping and/or homecare) and the popularity of the application or site (over 100 k downloads or views), we were able to collect and analyze documentation (e.g. conditions for use of online services, company income statements, press articles) of 9 digital care intermediaries: Aladom, Yoopies, Yoojo, Allovoisins, Wecasa, Oxilia, Ouihelp, Wanteez, Helpling. Finally, we interviewed the CEOs of two of these digital intermediaries, Ouihelp and Oxilia, which are representative of only one category, namely online employment agencies.

1 The Institutional Embedding of Platforms in Home Care and Personal Services

Home services can be provided under a variety of statutes and by different types of organizations. While the configuration in which a worker and beneficiary of the service are directly linked by an employment contract is still the majority, the intervention of a third-party organization that employs the workers and provides the service to the customer is increasingly common. The diversity of these intermediary configurations is reflected in the different digital intermediation models in the sector, which consist of a job board, an on-demand platform, an online employment agency, and an online service provider.

1.1 *The Diversity of Employment and Commercial Systems for Home Care Delivery*

Hiring home services, whether for personal care (assistance with the vital needs of vulnerable people) or for everyday life (cleaning, gardening, babysitting,

1 The Urssaf collects and distributes the social contributions from employers that finance the entire social security system.

etc.) entails choosing from five different possibilities for identifying work or commercial contracts.

a) *Informal work modality* (*travail dissimulé*): this modality uses neither work contract nor commercial contract. A survey conducted in 2015, showed that 20% of home service users chose undeclared work (Brice, Daudey, Hoiban, 2016). They might declare part of the worker's hours or use solely informal work. The survey estimates that the volume of informal working hours represents 15.6% of the declared working hours.

b) *Direct employment modality*: the user directly employs someone to work in their home. In this case the care recipient and the care worker are linked by a work contract, but there is no commercial relationship.

c) *Agency modality*: the user employs people through an organization that recruited them and manages their work. The household is the employer of the worker but the contract is commercial via an intermediary placement agency that manages the worker's schedules and does the paper work linked to the role of employer. The agency might be a for-profit company, a non-profit (NGO, association), or even a public organization.

d) *Service provider modality*: the user hires a domestic service provider organization that employs domestic and care workers. In this case, the household is the client of the provider, which invoices the service. There is no work contract between the household and the worker. The provider might be a company, a non-profit, or a public organization.

e) *Individual provider modality*: the user hires a self-employed service provider that falls under the category of "micro-entrepreneur," which comes under the micro-enterprise tax regime.[2] As any provider, the micro-entrepreneur sells a service to the care recipient who is the client.

As Ledoux and Krupka underscore, "collective agreements – all now legally binding – covering domestic workers and carers employed by households and service providers have existed for more than40 years too, making France the only country in Europe where a wide range of home-based care and domestic work is covered by binding collective agreements" (Ledoux, Krupka 2022: 72). Domestic workers under direct employment or agency modalities are covered by the national collective agreement of *Particuliers employeurs* (individual employers) negotiated between the individual employers' union (FEPEM) and representative workers unions. Employees in the home care sector benefit

2 The purpose of the micro-enterprise tax regime is to simplify business creation as it requires less administrative formalities, less tax returns, and less social declarations. Home care work can be carried out by a micro-entrepreneur if their annual income does not exceed €72,600.

TABLE 5.1 Work and commercial contracting parties for home-based care services

Modality of service delivery (% of paid hours in 2018)	Work contracts	National collective agreement or civil servant social protection	Commercial contracts
Informal work	None	No	None
Direct employment (54%)	Care recipient/ Care worker	Yes	None
Agency mode (5.3%)	Care recipient/ Care worker	Yes	Care recipient/ Agency
Service provider mode (45.7%)	Provider organization/Care worker	Yes	Provider organization/Care recipient
Individual provider mode (1.2%)	None	No	Care recipient/ self-employed care worker

from different branch agreements, depending on whether they work for an association or a private company.

A summary of the diversity of employment and commercial modalities of home service delivery can be seen in Table 5.1.

We have observed that the service-provider modality has gradually been substituting direct employment (See Graph 5.1). In 2018, the home services market was mainly driven by direct employment and individual employers, who accounted for 54% of all working hours in the sector. Still, this share (in terms of hours) has been declining since the 2000s, when it stood at 82% (Kulanthaivelu and Thiérus 2018).

Despite relatively important growth (+10.5% between 2017 and 2018), self-employed workers are still an extreme minority in home services, representing 1.2% of the total amount of paid working hours in 2018. Moreover, they are concentrated in everyday life services like housekeeping and tutoring. Only 5.2% of the 4.3 million hours provided by self-employed workers were dedicated to personal care for vulnerable people in 2017, i.e., 223,000 hours. Compared to the 217.6 million home care hours delivered by provider organizations, the

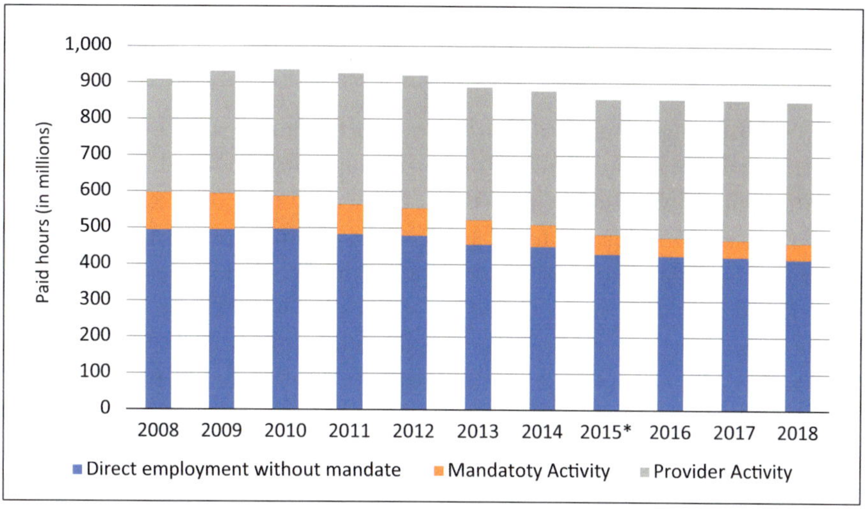

GRAPH 5.1 Evolution of paid hours in home services (2008–2018)
FIELD: FRANCE
SOURCES: IRCEM (UNTIL 2014), THEN INSEE (SINCE 2015) FOR INDIVIDUAL EMPLOYERS; DGE, NOVA, PROCESSING DARES FOR PROVIDER AND PLACEMENT AGENCIES ACTIVITIES. TAKEN FROM (KULANTHAIVELU AND THIÉRUS 2018)

weight of self-employment in home care work with vulnerable people seems close to insignificant.[3] Finally, following Sarah Abdelnour's work on the self-employed (Abdelnour 2017), many of the workers who use care platforms to find work are backed by salaried employment, whether a salaried spouse or their own salaried work done alongside their self-employed activities.

The growth of service provider organizations has caused home workers to move closer to what Bernard Fourcade called a "typical" situation of salaried employment, used to describe the wage-earner society of the post-World War II economy. The characteristics (Fourcade 1992) are:

a) more durable work contracts
b) the unicity of the employer and belonging to an organized service

3 However, a significant proportion of home service companies operate under the franchise model, whereby an entrepreneur buys the right to use one of the 206 brands of the sector (in 2022) and a certain number of its infrastructures, while having to comply with a set of specifications established by the brand. By employing home care workers, those 7149 "independent managers" can be also seen as disguised salaried employees. For the figures, see Fédération Française de la Franchise. https://www.franchise-fff.com/entreprendre/la-franchise-c-est-quoi/ consulted on January, 16th 2024.

c) full time contracts with time-oriented (not task) earnings depending on the function in the normal and permanent activity of a working organization.

Indeed, three characteristics can be seen in the home service sector today. First, illegal work tends to decline in the long term. Second, employment contracts are more durable. And third, the service provider modality means workers are part of an organized service that assumes the risks of decreased activity. The organization of workers' activities seems to be more intermediated and regulated by the collective entities in charge of the continuity of services, bringing a certain regularity and predictability to the work. This normalization of the employment relationship is also evident in the number of employers per worker in the home service sector. In 2014, home service professionals working only with service providers had an average of less than 2 employers (1.7), while workers employed by individual employers reached 3.6 employers (Kulanthaivelu and Thiérus 2018).

1.2 *Diversity Reflected in the Digital Labor Market of Intermediaries Landscape*

The diversity seen in the employment and commercial relationships between care workers, care recipients, and intermediaries in the sector is reflected in the platforms landscape. If care recipients or their families look for a care worker online, they will encounter very different types of immaterial organizations that connect them to different job markets. Some platforms will refer recipients to organizations that use provider or agency modalities approved by the State, or to freelance care workers. Finally, recipients can sign a contract as a client of the platform, with other care organizations that post their offers on the platform, or directly with care workers, either as clients or employers (see Table 5.2).

Not all digital platforms lead to the uberization (outsourcing or individualization) of home care workers. In fact, we observed four types of platform models:

- Recruitment or job board platforms intermediate collective or individual employers that want to recruit candidates. Aladom is a classic job board specialized in home care. Home care providers pay it to post job openings and to consult the CV bank. For example, Ouihelp, another platform in our sample, posts many job openings on Aladom. Job boards, in fact, operate as a disintermediation tool: candidate profiles and job posts are visible to each party and the platform does not interfere in the relationship between care workers and care recipients.

TABLE 5.2 Four intermediation models

Platform model	Employment status of care workers	Monetization of the care worker	Names of the platforms
Job board	Employee of the care recipient Employee of NGO, private company, or self-employed	Yes, if self-employed	Aladom
On-demand platform	Self-employed	Yes	Yoopies, Yoojo, Allovoisins, Wecasa
Digital home care agency	Employee of the care recipient	No	Oxilia, Ouihelp
Digital home care provider	Employee of the platform or its franchisee	No	Wanteez, Ouihelp, Helpling

- On-demand platforms or "jobbing platforms" promise caregivers access to a market of individualized paid tasks. They target self-employed workers or illegal workers. Allovoisins is developing a model where workers pay subscription fees to have priority in responding to a demand from a care recipient. The platform collects demands for care at an hourly rate proposed by the care recipient and organizes access to those offers for care workers. In this case, there is no contract of any kind between the platform and the care recipient. Yoopies takes a commission on each invoice it issues on behalf of self-employed workers. Some platforms are stricter (Yoopies, Wecasa) than others (Allovoisins, Yoojo) about workers being registered as self-employed, in order to avoid illegal work.
- Some platforms act as digital versions of a placement agency by offering a pre-selection service and administrative support for employment contracts. What marks these platforms are its collections of candidates. Oxilia boasts a database of 200,000 home helpers who registered on its website. It simply recommends an hourly wage rate to customers before pre-selecting candidates. Workers placed by Oxilia can therefore receive different wages

depending on the person they are caring for and who is paying them. The platform's strategy is to obscure the relationship between the two sides of the labor market: care workers register on the platform without knowing who is requesting services and clients have no direct view of the candidate pool. Some platforms, like Ouihelp, operate in both agency and provider modality.

– Some online home care agencies centralize requests for care work and dispatch their own staff. In this sense, Wanteez digitalized the old provider model. By investing in ads and digital marketing, the company works to gain visibility on the web and become a brand that attracts candidates and clients. Moreover, it saves on costs that are linked to physical agencies. What marks these platforms is essentially their ERP (Enterprise Resource Planning) and focus on an automated recruitment process. Some platforms, like the German company Helpling, chose the franchise system where domestic workers are employees of the franchisee company, not of Helpling directly.

As can be seen, these economic actors using digital platforms for home services or home care play very different roles in the job market. Most platforms fit into pre-existing employment norms of multi-employer salaried employment and employment in companies, mostly part-time. Furthermore, some of these actors are interdependent. Job boards that are financed by recruitment advertisements or actual recruitments benefit from high turnover and number of hires, which gives them a stable number of working hours. They live in perfect symbiosis with home service companies that have large recruitment needs and want to distinguish themselves with an identifiable brand and relatively higher hourly wages.

Platforms face a dual challenge of retaining an available workforce when recruitment is under pressure, and of generating margins in a labor-intensive sector. From these two perspectives, internalizing home care workers with permanent contracts is not necessarily a bad choice, and online, large-scale human services companies have significant economic advantages.

The different platforms are not supported by the State in equal proportions and through the same channels. Social and industrial policies are building an institutional framework that shapes profit opportunities for each type of digitalized intermediary.

2 How Public Policies Support and Shape the Development of Home Care Platforms

French platforms for the home service sector benefit from two public sources that shape their models. 1) French platforms get financial and professional support from the State through specific "patriotic" industrial policy tools. 2) Like any for-profit business, homecare platforms see their activities and possibilities for growth as conditioned upon a high level of State support in favor of formal employment and of implementing regulatory constraints that are unfavorable to self-employment in the sector.

2.1 *Public Support for the Financialization of French Platforms*

Home care and domestic work platforms are start-ups mostly supported by the State. Thus, they can easily benefit from the Research Credit Tax (*Crédit Impôt Recherche*) that is calculated based on research and development expenditures incurred by companies. For instance, Ouihelp benefitted from 241,736 euros in tax credit in 2021.[4]

However, the main driver of French platforms in the home care sector is the French Tech policy rooted in a long lineage of French industrial policies oriented towards the creation of national champions (Cohen 2007). Aladom, the first website for home services, was created in 2008, but the real boom of online intermediaries came in 2014, after the French government launched the French Tech label. French Tech is a label granted to metropolitan ecosystems that help start-ups successfully emerge. The initiative, led by the Digital Agency and linked to the Ministry of Economy, aims to unify the French digital ecosystem. The State has invested 200 million euros in mentoring programs and access to private investors to secure those start-ups, and another 15 million euros to ensure the international visibility of these new tech firms. The goal of this policy is to create various clusters (Bourdin, Nadou 2018), similar to Silicon Valley or Japanese clusters. These spatial configurations connect companies, local public authorities, and innovations to foster competitive actors at the global level.

> To be labeled French Tech, you have to meet a set of innovation specifications. It's an important part of the start-up project. And then there's the network aspect, where you can exchange ideas with your colleagues or other start-ups in other sectors of activity and innovation, which will help you open up your chakras a little and see what's going on next door, which can be a source of advice or perspective when you've got your head in the game.
>
> FRÉDÉRIC ARNAUD, CEO Oxilia, 19/10/2023

4 Ouihelp SAS, Annual account from 01/01/2022 to 31/12/2022, accounting documents registered at the Paris Commercial Court on 04/07/2023.

The French policy for innovation is now centralized by the Public Investment Bank (*BPI – Banque Publique d'investissement*), which has a number of financial tools for French start-ups at its disposal that range from repayable credits to zero-interest loans.

An economic model based on the financialization of a company is what drives this policy. Labelled French Tech companies have reputational benefits from being part of the French economic elite and being guaranteed by the State. The label also helps start-ups in large-scale fundraisings with business angels on the international market. The support of the French State to foster economic patriotism can explain the fact that very few home care platforms come to France from abroad. Only Helpling, a German platform, has managed to hold its own in the French market since its implementation in 2014.

The economic newspaper *Les Echos* used the Yoopies case to explain the interplay between government support, the accelerating financialization of the home services sector, and the internationalization of companies. In 2017, buoyed by a 4 million euro round of funding from XAnge and Runa Capital, Yoopies acquired the UK's number 2 babysitting service, Findababysitter.com. Its short-term goal was to become the UK's leader in this field, and then take the number one spot in the personal services market. The CEO of Yoopies underlines the role of BPI:

> At the same time, Bpifrance supported this operation with a grant to finance our international expansion. This autumn, we're preparing to launch our range of offerings in the Nordic countries, Sweden, Finland, and the Netherlands. … Bpifrance supports our international development, and the meetings organized with other entrepreneurs operating abroad are a great opportunity to better deal with the issues specific to each country. On the financial side, we're looking into the possibility of calling on Bpifrance Assurance Export at the end of the year. Last, but not least, the fact that we benefit from both the French Tech label and the Bpifrance Excellence label is a factor of credibility, whether we're talking to major accounts or establishing ourselves abroad.
>
> BENJAMIN SUCHAR, CEO Yoopies, in Les Echos, published June 28, 2018[5]

Allovoisins, a website started in 2013 offering commodities and home service rentals between individuals, acquired a 20% stake in its capital from the media

5 https://www.lesechos.fr/partenaires/bpifrance/yoopies-le-champion-tricolore-du-service-a-la-personne-133908.

group RTL in November 2015. The start-up raised 1.7 million euros, the majority of it by the radio station, in a "media for equity" deal. The principle behind this kind of fund raising is that start-ups exchange a part of their capital for visibility in press groups.

Between July 2016 and May 2022, the company Ouihelp, funded by Pierre-Emmanuel Bercegeay, Victor Sebag, and Bastien Gandouet organized four rounds of fund raising involving several business angels and venture capital firms for a total amount of 33.3 million euros. Wecasa, also established in 2016, had a similar financial trajectory. In 2017 it raised 250,000 euros and in July 2019, it raised 4.5 million euros from SERENA, ISAI, and KERNEL Investissement. Two years later, the round permitted a fundraising of 15 million euros to finance international development.

The research of investors is part of the start-up economic model that must establish several individual users and offer free intermediation services before building customer loyalty and monetizing the clients. For some years (up to five, in the case of Allovoisins) digital platforms remain unprofitable, seeing as most of the start-ups have negative operating income. The cash obtained from capital ventures is what sustains the business in the long run, as the CEO of Allovoisins explains to the web media Maddyness.

> We chose to start monetizing very late, since during our first four years, from 2013 to 2016, we didn't generate any sales. 2017 was devoted to refining and testing the subscription-based business model. 2018 was devoted to deploying and validating it.
>
> EDOUARD DUMORTIER, CEO of Allovoisins, 14/05/2019 in Maddyness[6]

This model of financialization marks the economic development of platforms.

> Platforms like ours, in fact, have much higher margins because there are no structural costs. On the other hand, platforms are often backed by financial investors. This is the case for us, so we're asked to reinvest, to reinvest everything, and to spend in order to take market share. As a result, when you look at the published accounts of care platforms in France today, they're not profitable. Despite everything today in the world of investment, start-ups and so on, we're back to growth at all costs,

6 Géraldine Russell, « Ce qu'*Allovoisins* a appris de sa levée de 3 millions d'euros », Maddyness, 14/05/2019. https://www.maddyness.com/2019/05/14/1anapres-allovoisins/.

> without looking at profitability. And investors are starting to say, "Oh yes, we should make our investments profitable." Today, in the last quarter of this year, we have achieved economic equilibrium. So, we put the brakes on. Today, we've slowed down our investments. It's okay, obviously, because in recent times, in recent years, we were easily growing at 20% a year, where the natural market is more like 4 or 5%. So we were outperforming, but because we were spending a lot. Today, I've put the brakes on investments, so I'm going to put the brakes on growth. I'm going to return to more normal growth. But on the other hand, I'll be balanced.
>
> FRÉDÉRIC ARNAUD, CEO Oxilia, 19/10/2023

The purpose of these start-ups is to grow until they are acquired by a traditional company that wants to integrate the service into its offer.

Some of the more recent platforms have been involved in international economic concentration movements. Yoopies, created in 2012, bought the French digital home services platform Yokoro (2009), that had 200,000 clients at the time. After two rounds of fundraising in 2015 and 2017, it purchased two more homecare platforms in the UK and in Asia.

2.2 *How Provider and Agency Platforms Get State Support to Develop Their Activity*

We identify two main instruments of financial support for developing home care services in a provider or agency modality. First, the State helps sustain a solvent demand for home care by helping care recipients pay for home care services. Second, public authorities reduce the cost of work for employers through specific social security exemption schemes.

The first justification for public intervention in home care services is providing access for vulnerable people. Public authorities provide direct assistance that can vary according to the level of dependence and income of older adults (APA), the disabled (PCH) or the parents of small children (PAJE). They enable reducing the remaining or final price for vulnerable users.

More general government support for domestic services has been implemented and expanded since 1992. NGOs and government-approved companies, and all associations and companies devoted to providing home services, benefit from a reduced VAT rate of 5.5% (for care) or 10% (for everyday life services) and an income tax reduction equal to 50% of the expenses incurred from employing a home care worker. FESP, the largest employers union in the private home service sector, was behind the immediate tax credit introduced in 2022, which enables individuals to pay only 50% of the actual cost of the home service, with the government paying the other half to the employee or organization providing the service, thus relieving families of the need to pay in advance for the costs covered by the State.

Furthermore, for nearly thirty years, private companies have been conducting service activities in the homes of vulnerable people. The law of January 29, 1996 authorized private companies working exclusively with household or family tasks to deliver home care services and therefore, to benefit from full social exemption on employment. The indirect costs of work are dramatically reduced for organizations and platforms that directly employ workers because of the socialization of employers' social security contributions.

This employment-oriented public policy tends to aggregate domestic work and care work in the home under a single banner of personal services (*services à la personne*). Moreover, while it was initially in favor of direct private sector employment or employment via an agency (association or public), it has gradually adopted a more neutral stance, allowing private companies to penetrate the sector more fully (Jany-Catrice 2010). For instance, the home service voucher originally reserved for individual employers to facilitate declaring their employees, was transformed in 1996 into a universal voucher for service payments, including those provided by private service providers. While the law of January 29, 1996, gave private, for-profit businesses access to accreditation and the right to operate in the social sector, it also gave them tax breaks to foster these actions. This was accelerated in 2005 with simplified procedures for services dedicated to all types of users (dependent older people and non-dependent working households).

The leading care work platforms are involved in the collective regulation of the sector, pushing the State to support the solvency of demands for care by increasing social assistance so dependent people can live at home. Ouihelp has a representative on the board of directors of the largest employer union (FESP). Oxilia is a member of 2 employer unions that negotiate with public authorities: FESP (*Fédération des Services aux Particuliers*) and SYNERPA (*Syndicat National des Établissements et Résidences Privés et Services d'Aide à Domicile pour Personnes Âgées*).

Public policy for the homecare sector specifically favors and encourages salaried employment in the home, whether directly (through an employment contract binding the employee to the individual employer) or indirectly (through an employment contract between the service provider and the home care worker). This makes being self-employed comparatively unattractive. Micro-entrepreneurs find it harder to obtain the approval of quality that is required to carry out personal care for vulnerable people. In particular, self-employed care workers have trouble meeting the specifications established by the State concerning exclusivity (the provider must be exclusively dedicated to this activity), continuity (be available 7 days a week, 24 hours a day), and the delivery and assessment of services. Furthermore, households cannot use their vouchers (APA, PCH, or PAJE) for services delivered by unapproved self-employed workers, who are also legally excluded from some activities, specifically regular childcare (for children under 3) at an employee's home (*assistante-maternelle*).

To summarize, social policies in favor of solutions for home service demands tend to position private investment towards agency or provider platforms instead of on-demand (or marketplace) platforms, especially in cases of home care for the vulnerable.

3 Home Services Platforms in the COVID-19 Crisis: Looking to the State Again

A study conducted by the OECD (OCDE 2020) showed that platform workers faced two major risks during the COVID-19 pandemic: 1) Those who played a key role in ensuring the continuity of essential services during periods of containment had increased activities, but also faced very high risks of exposure to the virus. 2) Others lost their income because of reduced demand, being ill and unable to work, being under quarantine, or having to care for children or relatives. But what were the consequences for the platforms themselves?

The first consequence was a drop in demand for home care services, which undoubtedly differentiates this market from that of delivery services. For fear of contamination, families curbed the entry of workers into their domestic space.

> So, 2018 is regional development in Provence-Alpes-Côte d'Azur, just before COVID. The idea was to really expand nationally. Then COVID came along. March 2020, we have 40% of our families calling us and saying, 'we're stopping our services because we don't want the virus to enter our home, whether it's through our homecare workers or not.' So, we're losing 40% of our customers.
>
> FRÉDÉRIC ARNAUD, CEO Oxilia, 19/10/2023

> What happened that year was that the market dropped about 20 to 25%, because people stopped arbitrable home services.
>
> VICTOR SEBAG, CEO Ouihelp, 06/10/2023

Provider registrations on on-demand platforms like Yoojo dropped by 60% during the first lockdown in March 2020.[7] It appeared that service providers were much less resilient to the pandemic than direct employment agencies. Indeed, the number of paid hours for all home services declined by 9% between 2019 and 2020 in service provider companies, while remaining nearly flat in direct employment. Additionally, the number of brands in the franchise system dropped by 6% between 2019 and 2022.

The high level of capitalization for home service start-ups enabled them to survive these drastic falls in business, probably more easily than traditional agencies that were not backed by large companies. They were able to wait for business to pick up (Oxilia), absorb heavy losses, or even, thanks to the visibility of their brand, forge partnerships with other players in the service providing sector (Ouihelp).

> Then we had to take some of these families back three months later, who couldn't take it anymore. They were fed up, because they wanted to take care of their father or their mother. But it didn't end well. Because when you combine a job with caring for your older dependent relatives, it's very complicated. So, we got calls for help from families we had before. 'We have to get back to work quickly. Dad, Mom, we can't take it anymore.' That's how it is.
>
> FRÉDÉRIC ARNAUD, CEO Oxilia, 19/10/2023

> But in fact, what happened is that we have very good relations with the hospital sector. And so, at the same time, the hospitals had to empty their wards to take in almost exclusively COVID patients. So, in the space of six weeks, over March, April, or April-May, over these three months, we managed a number of older patients returning home who would normally have had to stay in hospital longer, to free up COVID beds. So that, on the other hand, added to the workload.
>
> VICTOR SEBAG, CEO Ouihelp, 06/10/2023

By 2022, there was no trace of the COVID-19 crisis left in the accounts, and business generally returned to pre-COVID levels for the leading platforms. However, inflation took a heavy toll on living standards and purchasing power and has had contrasting effects on the activities of the various actors. The

7 Source:Yoojo.https://yoojo.fr/services-a-la-personne/etude-boom-services-a-la-personne-post-covid, consulted Oct. 27, 2023.

growing precariousness of part of the low-skilled workforce has boosted work providers registrations on jobbing platforms. Yoojo, for example, is reporting a 48% increase in registrations from 2021 to 2022, as care freelancers seek to supplement their income. Platforms that target affluent urban consumers looking for fast, low-cost services such as cleaning are also seeing their customer base expand, since the affluent segment of the population was spared during the pandemic.[8]

On the other hand, platforms that target customers with heavier and more expensivee needs, such as caring for dependent people, are caught between worker demands for higher wages to offset inflation and the decline in the purchasing power of families. As is often the case in France, and particularly in the home care sector, the reflex of economic actors is to turn to the State for help in supporting the supply and demand.

The CEO of Oxilia makes a strong case for government support through an increase in social assistance benefits for dependency care:

> It's worth noting that 80% of requests for home help for dependent people in France are covered by social assistance, known as the APA. For several months now, since the beginning of the year or so, the APA no longer covers the entire bill for families. This is because salaries that were extremely low have been raised. The home care sector is under pressure, just like the health and social services sector. And it's a sector with a shortage of personnel. So, salaries have been raised a little. As a result, today's families have what's known as a remainder. In other words, when they're presented with a bill, they're told that 80% of the cost is covered by social assistance, or the APA, and they have to add 20% out of their own pocket. Well, they can't do that anymore. Because with inflation and all, they tell us they have to pay €150 or €100 a month. ... So, the government isn't increasing social assistance at the moment. The employers' federations of home services are pushing the State to do so. But we're all aware of the State's cash-flow difficulties after the pandemic. They're being very careful, and today there's no movement. So, it's complicated. The demands are there, but it's complicated. To find a way around it, you'd have to crush the salaries of homecare workers. But it's already a high-stress, low-paying job, so that's not possible. And the structures, the classic structures, are a bit on their last legs. Margins are extremely low.

8 A study of the Conseil d'Analyse Economique on the French case showed that "while savings are well above normal for the most affluent households at the end of the period, they are below normal for the most modest households" (Bounie et al. 2020).

> We're in a business sector where we can quickly increase volume, but in terms of margins, it's complicated.
>
> FRÉDÉRIC ARNAUD, CEO Oxilia, 19/10/2023

Ouihelp is campaigning for the government to pay a bonus to all home care workers in the sector to make the occupation more attractive.

> But here we are, talking about an upgrade, talking about all that. In practice, nothing happened at all. But really, nothing at all. There was a bonus in nursing homes that wasn't even in home care, or that was at the whim of certain Departments. There has been an increase in the collective bargaining scale for the volunteer sector. In the for-profit sector, there's been nothing, so there hasn't been much. At the moment, they're talking about a national consultation on jobs in precarious situations, which is underway. Well, we'll see what comes out of it. But it would be nice if something could actually be done, because we don't see much, so there you go. These are people who aren't really valued by our society.
>
> VICTOR SEBAG, CEO Ouihelp, 06/10/2023

4 Conclusion

By exploiting the grey areas of labor legislation, the gig-economy actors are said to be waging a form of economic guerrilla warfare aimed at pushing the boundaries of the market in national legislation (Chan, Kwok 2021). However, the case of home care in France shows the strong institutional embedding of digital intermediaries, whose profit and development opportunity structures are clearly conditioned by public policies in social, fiscal, and industrial spheres (Au-Yeung, Qiu 2022). Their ability to expand in the home care market depends precisely on their ability to offer services adapted to the legislative and institutional framework, for example, by taking over and automating the bureaucratic work of individual employers. Far from trying to deregulate the sector, a number of new digital intermediaries actively support the demand for state intervention, particularly to support the welfare market after the pandemic. As a result, we do not believe that digital labor market intermediaries have yet called into question the French model of home care employment.

Platforms that present new digital tools for bringing together labor supply and demand are experiencing a relatively organized supply of labor while the demand remains highly fragmented. Therefore, we show that the platformization of home care services should not be confused with the uberization of home care work, and that we are perhaps a little too quick to equate the digitalization of matching service providers and service seekers with the desalarization of the employment relationship.

On-demand platforms seem to be the most fragile, at least in the field of home help, because of the administrative requirements that self-employed workers find difficult to overcome. Additionally, care recipients tend to use on-demand platforms less frequently because of the more durable nature of their relationship with their care workers. Nevertheless, the pandemic has not altered the trajectory of the main home care platforms, which continue, as in the past, to face the challenges of staff shortages and the solvency of demand.

References

Abdelnour, Sarah (2017) *Moi, petite entreprise. Les auto-entrepreneurs, de l'utopie à la réalité*. Hors collection. Paris: Presses Universitaires de France.

Abdelnour, Sarah, and Dominique Meda (2019) *Les nouveaux travailleurs des applis*. La Vie des Idées. Paris: Puf.

Andrada, Ana Carolina, Ana Claudia Moreira Cardoso, Nadya Araújo Guimarães, Renata Moreno, and Maria Julia Tavares Pereira (2023) Plataformas digitais de cuidado no Brasil : Acesso e controle do trabalho no entrecruzamento de múltiplas crises. *Tempo Social* 35 (3): 5–31. https://doi.org/10.11606/0103-2070.ts.2023.218376.

Apitzsch, Birgit, and Karen Shire (2021) Informalisation of Work and Workers' Voice in Welfare Markets for In-Home Domestic/Care Services in Germany. In *The Dynamics of Welfare Markets*, edited by Clémence Ledoux, Karen Shire, and Franca Van Hooren, 347–71. Cham: Springer International Publishing. https://doi.org/10.1007/978-3-030-56623-4_13.

Au-Yeung, Tat Chor, and Jack Qiu (2022) Institutions, Occupations and Connectivity: The Embeddedness of Gig Work and Platform-Mediated Labour Market in Hong Kong. *Critical Sociology* 48 (7–8): 1169–87. https://doi.org/10.1177/08969205221090581.

Bernard, Sophie (2023) *UberUsés. Le capital de plateforme à Paris, Londres et Montréal*. Paris: Puf.

Bounie, David, Youssouf Camara, Étienne Fize, John Galbraith, Camille Landais, Chloé Lavest, and Tatiana Pazem (2020) Dynamiques de consommation dans la crise : les enseignements en temps réel des données bancaires. *Focus*, nº 049.

Bourdin, Sébastien, and Fabien Nadou (2018) La French Tech : une nouvelle forme de mobilisation des territoires pour faire face à la compétition mondiale ? *Annales de géographie* 723–724 (5–6): 612–34. https://doi.org/10.3917/ag.723.0612.

Brice, Lucie, Emilie Daudey, and Sandra Hoiban (2016) *Le travail dissimulé en France : résultats d'une enquête pilote auprès des ménages*, rapport CREDOC.

Chan, Ngai Keung, and Chi Kwok (2021) Guerilla capitalism and the platform economy: Governing Uber in China, Taiwan, and Hong Kong. *Information, Communication & Society* 24 (6): 780–96. https://doi.org/10.1080/1369118X.2021.1909096.

Cohen, Elie (2007) Industrial Policies in France: The Old and the New. *Journal of Industry, Competition and Trade* 7 (3–4): 213–27. https://doi.org/10.1007/s10842-007-0024-8.

Devetter, François-Xavier, Florence Jany-Catrice, and Thierry Ribault (2015) *Les services à la personne*. Vol. nouvelle édition. Repères. Paris: La Découverte.

Doorn, Niels van (2020) Stepping Stone or Dead End? The Ambiguities of Platform-Mediated Domestic Work under Conditions of Austerity. Comparative Landscapes of Austerity and the Gig Economy: New York and Berlin. In *Working in the Context of Austerity*, 49–70. Bristol University Press. https://bristoluniversitypressdigital.com/edcollchap-oa/book/9781529208689/ch003.xml.

Flichy, Patrice (2017) *Les nouvelles frontières du travail à l'ère numérique*. Les livres du nouveau monde. Paris: Editions du Seuil.

Fourcade, Bernard (1992) L'évolution des situations particulières d'emploi de 1945 à 1990. *Travail et Emploi*, no 52 (février): 4–19.

Glaser, Alana Lee (2021) Uberized Care: Employment Status, Surveillance, and Technological Erasure in the Home Health Care Sector. *Anthropology of Work Review* 42 (1): 24–34. https://doi.org/10.1111/awr.12215.

Guiraudon, Virginie, and Clémence Ledoux (2015) The Politics of Tax Exemptions for Household Services in France In *The Political Economy of Household Services in Europe*, edited by Clément Carbonnier and Nathalie Morel, 39–59. London: Palgrave Macmillan UK. https://doi.org/10.1057/9781137473721_2.

Hooren, Franca van, Clémence Ledoux, Birgit Apitzsch, and Anja Eleveld (2021) Inclusive Advocacy? Trade-Union Activity in Support of the Rights of Domestic Workers in Continental Europe. *Politique européenne* 74 (4): 108–34. https://doi.org/10.3917/poeu.074.0108.

Jany-Catrice, Florence (2010) La construction sociale du "secteur" des services à la personne: une banalisation programmée ? *Sociologie du Travail* 52 (4): 521–37. https://doi.org/10.1016/j.soctra.2010.09.010.

Kulanthaivelu, Éric, and Lydia Thiérus (2018) Les salariés des services à la personne : comment évoluent leurs conditions de travail et d'emploi ? *Dares Analyses*, nº 038. https://dares.travail-emploi.gouv.fr/publications/les-salaries-des-services-a-la-personne-comment-evoluent-leurs-conditions-de.

Ledoux, Clémence, et Rachel Krupka (2022) Negotiating in a Highly Feminised Sector: The French Domestic Work and Home-Based Care Sector. In *Social Partners and Gender Equality*, edited by Anna Elomäki, Johanna Kantola, et Paula Koskinen Sandberg, 71–95. Gender and Politics. Cham: Springer International Publishing. https://doi.org/10.1007/978-3-030-81178-5_4.

Ledoux, Clémence, Karen Shire, and Franca Van Hooren (2021) Introduction: From the Emergence to the Dynamics of Welfare Markets. In *The Dynamics of Welfare Markets*, edited by Clémence Ledoux, Karen Shire, et Franca Van Hooren, 3–49. Cham: Springer International Publishing. https://doi.org/10.1007/978-3-030-56623-4_1.

Manriquez, Mariana (2019) Work-Games in the Gig-Economy: A Case Study of Uber Drivers in the City of Monterrey, Mexico. In *Work and Labor in the Digital Age*, edited by Steve P. Vallas and Anne Kovalainen, 33:165–88. Research in the Sociology of Work. Emerald Publishing Limited. https://doi.org/10.1108/S0277-283320190000033010.

OCDE (2020) Qu'ont fait les plateformes pour protéger les travailleurs pendant la crise du coronavirus (COVID-19) ? https://read.oecd-ilibrary.org/view/?ref=136_136531-lrd885qori&title=Qu-ont-fait-les-plateformes-pour-proteger-les-travailleurs-pendant-la-crise-du-coronavirus-%28covid-19%29%3F.

Rodríguez-Modroño, Paula, Astrid Agenjo-Calderón, and Purificación López-Igual (2022) « Platform work in the domestic and home care sector: new mechanisms of invisibility and exploitation of women migrant workers ». *Gender & Development* 30 (3): 619–35. https://doi.org/10.1080/13552074.2022.2121060.

Rosenblat, Alex (2018) *Uberland. How algorithms are rewriting the rules of work.* Oakland, California: University of California Press.

Ticona, Julia, and Alexandra Mateescu (2018) Trusted Strangers: Carework Platforms' Cultural Entrepreneurship in the on-Demand Economy. *New Media & Society* 20 (11): 4384–4404. https://doi.org/10.1177/1461444818773727.

CHAPTER 6

Care Work Platformization in Brazil: Exploring Workers' Narratives about Experiences during the Pandemic

Ana Carolina Andrada, Ana Claudia Moreira Cardoso, Nadya Araujo Guimarães, Renata Moreno and Maria Júlia Tavares Pereira

1 Introduction[1]

Care work is fundamentally diverse, whether its range of activities, organizational structures, or its distinct contexts. Extensive studies have thoroughly documented this heterogeneity (Carrasco, Borderías and Torns, 2011; Duffy, 2011; Duffy, Armenia and Stacey, 2015; Folbre, 2006 and 2012; ILO, 2018; Le Bihan, Martin and Knijn, 2013). From them, we gather that Brazil stands out as the largest market for paid home-based work in Latin America, and the most significant, in relative terms, on a global scale (ILO, 2018). This vast occupational sector is predominantly composed of racialized women (particularly those of African descent in the Brazilian context) who frequently face precarious working conditions (Guimarães and Pinheiro, 2023). In this chapter, we narrow our focus to care work performed within private homes as a paid service. This encompasses both direct care, which is provided to dependent individuals on a regular basis and under intense and direct interaction, and indirect care, aimed at preserving the household environment and the well-being of its residents.

According to official Brazilian statistics, some specific occupations play a significant role in the care labor market (Guimarães and Pinheiro, 2023; Almeida and Wajnman, 2023). In the realm of direct care, babysitters and caregivers for older adults are predominant, collectively constituting 99% of the

1 Research Supported by The National Council for Scientific and Technological Development (CNPq), Grant # 421754/2021/4, the São Paulo Research Foundation (FAPESP), Grant # 2021/07888-3 and Arymax Fountation (Arymax/Cebrap Grant July 2022). A preliminary version of this text appeared in *Tempo Social*, a journal from the University of São Paulo Sociology Department (Andrada et al, 2023). The authors wish to thank the editors for publishing this more extended and revised version in English, and Brill's reviewers for their comments and suggestions.

 | DOI:10.1163/9789004707009_007

workforce in this category. In indirect care, female domestic workers (especially cleaners and cooks) make up 99% of the workforce. When we consider the entire Brazilian home care service market, we find that out of every ten female workers, eight classify their primary occupation as general domestic service providers, while the remaining two are engaged in caregiving, with one focusing on care for older adults and the other on younger children (Fontoura and Marcolino, 2021; Guimarães and Pinheiro, 2023). Therefore, our focus will be on babysitters, caregivers, and general domestic service workers.

Studies on access to care work in Brazil have shed light on the growing importance of intermediaries, such as employment agencies specialized in domestic work (cooks, babysitters, cleaners). They have been present since the mid-20th century (Lima, 2023) and have continued to evolve and expand into new forms (Araujo, 2015). Nevertheless, the digitalization of economic activities and the emergence of digital labor platform companies have presented new analytical challenges (Ticona and Mateescu, 2018; Vallas and Schor, 2020). Platform companies, while frequently championing the narrative of worker autonomy, have introduced a range of algorithmic management tools designed for monitoring, controlling, and sometimes even punishing workers. These recent developments define a new agenda for studies on labor market intermediaries, urging us to understand the emergence of new forms of access, management, and control within the domain of care in Brazil. Therefore, in this chapter, we analyze how some platform companies function and their implications on working conditions and labor relations in the care sector, paying special attention to the possible effects of the COVID-19 pandemic.

To achieve this goal, considering that Brazil lacks statistics to accurately monitor the extent to which the digitalization process reaches the care sector and the impact of platform companies, we explored different types of sources.[2] In the following section, we provide information about the labor platform companies in general. Echoing Brazilian literature, we underscore their fast growth in the delivery and individual transport sectors between 2016 and 2019. However, during the COVID-19 pandemic, job opportunities dropped in location-based platform companies (where work is carried out locally and in person), except for the delivery sector, while web-based platform companies (where the results of work are delivered online) expanded. Such trends reflect the restrictions of face-to-face interactions and the increased use of digital media in social relationships.

2 Details regarding the methodology will be presented when we introduce the different sources.

Drawing on a database specifically designed to track the growth of app and platform companies operating in the care sector, section 2 traces the intense growth that began in 2016 and was reshaped during the 2020 health crisis. Growing digitization encompassed platform companies, job search apps, and apps designed to control and manage care work to be used by caregivers, intermediary agencies, care institutions, and even families.

In the third section, we amplify the voices of workers registered on digital labor platform companies. We draw from our qualitative research to analyze their perceptions of platform governance. Special attention is given to how workers in direct and indirect care described the impact of the pandemic on their experiences. This is justified by recent quantitative studies that reveal how the pandemic had unequal effects on the inclusion of indirect care workers like domestic workers, and direct care workers like babysitters and adult caregivers on the labour market (Almeida and Wajnman, 2023). However, the specific impact of the pandemic on platform care work remains relatively understudied and interesting features came from our fieldwork. If the context of the pandemic meant reduced work options, platform companies position themselves as an object of dispute between workers by rewarding those who respond first, have higher scores, or are more available.

We also observed that the governance used by these companies is based on a huge asymmetry of information where they control demands, define the form of communication with customers, and create prescriptive and punitive rating systems. This format is far from some expectations (Vallas and Schor, 2020) that foresaw a tendency toward relinquishing what literature calls hierarchical controls (Powell, 1990; Edwards, 1980), and replacing them with more distributed governance mechanisms. Nevertheless, there is room for variation, in line with Schor et al. (2020). This is especially true in a country like Brazil, where platforms are poorly institutionalized and care work is highly unregulated. Therefore, as we learned from our interviewees, indirect care platforms completely defined work relations in an automated way (including defining payment and required services), while companies in the direct care contexts we analyzed ended up inducing workers, rather indirectly, to perform tasks that went beyond the agreed-upon activity.

Thus, we conclude in the fourth and final section, that companies go far beyond the triadic model of intermediation between supply and demand. They interfere in, and define how the work itself is carried out, although management strategies seem to vary between direct or indirect care. Platforms are, in this sense, complex arrangements in line with evolving modern corporations, and for this reason we will refer them as "platform companies" and assume, like Vallas and Schor (2020), that platforms create value by adopting a business model that captures profits through digital intermediation without the encumbrances of fixed capital or the direct employment of labor. Nevertheless, as we highlight in the conclusion, the experiences we documented fall short of Kornberger et al.'s (2017) argument that a labor process grounded on evaluative infrastructures (as platforms are) will acquire a new geometry that combines distributed control and centralized power.

2 Platformization of Work, Care, and Care Work in Brazil

Platform companies in the Brazilian market became noticeable as early as the mid-2000s (Cardoso, 2022). They began in sectors characterized by precarious work, and within a few years had expanded into sectors hitherto characterized by formal employment and solid labor organizations. This expansion means platform companies are present across a wide spectrum of segments, including commerce, legal services, crowdwork, healthcare, finance, education, information technology, soccer, beauty, direct and indirect care, banking, road transport, real estate, and others (Cardoso, 2022).

While research in this area remains limited, specific findings have allowed us to discern a common *modus operandi* among these companies in Brazil (Kalil, 2019; Cavarzan, 2022; Ikuta; Santana, 2022; Rodrigues, 2022b). Their framework comprises some key elements, also referred to in the international literature (Vallas and Schor, 2020): 1) digital infrastructure and mediation; 2) platformization as a dimension of digitalization; 3) goal-based management, gamification, and use of algorithms; 4) disregard for legislation; and 5) datafication. It is important to note that within each sector or subsector, companies may vary in terms of their business models, customer and worker relationships, and work organization. While these differences are undoubtedly influenced by sector-specific characteristics, they also reflect strategic decisions and choices made by the platform companies themselves (Cardoso and Pereira, 2023).

Knowledge regarding care work platforms in Brazil mirrors the sector's expansion, as shown by our efforts to map companies operating as digital intermediaries for care services via apps and/or platforms in 2023. A significant share of them were launched after 2016, and even more after 2019 (Graph 6.1). Considering there are no official databases on digital intermediaries for care work in Brazil, our approach was to collect data through the automated retrieval of information from the country's most widely used app store. This database gathers different types of apps, including digital labor platforms, as well as apps that operate as job boards, not exclusively in the care sector.

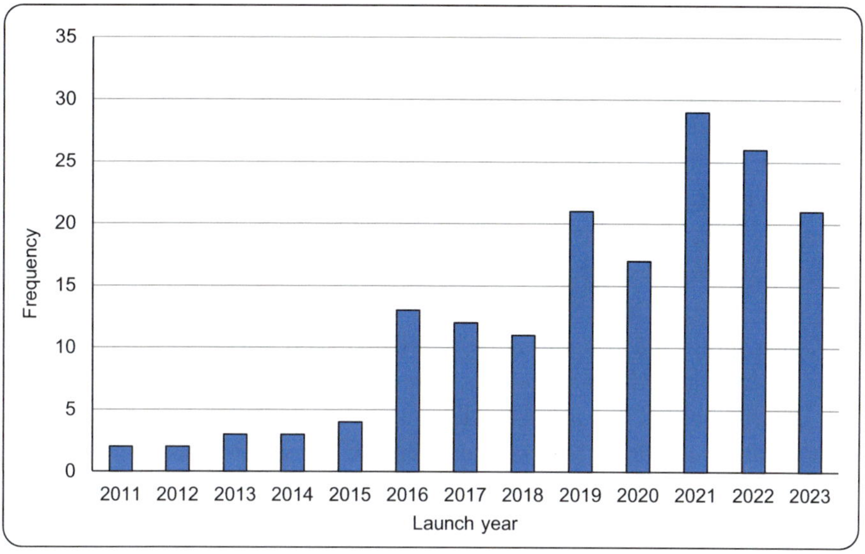

GRAPH 6.1 Launch year for care work intermediary apps in operation in 2023
SOURCE: INTERNET DATA COLLECTED THROUGH AUTOMATED RETRIEVAL FROM A LOCAL APP STORE, IN OCTOBER 2023

Automated searches were conducted in February and October 2023 using 168 keywords related to both direct and indirect home care. We identified 9,416 apps, which underwent an automated screening to exclude labels such as casino, photography, music, etc. This was followed by a manual screening that involved reviewing each app's description and assessing its relevance to our research interests. Apps were classified as 'care work intermediaries,' 'care work control and management,' and 'no interest'. The latter included game apps, as well as diet or weight loss apps. This process gathered 170 apps classified as care work intermediaries, including job boards that do not exclusively display care work opportunities, as well as care work platforms.

Our analysis points to a growing trend of digitalization within the sector, resulting in a diverse digital intermediation landscape. There are myriads of job board apps displaying opportunities (often long-term contracts) not exclusively in the care sector. The way information circulates and is displayed on the different apps also varies. Users might have access to all job openings (including details given by potential employers) or to just a few, depending, for instance, on fees. Apps that do not exclusively focus on care and that operate as job boards have a larger number of downloads. There is also a significant set of apps devoted to on-demand care services. They are almost exclusively dedicated to intermediating both direct and indirect care work. Automated matching between workers and clients is more widespread and tasks can be more narrowly defined by the app. We found less automated apps that match service providers and users. Clients can freely describe what their specific needs are, and providers can contact them and vice-versa. Algorithmic management and datafication, traits that set platforms apart from other ventures, can also be found on this kind of app, although not as much as on-demand platforms. The database also encompasses some traditional agencies that began operating through digital means, although not exclusively, while still contacting clients through phone calls, office visits, etc.

Our mapping also revealed that the digitalization of care extends beyond intermediating work opportunities. Some apps were not specifically created for intermediation, but for controlling and managing paid and unpaid care work. These apps allow caretakers to inform the exact time they complete a task, and other relevant information (e.g., each diaper change, bath, drug administered, etc.), thus making data immediately available to different app users, like other caretakers, employers, and companies (agencies or institutions). Furthermore, these management and control apps in operation in 2023 had been primarily launched in 2015, with a notable increase in 2020 (Graph 6.2). Our findings offer valuable insights into how digital technologies, initially introduced by intermediation agencies and care institutions, have extended into domestic environments to manage the unpaid care provided by families.

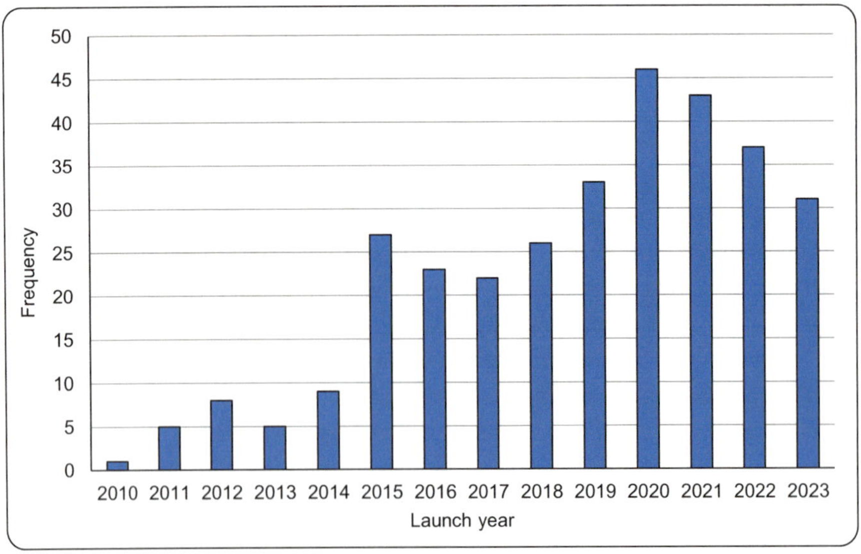

GRAPH 6.2 Launch year for control and management of care work apps in operation in 2023

In summary, existing literature and our mapping efforts show that the substantial growth of these companies in Brazil coincides with intersecting crises that began in 2016 during a labor market recession, which intensified with the Labor Reform in 2017, and took on new dimensions with the onset of the COVID-19 crisis in 2020. However, available secondary data does not allow us to pinpoint whether the expansion of platform companies in the care sector primarily resulted from the pandemic or from changes in the regulation of employment relationships stemming from new labor laws.

As for household workers, previous research has yielded intriguing findings. Guimarães and Hirata (2019) documented that until 2019, care workers, differently from general domestic service workers, experienced rapid growth in Brazil and appeared relatively resilient to the impact of economic downturns in the job market. However, Almeida and Wajnman (2023) revealed that transitions towards unemployment or inactivity during the pandemic affected female care workers more significantly than average female employees in Brazil. Notably, both unemployment and inactivity were more prevalent among female workers engaged in direct care (babysitters and caregivers for older adults) than among those in indirect care (domestic workers in general domestic services).

However, we currently lack national statistics to evaluate the impact of the pandemic on female employment in platform companies in the care sector. Thus, in the next section, we will rely on qualitative information provided by female workers using digital labor platforms to look at the effects of the pandemic on their working conditions.

3 Effects of the Pandemic on Domestic Care Work: the Perceptions of Female Workers on Platform Companies

In a heterogeneous labor market such as the care sector, the impact of the COVID-19 pandemic varied depending on the specific types of work and the nature of care provided. According to Almeida and Wajnman (2023), based on data from the Continuous National Household Sample Survey (*Pesquisa Nacional por Amostra de Domicílios Contínua*) for 2019–2021, workers engaged in home-based care experienced the most significant unemployment rates during the initial months of the pandemic. In contrast, workers in the public health and education sector experienced more employment stability. If we narrow our focus to private educational institutions, early childhood educators and employees in smaller establishments were the most severely affected by job losses early on (FCC, 2022).

A shortage of evidence and literature concerning the impact of the pandemic on different groups of home care workers hinders a precise understanding of what unfolded in the sector. Moreover, as highlighted earlier, acknowledging heterogeneity in care work is essential for conducting detailed analyses of the digitalization of care intermediation in Brazil. To address this analytical challenge, we sought the perspectives of care workers registered on digital labor platforms.

But, before proceeding with the analysis, a preliminary commentary is necessary to link empirical cases to theoretical departure points. Care platforms are location-based, i.e., they require the worker to be in the specific place where the service is provided. But even in this type of platform, the algorithmic management of work, the control over the worker, and the profiles of those engaged in the service are far from being homogeneous (Grohmann, 2020). Variability is greater where rules are scarce and environments are less institutionalized. This is true in the Brazilian case, where the rights and obligations of care workers and companies are negotiated without a legal framework to establish limits. Thus, informational asymmetries change the degrees of freedom available to each actor in the triad (worker/care provider, platform company, care beneficiary/consumer). This context makes analyzing specific cases especially valuable in that they document variations in management strategies and worker resistance, as well as (possible) movement of de-/re-concentration of power, as suggested in the literature referred to earlier. The heuristic value of this analytical strategy is in exploring singularities, not in searching for some kind of representativeness. The uniqueness of each situation is an opportunity to observe how asymmetry is negotiated and how different actors engage with it. It is important to emphasize that our doorway into each situation is the worker's experience, meaning their narratives will provide the starting point for reflections.

The case studies selected for this section encompass two Direct Care Platforms (DCPs) focused on care for older adults and babysitting, and one Indirect Care Platform (ICP) focused on cleaning services. We aim at understanding how specific platforms deal with care work specificities as well as how the pandemic shaped care workers' experiences and their use of platforms to find job opportunities.

Mindful of the methodological challenges to gather data in this understudied sector, especially in accessing the inner workings of platform companies (Moreno, 2023), we combined different information sources and empirical research approaches. Our investigation began with an examination of platform websites, observing the different accessibility layers made visible to visitors or users. Additionally, we looked closely at the companies' "Terms of Service" and "Conditions of Use".[3]

Research with digital platform workers faces the common challenge of finding and contacting potential participants. Our strategy was to contact participants "inside" the platforms, a procedure that allowed us to learn more about their design and function. We created "client" profiles from which we made requests for services in the city of São Paulo and then started conversations with the workers to invite them to take part in the research through an interview. We carried out 17 in-depth interviews with the aim of gaining deeper insights into the workers' perceptions of the companies' modus operandi. For this chapter, we selected four interviewees whose narratives provided richer reflections on their experiences related to the pandemic. They are two babysitters and a caregiver for older adults affiliated with two DCPs, and a female worker from an ICP. These interviews took place between September 2022 and March 2023. Two of them were conducted in person and two via online video calls.[4]

To enhance our understanding on the effects of the pandemic, we added complementary information on worker complaints sourced from the *Reclame Aqui* (*Complain Here*)[5] website that were posted between March and October 2020. That was a critical period for labor relations and care workers during the pandemic in Brazil, when social isolation measures were in place, deaths were accelerating exponentially, care needs increased as there was no access to vaccines, and contractions in the job market reached dramatic levels.[6]

3 Our analysis of the platform websites was carried out in two periods, in April and August 2023.

4 To ensure the anonymity of our interviewees in accordance with the Informed Consent Form (ICF) they signed, we adopt the following pattern when quoting excerpts from the interviews: (i) "Babysitter X_DCP", "Caregiver for Older Adults X_DCP" for DCP workers, where "X" will be replaced by a number to distinguish between speakers, and (ii) "Domestic Worker_ICP" for the ICP worker.

5 "*Reclame Aqui*" (*Complain Here*) is a Brazilian website for consumer complaints about customer service and purchases. The website provides free services for consumers to submit their complaints and for companies to respond to them. The website can be accessed at: <https://www.reclameaqui.com.br/login/>.

6 Of the sixteen complaints related to the Indirect Care Platform and categorized on the website under "COVID-19", we selected five submissions made by domestic workers to support our analysis. Our initial goal was to conduct a comparative analysis spanning 2019–2023 to examine any potential effects of the pandemic on workers' experiences. However, our attempts to access data on the *Reclame Aqui* website proved unsuccessful. Despite a total of over 3,000 complaints referring to the ICP over their nine-year existence, *Reclame Aqui* only allows access to posts within the last year. Consequently, we resorted to a special filter formed by the categories selected by the complainants themselves.

3.1 *Demands for Direct Care during the Pandemic*

Throughout the COVID-19 pandemic, a wide range of care demands emerged. These sometimes increased the unpaid workload of women within their families and communities, while also requiring domestic workers to spend extended periods in the homes where they worked, as demonstrated by Araújo (2023). From the interviews conducted thus far, we chose three cases that provide a more detailed perspective on this heterogeneous reality and directly pertain to the topic of intermediated job opportunities in the care sector.

Babysitter 1_DCP is a teacher at a public daycare center in metropolitan São Paulo and enjoys job stability as a public sector employee. Even before the pandemic, she supplemented her income by working as a babysitter on weekends and at night, jobs she secured through three platform companies. When reflecting on whether listing her credentials as a teacher in her DCP profile could influence the negotiation and hiring process as a babysitter, she said that, in general, this is not the case. According to her, the main concern of potential employers during interviews is whether the worker has prior references. Additionally, some families stipulate performing indirect care tasks alongside direct childcare. The DCP streamlines this by incorporating indirect care activities such as cooking and other household tasks into the list of duties that babysitters can include in their public profiles:

> some people say 'hey, when my child's here with me, I want you to sweep the house, take out the trash, tidy the bed' … So, it's not just being with the child, they want a more expanded work for this type of service.
>
> *Babysitter 1_DCP*

There appeared to be a shift in this dynamic during the pandemic. While employer demands generally tend to blur the lines between direct and indirect care in the work of babysitters and home caregivers, the pandemic saw a heightened demand for the educational dimension of care. This mirrored the inseparability of caregiving and education found in early childhood education institutions, which extends into households with young children.

> I worked a lot during the pandemic. I was teaching remotely, so being an educator was a big plus for my employers because their kids were studying from home, and I could help them. I even ended up tutoring them, even though my actual job was babysitting.
>
> *Babysitter 1_DCP*

However, employers' demands for more "skilled" work because of her background in education did not lead to increased appreciation in terms of higher pay, nor did it shield her from instances of discrimination, including those related to COVID-19.

> I once worked at this house where they had a camera with audio always keeping tabs on us. The maid had already had COVID, but I hadn't even stepped inside yet. Once inside, I found two children, each with their own babysitter. I was just filling in for someone's day off. During the week, they had a nurse for the baby, a maid, and a babysitter for the 2-year-old. On weekends, I covered for someone's day off. We all had to wear masks, but not the homeowners. I even asked her [employer]: 'With the virus going around, wouldn't it be safer for everyone to wear masks, including you?' But no, it felt like we were the only ones who could possibly spread the virus.
>
> *Babysitter 1_DCP*

Having a profile on the DCP can be either free or premium with a monthly fee. In the case of free profiles, the information about the workers and families is publicly listed. However, only those who pay the monthly fee have the option to start conversations to discuss job opportunities or hire a babysitter. According to the experiences shared by the women we interviewed, the workers typically are the ones to take the first step to initiate contact. Notably, many of the messages they send often receive no response from the hiring families, which suggests a search for work that surpasses the available job opportunities.

According to Babysitter 1_DCP, when she finds a work opportunity, she tries to make a direct connection with the hiring family in an attempt to secure regular work filling in for the regular babysitter's time off, usually on weekends. Once this direct contact is established, she no longer needs the platform to mediate her relationship with the family. However, she mentioned that she commonly receives requests from families she has previously worked for through the platform. It's interesting to note how the worker associates these frequent requests from families on the platform with her concerns about working conditions and the inherent asymmetry in how the DCP operates, which allows families to evaluate workers, but not vice-versa. This can result in recurring rights violations in the homes where care work takes place.

> Can we give and receive references about our employers? We do this informally, among ourselves, saying things like, 'Hey, watch out for that lady'. ... The website doesn't offer us a way to rate or review the employer.

> I see employers on the platform all the time, and it makes me wonder … if no one sticks around for long in their house, there might be something wrong. But we don't really know because there's no way for us to publicly evaluate them.
>
> *Babysitter 1_DCP*

Exchanging information outside the platform is a strategy workers use to navigate the lack of transparency in algorithmic management. In a separate case, a babysitter followed a colleague's suggestion and altered her residential zip code to increase job opportunities for her profile, effectively circumventing the platform's primary mechanism for job allocation.

In the two cases described below, the pandemic was an entry point into home care work. A caregiver for older adults, currently registered on a platform, started working in the sector following a request from within her college peer group, even though her degree had no actual connection to care work.

> A couple of days after my college closed, she messaged our group asking if anyone could help her during the pandemic. She wanted someone to stay with her boyfriend's grandmother at her home. Her children were worried about leaving her alone or that she'd want to go out. They couldn't take care of her themselves, so they reached out for help and asked if there was anyone available. Since I had taken care of my grandmother when she was sick, I thought of this as something that came at the right time, you know? So, I ended up taking care of her for six months. I'd come back home for a couple of days every month and then go back there. That's how I began working as a caregiver.
>
> *Caregiver for Older Adults 1_DCP*

After entering this market during the pandemic, this became the interviewee's primary occupation. The demand for care in this case focused on companionship and support for some of the older person's daily activities.

> She's remarkably sharp even at eighty. So, my role mainly involved keeping her company. I'd cook lunch, tidy up the house, help her up the stairs to her bedroom, because her place had stairs. She liked to stay in her bedroom. I'd make sure she took her medication on time. She's very independent, so I didn't have any major problems. There weren't many tasks in actually caring for her. I was more of a companion, a really enjoyable companion. This allowed me to look after her the way she preferred.
>
> *Caregiver for Older Adults 1_DCP*

Later on, the same family hired this caregiver once more to accompany a different older woman who was hospitalized. It was during this period that another caregiver introduced her to a care work platform.

In the case of Babysitter 2_DCP, her prior occupation as a child entertainer became unfeasible during the pandemic because of restrictions on gatherings and direct interactions.

> In fact, what led me to look for babysitting work was the pandemic. With all the restrictions, there was no way to throw a children's party, go on trips, or set up playdates – no chance of direct interaction. So, during the pandemic, I found this babysitting service, and I've been doing it ever since.
>
> *Babysitter 2_DCP*

The common thread in the experiences of these two workers is their entry into the home care labor market during the pandemic. They both subsequently became involved with platform companies in the sector, discovered through interactions with other babysitters and caregivers.

> I actually created my profile before the pandemic, around late 2019 or early 2020. But during the pandemic, I had no clue how to use it. I had downloaded the app and didn't really figure out how to use it until later. I didn't actually start using the platform until last year [2022], in March. Two of my friends were already using it and had found work there. So, I thought, 'Why not give it a shot? Let's see if it's any good.' I liked it, and I'm still using it to this day.
>
> *Babysitter 2_DCP*

The babysitters and caregivers for older adults that we interviewed engaged in multiple relationships, networks, and digital labor platforms in their search for job opportunities. It is worth noting that, in addition to using platforms, they all explored alternative avenues to find work opportunities and actively participated in WhatsApp or Facebook groups where various opportunities for care work for older adults are shared. These groups can be open to the public, managed by intermediation agencies, or created by the caregivers themselves. Interestingly, these groups also serve as spaces for babysitters to share information and alerts amongst themselves.

> There was this one situation where an employer actually asked a babysitter to breastfeed his older child. It became a hot topic of discussion in the

> babysitting groups. People in the group started saying things like, 'The platform should have noticed this. What if one of us went to work there and something even worse happened? How can they allow a request like that?'
>
> *Babysitter 1_DCP*

In another example shared by one of the interviewees, a message circulating in the groups warned about an individual that had a history of mistreating workers who was seeking babysitters on a platform. As mentioned earlier, the DCP lacks a mechanism for workers to evaluate the hiring families. This operational asymmetry within the DCP favors the families and introduces an additional layer of vulnerability for the workers. As per the accounts of interviewees, personal referrals and "word-of-mouth" recommendations continue to be effective methods for securing work, alongside the platforms, and/or for assessing whether an employer is "good" or "bad".

The vast and varied range of actors and scenarios caregivers engage with to search for jobs presents an intriguing area for further investigation. Such research could provide a deeper understanding of how specific actors interact in particular contexts, shed light on the experiences of caregivers, and explore the significant time and effort they invest in seeking work and/or the need to permanently search for work. This is especially relevant in the Brazilian context, marked by precarious and uncertain living conditions that extend beyond working conditions. This reality is also characterized by the multitude of tasks that caregivers are expected to perform, often without adequate protection or means to negotiate their roles securely. These challenges primarily stem from the lack of professional recognition of their work and the limited effectiveness of labor courts in enforcing the minimal rights established in domestic work regulations, secured a decade ago through the efforts of the domestic workers' movement.

3.2 *Lack of Protection during the Pandemic: a Case Study of an Indirect Care Platform (ICP)*

The ICP we researched was launched in Brazil in 2014, and in 2020 it merged with another company in the same sector, expanding its service capacity. Both companies had been market leaders, and it is noteworthy that they merged precisely in the year of the pandemic. According to reports from that period, the goal was to bolster the companies as they navigated the crisis caused by the low demand for their services.

The ICP considers the workers as autonomous partners. As outlined in its Terms and Conditions of Use, available jobs appear for workers on the platform, including dates, number of hours (calculated by algorithmic management based on data provided by customers about the number of rooms in the house), the type of cleaning required, the total payment, the specific tasks to be performed, and the customer's address.[7] The Terms also explain that customers must provide cleaning products and other tools for the service.

To use the platform, the worker is required to pay a monthly subscription fee of R$28.00 (US$5.70) to the platform company. According to the platform's Terms, this covers software development costs. Additionally, for each service performed, the ICP deducts a percentage of the amount paid by the customer, which can be as high as 30%. Although the company claims that this percentage is meant to "cover the intermediation services provided by the platform," it can be viewed as a means of extracting a surplus value through the exploitation of labor (Rodrigues, 2022a). There is an additional charge of R$1.50 (US$0.30) for each weekly payment the company sends to the domestic workers. Finally, company's practice of paying workers weekly while receiving daily payments from customers allows them to "generate income from the amount owed to the worker by placing the funds into the financial market" (Ferreira, 2022, p. 47), which illustrates the financial dimension of platformization.

There is a conspicuous lack of transparency in how the platform operates. In many instances, the domestic worker is unaware of how much the client pays the ICP for her work. This leads to an asymmetry of power between the platform and the worker as well as between the client and the worker. Consequently, rather than the autonomy described by the company, what we find are one-sided actions, largely underpinned by this lack of transparency (Ferreira, 2022).

Furthermore, the Terms specify a system for scoring and categorizing workers. Customers rate their performance based on criteria such as punctuality, friendliness, and the post-service cleanliness of the house. These ratings then classify the workers as "bronze," "silver," or "gold," which significantly influences all aspects of their work. For instance, "gold" workers can have shorter working hours with higher pay, in addition to being exempt from monthly fees. High ratings also give access to heavy cleaning jobs, which also means higher pay. As one interviewed worker explained, "*My chance to take on heavy cleaning tasks depends entirely on the scores I earned from my initial cleaning jobs. It's all about those scores*" (Domestic Worker_ICP). In other words, the entire process is tightly controlled by the platform's algorithmic management.

7 The platform categorizes the types of cleaning into standard, heavy, pre-move, post-construction, and express.

The ICP explains that a worker's ranking is tied to a "Retention Index," which reflects the worker's ability to retain a client, i.e., if the client continues contracting services through the platform. On its blog, the ICP states that a worker's Retention Rate can decrease if a customer does not request further services or cancels their subscription after a service. Thus, despite any other factors that might account for the client's lack of loyalty to the platform, the workers are held responsible and suffer the consequences.

Therefore, the platform's governance imposes control, regulations, protocols, and penalties on workers, despite categorizing them as "self-employed," "autonomous," and "partners". This results in problematic experiences for these domestic workers, prompting a new question: did the COVID-19 pandemic influence these already precarious experiences?

Despite the increased vulnerabilities for domestic workers during the pandemic, the ICP made no changes to provide a safety net for its workers. On the contrary, an analysis of five complaints posted on the website *Reclame Aqui* revealed various negative experiences, including: 1) Imposing fines on domestic workers for not showing up to work; 2) Deactivating accounts due to being absent from work; 3) A shortage of paid jobs available on the platform; 4) Continuing to charge a monthly fee even when there were no jobs available on the platform; 5) Workers feeling abandoned by the company.

The ICP continued to hold workers accountable during the pandemic, imposing penalties for absenteeism and charging monthly fees, despite the specific challenges brought about by the pandemic, such as a lack of clients and the platform's own suspension of activities. Indeed, customer complaints revealed that the platform suspended its services for a period, although we did not find more detailed information about this episode.

> Yesterday, May 16, 2020, I tried to request a cleaning service through the ICP app. I got an error message, so I reached out to their chat service for help. They were able to assist me with the error … and I made the payment using my credit card. Later, while waiting for confirmation of the cleaning service, and my payment already processed, I received a message on WhatsApp asking if I'd like to reschedule because, due to the COVID-19 pandemic, they had suspended their services until June 15, 2020. … Nowhere on the app or website did they inform users about this interruption. They let you pay first and only then ask if you want to reschedule for after the pandemic. That is a total lack of respect for the consumer
>
> *Reclame Aqui*, May 2020

Worker complaints on *Reclame Aqui* indicated they were directly affected by the pandemic, often citing it as the reason for their work absences. In one case, a worker reported being absent for a day due to COVID-19 symptoms, having informed the client about her condition and her inability to work. However, even though the client agreed with the worker's reason, the ICP did not and imposed a fine for the missed service. Another worker had her account deactivated because she missed work while taking care of her brother and mother who were infected with COVID-19. Because she was extremely worried about the situation, she did not inform the platform about her absence, and as a result her account was deactivated. In her complaint on *Reclame Aqui*, she sought guidance on resolving the issue, emphasizing that she relied on the platform for work to support her family.

As the pandemic escalated, the company displayed a glaring lack of sensitivity in handling absences justified by COVID-19 symptoms, whether related to the worker herself or her close contacts. The automated system provided no means for workers to engage with a human agent who could address issues such as low scores, fines, abrupt profile deactivations, or any other concerns they faced while providing services. Consequently, workers understood that the platform expected them to expose themselves to risks if they wanted to stay on the platform. For many workers, the platform represented their sole source of income, especially when customer demand was limited due to geographical distances.

This management model accentuates the illusion of the purported "worker autonomy" championed by the platform. By exerting disciplinary power (Ferreira, 2022), the platform erects communication barriers with workers, revealing its indifference to the intricate everyday experiences of service provision, which, especially amid a severe health crisis, entail complexities that extend beyond the narrow confines of algorithmic calculations.

In this regard, the automation embedded in algorithmic management exposes workers to a lack of transparency and to unilateral decision-making. This underscores the major problems that arise when technology eliminates the human element from relationships. As one of our interviewees succinctly described, "*this company is something we talk about all over the internet. Everything is online. Nobody sees anyone*" (Daily Domestic Worker_ICP). In many instances, this situation deprives workers of support as well as autonomy in making decisions without fear of punishment.

4 Concluding Remarks

The platformization of care work in Brazil has seen a significant surge since 2019. However, comprehending this evolving phenomenon poses a considerable challenge. A lack of disaggregated data pertaining to care work performed through platform companies, as well as the absence of precise statistics on the exact number of Brazilian workers registered on these platforms, hinders our understanding. In response to these limitations, we employed alternative strategies to provide a deeper insight about the Brazilian context. We gathered information from online sources, compiled a database of platforms and apps, and conducted in-depth interviews with workers in the care sector. By integrating these approaches with labor market statistics, we have gained valuable insights on the expanding presence of platform work in the care sector. Furthermore, this research has enabled us to assess the impact of the COVID-19 pandemic on the everyday lives of workers in this sector.

On one hand, our analysis of the ICP revealed the persistence of strict work control measures and inadequate protection for its workers during the pandemic. Furthermore, a significant lack of effective communication with workers became evident, as the platform's algorithmic management remained unchanged. Worker complaints on the *Reclame Aqui* website underscored their heavy reliance on the ICP as their primary source of income, particularly in the context of widespread job reductions in the broader domestic services sector. Conversely, the experiences of direct care workers during the pandemic encompassed a range of situations and diverse care demands, often accompanied by shifts in their career trajectories. In these cases, the platforms seemed to offer an additional avenue for accessing care work opportunities, working in conjunction with interpersonal networks, referrals, and agencies.

On other hand, the different governance models implemented by these platforms had a significant impact on the experiences of workers during the pandemic. For instance, in the case of the DCP, which uses a less automated matching process, workers expressed their concerns about their inability to evaluate the hiring families. They considered this information crucial, especially at a time when the risk of infection was a major concern. Conversely, the ICP uses an almost entirely automated matching process, but that allows workers to evaluate customers. However, the rating system imposes prescriptive and punitive functions on the workers. Based on the *Reclame Aqui* data, it becomes apparent that most of the workers' complaints arose from their interactions with the platform itself. These workers experienced a pervasive sense of injustice, since they were dependent on a management system that restricted their autonomy before the pandemic and even more so after. Why were monthly fees charged when there were no available jobs on the platform? If COVID-19 could potentially endanger the health of both workers and customers, why impose penalties for absences, even when they are justified by symptoms reported by the workers or their family members?

We also observed that both workers and customers on the platforms we studied are compelled to accept the Terms and Conditions that are unilaterally defined by the companies. For instance, on the DCP, client and worker must establish direct contact to negotiate fees and tasks. This operational model underscores the unique nature of recruitment for direct care, which is characterized by direct interactions. To some extent, this dialogue enables both parties to align their expectations and negotiate, even though the actual conditions in the client's home may occasionally diverge from the initial description. In contrast, ICP workers do not have the option to establish prior agreements with clients and have no choice but to accept the daily payment rate, along with all the associated demands. Furthermore, they must comply with customer requirements and fulfill the platform-imposed conditions, including the number of working hours (calculated by an algorithm and subject to customer adjustments), and potential penalties. None of these dynamics changed amid the challenging circumstances of the COVID-19 health crisis.

The findings we have presented also lead us to the conclusion that the operational methods of platform companies have a direct impact on the conditions in which care work occurs. Notably, the DCP provides a list of potential tasks that workers can undertake in addition to their primary responsibilities. The mere existence of this list exerts pressure on workers to accept tasks that expand the scope of their duties and blur the line between direct and indirect care. This pressure affects babysitters and caregivers for older adults and erodes the boundaries between the various forms of home care. In the cases we examined, for example, it induces babysitters to take on additional indirect care tasks. This fluidity underscores the platform company's capacity to extend its influence beyond mere job matching and intermediation by affecting how the actual work is performed and by exerting pressure on workers. Furthermore, it is essential to bear in mind that job opportunities on platforms are fiercely contested among the workers themselves. Factors such as quick responses to requests, high acceptance rates, profile visibility, and positive reviews ultimately limit workers' autonomy when handling demands, suggestions, or incentives shaped by the algorithmic management process.

The significantly higher level of work intensity is particularly noteworthy in the case of the ICP. This trend was not initiated by the platforms themselves. Brazil has seen a growing tendency of domestic workers transitioning from offering their services on a monthly basis (*mensalista*) to offering them on a daily basis (*diarista*), resulting in an increased concentration of tasks within a single working day. What distinguishes the ICP is the introduction of even more intense work patterns that involves scheduling at least two cleaning jobs in one day, each lasting 3 to 4 hours, according to the standards of the platform's algorithmic management. Based on our observations, this pattern eventually becomes a self-imposed goal for the workers themselves, as they are driven to achieve it in pursuit of higher income.

Two additional elements complete our concluding remarks. The first one pertains to information asymmetry, a recurring characteristic in both types of platforms. In fact, information asymmetry seems to be a distinguishing trait of digital labor platforms in general. This asymmetry skews the matching process, leading to an unequal connection between service providers and service seekers, primarily due to the significant concentration of power held by the latter. We believe this characteristic is particularly pronounced in the realm of paid domestic care, whether direct or indirect, which reflects the societal undervaluation of these occupations and their subsequent stigmatization through recurrent racialization. Within the realm of home-based care work, we find a convergence between platform algorithmic management and the evolving dynamics of control and discrimination that unfold within private residences. Furthermore, this was especially detrimental during the COVID-19 pandemic when equitable treatment of both caregivers and care recipients should have been a top priority.[8]

The second element leads us to infer that, despite stigmatization, care work does not deprive care workers of the power of agency. This agency can manifest itself in multiple ways, including the deliberate management of their image to enhance their reputational capital. For instance, workers on the DCP platform create personal profiles with photos of themselves engaged in activities that showcase their skills in dealing with children. Or, as another example, even without fully understanding the algorithmic logic of job allocations, workers find ways to influence the platform's modus operandi, such as modifying their addresses to optimize their access to job offers. The multiple manifestations of the power of agency preclude hasty and reductionist analyses that might

8 During the pandemic, however, we observed a worsening situation considering the specific context, as expressed in the report of the worker who had to wear a mask while her employers did not. In her opinion, the discrimination seemed clear, since the fact that they did not wear a mask revealed their belief that only she and the other workers transmitted the disease. These situations occurred regardless of any positive attributes that employers may have found in the worker's profile.

prematurely assume that inaction in the face of seemingly overwhelming control leaves no room for individual responses.

Finally, we have documented that platform companies have made deliberate efforts to oppose the demands advocated by care workers in Brazil. These include requests for employment formalization, non-overlapping tasks, equal rights compared to other workers, professional qualifications, and the right to unionize, all of which signal the potential for collective responses to emerge in the future.

References

Almeida, Mariana and Simone Wajnman (2023) Occupational transitions of paid care workers during the COVID-19 pandemic in Brazil. Working Paper Series "Documentos de Trabalho", Project "Who cares? Rebuilding care in a post pandemic world" and Network "Cuidados, direitos e desigualdades", São Paulo: Centro Brasileiro de Análise e Planejamento (Cebrap), n. 3. Available at: https://cuidado.cebrap.org.br/wp-content/uploads/2023/11/WhoCares_DT03.pdf. Consulted on Jan. 10, 2024.

Andrada, Ana Carolina, Cardoso, Ana Claudia, Guimarães, Nadya, Moreno, Renata, and Pereira, Maria Julia (2023) Plataformas digitais de cuidado no Brasil. Acesso e controle do trabalho no entrecruzamento de múltiplas crises. *Tempo Social* 35(3): 5–31.

Araújo, Anna Barbara "O trabalho doméstico remunerado durante a pandemia no Brasil. Um balanço bibliográfico da produção brasileira nas ciências sociais e na saúde coletiva". Working Paper, "Who Cares?" Project, São Paulo, July, 2023, 63p.

Araujo, Anna Bárbara (2015) *Gênero, profissionalização e autonomia: o agenciamento do trabalho de cuidadoras de idosos por empresas* (Master dissertation). Federal University of Rio de Janeiro, Rio de Janeiro, Brazil.

Cardoso, Ana Claudia Moreira and Maria Júlia Tavares Pereira (2023) A plataformização do trabalho no Brasil e o subsetor dos cuidados: uma revisão de achados bibliográficos. Working Paper Series "Documentos de Trabalho", Project "Who cares? Rebuilding care in a post pandemic world" and Network "Cuidados, direitos e desigualdades", São Paulo: Centro Brasileiro de Análise e Planejamento (Cebrap), n. 1. Available at: https://cuidado.cebrap.org.br/2023/02/15/a-plataformizacao-do-trabalho-no-brasil-e-o-subsetor-dos-cuidados-uma-revisao-de-achados-bibliograficos/. Consulted on Aug. 29, 2023.

Cardoso, Ana Claudia Moreira. (2022) Dossiê Plataformas Digitais II. *Revista Ciências do Trabalho* 21. Available at: https://rct.dieese.org.br/index.php/rct/issue/view/22. Consulted on Nov. 03 2023.

Carrasco, Cristina, Borderías, Cristina and Tereza Torns (2011) *El Trabajo de Cuidados. Historia, Teoría y Políticas.* Madrid: Los Libros de la Catarata.

Cavarzan, Gustavo (2022) Ensaios de plataformização do trabalho no setor financeiro: o modelo de negócios das Fintechs e corretoras de valores. *Revista Ciências do Trabalho* 21: 01–04.

Duffy, Mignon (2011) *Making Care Count. A Century of Gender, Race, and Paid Care Work.* Piscataway, N.J.: Rutgers University Press.

Duffy, Mignon; Armenia, Amy; Stacey, Clare (2015) *Caring on the Clock: the Complexities and Contradictions of Paid Care Work.* New Jersey: Rutgers University Press.

Edwards, Richard (1980) *Contested Terrain: The Transformation of the Workplace in the Twentieth Century.* New York: Basic Books.

FCC-Fundação Carlos Chagas (2022) Mercado de trabalho de professores durante a pandemia no Brasil: tendências e movimentações de empregos. Project "Educação escolar em tempos de pandemia na visão de professoras(es) da educação básica", n. 5. Available at: https://www.fcc.org.br/fcc/educacao-pesquisa/mercado-de-trabalho-de-professores-durante-a-pandemia-no-brasil-tendencias-e-movimentacoes-de-empregos/. Consulted on Feb. 05, 2024.

Ferreira, Mariana Maciel Viana (2022) *Trabalhadoras domésticas uberizadas: uma análise dos desafios do direito do trabalho a partir da Plataforma Parafuzo* (Final Paper). University of Brasília, Brasília, Brazil.

Folbre, Nancy (2006) Measuring Care: Gender, Empowerment, and the Care Economy. *Journal of Human Development*, 7 (2): 183–200.

Folbre, Nancy (ed.) (2012) *For Love and Money: Care Provision in the U.S.* New York: Russell Sage Foundation.

Fontoura, Natalia and Adriana Marcolino (2021) A heterogeneidade do trabalho doméstico no Brasil. Institute for Applied Economic Research (Ipea) and International Labour Organization (ILO). Available at: https://repositorio.ipea.gov.br/bitstream/11058/11444/1/heterogeneidade_trabalho_cap04.pdf. Consulted on Aug. 31, 2023.

Grohmann, Rafael (2020) Plataformização do trabalho: entre a dataficação, a financeirização e a racionalidade neoliberal. *Eptic*, 22 (1): 106–122.

Guimarães, Nadya and Hirata, Helena (2020) *O Gênero do Cuidado. Desigualdades, Identidades e Significações.* Cotia, São Paulo: Ateliê Editorial and USP Graduate Program in Sociology.

Guimarães, Nadya and Luana Pinheiro (2023) The halo of care. Measuring paid care work in Brazil. Working Paper Series "Documentos de Trabalho", Project "Who cares? Rebuilding care in a post pandemic world" and Network "Cuidados, direitos e desigualdades", São Paulo: Centro Brasileiro de Análise e Planejamento (Cebrap), n. 2.Available at: https://cuidado.cebrap.org.br/wp-content/uploads/2023/11/WhoCares_DT02.pdf . Consulted on Dec. 02, 2023.

Ikuta, Camila and Yuri Santana (2022) Manifestações do trabalho em plataformas na educação. *Revista Ciências do Trabalho* 21: 01–04.

ILO – INTERNATIONAL LABOUR ORGANIZATION (2018) *Care Works and Care Jobs: For the Future of Decent Work*. Geneva: ILO.

Kalil, Renan Bernardi (2019) *Capitalismo de plataforma e direito do trabalho: crowd work e trabalho sob demanda por meio de aplicativos* (PhD Thesis). University of São Paulo, São Paulo, Brazil.

Kornberger, Martin, Pflueger, Dane, and Mouritsen, Jan (2017) Evaluative infrastructures: Accounting for platform organization. *Accounting, Organizations and Society*. 60: 79–95.

Le Bihan, Blanche, Martin, Claude and Trudie Knijn (2013) *Work and Care under Pressure. Care Arrangements across Europe*. Amsterdam: Amsterdam University Press.

Lima, Léa (2023) The commodification of job vacancies: market practices of fee-charging employment agencies in Rio de Janeiro (1950–1975). *Sociologia & Antropologia* 13 (1): 1–26.

Moreno, Renata (2023) Plataformas digitais de trabalho de cuidado: um estudo exploratório com trabalhadoras. Working Paper, Project "Who cares? Rebuilding care in a post pandemic world" and Network "Cuidados, direitos e desigualdades", São Paulo: Centro Brasileiro de Análise e Planejamento (Cebrap).

Powell, Walter W. (1990) Neither Markets, nor Hierarchies: Network Forms of Organization. In: Barry M. Staw and Lary L. Cummints, eds., *Research in Organizational Behavior*, 12: 295–336. Greenwich, CT: JAI Press.

Rodrigues, Gabriel Ferreira (2022a) *Plataformização do trabalho doméstico: uma análise do processo de (des)valorização das diaristas na plataforma Parafuzo* (Master dissertation). University of Brasília, Brasília, Brazil.

Rodrigues, Ciane dos Santos (2022b) *Trabalho médico sob demanda por meio de plataformas digitais: controle por algoritmos e implicações às relações de trabalho* (PhD Thesis). Oswaldo Cruz Foundation, Brazil.

Schor, Juliet B.; Attwood-Charles, William; Cansoy, Mehmet; Ladegaard, Isak; Wengronowitz, Robert (2020) Dependence and Precarity in the Platform Economy. *Theory and Society*. 49(5–6): 833–861.

Ticona, Julia and Alexandra Mateescu (2018) Trusted strangers: Carework platforms' cultural entrepreneurship in the on-demand economy. *New Media & Society* 20 (11): 4384–4404.

Vallas, Stephen, and Schor, Juliet B. (2020) What do platforms do? Understanding Gig Economy. *Annual Review of Sociology* 46: 273–294.

CHAPTER 7

From "Wonderful" Profession to the Harsh Realities of Health as a Commodity: Colombian Nurses during and after the Turmoil of the COVID-19 Pandemic

Pascale Molinier

This chapter presents some of the results of a survey carried out among Colombian nurses about their experiences during the COVID-19 pandemic.[1] As a psychologist, I am interested in the issue of suffering and well-being at work. My aim is to better understand how nurses psychologically coped with the extremely stressful work situations they faced during the pandemic.

Research in the field of work psychodynamics has taught us that workers never remain passive in the face of work-generated suffering—in fact, they try to protect themselves using defensive strategies (Dejours, 1993; Molinier, 2006). These strategies may be individual or based on shared rules and standards that require cooperation and linguistic conventions. These are referred to as "collective defensive strategies" or "professional defensive ideologies." In other words, the discursive devices that prevent us from considering the causes of our suffering. My main question, therefore, concerns these defense mechanisms and their effectiveness in protecting one's mental health, as well as their possible role in phenomena of inertia related to collective struggles. This survey reveals a long-standing process of deterioration in working conditions that was exacerbated during the pandemic, and yet there appears to be no social movement to challenge it.

This chapter will present valuable data for understanding *objective* obstacles to collective struggles. In the final section, I will focus on a *subjective* barrier that I call *defensive professional ideology*, which consists of thinking how "wonderful" it is to sacrifice oneself for others. This ideology is far from being shared by all nurses, but insofar as it is held by some profesors, it maintains the fiction of, in the words of one of my informants, "an emotional wage," or the fiction of achieving work gratification through self-sacrifice.

1 Research carried out as part of the Who Cares? program.

 DOI:10.1163/9789004707009_008

1 Methodology

Fourteen interviews were conducted using the snowball sampling method via four different sources: a non-governmental organization, a professor working at a foundation, a professor in the History department of a private university, and a journalist. Eight of the interviews were conducted in July and August of 2022, and the other six in July and August of 2023. Nine of the interviewees were graduate nurses (GNs) in different positions: a head nurse in a private hospital, a nurse manager in a pediatric ward, four teachers from two different universities, a night nurse in a maternity hospital, a community health nurse, and the owner of a nursing home specialized in psychiatry. Four of the interviewees were nursing assistants: a trade unionist, a nursing assistant in the night ward of a private clinic (acting as a nurse), a nursing assistant in a psychiatric day hospital, and a nursing assistant in a blood sampling laboratory (acting as a nurse). The fourteenth and final interviewee was a lawyer and the director of a feminist NGO that supported caregivers during the pandemic. As of the writing of this paper, the interviewees have all been female. I had contacted two male nurses, but they did not respond. This field survey is therefore not yet complete, but it has already provided some perspectives. Furthermore, in terms of practice sites, I have yet to confirm an informant working in a public hospital.

The eight practice sites of the 14 interviewees described above were varied, comprising two large private university hospitals (which I will refer to as the Foundation and the History Department), a surgical clinic, a private psychiatric nursing home, a psychiatric day hospital, a municipal community health service, a municipal community mental health service, and a biology laboratory linked to another private hospital.

Interviews were conducted in cafeterias, or in the case of the head nurses and professors, in their offices. These took place in three stages: (1) an introduction of their professional background; (2) their experiences during the pandemic; and (3) the recounting, at my request, of one or two particularly significant situations. In 2023, I also investigated whether the changes that occurred during the pandemic had been sustained. In this chapter, I use "nurses" or "caregivers" generically to refer to the informants.

2 Contextual Framework

There are currently around 70,000 nurses and 280,000 care assistants in Colombia. The introduction of national Law 100 in 1993 and the consequent marketization of healthcare have led to significant increases in job insecurity for all categories of care workers. Many nurses and care assistants are now employed with "service provision" contracts, as part of a subcontracting system that implies the deregulation of social rights. Neither overtime nor vacations are paid, and contributions to social security, pensions, and health benefits are paid for by the individual. This means, for example, that sick leave due to COVID-19 contagion often resulted in uncompensated wage loss. Employment is also never guaranteed. In 2023, salaries for nurses and care assistants were generally low, ranging from 1.8 to 4 million Colombian pesos (COP) per month (between $447 and $993 USD). A salaried hospital nurse, working 48 hours/week with 15 vacation days/year earns on average 2.2 million COP/month (about $546 USD). Salary progression over the course of a career is practically nil, at around 400,000 COP (under $100 USD).

According to the trade unions, the minimum salary should be at least 3 million COP/month ($745 USD), buffered by employer-paid health insurance and pension. The professors I met were very happy with their salaries of around 5 million COP/month—double that of their hospital colleagues—especially because they are guaranteed a job until they turn 80, if they so wish. (In a country with a failing pension system, this is considered a privilege.) The salaries of care assistants, normally equivalent to the minimum wage (1 million COP/month or about $250 USD) is, in some establishments, considerably increased (1.5 million COP/month) when replacing nurses. The nursing assistants I met performed nurse-like tasks, such as inserting catheters, working in the operating room, and taking blood samples. Each technique mastered is the subject of a certificate of competence, acquired, of course, after paying for the corresponding training. Public health nurses earn more (3–4 million COP/month), but their salary is often subject to a contract of quantitative objectives during home visits and depends, to some extent, on the number of visits. Professional training is also expensive (6 million COP per semester at the Foundation, 8 million at the History Department).

Care workers go into debt, often owing the medical institutions where they train, the largest of which function as veritable banks. To get by financially, many of them work nights during their studies, perform multiple day shifts, or work in multiple establishments, as is also notoriously the case for doctors. Progressing to manager and team leader involves further studies (e.g., a master's degree in hospital management), and therefore more debt. Nurses with a master's degree in administrative sciences working in senior positions can earn up to 10 million COP per month (about $2500 USD). I met a nurse executive who held such a position during the pandemic. However, this relatively high salary implied permanent availability and, in her case, total submission to higher management decisions, even when they ran counter to the opinions of the healthcare teams, which partly explains why she did not remain in her position.

3 Results

The interviews lasted between 30 minutes and two hours. Except for differences related to place of work, patient flow, working conditions, and transport, which will be further detailed below, a level of saturation can be reached very quickly. During the pandemic, nurses in most healthcare establishments were restricted from speaking to the press about what was happening in hospitals. For example, one of the professors spoke of a colleague working in intensive care who was fired on the spot for talking to the media about the death of another colleague in his care. It seems there was a general rule to not foster panic in the population, which was indeed already terrified, as we shall see below. During the first months of the pandemic, as the number of patients in intensive care units (ICUs) doubled, nurses often found themselves trapped with no colleague to relieve them. They were therefore unable to rest, take turns, or take time off. Some were moved overnight from their usual department (e.g., the operating room or pediatrics) to the adult ICU, where they had no choice but to learn on the job with fear seizing their stomachs.

The number and quality of contamination protection devices varied by location and were unevenly distributed, depending on the profession. For example, the trade unionist said she heard of care assistants having to cobble together protective equipment from garbage bags, while one of the university hospital teachers recounted that cleaning staff were only given ineffective cloth masks. There were also conflicts between the hospitals and the occupational hazards managers (ARL: *administradora de riesgos laborales*)—private agencies meant to cover biosafety costs. According to my union informant, when these agencies finally began delivering equipment, it was inconsistent: one might receive a mask but no gown, or masks of insufficient quality for the intended purpose. The psychiatric orderly said she had to buy her own masks.

Furthermore, once masks, gloves, and gowns had been put on, they could not be removed without throwing them away. In order to use less supplies, physiological needs were rigorously controlled, for example, restricting fluid intake in order to not urinate. This practice was widespread, even at the Foundation where informants agreed supplies were relatively abundant—although one nurse recalled that bottled water was rationed. Likewise, there seems to have been a widespread practice of wearing urinary protection in areas dedicated to intensive care. Naturally, when temperatures outside were high, this work context became even more difficult.

In the early months of the pandemic, patients were dying in critically high numbers, caregivers were afraid of infecting their families, and some workplaces were experiencing desertions by people no longer willing to take the risk of coming to work, especially those whose loved ones were very ill. The risk was explicit—colleagues were dying. A nursing teacher recalled that the main mode of communication between caregivers from this period onwards was WhatsApp messaging groups. She recounted how, for example, while at home resting, she repeatedly received news of one of her colleagues dying. When this recollection made her cry, she was apologetic, "I am sorry, I am too sensitive." Nurses in maternity wards spoke of the sadness caused by the pandemic-related ban on fathers being present for their child's birth—a right that had only recently been granted. The informants repeatedly highlighted the isolation of patients who gave birth or died alone, and the pain of seeing families separated from their loved ones as they were induced into a coma, only to never see them again. Others described the moral torture involved in triaging patients. For example, one informant recounted asking a doctor she knew to revive her friend, a man in his fifties who she expected to be given low priority in triage. When he was treated and pulled through, she recognized that this had been unfair to the other patients and was disturbed by her own actions. She became emotional telling me. But could she have done otherwise?

Virtually all my informants had contracted COVID-19 at least once, many of them twice. I encountered no refusal to vaccinate among informants, nor any complaints about problems obtaining the vaccines. In working-class neighborhoods, particularly because of poverty, drug-addicted street dwellers, and lack of health education, they said the task of testing the population was very risky. They were required to set up and dismantle the medical tent themselves, which they found exhausting, while keeping an eye on valuable equipment to guard it from theft. They described working in the rain, sun, or wind to organize the queue while being insulted by passersby. Rumors of conspiracy were rife, with some believing that the nurses were trying to transmit the disease by inserting the swab into their nose. It was also very difficult to convince people to maintain the recommended social distance from their loved ones. The public health nurse sympathized with this resistance, having contracted COVID-19 herself, not in the course of her work, but at a family Christmas party. More generally, nurses were the target of a veritable onsloughts on public transport, where their customary uniforms made them easily identifiable.

Some refused to let them on buses, insulting and physically threatening them. "What kind of country are we in," said one informant, "where people attack the ones who care for others and risk their lives for them?" The violence of public reactions testifies both to a particularly high level of fear and to a lack of confidence in the healthcare system. NGOs and some institutions offered nurses cabs, which proved very popular as they also provided some rest, or set up transport services, sometimes unsuccessfully if bus stops were located in isolated areas or too far from the women's homes. One nurse conceded that although this was well-intentioned on the part of hospital management, the staff should have been asked first what their needs really were, to avoid situations where women were put in danger walking alone at night to a little-used bus stop.

Unsurprisingly, nurses described this period as a time of intense emotional exhaustion. It was impossible to find time to eat or rest, and some had to sleep in hotels to protect their families from contagion, which added to their stress. What's more, using hotels close to the workplace often proved to be a bad idea for women with children. In the private psychiatric clinic, some Venezuelan women were recruited for four-month cycles, sleeping inside the clinic. The NGO director recounted that the women they supported, most of whom were auxiliary nurses in different towns, described days that began at 3 a.m. and ended at 11 p.m., because in addition to their paid work, they were expected to prepare food for their entire family, including their confined adult children. One of the actions implemented—and which was much appreciated according to an informant—consisted of self-care workshops where the facilitator asked the participants to do at least one thing for themselves every day. The aim was to help them realize that they were caring for others, but never themselves.

At the hospital, there was no service to wash nurses' uniforms—even though, according to the pediatric nurse manager, doctors' scrubs were washed for them. There were also no washing machines, no showers, and no secure lockers for their personal belongings. Nurses had to wash their work clothes at home, and, as they pointed out, separately from the family laundry. Since then, nothing much has changed in terms of work clothes hygiene, but according to some informants, many nurses now go to work by bike or motorcycle to avoid public transit. One of the executive nurses emphasized the fact that doctors are provided showers and spaces to change their clothes and rest. These advantages materialize the inequality between the social classes, which had nevertheless faded during the pandemic through a relational fabric marked by the logic of solidarity.

4 Low Pay, Poor Working Conditions, Mistreatment: How Did Nurses Cope?

There are several discourses I would like to emphasize, especially those of professors at the Foundation. It should be noted that while these professors were not on the front line of care, they were responsible for educating those who were. Some of their speech simply lined up words to express the difficulty of dealing with COVID-19: "It was hard," "It was really hard," "It was really tiring," "I was fed up," "I couldn't take it anymore," without any trace of the idealization process or enchanted servility that will be the focus of analysis later in this chapter.

The discursive strategies of these nurse educators can be characterized by an exaltation of love and apologetic self-giving, combined with formulations of humility, remembering that *la humildad* is a typical feature of Colombian Catholic puritanism.[2] These ways of speaking are characteristic of a society still strongly marked by colonial social structures and are reflected in the recurrent use of diminutive formulation. For example, one asks for a *little* coffee (*un cafecito*) rather than a coffee. This is the rule when begging for alms: give me a little piece of bread (*a pancito*) or a little coin (*una monedita*). These diminutive formulations foster the idea that "we" (the poor) do not need much, we make do with little, or even that it would be disproportionate to give us more, as it is already a great favor to be given a little. Here is a particularly revealing excerpt, in which a professor talks about her own charity practices:

> My husband, for example, he has a good heart. He says, at Christmas time during the pandemic, 'Let's buy five roast chickens with potatoes and soda.' We put five chickens in the car and left. We found a family, I got out and told them ... to have a Merry Christmas with their family and we gave them their little chicken (*pollito*) and soda, then said goodbye. We do not give toys or second-hand clothes, no. I think if you give me a hamburger and a soda, I am happy, so we give people little meals (*comidita*), we give them their little chicken (*pollito*), their little potatoes (*papitas*) and little things (*cositas*).

This diminutive formulation—the same informant speaks of her little house (*casita*) in a pleasant neighborhood—is associated with expressing exaggerated gratitude to the Foundation's bosses, whose contributions are emphatically

2 Thank to Javier A. Pineda D. for his suggestive remarks on this subject.

judged as "great" (*grandioso*) when they are, in fact, quite ordinary: providing the necessary equipment to work safely, not laying anyone off during the pandemic, or maintaining salary levels, for example. Of course, in many institutions this was not the case, and in some there were frequent wage delays (see below). In the following testimonial from the same person, we observe both diminutive speeches related to employees, and emphatic formulations regarding employers.

> What do I like about my Foundation? I have said it many times before, they kept all our jobs, they have not fired anyone. Everyone has continued working in *their little house, their little salaries* have come in on the 15th and the 30th, their benefits, and with health as it is, no one has been suspended. I think these people ... are magnificent and divine and they do a lot from a human point of view. They did not fire anybody, anybody, it was respected, which is a great and wonderful thing. No contracts were cancelled, no contracts were changed or anything, it was all preserved and that is a great thing about this institution.

These discourses sometimes included explicit Catholic references. The same informant, for example, expressed her belief that if she did not fall ill during the pandemic, it was not only because of her strict observance of biosafety rules, but also because "her" God looked upon her with "very beautiful eyes" (*pienso que soy una afortunada en todo, todos los días digo que mi Dios nos mira con unos ojos muy lindos*). These forms of discourse, which value the positive role of employers and minimize the needs of employees, above all euphemize the social relations of domination and, more generally, embellish reality. In this discursive strategy, terms associated with the exaltation of love, like beautiful, marvelous, and pretty (*hermoso, maravilloso, lindo*), recur with some frequency. Here is another example, from a relatively progressive nurse educator who, on her part, makes no reference to God:

> *What was your professional background prior to your current position? Your education and where you obtained your diploma...*
>
> First of all, I would like to say that I am the mother of [x] beautiful children and the grandmother of a beautiful grandson, and that I am the widow of a man I loved very much, who left me too soon. An important fact in my life is that I was born in a very pretty little Colombian town called Armero, Tolima, which was swept away by an avalanche in 1985. I grew up in the countryside in the Cundinamarca and Tolima regions, then came to Bogota to study at [religious institution]. I then studied

> at the Universidad XX, graduated and went to do my rural internship in Barrancabermeja, Santander, at a level 3 hospital, in an area where violence was very high. I then came to Bogota, to a red zone, for a difficult six months, but I lasted a year, even though it was hard.

This informant's narrative strategy consisted of accentuating positive dimensions in tension with dramatic events, which has the effect of euphemizing them, even though her discourse ultimately aligned with the objective discourse of most informants: "It was hard." This strategy of embellishment (the beauty of children, the beauty of the town before its tragic destruction, true love) mitigates successive traumas: the Armero avalanche (35,000 dead), early widowhood, the civil war that raged in Barrancabermeja. This informant used the adjective *maravilloso* nine times and the word "love" four times in a 3,458-word interview. In this enchanted universe, love is the driving force behind the work:

> I think it is beautiful (*hermoso*) to work with students. Students have not lost their sensitivity, they have not lost their humanity, they have not lost their values, the great values of students. So, what is going on? When we welcome students, they leave with this great love for serving others.

She also discussed helping a teenager suffering from leukemia in a very disadvantaged neighborhood:

> Because it drives you to go to San Cristóbal del Sur with your partner and take food, it is something that fills your soul. I think that is how care should be, and we should have total dedication to give others the best, do we not? To give them the best when you take care of their health. So, I think nursing is wonderful (*maravillosa*) because it brings knowledge, but also the essence, the essence of care, dedication, love, perseverance, right? We nurses have all that.

This speech can be further analyzed through a political or psychological lens. Politically speaking, this discourse is undoubtedly right-wing. The teacher who uses it the most is the one who "does not need her salary to pay the bills," thanks to her doctor husband whose specialty pays well (the "good man" with his little chickens). She is also the one who was the most emotional during her interview, having only recently moved from nursing into teaching, and still mourning her colleagues who died in a private hospital, having paid a heavy price. Psychologically speaking, this enchanted discourse appears to be a defensive ideology that masks the reality of social injustice, malaise, and feelings of powerlessness expressed by other nurses, including teachers, who were less defensive and much angrier. The latter was by no means the majority view expressed in the interviews. However, some nurses, particularly the left-wing union members, critically and acerbically alluded to this discourse. They summed it up with the phrase "*Gracias a Dios,*" a motto that they believe stops mobilization against social injustice and justifies accepting everything as "wonderful."

Two informants shared their personal interpretation of this "enchanted servility." Both had wanted to study medicine but had not been accepted into med school. With a master's degree, they were able to hold non-subordinate positions (one resigned from a senior position because of a disagreement with management), and were among the most aware of class inequalities and the process of subordination to doctors. What their point of view suggests is that being a nurse is devalued, a second-best option.

> I wanted to go to medical school, but I did not succeed. I made other attempts, two more to be exact, and I still did not succeed, so I decided to stay here. And the second reason, which is perhaps more subconscious, I would say maybe it is throughout your career that you are encouraged to be altruistic, in a bad, bad way. To put it another way, when you are full of charity, it makes you feel selfish as soon as you think about yourself.

This enchanted discourse was absent from interviews with field nurses who found the pandemic period "hard" and were "upset" by it (*aburridas*). Enchanted discourse cannot stand up to the realities of care work, which has been doubly degraded by the commodification of healthcare and the pandemic crisis. This raises the question of how people managed to protect themselves psychologically from the suffering generated by the moral dilemmas of triage in intensive care, the fear of catching the virus and transmitting it to their families, and the helplessness in the face of mass death. While I cannot give an exhaustive answer to this question, several informants referred to forms of hyperactivity on the job. For example, caregivers worked to the point of complete exhaustion and sometimes despair, having breakdowns or becoming suicidal, unable to watch patients "die and die." This self-sacrificial level of commitment continued—in some cases, even without pay—right up to the point of collapse.

> But what I saw were people so committed that they could not stop. For example at M's public hospitals, not just professionals, but technicians

> too, I know a lot of them, they were doubling their hours, they were doubling them, can you believe it? Yes, that is to tell you that there were people in the pandemic who were not getting paid and who were going to work and doing their hours, yes, they were continuing to work, they were continuing … but there was no money to pay them, you understand? So, think how unbelievable it was.[3]

Did these people draw their strength from the discourse that "encourages you to be altruistic in a bad, bad way?" Or did these behaviors go beyond the level of ideology? Faced with the mass influx of patients and the multiple tragic aspects of the crisis, were these people unable to disengage? Did they act to the point of collapse because, faced with their responsibilities, they could *not*? Would any resignation have been seen as an ethical failure? Did they act out of a sense of responsibility to patients, but also to colleagues? Was it even possible to work through the crisis without a masochistic self-defense mechanism? How many sank into permanent depression, and how many changed professions?

Some left, too terrified to work. Others kept working, exhausted. While feelings of powerlessness were frequently expressed in the interviews, these were housed in a discourse of usefulness that gave meaning to the work. This was particularly the case in the account of a pediatric nurse who had taken charge of children from remote Indigenous communities who needed hospital treatment. New relationships had to be built between the children's caregivers who were sometimes a community representative who spoke a little Spanish, and the nursing staff. The care team also had to learn to work with the community's *Mamo*, a highly trained spiritual leader and healer. They agreed to bring the plants and other natural materials used for traditional rites into intensive care, sometimes agreeing to install elements so that a rite could take place around a child, with the Mamo in videoconference. It became necessary to weave an entire network, not only with Mamos and translators, but also with boat captains and bush pilots. In this story, powerlessness was replaced by genuine reflection on the relational dimensions of care. What heals? Which Western medicine is aligned with which ancestral and traditional knowledge? How

3 For more on nurses (specifically, Afro-descendant Columbians in the department of Choco) selling beauty products at home to cover expenses while waiting for their unpaid salary, see also: Notas sobre el círculo del cuidado. *Boletina 6 de la Red Cuidados y Ciudadanía*, https://redcuidadosyciudadanias.wordpress.com/2020/10/05/notas-sobre-el-circulo-de-cuidado/ [accessed 08/09/2021].

do we build unimaginable bridges between here and there, between people involved in caring for the same child?

5 Conclusion

The interviews revealed a diversity of positions, some of which do not seem to have evolved much from the era Edilma Suárez Castro described in her book *El jardín de rosas: la formación universitaria en enfermería en Bogotá, 1950–1970* (Suárez Castro, 2021). Throughout its development in the 20th century, the nursing profession in Colombia followed the North American model, with the Rockefeller Foundation investing heavily. The profession recruited upper class, "good" Catholic women that corresponded to the imaginary of whiteness and served capitalist prophylaxis. The relationship between a well-educated woman and healthcare was exalted, allowing patriarchal ideology to associate a high level of training with low wages and total subordination to doctors. For women from privileged backgrounds, the rewards of work were meant to be more spiritual than economic, linked to an ideology of loving one's neighbor. Some seventy years later, women from privileged backgrounds went into medicine or other skilled occupations, while nurses were downgraded and poorly paid, the ideology of love as a superior expression of femininity having been structurally maintained by a "defensive ideology of profession" that exalts the "emotional wage" in a situation of denied exploitation.

In this context, it is difficult to consider the ethics and work of care as they have been theorized within the French framework of care studies (Molinier, Laugier, & Paperman, 2009 Molinier, 2020 Hirata, 2021). Indeed, the ethics of care in Colombia continue to be—explicitly or more covertly—associated with the right-wing Catholic ethics and entangled in colonial values, which hinders the possibility of thinking of care as collective work rather than an individual virtue. Professional care is not a *little gift* to those more unfortunate or needy than oneself. In keeping with this systemic view, by not considering nursing care as a category of work, Colombian nurses deny themselves the capacity to recognize their own exploitation as well as the efforts and know-how they mobilize. They are therefore denied the necessary conceptual tools to capture in an analytical grid the structural and collective conditions of attention to others. Ultimately, this means confusing defense (hyperactivity and self-sacrifice) with desire (caring). This is where theorist Carol Gilligan's proposal of the opposition between a *feminine* ethics of care (feminine and masochistic) and a *feminist* ethics of care (open to collective and social transformations) comes into play (Gilligan, 2013).

Fourteen is a relatively small number of interviews, which is a limitation. The place of the Catholic religion in nurses' altruistic representations of their profession undoubtedly merits further investigation. Based on my research, it seems that the Catholic religion plays above all a defensive role, enabling some nurses (not all) to put up with poor working conditions and low pay. This masochistic ethos is still partly transmitted in nursing faculties. But it is important to stress that, among my informants, even the most Catholic of them are revolted by the gap between their pay and their skills. As for those who are union members, they joke about "*gracias a Dios*" (thanks be to God), a modism that is a watchword for some Colombians to prevent any discussion of the effects of social injustice, and thus not break Colombia's "*encanto*" (charm), to use the title of a famous movie about Colombia.

Other progressive groups, including academics, are prepared to recognise care as work, not a gift or an expression of the "female human spirit." Several of my informants were keenly aware that loving their patients or adopting a compassionate stance is not enough to care for them. They know that care involves complex work, particularly in understanding and adapting to the patient's social, cultural, and subjective position, as was particularly the case in the situation of the nurse manager who cooperated with the Mamo, or with the nurse who wondered about health education in working-class neighborhoods. The nursing profession in Colombia is thus a divided position, torn between two models: a vocational model that is no longer in tune with the realities of the profession, and a more professional model that is still trying to define itself. In the same way that speaking out on the pandemic and its impact on the healthcare system has been muzzled, censorship has prevented this debate from emerging. The absence of a way out of this conflictual situation, which is rarely, if ever, discussed, is reflected in individual strategies. Colombian nurses migrate, mostly to Spain—or dream of doing so. Professors are aware that they are ultimately training candidates for migration. I hope that this chapter, in its modest way, will help open the debate.

References

Dejours, Christophe (1993) *Travail: usure mentale*, Paris: Bayard.

Gilligan, Carol (2013) « Résister à l'injustice ». In: Gilligan, Carol, Hochschild, Arlie and Joan Tronto, *Contre l'indifférence des privilégiés. À quoi sert le care*. Paris: Payot: 35–67.

Hirata, Helena (2021) *Le* care, *théories et pratiques*. Paris: La Dispute.

Molinier, Pascale, Laugier, Sandra and Patricia Paperman (2009) *Qu'est-ce que le care? Souci des autres, sensibilité, responsabilité*. Paris: Petite Bibliothèque Payot.

Molinier, Pascale (2006) *Les enjeux psychiques du travail. Introduction à la psychodynamique du travail.* Paris: Petite Bibliothèque Payot.
Molinier, Pascale (2020) *Le travail du care.* Paris: La Dispute (2nd ed.).
Suárez Castro, Edilma (2021) *El jardín de rosas: la formación universitaria en enfermería en Bogotá, 1950–1970.* Bogotá: Editorial Pontificia Universidad Javeriana.

CHAPTER 8

Gender, Migration and Care Work: Analyzing the Impacts of the COVID-19 Pandemic through a Legal Case

Carolina Moreno and Camila Vega-Salazar

The purpose of this work is to highlight the unique challenges faced by a vulnerable group of women during the pandemic, specifically, Venezuelan migrant women engaged in care work in Colombia.[1] In this regard, it is sought to underscore the importance of adopting an intersectional perspective that integrates gender and migration considerations in the design of social policies. The approach relies on a legal research methodology employing normative frameworks and jurisprudence to analyze specific social issues, particularly the hardships experienced by some vulnerable migrant and refugee women in Colombia due to specific COVID-19 containment measures.

In the midst of the global COVID-19 pandemic, the Government of Colombia launched the Solidarity Income Program (hereinafter SIP) to provide financial assistance to those in need. This program was created during the pandemic emergency to address the economic hardships faced by impoverished communities. The SIP provided unconditional cash transfers to individuals in dire financial situations who were not already receiving assistance from other state social programs. While the program did not expressly exclude foreign individuals from accessing its benefits, in reality, it required migrants to have regular migratory status, which posed a challenge for the undocumented Venezuelan population, which at that moment outnumbered those with regular status.

One legal case that exemplifies this exclusion was heard by the Colombian Constitutional Court in 2023. 24 women, including Colombian domestic workers and Venezuelan migrant women working in the care sector, were denied access to the SIP. This left them struggling to support their basic needs and without access to essential resources. These women took legal action, represented by Colombian NGO Dejusticia, to protect their rights and demand

1 This chapter is a product of the research project *Who cares? Rebuilding care in a post pandemic world*, which is financed with resources from the Fondo Nacional de Financiamiento para la Ciencia, la Tecnología y la Innovación Francisco José de Caldas de Minciencias, Colombia.

 | DOI:10.1163/9789004707009_009

transparency in the selection process for the SIP. Despite initial rejection of their claims, the Constitutional Court later ruled in their favor, emphasizing the need for a gender-sensitive approach and recognizing the intersectional challenges faced by migrant and refugee women in caregiving roles. This legal case and the resulting judgment allow us to analyze the vulnerability of different groups of people to the effects of the pandemic. It also creates an opportunity to assess the impact of Government measures to contain the widespread COVID-19 virus.

To properly understand this legal case, it is crucial to contextualize the migratory landscape in Colombia. This country is highly relevant to current global migration issues for various reasons. Firstly, Colombia is widely recognized as a nation whose citizens emigrate and seek refuge from the internal armed conflict to save their lives and maintain their well-being. The internal conflict has resulted in a large number of internally displaced persons (IDPs) in Colombia. According to the United Nations High Commissioner for Refugees (UNHCR), there were 6.8 million IDPs in Colombia by the end of 2022 (2023). The UNHCR's Global Trends Report (2023) further confirms that "Colombia and Syria continued to report the largest number of people displaced within their own countries (6.8 million in each)" (p. 26). Secondly, Colombia serves as a crucial destination and transit country for immigrants. Over the past decade, the perception of Colombia as an emigration country has rapidly transformed in response to the significant influx of Venezuelans seeking refuge from the complex humanitarian crisis in their home country (Moreno & Pelacani, 2023).

When examining cross-border immigration in Colombia, two key factors to consider are the influx of Venezuelan immigrants and the flow of people crossing the Colombo-Panamanian border en route to North America. Notably, Colombia is the largest recipient of Venezuelan migrants worldwide. According to the Interagency Coordination Platform for Refugees and Migrants (R4V Platform), as of November 2023 over 7.7 million Venezuelan nationals have left their home country, with 6.5 million now residing in Latin America and the Caribbean, of whom 2.9 million reside in Colombia (R4V Platform, 2023c).

These latest figures align with the *Migracion Colombia* report indicating that, as of December 2023, there were 2,864,796 Venezuelans residing in the country (Migracion Colombia, 2024). Of this population, approximately 1.9 million held regular migratory status. At the same time, roughly 500,000 were undocumented, and another 400,000 were in the process of obtaining the Temporary Protection Permit (PPT in Spanish) to regularize their status. Despite the implementation of policies to regularize the migratory status of Venezuelans, there are still many undocumented individuals who are unable to access public services and fully exercise their rights.

According to Migracion Colombia (2023), as of August 2023, there were 1,484,413 Venezuelan women and 1,390,740 Venezuelan men in Colombia, representing 52% and 48% of the Venezuelan population in this country, respectively. This pattern is consistent across almost all age ranges, except for the 0–4, 5–17, and 30–39-year-old groups, where boys and men slightly outnumber girls and women. Overall, from ages 8 to over 70, there are more women than men among Venezuelan migrants in Colombia. These statistics demonstrate that the Venezuelan population in Colombia is feminized, with girls, adolescents, young adults, and women making up the majority of those who arrive and stay in the country.

In addition to the significant population of Venezuelans living in Colombia, the country is a destination for people from various countries in Asia, Africa, Latin America, and the Caribbean who are seeking to cross the Colombia-Panamanian border, commonly referred to as the 'Darien Gap', to reach North America (Moreno Velasquez, 2022). According to the International Organization for Migration (IOM), in 2023, there were 196,371 reported unauthorized entries at the land border between Panama and Colombia, representing an annual increase of 90 percent. (IOM, 2023).

The IOM issued a concerning warning about irregular migration in the Darien Province. According to Panamanian authorities, a staggering 458,228 migrants entered the region from the start of 2023 to October 31st, 2023. The majority of these migrants come from Venezuela, with 294,598 individuals making the perilous journey. Additionally, 51,129 Ecuadorians, 41,489 Haitians, 18,501 Chinese, 15,897 Colombians, and 5,090 Chileans have made the crossing. In October 2023 alone, the number of migrants reached 49,256 (IOM, 2023, p. 34).

As is clear from the above, there are complex, long-term and diverse fluxes, routes, and journeys of internal and international migration in Colombia. However, in this work, we will focus on the case of migrant women from Venezuela, particularly during the pandemic.

This chapter is structured as follows. Initially, we will provide a comprehensive overview of the context of the pandemic and the Colombian authorities' response to it. This review will aim to give the reader a broad understanding of the situation before delving into the specific issues facing migrant and refugee populations. In the following section, we will present a detailed analysis of how pandemic containment measures have had differentiated impacts on these populations, with a particular focus on those who are most vulnerable. Subsequently, we will explore the pandemic's effects on migrant women, including how the increased burden of caregiving responsibilities has exacerbated the difficulties of their situation during this time. We will examine this issue in depth, drawing on existing research and firsthand accounts from migrant women themselves. After that, we will turn our attention to a Colombian Constitutional Court case that recognizes the differentiated impacts of the pandemic on migrant and refugee populations. We will analyze the implications of this landmark ruling and what it means for the future of policymaking in Colombia. Finally, we will conclude with some reflections, drawing on the insights gained from our analysis.

1 The COVID-19 Pandemic: Context and Management

In 2019, the world witnessed the rapid spread of the 'coronavirus disease' (COVID-19) caused by the "severe acute respiratory syndrome coronavirus 2" (SARS-CoV-2) originating from China (WHO, 2020a). In response, various States implemented measures to control the spread of the virus, including physical distancing measures and movement restrictions, commonly referred to as shutdowns and lockdowns.

The Colombian Government implemented a series of measures in response to the declaration of COVID-19 as a Public Health Emergency of International Concern (PHEIC) by the World Health Organization (WHO) on January 30th, 2020 (WHO, 2020c). In its "Strategic Preparedness and Response Plan" (WHO, 2020b), the WHO advised States to swiftly enhance their readiness and response frameworks, covering aspects such as the identification, diagnosis, and management of cases, the identification and monitoring of contacts and infections, infection prevention and control measures in medical facilities, implementation of health measures for travelers, and the dissemination of information to the public on prevention and risks. To quote directly from the Plan,

> Countries must do everything possible to stop cases from becoming clusters and clusters from becoming explosive outbreaks. They must put in place the capacities for testing and diagnosis, isolation, contact tracing, and quarantine; they must engage everyone in the response.
>
> p. 4

In Colombia, in adherence to the guidelines issued by the World Health Organization, the Ministry of Health and Social Protection (MHSP) declared a health emergency on March 12th, 2020, through Resolution 385. The resolution sought to address the Coronavirus COVID-19 outbreak and to implement appropriate measures to contain the virus. Initially, the health emergency resolution was set to expire on May 30th, 2020; however, it was subject to an extension if the situation required it. As expected, the Government extended the health emergency ten times until it officially ended on June 30th, 2022 (MHSP, 2022).

The declaration of a 'Health Emergency' is a response to an extraordinary situation that requires immediate and significant action. These measures may include the suspension of large gatherings, the implementation of hygiene protocols in various settings, and the dissemination of information about preventive measures. Additionally, restrictions may be put in place for international maritime traffic.

It is important to note that the 'Health Emergency' is distinct from the 'State of Exception' outlined in the Colombian Constitution (Articles 213 to 215), which encompasses the 'Economic, Social, and Ecological Emergency'. The Colombian Government utilized both mechanisms to manage the COVID-19 pandemic. Indeed, only five days after declaring a 'Health Emergency', the former President, along with all his ministers, signed Decree 417 on March 17th, 2020, declaring a 30-day 'Economic, Social, and Ecological Emergency' (hereinafter 'ESEE')". On May 6th, 2020, through Decree 637 once again declared the aforementioned 'ESEE'. According to the Colombian Constitution, the 'ESEE' is one of the three 'States of Exception' reserved for situations where there is a "serious and imminent disturbance of the economic, social, and ecological order in the country" that is separate from external warfare or national security events.

The 'ESEE' declaration has significant implications, including granting the President the power to materially replace legislative power. This enables the President to pass decrees that hold the same force as laws, effectively taking the place of Congress in matters of legislation. Notably, the decree emphasizes the public budget as a crucial tool for addressing urgent social and economic needs resulting from the pandemic (Mendieta Gonzalez & Tobon-Tobon, 2021).

Based on the declared emergencies – 'Health Emergency' and 'ESEE' –, the Government enacted a series of measures to curb the spread of the virus. Among the earliest of these was the closure of the Colombia-Venezuela border (Ministry of Internal Affairs, 2020), which had a significant impact on the migrant and refugee population from Venezuela, as we will delve further in this chapter. Additional regulations followed, including a ban on gatherings of more than 50 people (MHSP, 2020), the indefinite closure of schools and universities (Ministry of Education, 2020), and a voluntary isolation period proposed by certain mayors and governors (Bogota Mayor's Office, 2020) (Boyacá Governor's Office, 2020). Eventually, the National Government instituted mandatory preventive isolation and restricted free movement, with penalties for non-compliance (President's Office, 2020).

Throughout the pandemic, decrees rather than legislative norms were the primary means of governance. The 'Health Emergency' and 'ESEE' gave the President and his ministries wide-ranging authority to address the health crisis caused by the pandemic. As was the case globally, these measures had a significant impact on people's human rights, including freedom, education, and work. For example, during lockdowns, many people were unable to work under the conditions they were accustomed to and had to work from home. Others were required to go to work despite rising infection rates and limited knowledge of how to manage the risks posed by this situation. For those who relied on informal work, the closure of economic activities and strict quarantines resulted in severe impoverishment.

The adverse impacts on the labor market did not affect all Colombians equally. In the October-December period of 2020, there was a 3.1 percentage point increase in the unemployment gender gap, with women experiencing a rate 8.4% higher than men in 2020, compared to 5.3% in 2019. Likewise, the gap between rural and urban areas widened by 3 percentage points, with a difference of 8.5% in 2020, compared to 5.4% in 2019 (DNP et al., 2021).

During the initial months of the pandemic, the impact of quarantine restrictions varied in different sectors of the economy. Commerce, for example, experienced a significant decline in activity levels in May 2020, resulting in adverse effects on employees in this sector. Conversely, the agricultural sector demonstrated remarkable stability in terms of employment levels (DNP, et al., 2021).

The care economy had a disproportionate impact on women during the pandemic, as stated by DNP, IPA, and UNICEF. Prior to the quarantine, women already faced lower levels of employment compared to men. However, the confinement measures exacerbated gender disparities in income attainment and productive activities. A comparison of employment changes from February to November 2020 reveals a significant widening of the gap between men and women. In February, the difference was 17 percentage points, but by November, it had nearly doubled to 30 percentage points. (DNP et al., 2021).

For the purpose of this work, it is essential to acknowledge the efforts made by the National Government to cater to the needs of disadvantaged communities. Specifically, we will focus on the 'Solidarity Income Program' (SIP), known as '*Programa Ingreso Solidario*' in Spanish, which was a key social policy implemented to alleviate the economic struggles of the most impoverished individuals during the pandemic. Legislative Decree 518 on April 4th, 2020, issued in accordance with the 'ESEE', introduced the SIP during the initial stages of the pandemic. As stated in Article 1 of the decree, the SIP was a social program managed by the Ministry of Finance that provided unconditional cash transfers to those living in poverty and vulnerability and who were not beneficiaries of other state social programs, such as 'Families in Action', 'Social Protection for the Elderly', and 'Youth in Action'.

According to the Inter-American Development Bank (Inter-American Bank, 2021), the program involved three monthly payments of 160,000 Colombian pesos (43 USD), of which approximately three million people were recipients. Based on data provided by the National Department of Statistics (DANE) (2020), this monthly household transfer accounted for 16.9% of impoverished households' average income in 2019 (Gallego et al., 2021). The program aimed to provide crucial financial assistance to households facing poverty and vulnerability, mitigating the negative impact of pandemic-related mobility restrictions. The program was extended multiple times and finally concluded in late 2022, with rapid response being a key strategy. This program managed to identify beneficiaries within two weeks through surveys conducted by the SISBEN (System for Identifying Potential Beneficiaries of Social Programs) before 2020 (Rodriguez, 2020).

The criteria for SIP eligibility did not distinguish between Colombians and foreigners, meaning that Venezuelan migrants affected by the pandemic could technically have applied. However, this did not translate into reality, and only a small number of Venezuelan migrants were able to benefit from the program. This situation sheds some light on the high number of non-voluntary returns from Colombia to Venezuela during the early stages of the pandemic, despite the official border closure. Venezuelan individuals faced various challenges in accessing the SIP, such as their irregular migratory status and underrepresentation within the SISBEN. We will delve deeper into this issue later in the text.

2 Distinct Impacts of Pandemic Measures on Migrant and Refugee Populations

The COVID-19 pandemic response measures implemented by Colombian authorities had significant repercussions on the migrant and refugee population, especially those without regular immigration status and living in impoverished conditions (Chaves-Gonzalez et al., 2021). These measures, such as border closures, economic activity cessation, protracted quarantines, and deportations, were put in place to combat the public health crisis, but they had a substantial impact on the livelihoods of migrants and refugees. Unfortunately, these measures also exacerbated the already precarious circumstances of economically disadvantaged migrant and refugee groups in Colombia (The New Humanitarian, 2020b). One of the first measures taken was the closure of the

Colombia-Venezuela border (Migracion Colombia, 2020), which made transit conditions considerably more arduous and dangerous and affected the mobility of the migrant population, although it did not entirely impede the flow of individuals (Acosta, 2020).

Since the start of the pandemic in 2020, one of its devastating consequences was the eviction of many impoverished Venezuelan migrants and refugees. These individuals rely on informal work for their income, which was severely impacted by mandatory lockdowns and the freezing of economic activity. Those who lived in daily rental accommodations, known as '*pagadiarios*', were unable to pay rent, resulting in sudden evictions (Mixed Migration Centre, 2020). In addition to losing their homes, their situation as homeless people, further aggravated by the prolonged closure of economic activities, made it impossible for them to engage in informal work (International Labour Organization, 2021).

The economic conditions of the most disadvantaged migrant and refugee individuals, particularly those with irregular migratory status, worsened due to their inability to access Government-provided social assistance (Mixed Migration Centre, 2020). For instance, only Venezuelan nationals with regular migratory status, as well as those registered in the SISBEN, were able to benefit from the SIP, which as mentioned above was the program implemented by the Colombian Government to alleviate the financial strain on the most vulnerable households. However, these beneficiaries accounted for less than 2% of the total number of recipients of the program (Castro, 2020).

Bitar (2022) stated that the vast majority of the migrant population had irregular migration status when the pandemic began (March 2020), which resulted in limited access to formal employment and health services.

To quote the author,

> In terms of the migrant population's income, according to the Pulse of Migration Survey, 38.8 percent of the migrant population did not receive any income in the month prior to the survey, while only 51.6 percent received income from work. Some 3.6 percent received money from the Programa de Alimentacion Escolar [School Meals Program] and 3.6 percent did so from Ingreso Solidario [the Income Solidarity Program]. Only 0.2 percent received money from Familias en Accion [Families in Action], 0.5 percent from Colombia Mayor [Older Colombia], and 0.1 percent from Jovenes en Accion [Young People in Action]. Some 48.3 percent of migrant women and 50.5 percent of young migrants did not receive any income.

The significance of migratory status in determining access to Government aid for the Venezuelan population cannot be overstated. It is particularly noteworthy that a disproportionately high proportion of individuals with irregular migratory status were negatively impacted at the onset of the pandemic in 2020. According to Migracion Colombia data, as of the end of 2019, there were 1,630,903 Venezuelan immigrants residing in Colombia, with 719,189 holding regular migratory status and 911,714 being undocumented (Migracion Colombia, 2019). This proportion remained unchanged throughout the first year of the pandemic, with approximately 1.7 million Venezuelan nationals living in Colombia in October 2020, of whom almost 1 million lacked the necessary legal documentation to remain in the country (Migracion Colombia, 2020).

Despite the ongoing humanitarian crisis in their home country, many Venezuelan individuals were forced to return due to the precariousness of their situation in Colombia (The New Humanitarian, 2020a). Even though the National Government closed its borders, this did not deter Venezuelan families who were unable to earn a living in Colombia from returning to their home country (UNHCR, 2020). Although the returns were deemed voluntary by Colombian authorities, in reality they were not. The impoverished foreign population had no other option in the face of a series of adverse factors that made it impossible for them to remain in the host country, compelling them to return (Centro de Derechos Humanos de la Universidad Catolica Andres Bello-CDHUCAB, 2020) (Moreno & Pelacani, 2021). In fact, some local authorities even encouraged these returns as a way to alleviate their responsibility to 'take care of' migrant individuals. For municipal governments, it was easier to provide financial support for transferring Venezuelan migrants and refugees to the Colombia-Venezuela border than to design measures to address the needs of this population (La Opinion, 2020).

Migrants and refugees, particularly those with irregular migratory status, faced pandemic containment measures that included migratory sanctions such as deportation and expulsion for non-compliance with the regulations set by the authorities. This posed a significant challenge to Venezuelan individuals who were unable to comply with the strict confinement measures due to their homelessness and lack of resources. Additionally, migrants and refugees could be expulsed or deported if they were deemed a 'risk to public health', as stipulated by Colombian migratory regulations (Moreno Velasquez, 2023). Deportations and expulsions are especially detrimental to sanctioned individuals and their families since, as well as being forced to leave Colombia and suddenly separated from their families, they are unable return to the country for up to five years or even longer (Border Criminologies Blog, Law Faculty, Oxford University, 2020).

Regarding the vulnerabilities faced by migrant and refugee populations during the COVID-19 pandemic, it is important to highlight the recommendations made by the Inter-American Commission on Human Rights (IACHR) to States. According to the IACHR, States should avoid detention strategies and other measures that increase the risk of contagion and vulnerability of migrant people, guarantee access to health services without discrimination, and include migrant populations in economic recovery policies and other actions that become necessary throughout the crisis caused by the pandemic (Inter-American Commission on Human Rights, 2020).

3 The Situation of Venezuelan Migrant Women during the Pandemic and the Barriers to Access to Social Programs

The COVID-19 pandemic had a global impact, affecting people in various ways, but it had more severe and distinct consequences for specific groups, especially the most vulnerable. According to the Economic Commission for Latin America and the Caribbean (ECLAC), despite the measures taken by Governments to address the pandemic, poverty and extreme poverty in Latin America reached unprecedented levels in 2020. Inequality also worsened, with significant reductions in employment and labor force participation rates, especially among women (ECLAC, 2021).

Women in Latin America are typically relegated to unpaid caregiving roles, which limits their opportunities for education, leisure, and political engagement. This disparity is even more pronounced for women in impoverished households, leading to greater marginalization and exclusion. For Venezuelan migrant women in Colombia, the pandemic has exacerbated existing challenges. These women have struggled to obtain recognition for their academic credentials and have found it challenging to secure employment in line with their qualifications. Due to traditional gender norms and the undervaluing of caregiving roles, many of these women have had to accept jobs that they are overqualified for, with nearly half employed in informal trade, domestic work, and caregiving, compared to only 23.1% of men (Valenzuela et al., 2020).

The situation is even worse for Venezuelan women without regular migratory status, resulting in their being trapped in the informal sector and forced to balance unpaid caregiving duties with work at home. Many Venezuelan families, often headed by women, have been severely affected by economic closures and strict lockdowns, leading to a sudden and significant reduction in daily incomes, particularly for those who rely on informal work (Inter-American Development Bank, 2020). As a result, Venezuelan women working in the informal sector have felt the full impact of the pandemic on their employment circumstances.

The DANE Integrated Household Survey and the Quanta-Care and Gender project's microdata analysis reveal significant disparities between migrant women and Colombian women, as well as between migrant and Colombian men. Notably, the unemployment rate for migrant women in 2020 was 29.2%, compared to 18.1% for Colombian women, while for migrant men it was 22.9%, compared to 15.8% for Colombian men. Furthermore, the participation of migrants in informal work is approximately 77%, which is significantly higher than the 39% rate for Colombians (Tribin-Uribe et al., 2022).

Regarding unpaid care work, during the pandemic migrant women dedicated an average of 32.16 hours to this per week in 2020, compared to 27.45 hours for Colombian women. In contrast, both migrant and Colombian men dedicated approximately 11.2 hours per week to unpaid care work (Departamento Administrativo Nacional de Estadistica, 2024). These findings highlight the unique challenges faced by migrant women and the need for targeted support to address these disparities.

In addition to the vulnerability, increasing levels of poverty and limited access to services and rights described above, access to social programs was another situation where women, particularly migrants engaged in care work, were disadvantaged. Access to the SIP is dependent on the score assigned by SISBEN. However, the government failed to update SISBEN registrations at the beginning of the pandemic, meaning they were unaware of a surge in the number of Venezuelan registrations from 32,570 in 2020 to 148,276 in 2022 (Departamento Nacional de Planeacion, 2024). This resulted in the exclusion of many individuals, as only those registered before the pandemic were eligible for the SIP. Thus, the population at greater risk found itself excluded. The impacts of this exclusion were felt by migrants with regular status, but undocumented people, who represented the vast majority of Venezuelan people in Colombia, were fully excluded and persecuted by the State.

4 The Legal Case of Care Workers Excluded from the Solidarity Income Program: Consequences and Opportunities

In October 2020, a group of 24 women filed a legal action known as 'tutela', which is a legal remedy that anyone can use to request protection for their fundamental rights before a judge against the President's Office and other public authorities, such as the National Planning Department [Departamento Nacional de Planeacion] and the Administrative Department for Social

Prosperity [Departamento Administrativo de Prosperidad Social]. Nine of the plaintiffs were domestic workers, and 15 were Venezuelan migrant women with regular migratory status engaged in caregiving work. They were represented by the Colombian organization Centro de Estudios de Derecho, Justicia y Sociedad (Dejusticia), which focuses on legal research for advocacy and strategic litigation. The legal action sought to protect their rights to a dignified life, minimum subsistence, health, food security, housing, information, and equality (Dejusticia, 2020).

Due to the pandemic, many women lost their jobs or sources of income from informal work, which made their situation more precarious by depriving them of resources for necessities such as food, rent, and utilities. Additionally, they lacked protective equipment against the virus, which left them extremely vulnerable and exposed. The Government initiated the Solidarity Income Program to support the most vulnerable, but its coverage was limited. The program only benefited people registered on the system until March 2020, before pandemic-related restrictions were imposed.

The women bringing the legal claim argued that there was insufficient information regarding their exclusion from the program. They speculated that their SISBEN score, or the opening of a bank account may have been the reason behind it. They suggested that the SIP website and institutional channels should have provided more comprehensive information about the selection criteria for program beneficiaries to help participants gain a better understanding of the program's selection process.

They highlighted the importance of a sensitive selection process that encompassed cross-sectional factors, while also considering the disproportionate impact of poverty, domestic work, and migration conditions on women. As a result, they demanded protection of their rights and inclusion in the SIP in order to receive monetary transfers starting from April 2020. Additionally, they urged for the creation and implementation of mechanisms to provide access to social programs without requiring identification documents that pose obstacles for migrants.

The legal action was first rejected by the lower courts. However, Colombia's highest judicial authority, the Constitutional Court, reviewed the case and made a new decision through judgment T-159 of 2023 (Corte Constitucional, 2023). The outcome of the specific case may be questionable, due to the considerable delay between the filing of the action and the court ruling, which occurred in June 2023. It is worth noting that the SIP, which was intended as a pandemic relief mechanism, had already expired by then, which could have affected the case's overall outcome.

The Court determined that the vulnerability of some women had been taken into consideration, as they could access the PIS after requesting a modification of their SISBEN score. This meant that they were no longer in need of special protection, as they had been able to access the necessary resources to overcome their precarious situation. However, the Court found that the other women had not received an appropriate SISBEN modification. This meant that they were still in a vulnerable position and in need of special protection. Unfortunately, since the damage had already occurred and the PIS had ceased operation, it was not feasible to include them in the relief program. Additionally, the Court criticized the delay of the second instance court in sending the case file, resulting in an irreparable delay in the legal claim process. This delay could have further contributed to the difficulty in providing adequate relief to the affected women.

The Court acknowledged the damage that had already occurred and accepted its own limitations in protecting the rights of women. However, it urged the President's Office to act by creating a public policy specifically designed for female informal caregivers and household heads. The policy should incorporate an intersectional approach to cater for their diverse needs. The Court emphasized that the Government had failed to ensure minimum subsistence and material equality for these women. It had excluded them from the SIP, used SISBEN without considering gender, and did not publish selection criteria. These actions were deemed to be violations of the rights of these women. Thus, the Court recommended the design of a policy that would address the needs of female informal caregivers and household heads and guarantee their rights to minimum subsistence and material equality.

The Court recognized the significance of incorporating an approach that acknowledges not only economic vulnerability but also the caregiving work provided by women to minors, persons with disabilities, and older adults. They also acknowledged that many women depended on informal work for family income. As a result, the Court ruled that the President's Office failed to a) consider the social and cultural context, which entails a caregiving burden disproportionately affecting women, and b) fulfill the State's duty to provide protection.

As per the Court's ruling, the Office of the Ombudsman is now responsible for setting up mechanisms that effectively assist and support individuals who seek to benefit from public policies but may require further clarification or assistance in accessing them. This directive aims to ensure that every individual has equal access to the benefits of Government public policies without any hindrance or difficulty.

This legal case has been instrumental in shaping the discourse around caregiving work. The case has established several alternatives to the traditional approach, including setting up support networks, childcare facilities, improving working conditions for informal workers, or providing direct aid to women instead of making them rely on family assets. Furthermore, this case has highlighted the vulnerabilities faced by migrant women who engage in caregiving, whether paid or unpaid, and the additional challenges they face, such as homelessness or forced returns without any means of livelihood.

The legal decision made in this case has the potential to create significant ripple effects across various areas, most notably in the development of the National Care System. This system is a crucial framework that comprises the Intersectional Commission for National Care Policy, which is responsible for coordinating interdisciplinary efforts to implement policies for care. These circumstances of the case have highlighted the need for the Commission to perform intersectional analyses that specifically address the unique challenges faced by migrant and refugee women.

Although the verdict was highly favorable to the women who brought the legal claim, implementation of it by the government is still pending. There remain challenges to be overcome in the design of policies that take into account the vulnerability of migrant and refugee women, particularly those engaged in caregiving roles, regardless of their migratory status. This requires a comprehensive approach that encompasses migration policy, social policies, and socioeconomic inclusion of the migrant and refugee population in Colombia. Additionally, social policy designs must be transparent and based on clear criteria to enable individuals to understand the requirements for beneficiary selection.

Additionally, there is an ongoing legal discussion at the Inter-American Court of Human Rights (IACrHR) regarding the right to care. This has been triggered by an advisory opinion petition filed by Argentina, which is generating a regional debate (IACrHR, 2023). The Colombian Court's analysis sets an important precedent that the IACrHR must consider when evaluating the intersection of the vulnerability of migrants and women care workers and how this relates to international rules. The case's outcome will have far-reaching implications for the promotion and protection of the rights of vulnerable communities across the region.

5 Concluding Remarks

Our research aims to provide a legal analysis of the measures taken by the Colombian Government during the COVID-19 pandemic and to explore the disproportionate impact of the pandemic on women. Specifically, we examine how these decisions have disproportionately affected impoverished Venezuelan migrants, particularly women. To do this, we first present an overview of the current migratory profile in Colombia, highlighting the large number of Venezuelan nationals who have arrived in this country. We also discuss the legal norms that the Colombian authorities invoked to manage the pandemic, as well as some of the decisions and their consequences, especially for migrants and refugees. Our focus is primarily on the Solidarity Income Program (SIP), which was intended to support the most vulnerable populations in Colombia. However, we show that despite being open to foreign populations in Colombia, this social program required a regularized status, which excluded the majority of Venezuelans, who are among those most affected by the pandemic.

We carried out an analysis of the available data on Venezuelan women in Colombia, which revealed that they are underrepresented in formal employment and face challenges in accessing social programs provided by the State to alleviate their situation. Additionally, migrant women are burdened with a significant amount of unpaid caregiving work, which is further compounded by the previously mentioned barriers. To provide an illustrative example, we highlighted a case that was presented before the Colombian Constitutional Court, which involves the exclusion of caregiving women, including migrants, from the Solidarity Income Program. Our analysis of the case demonstrated the implications of these issues and the need for public policies to recognize and address the vulnerabilities faced by migrant women and caregivers. We hope this contribution will enhance gender, migration, and socioeconomic inclusion policies. We urge approaches to care policy that consider the specific vulnerabilities experienced by migrant women.

References

Acosta, L. J. (2020, November 1). Despite closed border and pandemic, desperate Venezuelans return to Colombia. *Reuters*. Available at: https://www.reuters.com/article/us-venezuela-migration-colombia-idCAKBN27H1FB.

Bitar, S. (2022). *Policy Documents Series. Elements to understand the challenges of migration UNDP LAC PDS N°. 34 Migration in Colombia and Public Policy Responses.*

Available at: https://www.undp.org/sites/g/files/zskgke326/files/2022-11/PNUDLAC-working-paper-34-Colombia-EN.pdf.

Bogota Mayor's Office. (2020, March 19). *Decreto de Simulacro Vital que aplicará en Bogotá de viernes a lunes | Bogota.gov.co*. Bogota.gov.co. Available at: https://bogota.gov.co/mi-ciudad/salud/coronavirus/decreto-de-simulacro-vital-que-aplicara-en-bogota-de-viernes-lunes.

Border Criminologies Blog, Law Faculty, Oxford University. (2020, November 23). *El debido proceso legal: Un vacío de protección que experimentan los migrantes en Colombia | Oxford Law Blogs*. Available at: Blogs.law.ox.ac.uk. https://blogs.law.ox.ac.uk/research-subject-groups/centre-criminology/centreborder-criminologies/blog/2020/11/el-debido-proceso.

Boyaca Governor's Office. (2020, March 20). *Gobernador de Boyacá anuncia simulacro preventivo a partir de las 12:00 m. del viernes 20 de marzo – Secretaría de Educación*. Sedboyaca.gov.co. Available at: http://sedboyaca.gov.co/2020/03/20/gobernador-de-boyaca-anuncia-simulacro-preventivo-a-partir-de-las-1200-m-del-viernes-20-de-marzo/.

Castro, F. (2020, May 21). *¿Qué deben hacer los venezolanos que son beneficiarios de Ingreso Solidario?* Semana.com Últimas Noticias de Colombia Y El Mundo. Available at: https://www.semana.com/opinion/articulo/que-deben-hacer-los-venezolanos-que-son-beneficiarios-de-ingreso-solidario/673021/.

Centro de Derechos Humanos de la Universidad Católica Andrés Bello (CDH-UCAB). (2020). *Violaciones a los derechos de los retornados a Venezuela durante la pandemia de COVID-19*. Available at: http://w2.ucab.edu.ve/tl_files/CDH/Lineastematicas/El%20espejismo%20del%20retorno%20FIN.pdf.

Chaves-Gonzalez, D., Amaral, J., & Mora, M. (2021). *Socioeconomic Integration of Venezuelan Migrants and Refugees*. Available at: https://www.iom.int/sites/g/files/tmzbdl486/files/press_release/file/mpi-iom_socioeconomic-integration-venezuelans_2021_final.pdf.

Corte Constitucional [Colombian Constitutional Court] (2023, May 16). *Sentencia T-159 de 2023*. Magistrado Ponente: Jose Fernando Reyes Cuartas. Available at: https://www.corteconstitucional.gov.co/relatoria/2023/T-159-23.htm.

Dejusticia. (2020, October 22). *El Programa Ingreso Solidario estaría excluyendo a mujeres en condiciones críticas de pobreza*. Available at: https://www.dejusticia.org/el-programa-ingreso-solidario-estaria-excluyendo-a-mujeres-en-condiciones-criticas-de-pobreza/.

Departamento Administrativo Nacional de Estadistica [National Statistics Administrative Department] (2020). *Principales indicadores del mercado laboral Diciembre 2020*. Boletin Tecnico Gran Encuesta Integrada de Hogares [Great Integrated Household Survey]. Available at: https://www.dane.gov.co/files/investigaciones/boletines/ech/ech/bol_empleo_dic_20.pdf.

Departamento Administrativo Nacional de Estadistica [National Statistics Administrative Department] (January 31, 2024) *Mercado Laboral. Gran Encuesta Integrada de Hogares* [Great Integrated Household Survey]. Available at: https://www.dane.gov.co/index.php/estadisticas-por-tema/mercado-laboral/empleo-y-desempleo/geih-historicos.

Departamento Nacional de Planeacion [National Planning Department] (2021). Mercado laboral en la crisis del COVID-19. Resumen de politicas según la iniciativa Respuestas Efectivas contra el COVID-19 (RECOVR). Available at: https://colaboracion.dnp.gov.co/CDT/Sinergia/Documentos/Notas_politica_publica_EMPLEO_09_04_21_v4.pdf.

Departamento Nacional de Planeacion [National Planning Department] (2024). Observatorio Nacional de Migracion [National Migration Observatory]. Tablero de control sobre afiliaciones al SISBEN. Available at: https://2022.dnp.gov.co/DNPN/observatorio-de migracion/Paginas/Sisb%C3%A9n.aspx.

ECLAC (2021). Pandemic Prompts Rise in Poverty to Levels Unprecedented in Recent Decades and Sharply Affects Inequality and Employment. Available at: https://www.cepal.org/en/pressreleases/pandemic-prompts-rise-poverty-levels-unprecedented-recent-decades-and-sharply-affects.

Gallego, J., Hoffmann, B., Ibarran, P., Medina, M.P., Pecha, C., Romero, O., Stampini, M., Vargas, D., Vera-Cossio, D.A. (2021) *Impactos del programa Ingreso Solidario frente a la crisis del COVID-19 en Colombia*. http://dx.doi.org/10.18235/0003261.

Inter-American Commission on Human Rights (IACHR). (2020). *Pandemic and Human Rights in the Americas*. Available at: https://www.oas.org/en/iachr/decisions/pdf/Resolution-1-20-en.pdf.

Inter-American Court of Human Rights (2023). *Request for an Advisory Opinion to the Inter-American Court of Human Rights "The content and scope of care as a human right, and its interrelationship with other rights"*. Available at: https://www.corteidh.or.cr/docs/opiniones/soc_2_2023_en.pdf.

Inter-American Development Bank (2020). *Politicas sociales en respuesta al Coronavirus. La migración en América Latina y el Caribe ante el impacto del Coronavirus.* Available at: https://publications.iadb.org/publications/spanish/viewer/La-migracion-en-America-Latina-y-el-Caribe-ante-el-impacto-del-Coronavirus.pdf.

International Labour Organization. (2021). *Promoting Decent Work in Refugee and Mixed Migration Contexts A South-South Triangular Cooperation (SSTC) Initiative Between Turkey and Colombia*. Available at: https://www.ilo.org/wcmsp5/groups/public/---europe/---ro-geneva/---ilo-ankara/documents/publication/wcms_828647.pdf#page29.

International Organization for Migration. (2023). *Migration trends in the Americas*. Available at: https://rosanjose.iom.int/sites/g/files/tmzbdl1446/files/documents/2023-12/trends-september.pdf.

La Opinión. (2020, April 24). *No pueden presionar a migrantes a abandonar las ciudades: Defensor del Pueblo*. Noticias de Norte de Santander, Colombia Y El Mundo. Available at: https://www.laopinion.com.co/frontera/no-pueden-presionar-migrantes-abandonar-las-ciudades-defensor-del-pueblo#OP.

Mendieta Gonzalez, D., & Tobon-Tobon, M. L. (2020). La pequeña dictadura de la COVID-19 en Colombia: uso y abuso de normas ordinarias y excepcionales para enfrentar la pandemia. *Opinión Jurídica, 19*(40), 243–258. https://doi.org/10.22395/ojum.v19n40a12.

Migracion Colombia (2019). *Venezolanos en Colombia Corte a 31 de octubre de 2019. Radiografía Venezuela*. Available at: https://unidad-administrativa-especial-migracion-colombia.micolombiadigital.gov.co/sites/unidad-administrativa-especial-migracion-colombia/content/files/000041/2039_venezolanos-en-colombia_31-oct.pdf.

Migracion Colombia (2020). *Distribucion de venezolanos en Colombia*. 31 de octubre de 2020. Available at: https://unidad-administrativa-especial-migracion-colombia.micolombiadigital.gov.co/sites/unidad-administrativa-especial-migracion-colombia/content/files/000042/2059_distribucion_venezolanos-en-colombia_oct.pdf.

Migracion Colombia. (2020, March 13). *Cierre de frontera con Venezuela y restricción de entrada al país para extranjeros provenientes de Europa y Asia, nuevas medidas para contener el coronavirus*. Bit.ly. Available at: https://bit.ly/3kWhsqi.

Migracion Colombia. (2023). *Distribución de venezolanas y venezolanos en Colombia*. Available at: https://unidad-administrativa-especial-migracion-colombia.micolombiadigital.gov.co/sites/unidad-administrativa-especial-migracion-colombia/content/files/000112/5575_distribucion_venezolanos_2022_octubrepdf.pdf.

Ministerio de Educacion Nacional [Ministry of Education]. (2020, March 16). *Circular 020 de 16 de marzo de 2020*. Available at: https://www.mineducacion.gov.co/1780/articles-394018_recurso_1.pdf.

Ministry of Health and Social Protection. (2020, March 16). *Por COVID-19, se limitan eventos masivos a 50 personas*. Minsalud.gov.co. Available at: https://www.minsalud.gov.co/Paginas/Por-COVID-19-se-limitan-eventos-masivos-a-50-personas.aspx.

Ministry of Health and Social Protection. (2022). *Resolution 666, April 28th, 2022, "Por la cual se prorroga la emergencia sanitaria por el coronavirus COVID-19, declarada mediante Resolución 385 de 2020, prorrogada por las Resoluciones 844, 1462, 2230 de 2020, 222, 738, 1315, 1913 de 2021 y 304 de 2022"*. Available at: https://www.minsalud.gov.co/Normatividad_Nuevo/Resoluci%C3%B3n%20No.%20666%20de%202022.pdf.

Ministry of Internal Affairs (2020, March 13). Decreto 402 de 2020 *"por el cual se adoptan medidas para la conservacion del orden publico"* Available at: https://www.suin-juriscol.gov.co/viewDocument.asp?ruta=Decretos/30038935#:~:text=DECRETA%3A,30%20de%20mayo%20de%202020.

Mixed Migration Centre. (2020, November). *Urban Mixed Migration Bogota Case Study*. Unhcr.org. Available at: https://data.unhcr.org/en/documents/download/83819.

Moreno Velasquez, C. (2022, March 21). Refugio y desplazamiento interno: entrecruzamientos de las migraciones en Colombia. *Researching Internal Displacement*. Available at: http://bit.ly/3xODSjd.

Moreno Velasquez, C. (2023). El debido proceso en el marco de los procedimientos sancionatorios migratorios: la fragilidad de un derecho. In C. Moreno Velásquez & G. Pelacani (Eds.), *Perspectivas sociojurídicas de la migración: aprendizajes a partir de la experiencia venezolana*. (pp. 31–56). Facultad de Derecho, Ediciones Uniandes.

Moreno, C., & Pelacani, G. (2023). Refugee System in Colombia: The Silent and Prolonged Throes of an Outdated System. In A. Vila-Freyer & I. Sirkeci (Eds.), *Global Atlas of Refugees and Asylum Seekers*. Transnational Press London.

Moreno, C., & Pelacani, G. (2021). *Comunidad Venezuela. Una Agenda de Investigación y Acción Local* (A. Fajardo & A. Vargas, Eds.). Available at: https://cods.uniandes.edu.co/wp-content/uploads/2021/04/Comunidad-Venezuela.pdf.

Pelacani, G., & Moreno, C. (2023). La respuesta del Estado colombiano frente a la migración proveniente de Venezuela: la regularización migratoria en detrimento del refugio. *Derecho PUCP*, (90), 497–522. https://doi.org/10.18800/derechopucp.202301.014

Presidencial Office. (2020, March 22). *Decreto 457 de 2020 – Gestor Normativo – Función Pública*. Www.funcionpublica.gov.co. Available at: https://www.funcionpublica.gov.co/eva/gestornormativo/norma.php?i=110674.

R4V Platform. (2023, November). *Refugees and Migrants from Venezuela | R4V*. Www.r4v.info. Available at: https://www.r4v.info/en/refugeeandmigrants

Rodriguez, Luis Alberto (2020). Programa Ingreso Solidario. Departamento Nacional de Planeacion. [National Planning Department]. Available at: https://ingresosolidario.dnp.gov.co/documentos/Ingreso_Solidario%20_Plenaria.pdf.

The New Humanitarian. (2020a, April 22). *COVID-19 lockdown means tough choices for Venezuelan migrants in Colombia*. Available at: Www.thenewhumanitarian.org. https://www.thenewhumanitarian.org/feature/2020/04/22/Venezuela-Colombia-migrants-coronavirus.

The New Humanitarian. (2020b, October 15). *COVID-19 stalls legal reforms for Venezuelan migrants*. Www.thenewhumanitarian.org. Available at: https://www.thenewhumanitarian.org/analysis/2020/10/15/Venezuela-Colombia-migrants-legislation-documents.

Tribin-Uribe, A. M., Gómez-Barrera, A. D., & Mojica-Ureña, T. (2022). Desigualdad laboral: Migración y género. In *Quanta – Cuidado y Género*. Available at: https://cuidadoygenero.org/wp-content/uploads/2022/01/Desigualdad-laboral.pdf.

United Nations High Commissioner for Refugees (UNHCR). (2020, December 10). *Forced Back Home by The Pandemic, Venezuelan Grandmother Sees No Choice but to Flee*

Once Again. UNHCR. Available at: https://www.unhcr.org/news/stories/forced-back-home-pandemic-venezuelan-grandmother-sees-no-choice-flee-once-again.

United Nations High Commissioner for Refugees (UNHCR) (2023. *Global Trends Report. Forced Displacement 2022*. Available at: https://www.unhcr.org/global-trends-report-2022.

Valenzuela, M.E., Scuro Somma, L., Vaca-Trigo, I. (2020). *Desigualdad, crisis de los cuidados y migración del trabajo doméstico remunerado en América Latina*. CEPAL y Cooperación Española. Available at: https://www.cepal.org/es/publicaciones/46537-desigualdad-crisis-cuidados-migracion-trabajo-domestico-remunerado-america.

World Health Organization. (2020a). *Naming the coronavirus disease (COVID-19) and the virus that causes it*. Available at: Www.who.int. https://www.who.int/es/emergencies/diseases/novel-coronavirus-2019/technical-guidance/naming-the-coronavirus-disease-(covid-2019)-and-the-virus-that-causes-it.

World Health Organization. (2020b, February 4). *Strategic preparedness and response plan for the novel coronavirus*. Www.who.int. Available at: https://www.who.int/publications/i/item/strategic-preparedness-and-response-plan-for-the-new-coronavirus.

World Health Organization. (2020c, April 27). *Archived: WHO Timeline – COVID-19*. Www.who.int. Available at: https://www.who.int/en/news/item/27-04-2020-who-timeline---covid-19.

CHAPTER 9

Domestic Workers, Pandemic and Social Outbreak in Cali, Colombia

Jeanny Posso and Javier A. Pineda D.

1 Introduction[1]

The health emergency caused by COVID-19 focused society's attention on the tensions between paid work and unpaid domestic work within homes, given the limitations on mobility and the restrictions imposed on various care services. This situation highlighted the importance of care work, showing it to be essential for the well-being of the entire population. Among the care services that were subject to the most restrictions and whose workers were most significantly affected, was domestic work. Workers in this sector were forced to restrict their mobility and the vast majority lost their jobs.

This chapter focuses on the experiences of domestic workers in the city of Cali, Colombia. They experienced not only unemployment but also, a year later, what was called the "social outbreak". This occurred throughout Colombia but was most prominent in this city. Many analysts consider this social and political protest movement to be the longest-lasting in the entire two century-long history of the Republic of Colombia (Medina, 2023). For domestic workers, the difficulties caused by national strike were even worse than those they had faced during the pandemic; they experienced despair, food shortages, unemployment, violence and more.

Thus, based on conversations in different focus groups and interviews with workers, this chapter will show the effects of the health emergency, as well as those of the social outbreak in Cali, on paid domestic work in the city. Along with this, processes of change, modernization, and formalization of domestic work, as well as a continuous long-term reduction of these workers as a percentage of the female workforce, are presented. These processes occur in tandem with a reduction of work times – more work in less time –, lower income

1 This chapter is a product of the research project *Who cares? Rebuilding care in a post pandemic world*, which is financed with resources from the Fondo Nacional de Financiamiento para la Ciencia, la Tecnología y la Innovación Francisco José de Caldas, Minciencias, Colombia.

 | DOI:10.1163/9789004707009_010

and multiple negotiations with different employers, in unequal conditions of power.

In section 2, the context of paid domestic work in Latin America and Colombia will be presented. In the third section, some statistical data on the effects of the pandemic on domestic work will be analyzed. In section 4, analysis of five focus groups and three interviews carried out in Cali between April and August 2023 is carried out, in order to delve deeper into what happened during the COVID 19 health crisis and the social outbreak in the post-pandemic. In the last section we will include some final thoughts.

2 Dynamics of Paid Domestic Care Work

In Latin America, social care policies and programs to support families have attracted growing attention, especially since the Regional Women's Conference of Latin America and the Caribbean held in Quito in 2007 and until the most recent one, held in Buenos Aires in 2022 (Pautassi, 2007; ECLAC, 2022). Despite the advances of recent decades, familism by default is maintained in the region (Barbosa et al., 2023). This type of welfare regime is characterized by placing responsibility for care services on families, with women notably doing unpaid care work (Sátyro and Midaglia 2021; Cepal, 2021).

The two groups of women on whom responsibility for care work mostly falls are, on the one hand, women who are outside the labor market and are exclusively dedicated to unpaid care, who have traditionally been called "housewives,"; and on the other hand, domestic service workers, who undertake paid care work of all kinds (Pineda, 2011). Paid domestic work in Latin America and the Caribbean employs around 15 million people and represents 6.8 percent of total employment (OIT, 2021). In the region, domestic work has historically stood out for its characteristics of servitude and exploitation and has been widely documented since the last century due to its vertiginous growth resulting from processes of rural-urban migration and accelerated urbanization in the mid-twentieth century (León, 1991; Chaney and García Castro, 1993).

The first studies on domestic service workers addressed different issues that reflected the context of globalization and migration at the end of the last century, analyzed global inequalities and the crisis of social reproduction (Benería, 1979; Molyneux, 1979), and also observed the interweaving of multiple and simultaneous oppressions (Chaney and Garcia Castro, 1993) that, in this century, were consolidated through discussions on intersectionality (Viveros, 2016; Acciari, 2021).

The colonial legacies in the region, which have led to processes of marginalization and subordination of ethnic groups and social groups and were articulated in internal and international migration processes, have shaped domestic work in recent decades in the different realities of Latin American countries, based on gender, race and class (Rivera Cusicanqui, 2010; Gil Araujo and González-Fernández, 2014; Casanova, 2019).

In the Colombian context, continuous processes of migration from the countryside to the cities increased in the context of armed conflicts since the mid-20th century and in an anti-peasant and primary exporter development model (Pineda, 2015). This nourished the domestic service labor market, which is composed largely of peasant, indigenous and Afro-Colombian women working on a permanent basis (García López, 2012). Following significant growth from the 1950s to the 1980s, domestic service work began to decrease as a percentage of female employment, and then increased again due to the massive phenomenon of forced displacement at the end of the century (Escobar Cuero, 2022). Several recent studies have analyzed this phenomenon of forced displacement and its effects on domestic service as an employment option for thousands of female victims of the armed conflict in Colombia (Meertens, 1999; Osorio Pérez and Jimenez Torrado, 2018; Escobar Cuero, 2022).

By 1976, the percentage of domestic service workers as a proportion of the employed female population in the main Colombian cities was 25%, that is, one in four employed women worked in domestic service. By 1985, this percentage had reduced to 16% (Forero et al. 1991, p. 63). This significant drop in the proportion of the female labor force engaged in domestic work is not due to an absolute reduction in the number of domestic workers, but rather to the significant increase in female labor participation in other activities, which went from 34% to 41% in the same period. By 1997, the proportion of the female labor force in domestic work had fallen to 8%. However, with the economic crisis at the end of the century, this percentage rose again to the level of the early 1990s (13%) in 2002, then gradually declined to the current figure of 6.7% of the female workforce, representing a total of 656,000 women across the country (DANE, 2023).[2]

Thus, paid care work in domestic service has been, due to its historical conditions of subordination, raciality, precariousness and gender relevance, a job of survival in the face of better alternatives and, therefore, one characterized by great mobility. 97% of this work is performed by women. The processes

2 The figure corresponds to the average domestic employment for the first post-pandemic year, from July 2022 to July 2023.

of modernization, commercialization of care and accelerated growth of the commerce and service sectors have contributed to this significant percentage reduction of the female workforce employed in this sector in recent decades. Nonetheless, despite its relative decline and special regulation efforts directed towards it, the presence of domestic work has been persistent both in its size and in its characteristics of precarious and informal employment, which devalues women's care work in favor of households from middle- and high-income sectors (Pineda, 2019).

One of the main factors that has traditionally characterized domestic work is the relationship of servitude that is presented as part of cultural patterns for reasons of class, race and gender. In this regard, it is worth mentioning the reflection of Pascale Molinier (2011) "in my encounter – as a French woman – with the cultural difference between my country and Colombia." She notes the omnipresence of domestic employees in middle- and upper-class homes in Colombia, which

> is experienced by Colombians as if it were evident and, although no one would say that the relationships between employers and domestic employees are simple and "natural", from an external perspective it would seem that everyone knows how to assume them and get ahead.
>
> p. 229

To understand humiliation or trivialized servitude, which cannot be questioned, Molinier adopts the notion of close domination proposed by Dominique Memmi, which is understood as that which occurs in the home, in privacy, redefining the division between the public and the private, and rescuing the dimension that the personal is political. Although the author focuses on the case of French feminist employers, she shows, from the psychodynamics of work, key notions to understand the suffering, affectivity and complexity of the relationships between domestic care workers and their employers.

For their part, studies on internal forced displacement in the context of the armed conflict, which began to be produced in the mid-nineties, documented both the feminization of displacement – a high percentage of women – as well as the re-establishment of employment in places of arrival through domestic service jobs (UNHCR–CODHES, 2001; Meertens, 1999). Without a doubt, the massive, forced displacement in the Colombian countryside that, in recent decades, affected millions of inhabitants, nourished the female labor supply for domestic service. Although this effect is only observed in the statistics in the period of the economic crisis at the end of the 20th century and until 2002, this situation has affected the composition of domestic service, to the extent that qualitative work to date shows that domestic service is an occupation available to victims of internal displacement (Osorio Pérez and Jimenez Torrado, 2018; Esguerra et al., 2018).

In this regard, Jeanny Posso (2008a) analyzes in detail the domestic service work of black immigrant women from the Colombian Pacific Coast in the labor market of the city of Cali. This study, in addition to recognizing that domestic service is perhaps the most representative employment for Afro-Colombian migrant women, investigates how the different types of social inequality marked by gender, class and race discrimination operate in the work context of Western Colombia.

In the Colombian context, the progressive commercialization of many services previously performed at home (health care, restaurants, kindergartens, beauty salons, etc.), sociodemographic factors (urbanization, reduction in the size of families and homes, etc.) and cultural changes (delegitimization of privileges, dismantling of hetero-patriarchy, etc.), have led servitude to be questioned and made domestic service less necessary, going from 25% to 6% of the female workforce in the last half-century. This has led to the forms of domestic work being transformed, with a significant decrease in internal work – with residence in the workplace -, an increase in work per day and relationships with different employers, claiming of rights and creation of organizations, and emerging use of digital platforms that formalize labor relationships (Posso, Castiblanco and Pineda, 2024).

3 Pandemic and Domestic Work

In the second quarter of 2020, during the COVID-19 pandemic confinement, 42% of domestic workers in Colombia lost their jobs.[3] Subsequently, a slow recovery began, with fluctuations depending on health restrictions and during the post-confinement period; only at the end of 2022 were 2019 levels recovered. This year, before the pandemic, paid domestic care work represented 3.05 % of the country's total employment and 7.05% of female employment. In the post-pandemic,[4] from July 2022 to June 2023, the proportion of domestic work in the total number of employed people fell slightly to 2.93% and to 6.76% of female workers. This means that the number of domestic workers

3 Estimation based on data from the Great Dane Integrated Household Survey, national total, monthly series. https://www.dane.gov.co/index.php/estadisticas-por-tema/mercado-laboral/empleo-y-desempleo.

4 The end of the health emergency is declared in Colombia on June 30, 2022.

is maintained in absolute terms (656,000), but the decreasing trend of lower participation in the female labor force continues.

It can be observed that the COVID-19 pandemic generated a sharp drop in the employment of domestic workers, with a loss of 300,000 jobs, only half of which were recovered during the reactivation of the first year. This meant that, for nearly two years, those who were left without work entered mostly unpaid care work outside the labor market, and a smaller proportion entered informal work in commerce (Pineda and Castiblanco-Moreno, 2024). This led to a significant loss of economic autonomy for many women and a fall into poverty for their households.

These changes in the labor market have also led to changes in the socio-economic characteristics of domestic workers. The most significant of these is the increase in educational levels. The pandemic crisis generated a marginal replacement percentage in female workers, as women with better educational levels entered this sector, caused by the crisis in job opportunities. However, this trend was also caused by two other factors: the increase in work per day, with greater work intensity, but higher remuneration, and the increase in work through digital platforms.

The increase in the average years of education of domestic workers is historically in line with the general increase in the educational levels of women in the country. Over the last two decades of the 21st century, domestic workers have gone from having an average of around six years of education to around eight years. Although, in 2022, the highest proportion of domestic workers had basic primary education (30.8%) and middle or basic secondary education (15.7%), between 2019 and 2022, the proportion of domestic workers with higher education, especially technical, increased from 8.6%. to 10.8%. Given the difficulties of the labor market, some students or graduates of technical schools enter domestic service due to the lack of other job opportunities.

In an apparently contradictory way, the average age of domestic workers is also increasing, in accordance with the aging rate of the urban population. In the last decade, the percentage of workers over 49 years old went from 20% to 38% and those under 30 years old went from 35% to 20%.[5] Greater education and experience with age are generally associated with higher labor income. However, the pandemic crisis further led to over-qualified. Income also depends on the number of hours worked (given that workers combine paid and unpaid care work in their own homes) and the type of work, especially with the increase employment on a daily basis and the use of digital platforms.

5 Estimated data based on Jiménez Restrepo (2018) and recent data from DANE (2023).

Since domestic work has historically been one of the most devalued jobs, and that many work less than 48 hours a week, in 2022 more than half of domestic workers (58.5%) earned less than the current legal monthly minimum wage (SMMLV) (251 USD) and 26.1% earned the SMMLV. However, between 2019 and 2022, the proportion of women earning the SMMLV increased by about 7 pp (percentage points), while the proportion of women earning less than the SMMLV decreased by almost the same amount (Pineda and Castiblanco-Moreno, 2024). As a result of the aging process, the replacement rate meant that the youngest domestic workers in daily work or through platforms achieved better income, while those who left the market during the crisis had the worst working conditions.

As has been widely documented, the working conditions of domestic workers have also been characterized by their informality. Only one in five had a written contract in 2022. But what is most worrying is affiliation to the social security pension system, which has traditionally been low. At the beginning of this century, only one in ten working women contributed to pensions. By 2008 this percentage reached 12%, by 2016 18%, and from 2016 to 2022 increased to 28%.[6] This is largely because of the formalization of domestic work by digital platforms.

Although the emergence of digital platforms and Uberization processes have caused a loss of social protection for workers, as widely shown in the literature on passenger transport platforms, homes and crowdsourcing, (O'Farrell & Montagnier, 2019), in the case of domestic work, the effects seem to be less clear (Pereyra, Poblete and Tizziani, 2023; Rani et al., 2022). Digital platforms can offer many services and their business models for domestic work vary significantly. In the Colombian context, the main digital platforms have contributed to the formalization of domestic workers, facilitating the process of affiliation to social security and encouraging employers to comply with this obligation (Posso, Castiblanco and Pineda, 2024).

4 Cali as a Labor Market for Black and Indigenous Domestic Workers

Since the middle of the last century, Cali and its metropolitan area have been the receiving focus of migrations from southwestern Colombia. As has happened with other large urban centers in the country, migrations have

6 This is also influenced by the approval of ILO Convention 189, ratified by Colombia in May 2014, as well as the new organizations of domestic workers and the support of civil society groups for their rights.

been linked to regional socioeconomic inequalities and, of course, with the country's internal armed conflict in recent decades, as has been mentioned before. Due to its proximity to territories inhabited by indigenous and Afro-descendant populations, these ethnic groups make up a significant part of the population that has immigrated to Cali (Urrea and Barbary, 2004). As is the case in other capitals of the Andean zone, although the majority population has always been white and mestizo, as Urrea (2021) points out, the presence of black and indigenous people in the city dates back to the colonial and republican era, and this population has been further increased by the migrations of the 20th and 21st centuries.

Due to the characteristics of these migratory processes towards the city, racialized women have had an important representation in these migratory flows and their labor income has come mainly from informal jobs such as domestic service. Thus, in the 20th and 21st centuries, as Fernando Urrea (2021) explains:

> The city has had a labor market for black and indigenous domestic workers, partly a result of the colonial heritage of slavery and indigenous servitude that has survived the processes of modernization and the emergence of the middle and upper classes.
>
> p. 168

Research that documents the migratory processes of women from rural environments to Cali shows how, in the cohorts of 30 and 40 years ago there were many indigenous, Afro-descendant and peasant girls and adolescents who came to work as boarders, pushed by conditions of poverty, lack of educational and work opportunities, and situations of gender violence (Arias, 2015; Urrea and Posso, 2015). In the first decades of the 21st century, entire families displaced by violence arrived in the city, including women heads of households in charge of children and grandchildren. In 2005, when the question regarding ethnic belonging was refined in the National Census, Cali was one of the large cities in the country with "the largest participation of black, indigenous women, in addition to white-mestizo women, as live-in domestic employees" (Urrea, 2021: 168). In a December 2022 survey, it was estimated that 46% of the city's domestic workers were black/Afro-descendant and 14% were indigenous (Bermúdez, Posso and Melo, 2022).

5 The Characteristics of the Women Participating in the Focus Groups[7]

A total of five focus groups were carried out, as well as three in-depth interviews with women who participated in the focus groups. Two of the focus groups were carried out in two areas of the city where the workers live,[8] another two focus groups were carried out with organizations of domestic workers[9] and the other was with a group of workers from a digital platform that offers cleaning services for homes and offices.[10] In total, 47 women between 23 and 78 years old who work or have worked as domestic workers participated, 92% of whom live in strata 1 and 2.[11] 39% of the women are black or Afro-Colombian, 15% indigenous and the remaining 46% are white/mixed race. Regarding their educational levels, of the 45 women who provided this information, one had no training, 19 had some level of primary school, 3 reached basic secondary school (9th grade), 15 completed secondary education, 6 had received technical training and one had completed university studies. With the exception of the 8 workers from the digital platform who had a formal connection to the company, only 6 other women participating in the focus groups had a written employment contract and received their labor benefits.

6 What Consequences Did the Pandemic Have on the Lives of Domestic Workers?

As already noted, when the confinements began, a significant percentage of female workers lost their jobs. In the focus groups, only one worker in each group had continued working, but in order to keep their jobs, several of them had to stay working as live-in staff. This was something that they had either

7 The focus groups were carried out within the framework of the project Who Cares, Rebuilding Care in a Post-Pandemic World, in collaboration with researchers Louisa Acciari, University College London (UCL), Sabah Boufkhed, University of Manchester y Suelen Castiblanco, Universidad de la Salle.

8 In Siloé 8 participants and in Alto Nápoles 8 participants.

9 A first group of 12 women with the *Sindicato de Trabajadoras Domésticas* (Sintrasedom) and a second group of 11 women with members of the *Unión de Trabajadoras del Hogar* (Utrahogar) and the Néctar Foundation.

10 8 workers from the Hogarú platform participated.

11 Socioeconomic stratification in Colombia is a classification of homes for differential charging of home public services, allowing subsidies to be assigned. There are six strata, 1 and 2 are the lower strata.

never previously accepted, or had not accepted for years, in which case it represented a kind of setback. It was possible to identify that the women who accepted these conditions were coerced by difficult personal situations such as the illness of a close relative, having dependent children and, in general, not having other income or support from family. This can be observed in the contrast from the following two testimonies from workers who, prior to the pandemic, worked daily:

> I needed the job because I had my mother in the Social Security clinic with cirrhosis and I had to contribute, so she had to stay.
>
> Participant 17, Utrahogar, 55 years old, white-mixed race

> In other words, the condition was either you stay in and forget about your family, because you are not going out to bring us diseases, or you go home, and if they make me choose between staying in a stranger's house all the time, even if I was going to earn my salary, and leave my family stranded, well I decided to go to my family, to where my family is, although I knew that I was going to have trouble because without working, I was going to have difficulties.
>
> Sintrasedom Participant

Confinement under these conditions was a difficult experience and, in the case in which the worker could not go home regularly, it was so traumatic that she required subsequent psychological treatment.

> She paid me the nurse to stay with my mother at night at the insurance clinic, a nurse charged ninety thousand pesos, they preferred to pay that so that I wouldn't go out … Then one day I said, no more. When they caught me crying when the food arrived from Club Colombia, I told them, I don't want food, what I want is freedom, I want to go home, I want to get out, I've been locked up here for three months, now four months, I want to leave, I want to go. Ah well, then go out and you know (what'll happen)!
>
> Participant 17, Utrahogar, 55 years old, white-mixed race

Of the workers who could not continue going to their workplaces, the situations were diverse, but the majority lost their jobs and did not receive any help from their employers. Exceptionally, a few retained their employment and continued to receive their salary; some of those who had a longer employment relationship received partial payments or specific aid in money or in kind. It was mainly these workers who were able to resume their jobs as the movement of people became normal. However, several refused to return to their old jobs because they felt mistreated during the pandemic.

In general, domestic workers during the confinement periods had to draw on the solidarity of their families, neighbors, friends, popular organizations, associations, charities, unions and organizations of domestic workers, and, in some cases, the specific aid provided. by the government at different levels (national and local).

> People who had never been close to us, we became closer and ate from the same plate, we passed food to each other.
>
> Participant 6, Siloé, 40 years old, Misak indigenous

> From Utrahogar, thank God, from the council we also received aid, that was an incentive for us because everything was running out and we had no means, thank God the group was very attentive and the Casa del Chontaduro as well with some groceries that were very good and to this day, I am grateful to them.
>
> Participant 20, Utrahogar, 60 years old, white-mixed race

The last testimony is useful as it illustrates one of the "repertoires of care-resistance" identified by Acciari (2023) that was put into practice by domestic worker organizations in Latin America during the health crisis; the distribution of humanitarian aid among their members. The promotion of self-care and well-being of the members of the two organizations included in this analysis (Sintrasedom and Utrahogar) involved helping them learn about virtual communication tools. According to Acciari (2023), these actions allow domestic workers to be seen not just as a vulnerable group, but as proactive actors in maintaining their well-being and defending the right to care and to be cared for in times of crisis.

However, the aid provided for the most vulnerable was not enough. This was apparent in many cities in the country where the use of a red cloth to indicate that the fundamental needs were not being covered in that home was widespread, as happened to this worker who did not receive any help from her employer during the first confinement:

> So, I spent all my time at home, there with what I could, maybe my son sent me money and that was it, it went by, but it was very tormenting, because if you don't have a salary, then sometimes it was all day with coffee and bread and things like that.
>
> Participant 18, Utrahogar, 63 years old, white-mixed race

The return to work was not easy due to fear of contagion, difficulties in transportation and intermittent calls for confinement during the peaks of the pandemic. Work had accumulated in the houses where they came to work again and employers also began to adopt health protocols, additional cleaning protocols to those they were already accustomed to, in some cases exaggerated by the anxiety generated by the health emergency. Multiple procedures were added for the domestic worker and for the jobs to be performed. For the worker, the mandatory shower upon arrival and a complete change of clothes and, of course, the use of facemasks and gloves were common. For the work itself, the meticulous cleaning of all spaces was required, with the number cleaning implements used multiplying.

> After the pandemic the work increased because before you washed the bathroom as usual, in the pandemic you had to put alcohol on everything, you had to wear a mask, you had to have a mop for the room, a mop for the entrance to the living room, a mop for the bathroom and everything had to be impeccable.
>
> Participant 10, Alto Nápoles, 29 years old, white-mixed race

For the workers, it meant a longer working day, a greater mental workload, and a reduction in time for their families and themselves, as this participant commented when the topic of health effects was mentioned:

> It affected me a lot, because you imagine more work and say, My God, what time am I going to finish? I arrived at six, six thirty in the morning and it stressed me out to know it was past midday and I wasn't done, because there was more disinfection in the rooms, practically all day I had to be in the apartment, so I had the anxiety that I got up early to be able to leave early but no, I still left at the same time.
>
> Participant 14, Alto Nápoles, 26 years old, white-mixed race

However, the value of the daily wage did not increase; on the contrary, several women report that they had to work with lower remuneration than the period prior to the health emergency or include additional tasks or time without the corresponding monetary recognition, while the prices of the basic basket of food and transportation were on the rise.

> In my lifetime, I had never seen a tuna can worth twenty thousand pesos.[12] Let's remember all the prices from that time, from the time of the pandemic, that potatoes were expensive, that food implements went up.
>
> Participant 6, Siloé, 40 years old, Misak indigenous

The situations described above confirm research carried out on the effects of the pandemic on domestic workers in Latin America regarding loss of employment and/or reduction in income, and the dramatic consequences on the health and well-being of those who continued working, their overexploitation in time and volume of work, and their forced quarantines in their workplaces, among others (Acciari, 2023).

7 The National Strike Was Worse

In 2021, during the second year of the pandemic, Colombia experienced a popular uprising that lasted around four months after the call for a national strike on April 28 which has been commonly called "the social outbreak." From a historical perspective "it has been the longest-lasting social and political protest movement in the republican history of Colombia" (Medina, 2023, p. 49). It was characterized by the diversity of protest scenarios, its long duration and diverse social composition in which the youth population was prominent and the broader sectors to which was linked. According to social movement scholars, "it has been the protest with the greatest territorial coverage in the history of the country since the Bogotazo of 1948" (Archila and García, 2023, p. 83), it can be considered as a single protest of national character that, according to police reports, covered 860 municipalities (Ibid.), representing 77% of the 1,123 municipalities in the country. On the other hand, the delay and postponement of the negotiation with the representatives of the strike by the national government was widely reported by international organizations, such as the Office of the United Nations High Commissioner for Human Rights,[13] as well as in the international press. Moreover, there were reports of the denunciation of the

12 It refers to a can of tuna, which according to the value of the dollar in 2022 was equivalent to 4.7 dollars.

13 Colombia must urgently reform protest management to prevent further human rights violations – United Nations Report, Press release published December 15, 2021. https://www.ohchr.org/es/press-releases/2022/01/colombia-must-urgently-reform-how-it-polices-protests-avoid-further-human.

violation of human rights during the protests by the public forces, "including brutal attacks not only against the protesters but also against the population in the vicinity of the protest" (Ortiz, 2021. P. 43). It is worth reflecting on this recent episode in the country's history because Cali was the most affected city and became the epicenter of the social outbreak.

The 2021 national strike is considered a response to the government's failure to meet the demands of the less favored populations, which had as a precedent social protest led by different actors since 2017 and a national strike that occurred in 2019 (Gaviria, 2023). Added to this was the exacerbation of precariousness caused by the health emergency, with little aid to alleviate the economic paralysis, and the regressive economic policies proposed by the government of that time (Ortiz, 2021; Urrea, 2021). In Cali the youth revolt "from the first day went from mobilization to the creation of resistance points and barricades" (Castillo-Valencia et al., 2023. P. 8). In the city, a total of fourteen resistance points were established at different vital crossroads, mostly close to the neighborhoods of the popular sectors where the protesters lived. Attributing the popular mobilizations in Cali to external criminal actors, was, as Urrea (2021) points out, implausible, and they had more to do with fact that in no other major city has poverty increased so much. According to Ortiz (2021), from 2019 to 2020, Cali's monetary poverty increased from 21.4% to 36.6%, and according to DANE, in the quarter from November 2020 to January 2021, only 76% of households had three meals a day, that is, one in four homes was suffering from hunger. Moreover, youth unemployment in 2021 had reached 25.8%, with that of young women being 31.9% (Ortiz, 2021, p. 43–44).

To understand the experience of domestic workers, the object of our analysis, who were among the most vulnerable sectors of the population, it should be noted that, in addition to the barricades that prevented circulation within the city, there were protests and barricades in most of the municipalities of the Valle department and southwestern Colombia, especially those that were located along the main roads. This meant that communications were interrupted on the main entrance roads to the city. Towards the end of May, food shortages were already noticeable, as well as the interruption in the supply of gasoline. According to a bulletin from the Government of Valle, between April 3 and May 26, the entry of food into the city of Cali was reduced by 42.3%, with the food groups most affected being fish, -84.5% and cereals and grains, -73.7%. Supplies of other important food groups such as meat, eggs and dairy products were reduced by 51.0% and 50.7% respectively (Torres, 2021, p. 7). On the other hand, according to a report from a survey carried out in May 2021 among companies registered in the chambers of commerce of Valle del Cauca and Cauca, 26.9% were not operating at that time, 63.3% were working at 39.2% of their installed capacity and only 9.8% was operating at full capacity. 69.9% of companies reported difficulties in supplying raw materials or inputs (Cámara de Comercio de Cali, 2021). Thus, inflation, which as a result of the fall in consumption was at 1.61% in 2020, the lowest in the country's history, in 2021 shot up to 5.62%, as described by this worker:

> I think that the National Strike has been harder than even the pandemic itself at that time, because since the national strike the economy changed a lot, everything has changed for us, because let's say inflation began to rise, what was done before is no longer possible. If before you ate an egg, now you have to think about how many eggs a week, whether you eat it or not.
>
> Alto Nápoles Participant

The women in the different focus groups agreed with the previous participant that the national strike was a situation even worse than what they had experienced up to that point with the pandemic and confinements. The narration of some of the women reflects the desperation, sensation of cornered that they found themselves faced with. Again, many were without work, had exhausted all their savings in 2020 and faced the pressure of accumulated debts, and were without support because much aid from organizations and the government had already been exhausted.

> We came out of the pandemic, and we became unemployed and what we did not have in the pandemic got worse with unemployment because there was no money, we could not work because we could not go out either, everything was very expensive, we could not go out to work, we all stayed ... because we couldn't pass.
>
> Sintrasedom Participant

For those who still had their jobs, long walks awaited them to their workplaces due to the interruption of the roads by the demonstrations and barricades, having to cross several of these points where some felt afraid, since the confrontations with the police force occurred daily and the protesters only allowed passage to health personnel or those transporting food. In the most remote places of the city, informal transport such as jeeps, motorcycles and pirate taxis[14] continued to provide their services, but as the strike progressed,

14 They are private vehicles that offer public transportation services without authorization.

prices increased both due to the risk that the owners of the vehicles ran and due to the shortage of vehicle fuel.

> At least I worked in Valle de Lili and a pirate taxi charged me $15,000 to take me there, he told me, I'm taking the risk of taking four people, so I'm going to charge you $15,000 per person, so, he made good cash, … and there I was left stranded and I had to beg another pirate taxi to come back, because, of course, there were barricades in the middle of the journey, so they took risks because some young people were protesting and others were about to do harm, just for the sake of fighting with the authorities and throwing stones, everything was seen there, it could not be said that all those who were protesting were vandals, there were people who were tired of being oppressed, the poor man is already tired of there being no opportunities.
>
> Sintrasedom Participant

8 Working Conditions and Rights of Workers after the Pandemic

The ending of confinements and the gradual normalization of daily life in Cali after the social outbreak led to a slower recovery of economic activity and income compared to other regions of the country. This was reflected for domestic workers in a reduction in the demand for work; working in different homes on a weekly or biweekly basis became much more common as a way to top up income.

> Now the job instability is more noticeable, they no longer call us like before, before they called you two days a week, now it is once every 15 days, at most once every 8 days.
>
> Participant 9, Alto Nápoles, 41 years old, black-Afro-Colombian

According to a survey on care work carried out in Cali in December 2022, representative of the entire city, 70% of paid domestic workers worked between 1 and 15 days a month, 13% between 16 and 20 days a month and only 17% worked between 21 and 30 days a month (Bermúdez, Posso and Melo, 2022). That is, less than 20% had full-time work. The reduction in the number of days of work translated into an intensification of it, as illustrated in the following example in which the worker returns to her old job, but is hired to do in two days everything that she used to do in a week:

> I mean, I went on Monday, and I had to leave food ready for them until Wednesday, clean the house, put the clothes in the washing machine, iron some shirts … and I got stressed because it becomes too much to complete all the requests. So I didn't have a good lunch, and to fulfil it all you run there and run here, you come home with a headache … she cut the time, but I had to clone myself to cover the time that I wasn't going to work, So I told them, I am very sorry, but no more, my arms hurt, because of that I acquired a cervical hernia and it stayed that way.
>
> Participant 18, Utrahogar, 63 years old, white-mixed race

Another similar situation is the following for a full-time worker:

> I work in a family home, I started with three people, now I have like seven in two houses and for the same salary, because she told me that since the son got married then I should go three days to their house and three days to their son's.
>
> Participant 26, Utrahogar, 56 years old, black-Afro-Colombian

It is evident that the consequences of the health emergency and the social crisis have fallen on the most vulnerable sectors of the population, such as domestic workers. Although compliance with labor standards has been gradually increasing, what can generally be perceived is a deepening of the precariousness of working conditions for those who have greater social disadvantages, whether due to age, dependent people in your care, etc., as the following worker acknowledges that some women are not able to negotiate payment for their work:

> I was one of those, "it's not like I pay that much" and put my head down and "well." No, we are the ones who have to value our work, not someone else, and we have to learn to negotiate … Although we must keep in mind that many people, many women, have too much need, because we all have needs, but there are some who have more need than others because they pay rent, they have a mother, for example, who is sick, they have many expenses and live from day to day, they do not have support of any kind, they have a boy or girls studying, so often they have to.
>
> Participant 19, Utrahogar, 55 years old, Nasa indigenous

Although day-to-day domestic work is becoming more and more important, it was possible to perceive in the interviews and focus groups that the regulation of domestic work is more designed for a full-time worker. The calculations and rules for contribution and payment of social benefits are quite confusing for both workers and employers. The latter often mistakenly consider the amount paid on the day as a comprehensive salary in which the payment of all the worker's rights is included. Even more worrying is that no obligation is assumed with this, her work is considered in a certain way as a piecework that can be extended until the next day and that when the employer does not require it, they simply do not pay for it.

> and sometimes they pay you, if you finish, they leave you the money, if you don't finish, they leave it to the next day.
>
> Participant 2, Siloé, 61 years old, white mixed race

> The vast majority want to make a verbal arrangement, so that when he no longer needs her he just tells her, don't come back and that's it, they believe that's how it is.
>
> Sintrasedom Participant

In these conditions, the negotiation of the content of the work and the value of the day becomes a crucial aspect. Decades ago, the worker negotiated her salary and working conditions with a single employer in a verbal contract (Posso, 2008b), now this negotiation is multiplied with several employers in the midst of precariousness, economic vulnerability and the constant rotation at work, considering that in Cali 81% of domestic workers still have verbal contracts (Bermúdez, Posso and Melo, 2022). Time and time again, the domestic worker must negotiate the value of a day that can be arbitrarily lengthened or to which multiple tasks can be added, intensifying the volume, variety of tasks and work stress. Domestic workers struggle to set clear limits on tasks and/or hours, but often, at the last minute, must give in to non-compliance with what was agreed upon for fear of losing payment for the work done or losing the job if there is a fixed weekly agreement. In this bid for the payment of their wages, the employer continues to have the last word in most cases.

The experiences collected here to illustrate the post-pandemic situation of domestic workers in Cali are very similar to the testimonies of Brazilian domestic workers analyzed by Ana Cleaver in that they "reveal a reality in which various types of violence, oppressive practices and overexploitation are recurrent." (Cleaver, 2022, p.112). The analysis carried out on domestic work as a socio-professional category from the perspective of the coloniality of power vis-à-vis the Brazilian State is very useful in understanding the persistent situation of denial of rights of domestic workers in a country like Colombia in which inequal categories of domestic workers operate, such as gender, class and race, and for which reason these workers have been constituted as an internal alterity, which leads to the non-recognition of their civil and political rights (Ibid.: p.118).

The above explains the ineffectiveness of the State in the regulation and supervision of the conditions in which paid domestic work is carried out, which leads to the isolation of workers, allowing their recurrent subordination, super-exploitation and vulnerability, and in general, the constant violation of their rights, as is currently the case with the increasing number of daily domestic employees in the post-pandemic period. It is no coincidence that the women in the focus group belonging to the Hogarú digital platform are the group of workers with the lowest average age of all the groups, at 33.8 years, and that all of them had completed secondary education, two of them with complete technical studies. These workers have a formal connection with the company, receive all its social benefits, have clear rules that delimit the times and tasks to be carried out and, in general, have better working conditions than domestic workers hired directly by households (Posso, Castiblanco & Pineda, 2024). In the remaining focus groups analyzed we found various examples of impoverished middle-aged and elderly women who have not achieved their own assets after several decades of work, some with chronic illnesses or work-related disability situations and as yet without the possibility of receiving a pension in old age and, therefore, forced to continue working paid or unpaid, in the latter case with the loss of their economic autonomy.

9 Final Thoughts

In Latin America, paid domestic work has gradually lost relative importance in female employment as women from middle and upper sectors gained access to education and the labor market. However, this trend was slowed down in Colombia due to the economic crisis at the end of the century and the forced displacement processes that occurred as a result of the internal armed conflict. Other processes such as the commodification of various specific care tasks, modernization processes and the growth of employment in commerce and services continued to reduce the proportion of the female workforce engaged in domestic work. However, in recent decades, the importance of domestic work in absolute values and its characteristics of precariousness and informality have been maintained, with advances in the recognition of rights, but these have been more formal than real.

In Colombia, a country with its origins in a colonial past, like the other countries in the region, paid domestic work was configured to processes of marginalization and subordination of ethnic groups and social groups. Thus, this work, in addition to being characterized by gender, is linked to differences and inequalities of race, class, and other disadvantages such as age, national origin and situations of disability.

The investigation with various groups of workers showed that the majority could not continue working in the first periods of confinement; exceptionally, some continued to receive their salary, despite not being able to effectively carry out their work. However, the vast majority of employers did not continue paying salaries to their workers and in some cases provided them with specific monetary or in-kind aid (mainly food). A few had to go from day-to-day work to working on a live-in basis to maintain their employment and salary. In the face of the unprecedented situation of health and economic emergency, combined with the lack of social protection that most workers experienced, it is mainly the solidarity of family, friends and neighbors along with the help of community organizations, domestic workers, charities and specific measures of the State, which allow survival in this difficult situation.

In the gradual return to work in the midst of the pandemic, workers found a lengthening of the day due to health protocols and transportation difficulties that were generally not reflected in the value paid for their work. Added to the health emergency, Colombia in 2021 experienced a popular uprising for around four months that covered nearly 80% of the national territory. This broad social protest had special consequences in Cali, as one of the large cities in which the health crisis generated the greatest setbacks in social indicators. Due to its spatial and temporal extension, the popular revolt deepened the economic paralysis in the city with immediate effects on employment and the supply of essential goods. The most vulnerable population groups in the city, including domestic workers, were the most affected. Thus, social and economic recovery in the post-pandemic stage in southwestern Colombia has been slower and purchasing power has been reduced for the average population.

The gradual reduction in the importance of domestic work in female employment has continued during the post-pandemic, as well as other transformations in domestic employment in recent decades, such as the reduction in working on a daily basis and the shift to working as live-ins, and a shift from working in the same house during the week to working in different homes. This last type of work, in which the domestic worker goes to different homes during the week, increased in Cali, reflecting a reduction in demand. This reduction in the number of weekly hours of work at home in the post-pandemic is accompanied by an intensification in the content of the work, whereby the worker must perform tasks in fewer hours. The effects of this on work stress and physical consequences due to overwork are already beginning to be noticed.

Such changes in a profession whose hiring is still done verbally in 80% of cases translate into a greater violation of labor rights, especially for the most vulnerable women, that is, those who simultaneously experience several disadvantaged situations such as being racialized, having dependents, being the head of the household, being elderly, having a disability, among others. This becomes more acute for them, especially because labor legislation in Colombia seems to have been designed for full-time domestic workers in a single home. Thus, their battle to preserve the purchasing power of their salary and define tasks and schedules multiplies according to the number of families they work with. As Luz Gabriela Arango and Pascale Molinier (2011) have warned, there is a need not only for the establishment of laws to guarantee the rights and exercise of the profession in decent conditions, but also for these laws to be applicable, because due to their disadvantaged situation, many workers are pushed to receive payments with unacceptable terms, as shown in this chapter. In this sense, we agree with them that "Justice cannot be achieved at the individual level but through collective actions" (Arango and Molinier, 2011: 21).

References

Acciari, L. (2021) Practicing Intersectionality: Brazilian Domestic Workers' Strategies of Building Alliances and Mobilizing Identity. *Latin American Research Review* 56(1): 67–81.

Acciari, L. (2023) Caring is resisting: Lessons from domestic workers' mobilizations during COVID-19 in Latin America. *Gender, Work & Organization* 31(1): 319–336.

ACNUR – CODHES (2001) *Desplazamiento Forzado Interno en Colombia: Conflicto y Desarrollo*, Bogotá, Alto Comisionado para los Refugiados de Naciones Unidas y Consultoría para los Derechos Humanos y el Desplazamiento.

Arango, L.G. y Molinier P. (2011) El cuidado como ética y como trabajo. In: Arango L. and Molinier P. (comps) *El trabajo y la ética del cuidado*. Bogotá: La Carreta Social and Universidad Nacional de Colombia, 15–21.

Archila, M. y García Velandia M. (2023) Novedades y continuidades del estallido social del 28A. In: Celis J. (coord) *Estallido social 2021: Expresiones de vida y resistencias*. Bogotá: Siglo del Hombre Editores, Universidad del Rosario, Fundación Rosa Luxemburgo y Corporación Colectivo La Mariacano, 67–106.

Arias, W. (2015) La constitución de subjetividades femeninas indígenas en la ciudad de Cali. In: F. Urrea y J. Posso (eds) *Feminidades, sexualidades y colores de piel. Mujeres negras, indígenas, blancas mestizas y transgeneristas negras en el suroccidente colombiano*. Cali: Programa Editorial Universidad del Valle, 181–216.

Barbosa, P., Fabris L., Abbas, L., Caruso, G., Giusti V., and Coimbra B. (2023) Moving away from familism by default? The trends of family policies in Latin America. *Third World Quarterly* 44 (8): 1865–1883.

Benería, Lourdes (1979). Reproduction, production and the sexual division of labor. *Cambridge Journal of Economics* 3(3): 203–225.

Bermúdez, R., Posso, J., and Melo, P. (2022) Oferta y demanda de cuidado en los hogares en el distrito Santiago de Cali, diapositivas primera devolución de resultados de la *Encuesta sobre oferta y demanda de cuidados en los hogares de Cali, ENDEMOFERCUIH – 2022*, Alcaldía de Santiago de Cali and Universidad del Valle.

Cámara de Comercio de Cali (2021) Encuesta Ritmo Empresarial, Especial Valle del Cauca y Cauca, Diapositivas. Available (consulted 18 September 2023) at: https://www.ccc.org.co/file/2021/06/ERE-Especial-Valle-del-Cauca-y-Cauca-mayo-2021-VF2-1.pdf.

Casanova, E. (2019). *Dust and Dignity: Domestic Employment in Contemporary Ecuador.* First edition, Itaca and London: Cornell University Press.

Castillo-Valencia, M., Jiménez, D. M., Valdés, D. P., and Salazar, B. (2023) *Mujeres al oriente de Cali: Desigualdades al descubierto.* Bogotá: Editorial Universidad del Rosario.

Cepal (2021) *Hacia la sociedad del cuidado: los aportes de la Agenda Regional de Género en el marco del desarrollo sostenible* (LC/MDM.61/3). Santiago: Comisión Económica para América Latina y el Caribe.

Chaney, E. and García Castro, M. (eds) (1993) *Muchacha/cachifa/criada/empleada/empregadinha/sirvienta y… más nada: trabajadoras del hogar en América Latina y el Caribe.* Caracas: Editorial Nueva Sociedad.

Cleaver, A. (2022) Colonialidade do poder e precariedade Governamental: uma reflexão sobre o Estado brasileiro à luz do trabalho doméstico remunerado. In *Revista Cadernos de Campo* 32: 109–136.

DANE (2023) *Boletín técnico.* Departamento Administrativo Nacional de Estadística. Boletín del 31 de mayo. Available (consulted 25 August 2023) at: https://www.dane.gov.co/files/operaciones/GEIH/EMPLEO_DESEMPLEO/bol-GEIH-abr2023.pdf.

ECLAC (2022) *The care society: a horizon for sustainable recovery with gender equality* (LC/CRM.15/3). Santiago: Economic Commission for Latin America and the Caribbean.

Escobar Cuero, G. P. (2022) Internally displaced women from ethnic minority communities in Colombia, domestic work, and resilient strategies. *Revista Interdisciplinar da Mobilidade Humana* 30 (65): 91–104.

Esguerra, C.; Sepúlveda, I., and Fleischer, F. (2018) *Se nos va el cuidado, se no va la vida: Migración, destierro, desplazamiento y cuidado en Colombia.* Universidad de los Andes, Cider, Documentos de política.

Forero, M. T., Cañón, L. and Pineda, J. (1991) *Mujer trabajadora. Nuevo compromiso social.* Bogotá: Instituto de Estudios Sociales Juan Pablo II.

García López, A. C. (2012) Trabajo a cambio de pertenencia. Empleadas domésticas en Bogotá, 1950–1980. In *Revista Grafía* 9: 159–174.

Gaviria, V. (2023) El paro nacional desde el comité del paro. In: Celis J. (coord) *Estallido social 2021: Expresiones de vida y resistencias*. Bogotá: Siglo del Hombre Editores, Universidad del Rosario, Fundación Rosa Luxemburgo y Corporación Colectivo La Mariacano, 243–288.

Gil Araujo, S. and González-Fernández, T. (2014) International migration, public policies and domestic work Latin American migrant women in the Spanish domestic work sector. In: *Women's Studies International Forum* 46: 13–23.

Jiménez Restrepo, Diana M. (2020) *Las y los trabajadores del servicio doméstico en Cali y su área metropolitana: algunas Características de quienes ejercen esta ocupación*. Universidad del Valle, CIDSE, Documento de Trabajo #185.

León, M. (1991) Estrategias para entender y transformar las relaciones entre trabajo doméstico y servicio doméstico. In: Luna L. (comp) *Género, clase y raza en América Latina, algunas aportaciones*. Barcelona, Seminario Interdisciplinar Mujeres y Sociedad, Universitat de Barcelona, 25–61.

Medina, M. (2023) Inscripción histórica, personalidad sociocultural del estallido social 2021. In: Celis J. (coord) *Estallido social 2021: Expresiones de vida y resistencias*. Bogotá: Siglo del Hombre Editores, Universidad del Rosario, Fundación Rosa Luxemburgo y Corporación Colectivo La Mariacano, 25–66.

Meertens, D. (1999) Desplazamiento forzado y género: trayectorias y estrategias de reconstrucción vital. In: Cubides F. and Domínguez C (eds) *Desplazados, Migraciones Internas y Reestructuraciones Territoriales*. Bogotá: Universidad Nacional de Colombia, 406–455.

Molinier, P. (2011) Empleadoras y empleadas domésticas: ¿las feministas son mejores patronas? In: Arango L. and Molinier P. (comps) *El trabajo y la ética del cuidado*. Bogotá: La Carreta Social and Universidad Nacional de Colombia, 229–255.

Molyneux, M. (1979) Beyond the domestic labour debate. *New Left Review* 115: 3–28.

O'Farrell, R. & Montagnier, P. (2019) Measuring digital platform-mediated workers. New Technology. *Work and Employment* 35(1): 130–144.

OIT (2021) *El trabajo doméstico remunerado en América Latina y el Caribe, a 10 años del Convenio núm. 189*, Lima: OIT, Oficina Regional para América Latina y el Caribe.

Ortiz, C. (2021) Otra Vuelta de Tuerca. La codicia de las élites en la pandemia. In *Pensar la Resistencia. Mayo de 2021 en Cali y Colombia*, Documentos Especiales del CIDSE No. 6. Cali: Universidad del Valle, 41–51.

Osorio Pérez, V. and Jiménez Torrado, C. (2018) *Historias tras las cortinas: cifras y testimonios sobre el trabajo doméstico en Colombia*. Medellín: Ediciones Escuela Nacional Sindical, Universidad de Cartagena and Unión de trabajadoras del Servicio Doméstico.

Pautassi, L. (2007) El cuidado como cuestión social desde un enfoque de derechos. NU, CEPAL, *Serie Mujer y Desarrollo* No. 87.

Pereyra, F., Poblete, L. & Tizziani, A. (2023) *Plataformas digitales de servicio doméstico y condiciones laborales. El caso de Argentina*. Organización Internacional del Trabajo. Available (consulted 18 August 2023) at: https://www.ilo.org/buenosaires/publicaciones /WCMS_877416/lang--es/index.htm.

Pineda, J. (2011) La carga del trabajo de cuidado: distribución social y negociación familiar. In: Arango L. and Molinier P. (comps) *El trabajo y la ética del cuidado*. Bogotá: La Carreta Social and Universidad Nacional de Colombia, 135–155.

Pineda, J. (2015) Colombia: el sesgo antilaboral del modelo de desarrollo y las políticas de formalización. *Revista Cuadernos del Cendes* 89: 103–139.

Pineda, J. (2019) Trabajo de cuidado: Mercantilización y desvalorización. *Revista CS* núm. especial:111–136.

Pineda, J. y Castiblanco-Moreno, S. (2024) Mercado de trabajo, cuidado y pandemia. El caso colombiano. In Leite M. (comp) *La crisis de la Reproducción Social*. México: Universidad Autónoma Metropolitana UAM, Unidad Cuajimalpa, in print.

Posso, J. (2008a) *La inserción laboral de las mujeres inmigrantes negras en el servicio doméstico de la Ciudad de Cali*. Cali: Programa Editorial Universidad del Valle.

Posso, J. (2008b) Mecanismos de discriminación étnico-racial, clase social y género: la inserción laboral de las mujeres inmigrantes negras en el servicio doméstico de Cali. In: Zabala M. C. (comp) *Pobreza, exclusión social y discriminación étnico-racial en América Latina y el Caribe*. Bogotá: Siglo del Hombre Editores, y Clacso, 215–240.

Posso, J., Castiblanco, S., and Pineda, J. (2024) "Ni aseadoras, ni empleadas domésticas: somos profesionales de la limpieza". Plataformas digitales del trabajo de cuidado doméstico en Colombia. *Revista de Estudios Sociales*, in print.

Rani, U., Castel-Branco, R., Satija, S and Nayar, M. (2022) Women, work, and the digital economy. *Gender & Development* 30(3): 421–435.

Rivera Cusicanqui, S. (2010) *Ch'ixinakax utxiwa. Una reflexión sobre prácticas y discursos descolonizadores*. Buenos Aires: Editorial Tinta Limón.

Sátyro, N., and C. Midaglia (2021) Family Policies in Latin American Countries: Re-Enforcing Familialism. In Sátyro N., Midaglia, C. and del Pino E. (eds) *Latin American Social Policy Developments in the Twenty-First Century*. Cham: Palgrave Macmillan, 287–314.

Torres, S. (2021) *Análisis del impacto del Paro Nacional en el Valle del Cauca*. Gobernación del Valle del Cauca, Departamento Administrativo de Planeación, Subdirección de Estudios Socioeconómicos, Ciencia, Tecnología e Innovación, Boletín.

Urrea, F. y Barbary, O., Eds. (2004) *Gente negra en Colombia. Dinámicas sociopolíticas en Cali y el Pacífico*. Medellín: Lealon, CIDSE-Universidad del Valle, IRD and COLCIENCIAS.

Urrea, F. y Posso J. (2015). Sexualidades y feminidades de mujeres de clases subalternas: una mirada comparativa de múltiples identidades femeninas. In: Urrea F. y Posso J. (eds) *Feminidades, sexualidades y colores de piel. Mujeres negras, indígenas, blancas mestizas y transgeneristas negras en el suroccidente colombiano.* Cali: Programa Editorial Universidad del Valle, 31–127.

Urrea, F. (2021) Algunos factores desencadenantes del levantamiento popular en Cali y su región metropolitana. In *Pensar la Resistencia. Mayo de 2021 en Cali y Colombia*, Documentos Especiales del CIDSE # 6. Cali: Universidad del Valle, 167–182.

Viveros, M. (2016) La interseccionalidad: una aproximación situada a la dominación. *Debate Feminista* 52: 1–17.

CHAPTER 10

The Daily Grind of Care: a Retrospective of Care Worker Experiences during the Pandemic in France

Aurélie Damamme, Helena Hirata and Michelle Redondo

1 Introduction[1]

On March 11, 2020, the World Health Organization (WHO) declared that COVID-19 was a global pandemic. Five days later, President Emmanuel Macron addressed the French people from the Élysée Palace to announce measures against the pandemic.[2] "We are at war", he declared repeatedly, warning that the enemy was invisible and elusive.

"Care is not war, caregivers are not soldiers", wrote Pascale Molinier (2020) in an article published in the French daily newspaper *Libération*, recalling the importance of human contact in care and the paradox imposed by confinement. In other words, caring for others meant depriving them of the presence of other people, even though:

> the older we are and the more we are locked up in the prison of our bodies, seeing less, hearing less, understanding less, worrying more, the more indispensable the body of the other is to us, the hand we shake, the face that leans in, the voice that teases, we can't do without it.
>
> MOLINIER, 2020, p. 2

---

1 This chapter is based on research carried out as part of an international project entitled "Who cares? Rebuilding care in a post-pandemic world" (T-AP-RRR), the French section of which was funded by the French National Research Agency (*Agence nationale de la recherche – ANR*), Project ANR-22-RRRP-002.

2 "Tomorrow, from midday onwards and for at least a fortnight, our movements will be severely curtailed", announced the head of state. "The only outings that can continue are those that are necessary, to go shopping or for medical treatment"(From « Nous sommes en guerre »: le verbatim du discours d'Emmanuel Macron (lemonde.fr). (Transl: "We are at war": Emmanuel Macron's speech, verbatim). lemonde.fr. https://www.lemonde.fr/politique/article/2020/03/16/nous-sommes-en-guerre-retrouvez-le-discours-de-macron-pour-lutter-contre-le-coronavirus_6033314_823448.html Accessed on: 21/03/2023.

 | DOI:10.1163/9789004707009_011

Confinement once again accentuated the relational dimension of care and the importance of caregivers in the daily lives of older adults. The pandemic also made it difficult for caregivers to reconcile the "body to body" aspects of their work with the task of protecting the people they cared for from the risks of contamination (Molinier, 2020, p. 2). In that scenario, workers were additionally responsible for protecting their loved ones and themselves.

Care work in the pandemic context clearly illustrated the difference between care and war, wherein the challenge of care[3] is that it can only be achieved through relationships (Borgeaud-Garciandia, 2023, p. 55–56).

Fisher and Tronto (1990) defined care as a generic activity comprising everything we do to maintain, perpetuate and repair our world in order to live in it as well as possible (Tronto, 2008). Later, the centrality of work in the activity of care would be emphasized by authors such as Evelyn Nakano Glenn (2000) in the United States, and Pascale Molinier (2013) and Helena Hirata (2021) in France. According to Hirata (2021), "care is material, technical and emotional work, not just a caring attitude. It is work that covers a set of material activities and relationships that consist of providing a concrete response to the needs of others" (p. 9).[4] In this sense, care can also be defined as a relationship of service, support, and assistance, which may or may not be remunerated, and which implies a sense of responsibility for the lives and well-being of others. This definition enables us to observe the hierarchies that distinguish the professions that fall under the umbrella of "care", as well as the differences between paid care and so-called domestic care (Damamme & Paperman, 2009).

Similarly, the social status of doctors and workers presence in the media contrast sharply with the situations of care work rs like home helpers, care assistants and nursing assistants. Despite the difficulties doctors have in public hospitals to assert the value of those spaces for the common good, the situation of female care workers is far less visible. This makes it all the more crucial to report on their experiences during the pandemic.

In this chapter, we will first review the context in which care work took place during the pandemic in France, focusing mainly on government measures adopted at the time and the social, economic, and health contexts. Secondly, after reviewing these contours of care work, we will examine different experiences of the pandemic, focusing on the tensions felt by women care workers,

3 This reminds us of the value of using the English term "care" instead of the French "*soin*", which refers mainly to the therapeutical dimension.

4 Hirata (2021) noted that her definition was developed collectively within the organizing committee of the international colloquium "Theories and practices of care: International comparisons", held in Paris in 2013.

both in terms of managing emotional work and the problems generated by new tasks imposed by the pandemic, to portray the intensification of their work. Finally, we will talk about the mobilizations that emerged in the wake of the pandemic's first phase.

2 Government Action and Social Inequality: a Difficult Road for Care Providers

The pandemic highlighted the centrality of care, not only as a necessary service performed by care workers, but also as an activity that concerns everyone. The pandemic made everyone feel vulnerable, not just those considered dependent, like children, older adults, the disabled people, and the sick people also (Tronto, 2009; Glenn, 2000). It also revealed how fragile our living organizations were and underscored the importance of paying attention to "care infrastructures" (The Care Collective, 2010).

However, this vulnerability did not play out in the same way for everyone, seeing as the period was marked by increased social inequalities in the areas of health and employment (Bajos, 2020). Inequalities in the experience of work were also substantial in terms of gender, race, and social class.

2.1 *Growing Inequalities during the Pandemic*

The many surveys on social inequalities carried out in France during the pandemic unanimously showed increasing disparity, indicating that "the health crisis has revealed and exacerbated social inequalities" (Méda, 2021, p. 7). These inequalities are "well known to researchers, but their multi-dimensional nature and cumulative logic appear even more concretely and urgently, with the rapid and uncontrolled circulation of the virus across the territory" (Lambert & Cayouette,2021, p. 24). They emphasize "the reinforcement of inequalities in every dimension: housing, employment, working conditions, income, social relations (age, gender, social background)" (Idem, p. 38). These findings are taken from Coconel, a longitudinal 'coronavirus and confinement' survey focused on housing and living conditions, conducted by the French Institute for Demographic Studies (*Institut national d'études démographiques* – INED).[5]

5 Survey carried out by Ined in partnership with Coconel (a consortium of the vector-borne disease division of the Méditerranée Infection University Hospital Institute [VITROME IHU *Méditerranée Infection*], the Cochin-Pasteur Clinical Investigation Centre [CIC *Cochin-Pasteur*], the French School of Public Health [*École des hautes études en santé publique* – EHESP], and the Provence-Alpes-Côte d'Azur Health Observatory [*Observatoire Régional de*

According to Dominique Méda (2021) the effects of the crisis are linked to inequalities in employment status, where those on fixed-term contracts, temporary agency workers, casual workers, and undeclared workers bearing the brunt of the pandemic. As pointed out by the authors of the Ined Coconel survey, almost three-quarters of employees with stable employment (permanent contracts as of March 1, 2020, or civil service posts) continued working, as compared to only one in two people with fixed-term contracts, temporary contracts, or internships. The unequal effects of the crisis are also linked to the differences between those who were able to work remotely and those who had to risk exposure in public places and transport because they needed to be physically present to carry out their work. Hospital staff, home helpers, and all care providers were required to be present so that others could confine themselves. Méda (2021) referred to the "excess mortality among care workers, bus and cab drivers, security and sales staff" (p. 8), with COVID-19 and lockdowns disproportionately affecting the most vulnerable populations (residents of impoverished suburbs, undocumented migrants, the homeless, prisoners, etc.). She also mentioned the overexposure of women, low-income earners, and racialized people.

The EpiCoV (epidemiology and living conditions) survey[6] examined the effects of living conditions on exposure to the virus, and the effects of the epidemic on living conditions. Like Lambert and Cayouette's study, it highlighted the cumulative effect of inequalities (Bajos and al., 2020, p. 1), showing, for example, the role of factors such as communal density and overcrowding. The

la Santé – ORS Paca]), the French National Research Agency [*Agence nationale de la recherche – ANR*], the French National Research Institute for Sustainable Development (*Institut de Recherche pour le Développement – IRD*) and the Ifop international market research group. A sample of 2,003 people, representative of adults living in Metropolitan France, was drawn using the quota method (categories of age, gender, education, socio-professional group, region, and community). The online survey was conducted from April 30, 2020, to May 4, 2020. It covered the situation before and during confinement and addressed various themes: housing and living conditions; employment and working conditions; children and educational work; neighborhood and feelings of isolation.

6 Produced by France's National Institute of Health and Medical Research (*Institut national de la santé et de la recherche médicale – INSERM*) with the support of the French Directorate for Research, Studies, Evaluation and Statistics (*Direction de la recherche, des études, de l'évaluation et des statistiques – DREES*), INSEE (2020) and *Santé Publique France*, the national public health agency, with the participation of researchers from Ined, the French National Centre for Scientific Research (*Centre national de la recherche scientifique – CNRS*), Université Paris-Saclay and Université Paris Dauphine–PSL, this was a multi-wave survey with a representative sample of 135,000 people, surveyed by telephone and online between May 2, 2020 and June 2, 2021 (cf. Bajos et al., 2020).

survey revealed that 13.1% of care assistants and 18.1% of home helpers lived in overcrowded accommodations. It also showed that 27.9% of care assistants and 36.5% of home helpers felt that their financial situation worsened due to the pandemic. Only artisans and construction workers reported a higher percentage of pandemic-induced financial deterioration at 44.8%.

Territorial inequalities were also exacerbated. The COVID-19 pandemic hit the poorest areas the hardest, both in northern France and in the Île-de-France region. In Île-de-France, Seine Saint-Denis is the poorest department in mainland France and has experienced excess mortality linked to the factors clearly identified above, and also to the factors found in an Ined study (Brun & Simon, 2020) as early as July 2020. Seine Saint-Denis's high proportion of racialized people who are over-represented in precarious service occupations has led to their over exposure to the virus, which is reinforced by their use of public transport. Furthermore, as Mariette and Pitti (2020) point out, the inhabitants of Seine Saint-Denis have a higher frequency of chronic illnesses that are "important co-morbidity factors in the case of COVID-19. This has made the area's working classes more vulnerable to the virus."[7] The authors go on to explain how the stigmatization suffered by these populations further exacerbates inequalities in access to healthcare in a region that is already less equipped than others in Ile-de-France.

2.2 *The State during the Pandemic: between Protection and Sanctions*

As soon as the first lockdown was announced,[8] the French government set up a job retention scheme and introduced childcare leave, including for care workers[9] (Eydoux, 2023). The French government implemented a series of measures to help many categories of the population maintain their salaries so as to prevent the economy from collapsing at a time when many job sites were

7 "Seine-Saint-Denis ranks first among French départements for diabetes, after La Réunion and Guadeloupe, eighth for respiratory diseases and fourteenth for hypertension. The proportion of adults suffering from obesity is also very high, much higher than in Paris, for example" (Mariette and Pitti, op.cit.).

8 France declared its first lockdown from March 17, 2020 to May 11, 2020. A second lockdown was ordered from October 30, 2020 to December 15, 2020, and the third from April 3, 2021 to May 3, 2021, despite the start of vaccinations for those considered most vulnerable on December 27, 2020.

9 As mentioned by Anne Eydoux (2023), it is interesting to note that care professions were not initially included on the list of occupations eligible for short-time work to look after their own children or because of a vulnerable loved one at home. They were added after a slight delay, but the new measure was nonetheless significant for various care workers (home helpers, maternity assistants, care assistants, etc.), as it reflected a greater recognition of these workers' entitlement to social rights.

unexpectedly closing, in addition to businesses deemed "non-essential" and schools.[10] However, the French government drew criticism for its measures to support vulnerable people, specifically for its delays in supplying protective equipment to healthcare personnel, especially professionals working in others' homes (Handéo, n.d). The state did not have sufficient masks and protective equipment in stock. In addition, public authorities encouraged the adoption of measures to restrict the freedoms of vulnerable people, particularly those living in medical-social establishments (Fillion, 2020).

While public authorities took into account the risks of job losses and tried to limit the effects, the vulnerability of care workers was reinforced by several factors: the higher number of fixed-term contracts, greater exposure to the virus due to contact with people, and the living conditions described above. Given the low remuneration for these professionals and the precariousness of their employment, care workers are among those who have seen their economic situation worsen. As Valérie Albouy and Stéphane Legleye (2020) reported, those with modest incomes most frequently reported the negative consequences of confinement. Thus, short-time work measures did not always enable care workers to safeguard their financial or professional situation.

According to the TraCov survey[11] conducted by the Direction for Research, Studies, and Statistics (*Direction de l'animation de la recherche, des études et de la statistique – dares*), the group that includes home helpers and care assistants reported a deterioration in working conditions and an increase in emotional demands. Thus, care workers were affected by government measures implemented during COVID in two ways. First as professional care providers, due to the regulations that were put in place as the pandemic unfolded, and second as domestic care providers, because they had to cope with an increased workload of also helping vulnerable people in their own homes (children, older adults), a situation widely observed for all women. According to the survey carried out by the French National Institute of Statistics and Economic Studies (*Institut national de la statistique et des études économiques – insee*), at the end of the first lockdown (March to May, 2020), mothers were twice as likely as fathers to take time off work or to obtain special permission to look after children under

10 Schools continued to welcome caregivers' children.

11 The "Experience of work during the COVID-19 health crisis" survey, in its two versions (TRACOV and TRACOV 2), was a one-off survey carried out by DARES (2022,2023) under the French Ministry of Labor, targeting employed people aged 18 to 64 by Internet and telephone. The geographic scope of the survey included Metropolitan France, Guadeloupe, Guiana, Reunion and Martinique.

14 (21% vs. 12%), and more mothers had to combine their professional working hours with time spent with their children (Albouy & Legleye, 2020).

To better understand the experience of care workers during the pandemic, it is also necessary to reflect on the main features of public policies that target people suffering loss of autonomy.

2.3 *Autonomy Policies in France: between Deinstitutionalization and Refamilialization*

As many authors have pointed out (Giraud & Le Bihan, 2022; Eydoux, 2023), home care has been favored by dependent senior citizens since the end of the 1990s, followed by the introduction of the personalized autonomy allowance (APA) in 2002 to allow seniors a "free choice" between their home or an institution. This has fostered the development of the home care profession and of professional family care workers, albeit not as well developed as the field of home care for people with disabilities. The process commodifying older adult care has been ongoing for the last twenty years (Ledoux et al, 2021). However, commodification modalities differ according to the political orientations of government administrations and have an impact on care workers. Under right-wing administrations that favor a seller-dominated home care market, workers have to negotiate their value directly with their employers, whereas under left-wing administrations that value a state-dominated market, negotiation takes place within a framework established by the state, as Clémence Ledoux's article (2023) brilliantly shows.

As recalled by Anne Eydoux (2023), the fragmentation of the job market for care workers hinders their recognition, where workers in households enjoy less recognition than those working in institutions (nursing homes or hospitals). However, even recognized qualifications such as diplomas or experience in an institution were not enough to guarantee good working conditions due to the ongoing "industrialization of care work" (Sahraoui, 2018, p. 35–40), the intensification of work, and the extent of arduous working conditions (Eydoux, 2023). Stating that precariousness in care professions is linked to their female nature can also be seen in how the care sector always comes in second to the health sector, which is already under pressure.

In the next section, we adopt a methodology to observe everyday experiences as a way of understanding social relations and organization (Smith, 2005). We thus recognize that the epistemological relevance of the everyday experience of "care workers" is the first to be affected by this invisibilization of care work (Sahraoui, 2018).

2.4 *Care Workers during the Pandemic*

Care workers have had to face exacerbated daily difficulties. In addition to the context of uncertainty caused by an unprecedented situation, we will show that their working conditions often furthered fear of contamination and reinforced the need to adapt quickly. This context served to compound the intensity of physical and emotional labor.

But who are these workers looking after older adults at a time of global uncertainty?

It is well known that the majority of care-related workers are women. A study carried out in 2021 by the Employment Survey (see Table 10.1) showed that women account for 87% of the profession. They also represent 24% of all employed women, which means that one in every four working women is a care professional. However, while women form the majority of care professions in France, they make up a significant but clear minority of total female employment, since almost eight out of ten (76%) employed women work outside the sector. In this sense, if we consider nurses and related professions; physiotherapists, nursery nurses, babysitters; home helpers, domestic helpers, family workers; domestic workers, and cleaning staff in private homes, they amount to 3,245,000 female workers out of a total of 13,630,000 employed women in France on average in 2021. In other words, 24% of all employed women.

Quantitative data were also provided for home helpers in a recent book (Devetter et al., 2023). Figures sourced from the DARES 2022 Working Conditions Survey[12] for 2019 indicated a workforce of over 550,000 home care workers in France, with salaries "averaging 874 euros in 2019 for a minimum wage of 1,204 euros – due to so-called 'part-timers'" (Devetter et al., p. 17). This does not take into account the arduous nature of the work and the risk of occupational hazards, to which home helpers are highly exposed (Id. ibid., p. 26).

The finding that most care workers are women was also noted in our sample. Of the 39 interviewees (home helpers, social workers, and care assistants), only four were male. These interviewees work in Paris and its surrounding regions. It is through their experiences, related to us between November 2022 and October 2023, that we will learn about the struggles undergone during the pandemic.

12 The French Ministry of Labor's DARES Working Conditions Survey is carried out every three years, with an "individual" section (face-to-face) and an "employer" section. It covers working conditions, organization of work, and health.

TABLE 10.1 Women in care-related occupations in France in 2021[a]

INSEE code	Socio-professional categories	Number of women	% of women in the profession	% of all employed women
43A1–5	Nurses, midwives, and healthcare managers	698	87%	6%
43B1–2 and 43D6	Physiotherapists and early childhood educators	208	69%	1.50%
52B3	Healthcare facility service agents	275	79%	2%
52C1* and 52C2* and 52C5 and 52C6	Care assistants, medical and psychological assistants (AMP) and similar positions, medical and paramedical assistants, paramedics	861	87 %	6%
52C3* and 52C4	Childcare assistants, nursery, and nursery school agents	335	98%	2.5%
56D1–2:	Home helpers, home support for vulnerable people, other home help employees and family caregivers; social assistants	669	93%	5%
56 E2	Housekeepers and cleaning staff for private households	199	92%	1.5%
Total caregivers according to strict definition		3,245,000	87 %	24%
31A1–4* and 34C1–3*	Self-employed healthcare professionals (except veterinarians and pharmacists)	292	52 %	2 %
56B1–2	Body care employees	126	90%	1%
Total caregivers by broad definition		418	66%	3 %
Total female employment in France		13,630,000	49%	100%

a This survey does not provide data on non-binary gender.

SOURCE: EMPLOYMENT SURVEY 2021

2.5 *The Intensification of Emotional and Physical Work*

For those who look after older adults, the relational dimension of care work is often linked to physical effort. When handling bodies, it is important to create a bond by explaining what is happening, which part of the person's body is going to be lifted, turned, etc. The unexpected can happen and there can be resistance, aggression, bad smells, and fear (on both sides). So, the close physical contact that is part of the daily practice of this work requires not only mastery of strength, but also of emotions.

Hochschild (1983, 1993) defines the mastery of emotions as "emotional work," which involves understanding, evaluating, and managing one's own emotions, as well as the emotions of others. During the pandemic, it became clear that care did not solely require one's physical availability to others, and that responding to the vulnerability of others also required mobilizing one's own sensitivity (Molinier, 2020).

To help us understand this, we will describe the daily lives of care workers. Our aim is to understand the specific forms of these workers' experiences by analyzing their work environments and daily activities. This will enable us to better understand how, if in "normal" working conditions, these workers are already overloaded and exposed to the ontological precariousness of life[13] (Sahraoui, 2018), and how this intensified in the context of the pandemic, as did their emotional and physical labor.

2.6 *Protection at Work – Managing the Emotional Burden*

2.6.1 Coping with Lack of Protective Equipment

At the start of the pandemic in France, the lack of masks was widely discussed in the media and caused intense fear among the population. To deal with this, the government reserved protective equipment for people working in the medical field, however omitted home care workers from the priority access list. As a result, in addition to suffering from a short supply of masks like the rest of the population, care workers had no other protection either, like face shields, gloves or gowns.

When we asked our interviewees about access to protective equipment during the pandemic, most instantly recalled the absence of masks. We can thus confirm that this was an important issue for them.

Therefore, seeing as the activities of these workers requires physical contact with patients, and that one way to avoid COVID-19 contamination was

13 On the precariousness of life, see also Butler, 2016, and Hirata, 2021.

distancing, it is clear that the absence of protective equipment fostered great fear on a daily basis, as well as a "heavy responsibility," as Molinier (2020) recalled:

> This body-to-body work—toileting, changing, feeding—does not respect the prescribed distance. It is a heavy responsibility not to spread the virus for people who move from one home to another, from one room to another, often under time constraints, while their presence is indispensable, more than ever.
>
> p. 2

Thus, fear and a deep sense of responsibility were unmistakably a common thread in the work. In our analysis, we consider these aspects to be part of the added mental load that intensified the work.

Once care workers finally had access to protective equipment, a certain relief was expressed, albeit their work remained difficult. While their activities were already carried out in a time-constrained environment before the pandemic, things became even more complicated during the pandemic, as new barrier gestures were required to prepare for work and respond to all its new demands (Nerot, 2021).

2.6.2 Consequences of Barrier Gestures

Work needed to be carried out in accordance with the guidelines established to avoid contamination. This called for greater attention to the preparation involved before beginning the actual care work. That added time was described by one of our interviewees, when she explained why there was more work during the pandemic:

> Because actually, there was already a lot of wasted time because of … how can I put it? The fact that we had to put on the whole outfit, it was a waste of time. It took a long time. But it was compulsory. Those were the rules.
>
> Care assistant, 48 years old

The process of getting dressed for those starting their workday in a nursing home was not necessarily the same as for those working in homes. The former wear scrubs, for example, while the latter do not. However, barrier gestures also changed the daily lives of home care workers and assistants. They even influenced relationships between workers and the resident families:

> Regarding the families, it was a bit hard for us. It was really a very difficult time. It had mainly to do with the barrier gestures, because we had to take extra care for the families' sake and we had to be careful for ourselves, too, so there was stress and fatigue at the same time.
>
> Care assistant, 33 years old

Fatigue and stress increased the mental workload of workers, who had to prove to beneficiaries that they were complying with the procedures required to avoid contamination.

> People were scared, too, so we had to reassure them. Some people were scared when we came into their homes, which was normal. So we reassured them. We told them that we disinfected our hands properly, and that we had a different outfit for each person. So, you see, they needed a lot of reassurance.
>
> Care assistant, 51 years old

In this way, barrier gestures brought about changes in the daily lives of care workers, both in terms of time management and in their relationships with the families.

2.7 *Setting Up New Task*

The idea of work intensification is often linked to the quest for productivity (Hatzfeld, 2004). Intensification within the Taylorist framework takes on new contours in the service sector, where the management of emotions must be taken into account. In this section, we will highlight the new tasks defined during the pandemic.

Work overload was not necessarily due to the increase in the number of beneficiaries of an association or institution, but rather to the need to replace colleagues. These replacements due to the pandemic increased both the workload and the intensity of work because of neoliberal policies focused on cutting labor costs and reducing the number of available caregivers to a minimum.

During the pandemic, absences were often linked to colleagues having contracted COVID-19, needing to stay at home to look after their children, or being eligible for leave.

> The situation actually intensified, in the sense that we had colleagues at risk who weren't necessarily able to come to work. So, basically, we had to take on the beneficiaries they usually managed, and so we had more

> beneficiaries to manage, and consequently more work and slightly longer, necessarily more tiring days.
>
> Care assistant, 23 years old

In addition to replacing colleagues, nursing home workers faced other problems. While the number of beneficiaries did not increase, some had contracted COVID-19 and required more attention, as described in the following statement:

> And so then, more sick people, so more supervision, much weaker people; people we normally wouldn't need to do much for. Now, we had to feed them and monitor them, whereas normally, they could do it themselves.
>
> Care assistant, 48 years old

In addition to caring for the sick, contamination had to be avoided, and isolating older people within their nursing homes meant added tasks. In this new context, the staff had to go to each room to deliver meals, which modified daily logistics and increased, for example, the amount of time needed to distribute and remove food. Residents also took advantage of this opportunity to strike up a conversation and have a chat with the staff, delaying things further.

Another new task was coordinating times for residents to talk to their families using tablets or cell phones to make calls. In a number of nursing homes, female workers were required to add to their task list the organization of room visits and assisting the seniors in communicating with their families.

Increased administrative tasks (filling in forms, contacting suppliers for protective equipment, etc.) also had an impact. Although this was more evident for those who did not provide direct care for the residents, those who did were forced to develop additional means of communication with their colleagues (WhatsApp groups, for example) and to submit reports. Furthermore, the number of deaths that had to be dealt with, both emotionally and administratively, also increased significantly. In this context, the intensification of administrative work was enormous and sudden, as reported by one of the care assistants:

> We had to manage confined cases. We also had to handle the psychological aspect of that, and we had to deal with people who had died. All that was intense. Because we weren't expecting it.
>
> Care assistant, 42 years old

Thus, it can be concluded that the pandemic multiplied the tasks of care workers on two important fronts: the emotional and the physical. While relationships with residents had always been part of the job, new tasks emerged and had to be addressed in situations of repeated isolation, illness, and death. In this context, significant emotional efforts combined with an increase in material tasks resulted in the intensification of work.

This intensification of physical and emotional work led to a search for common organization among workers and beyond the workplace, as we will see below.

3 Inequalities and Mobilization

The rise in social inequalities and the precariousness of care workers during the pandemic led to unprecedented forms of mobilization, like, for example, how home care workers came together to demand better recognition of their work and an upgrading of their skills.

Hospital nurses and nursing assistants, who had long fought against bed closures and the lack of resources for hiring care workers[14] continued to mobilize during the pandemic in 2020 and 2021. Nurses, nursing assistants, and hospital staff held demonstrations in June-July 2020 and in subsequent years, asking for higher salaries and improved working conditions, demands that had been put forward by public hospital staff for over ten years. One example is the *Collectif Inter Hôpitaux* (2020) and its proposals for the "transformation and enhancement of care professions."[15]

Many care workers refused the bonuses and medals proposed by the Macron administration and considered the *Ségur de la Santé* agreements to be inadequate and falling short of the demands made during the pandemic.

Unlike hospital caregivers, many home care workers participated in demonstrations for the first time during the pandemic. We interviewed activists from two collectives, *la force invisible des aides à domicile* (the invisible force of home helpers) and the *collectif des aides à domicile du Loir et Cher* (the Loir and Cher home helpers collective), who mobilized in 2020 and 2021 with a series of demands. While activism in the home care sector has been very rare (Béroud, 2013), their heightened feeling of isolation during the pandemic and

14 See the CGT's monthly women's magazine, *Antoinette* (1979-1982), on the mobilization of nurses and orderlies in hospitals and maternity wards between 1969 and 1982, and the book by Danièle Kergoat et al., *Les infirmières et leur coordination, 1988–1989*, 1992 .

15 Following the *Ségur de la santé* agreement in July 2020, non-medical staff, without distinction, obtained a salary increase of 183 euros net per month in the public and private non-profit sectors.

the non-recognition of their work prompted care workers to organize, strike, and demonstrate.

During an unprecedented "three-month unlimited" strike in early 2023, the General Confederation of Labor's (CGT) ADMR[16] section made the following demands:

> An increase in hourly rate to a minimum of 15 euros net for all employees; the reclassification of all grade 1s to grade 2s;[17] all journeys paid for; all kilometers and travel time paid for in real terms; a kilometric allowance of 1 euro; professional vehicles or a 500-euro allowance for wear and tear on personal vehicles; a 500-euro end-of-year bonus; full-time contracts for employees who so wish; a 20-euro cleaning allowance for professional uniforms; no more pressure on employees; and respect for the union organization and union representative.

To date, these demands have not been met.

La force invisible des aides à domicile demonstrated in 2020 and 2021 during the pandemic. This collective was formed in June 2020 and connected home care workers—largely via Facebook—to discuss working conditions and fears about the future of their profession, as well as to alert as many people as possible and bear witness to the realities in the field. The collective was officially transformed into an association on December 22, 2020, by and for agents in the sector who realized that the status quo was unsustainable. The declared aim of this non-partisan, non-union organization, which you can read about on its website, is to "sound the alarm to the entire French population and work for the restructuring of the sector on a national scale."[18]

In terms of working conditions, the association demands: "better sectorization, paid listening time to reduce the mental workload, training—because there are many pathologies at home—recognition of 'their' skills, recognition of 'their' kilometers, of all 'their' kilometers" (Interview with an activist from *La force invisible*, AL, age 51, 01/17/2023). Another home care worker from this collective elaborated on the issue of work journeys:

---

16 ADMR: *Aide à domicile en milieu rural* (Home care workers in rural areas).

17 Grade 1 = home helper; grade 2 = care assistant. "Rider 32 offers good increases, but only if we're classified as grade 2, which corresponds to care assistant" (Interview with AF, age 55, CGT- Loir and Cher collective activist, 02/04/2023).

18 "Le Collectif National la force invisible des aides à domicile", Available at: https://laforceinvisible.fr/asso/.Accessed on: (05, 02.2024).

> Because … when you start the day, your commuting time, the time you spend going to the first person, is not counted as … working time. … kilometers are only paid at 60% of the total, for the first trip. For the second trip, if it lasts less than half an hour, the time you spend driving to the next person's home is counted as working time. Your kilometers are paid at 100%. On the other hand, when you go home … at lunchtime, or because you've only had two operations and you go home, and you've got a big gap, your kilometers, you get nothing. And the time you spend in the car, you've got nothing.
>
> Interview with a collective activist, AL, age 51, 01/17/2023

As for wages, they demand 1,500 euros net for 30 hours of work a week. It is also notable that both collectives asked to be differentiated from housekeepers, considering that they are home helpers who take care of the older adults and do not do housework, which is the specific work carried out by other care workers identified primarily by the performance of domestic work (Redondo, 2018).

The social movement called "Invisible Force" continued after the peak of the pandemic in 2020 and 2021. Home care workers linked to the association in Nouvelle-Aquitaine have gatherings planned for 2024:

> We're in the process of organizing a home care worker day, created by the home care worker, which will take place in 2024; the date has yet to be determined; a questionnaire has been circulated. It will take place in the Nouvelle-Aquitaine region, and if the response is good, we'll do it in Occitanie, as there's also a demand for it there. From there, we'll organize themed evenings.
>
> E-mail from the collective's leader, AL, age 51, 09/25/2023

This "Invisible Force" of home care workers that emerged from the pandemic continues to structure itself across the country, reflecting the need to mobilize and fight for better recognition and rights.

One report (Chassoulier et al., 2023) proposed an estimate of the cost and the level of jobs created by public investment in the care sector. It refers to a study by the International Trade Union Confederation (ITUC) which suggests that "with an investment of 2% of GDP in the care economy, the total number of jobs could increase by 2.4 to 6.1% depending on the country" (Chassoulier et al., 2023, p. 15).

4 Conclusion

During the COVID-19 pandemic, the pervasiveness of care in our lives was placed in the spotlight, and its structuring dimension was emphasized both in the individual sphere and in the more general organization of the social world. In this context, confinement illustrated the relational and political dimensions of care. It highlighted the importance of the bond within care actions, and the fact that part of the population and professionals were less able to protect themselves, making them more vulnerable than others who were able to stay at home due to exceptional salary maintenance measures when they could not work remotely.

In this article, guided by the question posed by the care perspective, "Who cares for what and how?" (Paperman, 2005), it has been possible to describe, analyze, and critique the political and social organization of care activities carried out by female care workers. Thus, by observing the activities of these workers and the sensitivity they mobilize, particularly under exceptional conditions, we have been able to contribute to a portrait of the social world during the pandemic.

Care work has thus been marked by new constraints linked to a social and political context. In addition to the organizational difficulties associated to work intensification, the emotional demands of care work have increased dramatically. Managing emotions in the face of illness and death, as well as the fear of dying on the part of beneficiaries, their families, and the caregivers themselves, has made care work particularly arduous. However, care workers have developed various kinds of resistance strategies, as seen in associations and collectives they created. In so doing, they have contributed to two important questions: What perspectives of care can emerge from surveys of their experience during the pandemic? And, how can their work be recognized?

References

Albouy, Valérie and Legleye, Stéphane (2020) "Living conditions during confinement: discrepancies by standard of living and socio-professional category", *INSEE FOCUS* no. 197, June.

Antoinette, cgt women's magazine, several issues from 1979 to 1982.

Bajos, Nathalie, Warszawski, Josiane, Pailhé, Ariane and et al. (2020) "Les inégalités sociales au temps du COVID-19" ("Social inequalities during COVID-19"), *Questions de santé publique*, no. 40 : 1–12.

Béroud, Sophie (2013) Une campagne de syndicalisation au féminin, in *Travail, Genre et Sociétés*, 30/2013 : 111–128.

Borgeaud-Garciandia, Natacha (2023) *Dans l'intimité du care*, Paris : La Dispute.

Brun, Solène and Simon, Patrick (2020) "L'invisibilité des minorités dans les chiffres du Coronavirus: le détour par la Seine-Saint-Denis" ("The invisibility of minorities in the figures for COVID-19: a detour by Seine-Saint-Denis"), in: Brun Solène and Simon Patrick (dir.), Dossier "Inégalités ethno-raciales et pandémie de coronavirus", *De facto* [Online], 19 | May 2020, uploaded May 15, 2020. Available at: https://www.icmigrations.cnrs.fr/2020/05/15/defacto-019-05/.

Butler, Judith (2016) "Vulnerability, Precarity, Coalition" in Gardey D., Kraus, C. (dir./eds) *Politics of Coalition. Thinking Collective Action with Judith Butler*, Zurich/Geneva: Ed. Seismo.

Chassoulier, Louisa, Devetter, François-Xavier, Lemière, Séverine, Pucci, Muriel, Silvera, Rachel (coord.), Valentin, Julie, Erb, Louis Alexandre (2023) *Investir dans le secteur du soin et du lien aux autres: un enjeu d'égalité entre les femmes et les hommes*, ("Investing in the care sector and connections with others. Equality issues between women and men"), Final report, IRES-CGT. https://ires.fr/publications/cgt/investir-dans-le-secteur-du-soin-et-du-lien-aux-autres-un-enjeu-degalite-entre-les-femmes-et-les-hommes/

Collectif Inter-Hôpitaux (2020) "Ségur de la Santé, motion voted October 2020, Pillar 1".

Damamme, Aurélie and Paperman, Patricia (2009) «Care domestique: délimitations et transformations » ("Home care: demarcations and transformations"), dans Molinier Pascale, Laugier Sandra, Paperman Patricia (dir.), *Qu'est-ce que le care?Souci des autres, sensibilité, responsabilité*, Paris: Payot & Rivages, Petite Bibliothèque Payot.

DARES (2023), *DARES Analyses* no. 22, April. https://dares.travail-emploi.gouv.fr/publication/lactivite-partielle-pendant-la-crise-sanitaire-quelles-consequences-sur-la-sante-debut-2021.

DARES (2022) Rapport d'Etudes n° 48, November, Didry, Claude, Giordano, Denis, and Cartron, Damien (2021), *Le travail à l'épreuve du covid. Sept portraits sectoriels à la lumière des relations professionnelles* ("Work put to the test by COVID-19. Seven sectoral portraits in the light of professional relationships"), Maurice Halbwachs Centre (CMH) (CNRS-ENS-EHESS).

Devetter, François-Xavier, Dussuet, Annie and Puissant, Emmanuelle (2023) *Aide à domicile, un métier en souffrance. Sortir de l'impasse* ("Home help, a suffering profession. Breaking the deadlock"). Ivry-sur-Seine: Les Éditions de l'Atelier.

Eydoux, Anne (2023) "Care policies in France. Segmented policies in a fragmented landscape", International Conference "Who cares? Care and Pandemics in Transnational Perspective", Paris, May 26.

Fillion, Emmanuelle (2020), "Confinement: quel impact dans les établissements pour personnes âgées et handicapées" ("Lockdown: the impact on institutions for the elderly and the disabled"), *The Conversation*, The Conversation France, March 25.

Fisher, Berenice and Tronto, Joan (1990) “Toward a Feminist Theory of Caring” in Abel Emily and Nelson Margaret (eds) *Circles of care: Work and Identity in Women's Lives*, Albany/NY:State University of New York Press. https://fr.scribd.com/document/330973025/Fisher-Tronto-Toward-a-Feminist-Theory-of-Caring-1.

Giraud, Olivier, and Le Bihan-Youinou, Blanche (2022) “Les politiques de l'autonomie: vieillissement de la population, handicap et investissement des proches aidants” (“The politics of autonomy: aging of the population, disability and the investment of family caregivers”), Giraud Olivier (ed.), *Politiques sociales: l'état des savoirs*. Paris : La Découverte : 115–133.

Handéo (s/d), Retour d'expérience COVID-19 (Exchanging experiences on COVID-19), report, 15 p.

Hatzfeld, Nicolas (2004) L'intensification du travail en débat. Ethnographie et histoire aux chaînes de Peugeot-Sochaux. Sociologie du Travail Volume 46, Issue 3, 291–307p

Hirata, Helena (2021) *Le care, théories et pratiques* (“Care: theories and practices”). Paris: La Dispute.

Hochschild, Arlie Russel (1983) *The managed Heart, Berkeley*: University of California Press.

Hochschild, Arlie Russel (1993) « Preface », in S. Fineman (Dir.), *Emotion in Organizations*, London: Sage.

INSEE (2020) “Les inégalités sociales à l'épreuve de la crise sanitaire: un bilan du first confinement” (“Social inequalities tested by the health crisis: an overview of the first lockdown”), in *France, Portrait Social 2020*.

Kergoat, Danièle, Imbert, Françoise, Le Doaré, Hélène and Senotier, Danièle (dir.) (1992). *Les infirmières et leur coordination* (“Nurses and their coordination”)*, 1988–1989*, Paris : Ed. Lamarre.

Lambert, Anne and Cayouette-Remblière, Joanie (2021) *The explosion of inequalities. Class, gender and generation in the face of the health crisis*. La Tour d'Aigues: L'aube.

Lambert, Anne and Cayouette-Remblière, Joanie (2021) “Introduction”, in Lambert Anne, Cayouette-Remblière Joanie *The explosion of inequalities. Class, gender and generation in the face of the health crisis*. La Tour d'Aigues: L'aube.

Ledoux, Clémence, Shire, Karen and Van Hooren, Franca (2021) Introduction: From the emergence to the dynamics of welfare markets, in C. Ledoux, K. Shire and F. Van Hooren (eds) *The Dynamics of Welfare Markets: Private Pensions and Domestic/Care Services in Europe*, Cham: Palgrave: 3–49.

Ledoux, Clémence (2023) Political parties, interest groups and the contestations of home care: the case of France, *European Journal of Politics and Gender*, 6(2): 240–257.

Mariette, Audrey and Pitti, Laure (2020), COVID-19 en Seine-Saint-Denis (1/2) : quand l'épidémie aggrave les inégalités sociales de santé, *Métropolitiques*, 6 juillet 2020, https://www.metropolitiques.eu/Covid-19-en-Seine-Saint-Denis-1-2-quand-l-epidemie-aggrave-les-inegalites-de.html.

Méda, Dominique (2021) Preface, in Lambert, Anne, Cayouette-Remblière, Joanie (2021) *The explosion of inequalities. Class, gender and generation in the face of the health crisis.* La Tour d'Aigues: L'aube.

Monde (Le) (2020) "On est prises pour des rien du tout, mais on est essentielles" ("We're considered good-for-nothings, but we're essential"), February 13, p. 16.

Molinier, Pascale. (2013) *Le Travail du Care* ("The work of care"), Paris : La Dispute.

Molinier, Pascale (2020), "Le soin n'est pas la guerre" ("Care is not war"), *Libération,* March17.https://www.liberation.fr/debats/2020/03/17/coronavirus-le-soin-n-est-pas-la-guerre_1782052/.

Nakano Glenn, Evelyn (2000) "Creating a caring society", *Contemporary Sociology*, no. 29: 84–94.

Nerot, Jocelyne (2021). *L'analyse de situations de l'aide-soignant. Pour une démarche clinique de qualité* ("An analysis of nursing assistants' situations. For a quality clinical approach"), Paris: Vuibert.

Paperman, Patricia (2005) "Les gens vulnérables n'ont rien d'exceptionnel" ("Vulnerable people are not exceptional"), in Paperman, Patricia, Laugier, Sandra (Eds.) *Le souci des autres. Éthique et politique du care.* Raisons Pratiques, Paris : Éditions de l'École des hautes études en sciences sociales : 281–298. Cf. 2011, https://books.openedition.org/editionsehess/11719.

Redondo, Michelle (2018) "Trajectoires du care: de au pair à nounou" ("Care pathways: from au pair to nanny"), PhD thesis in political and social science, Université Paris 8, Paris.

Sahraoui, Nina (2018) "De la précarité du travail émotionnel du care: Les apports d'une philosophie morale féministe à l'analyse de la précarité du travail" ("On the precariousness of the emotional labor of care: the contributions of a feminist moral philosophy to the analysis of job insecurity"), *Emulations – Revue de sciences sociales*, (28) : 31–45. Cf. 2019, https://www.librairie-gallimard.com/ebook/9783030143978-racialised-workers-and-european-older-age-care-nina-sahraoui/.

Ségur 02 de la santé (2020). Ségur de la santé agreements. Careers, professions and remuneration. July 2020.

Smith, Dorothy E. (2005) *Institutional ethnography: a sociology for people*, Oxford: Rowman Altamira Press.

The Care Collective (Chatzidakis, Andreas, Hakim, Jamie, Litter, Jo and Rottenberg, Catherine) (2020) *The Care Manifesto: The Politics of Interdependence*. London: Verso Books.

Tronto, Joan (2008) "Du care" ("On care"), *Revue du MAUSS*, Vol. 32, no. 2 : 243–265.

Tronto, Joan (2009) *Un Monde vulnérable. Pour une politique du care* ("A vulnerable world. For a politics of care"), Paris: La Découverte.

CHAPTER 11

Stay Home in the Closet: LGBTQIA+ Care Spaces and the COVID-19 Pandemic

Marcelo Maciel Ramos, Pedro Augusto Gravatá Nicoli and Gabriela Alkmin

> It's not time to go back into the closet,
> but time to care for oneself more.
>
> Older lesbian woman, *Longeviver* LGBT+ Project

1 Introduction: a Glance

Paulo and Angela's eyes met quickly one afternoon in March 2020. He was sitting on a bench in the middle of *Praça da Liberdade*, under a centuries-old imperial palm tree, enjoying the calm rhythm of his days. Today his habit of watching people passing by was accompanied by a distressing thought. What would come of this new pandemic? Another pandemic in his lifetime, he thought. Angela walked quickly, hand in hand with her "almost-girlfriend" whom she had met when she moved to Belo Horizonte. Coming from a small town in the countryside to study in the capital, she felt increasingly better in the city. It was as if she finally felt alive, life's true beginning. Paulo and Angela's eyes met and locked for a fraction of a second. Paulo, seeing the couple, could not help but think about how much times had changed. He himself would have never been seen like this, holding hands with one of his past boyfriends. A delicate smile played across his lips. Angela, whose eyes had perhaps been drawn to the little dog lying on Paulo's elegantly crossed legs, smiled back.

The years to come would radically change the lives of Paulo and Angela, in a way that was different from the structural changes that the pandemic would impose on the lives of everyone else. Paulo, a gay man in his late seventies, would spend very long periods in absolute isolation, without setting foot outside his house, not seeing or interacting with anyone. If loneliness was in some way already his companion, things were about to get worse. It would trigger

 | DOI:10.1163/9789004707009_012

two very intense depression crises and a disillusionment with life he had never known before. Angela, forced to return to her parents' home in a small town in the state of Minas Gerais, would find herself once again dealing with what she thought had been left in the past. She would re-live her family's everyday resistance to who she was. Comments, jokes, fights, awkwardness, rules. It meant going back to her space, her room, a world within herself. For both Paulo and Angela, what they considered most essential, most precious in their lives would be lost. It was as if, locked away at home and in their circumstances, they would cease to exist. A new closet. A closet at home.

This chapter wants to make your eyes, dear reader, meet those of Paulo and Angela. They are characters that we have fictionalized here, of course. But it is a fiction, as we will see, that is absolutely connected to reality – which, in one way or another, are our realities. Here, we align a theoretical exploration of the idea of LGBTQIA+ care and its correlations in the field of care and LGBTQIA+, based on empirical data, fragments of life stories, and the experiences of people with dissident gender identities and sexualities in the city of Belo Horizonte, Brazil. The focus is especially on the experiences they reported having during the COVID-19 pandemic.

We will discuss the empirical data, methodological structure, collection processes, and theoretical angles that we intend to analyze. But first, let us focus on a looser, freer, more intuitive, more provocative – perhaps queerer perspective for this chapter. We want to begin to understand what is not exactly visible in the process of producing the material and subjective lives of LGBTQIA+ people – in their spaces, relationships, and practices – through the analytical lens of care.

The intention here is perhaps just that, of trying to see something that is not visible. Trying to attract people's eyes, without necessarily giving them something defined or clear to look at. While this type of attempt promises something slightly opaque, diffused, and elusive, we hope it will be sufficiently outlined so as to at least *be seen*. There is a certain set of practices, spaces, and relationships that are vital elements for LGBTQIA+ people to be who they truly are, even if they are socially understood as unimportant or trivial, undesirable or dispensable, or even as repulsive or abject. We will identify some of these elements to try to understand the effects of the COVID-19 pandemic on the dissolution of these arrangements, and how this impacted LGBTQIA+ lives in an unequal distribution of the effects of the pandemic.

Our perspective developed in three parts. First, was looking. Two projects supported by the research and extension program of the Federal University of Minas Gerais (UFMG) called *Diverso* – Legal Center for Sexual and Gender Diversity, allowed us to listen to the life stories of LGBTQIA+ people in Belo

Horizonte. In this context, we also listened to their narratives about how pandemic affected their lives. Listening to these many stories opened the door to the second part, which is the resumption of previous attempts to develop an LGBTQIA+ concept of care. These attempts anticipated dimensions present in narratives about the material and symbolic modes of LGBTQIA+ production, in the most elementary sense of what can be understood as care. These theoretical and conceptual attempts aim to dialogue with the emerging idea of LGBTQIA+ care. Finally, the third part provides a deeper analysis based on the life stories and on how the pandemic interrupted these already traditionally illegible and fragile flows of care.

Basically, we want to build on a set of questions that are starting to be developed in the literature and activism of LGBTQIA+ people (Malatino, 2020). They are: How do LGBTQIA+ people experience care? Are they deprived of care? Do they have unequal access to care because they are LGBTQIA+? What position are they in regarding care relationships in the face of social vulnerability due to their sexualities and gender identities? How do they rebuild bonds of care based on producing their lives as LGBTQIA+ people? In which spaces, with which practices, in what relationships? Would all of this put together allow us to formulate an idea of LGBTQIA+ care? Our journey through all these questions, without any promise of definitive answers, comes with a specifier: the COVID-19 pandemic. It serves, perhaps, to elucidate, in its profoundly life-affecting processes, this particular design of LGBTQIA+ care.

2 Looking at LGBTQIA+ People in Two Projects: *Longeviver* and the Violence Against LGBTQIA+ People Observatory

The empirical data to be discussed in this chapter comes from two projects conducted by the research and extension program called *Diverso* UFMG – Legal Center for Sexual and Gender Diversity. One is *Longeviver* and the other is the Violence Against LGBTQIA+ People Observatory. Both projects were created to address the same problem, namely the notable gap in systematic statistical data on the LGBTQIA+ population in Brazil (Silva, Lena and Miranda-Ribeiro, 2018). It is enormously difficult to find information and solid reflections based on empirical data about the LGBTQIA+ population, which affects studying this population's access to the sphere of rights.

The research conducted under the *Longeviver* Project is entitled "Aging in the LGBT population: *Longeviver* Diagnosis and Access to Municipal Public

Services."[1] The Project seeks to provide a broad diagnosis of the living conditions of older LGBTQIA+ people in the city by outlining a number of issues: socioeconomic profile; family structure and background of weak family ties; mental health and illnesses in old age; rights violations and background of LGBT-phobic violence; perception of security; experience of sexuality, marriage, and other affective relationships; consumption, assets, and tourism. In this sense, the Project's starting point is an empirical "bottleneck" that is even more socially and scientifically invisible– the life experiences of people who, in addition to identifying as sexual and gender dissidents, make up an age group marked by violence and exclusions amplified by the aging process.

To conduct its research, the *Longeviver* team designed a general methodological strategy that applied online exploratory questionnaires to form a database of people interested in participating in the research. This was followed by in-depth interviews using the life history approach in a snowball sampling method. A central challenge to the research was accessing the target audience, since the older LGBTQIA+ population suffers from stigma, invisibility, and very particular fears of exposure. Furthermore, they have limited access to the internet. Thus, the project sought to combine virtual and in-person diffusion initiatives. Questionnaires were circulated in virtual forums for older adults, groups, and direct messages via WhatsApp; published in the capital's online and printed media; and propagated through active search and placement of materials in locations frequented by older LGBTQIA+, such as health clinics, bars, cultural spaces, nightlife venues, and bathhouses.

Despite all the difficulties, in this first phase we obtained 114 responses to the online questionnaire from LGBTQIA+ people over the age of 60. This permitted us to outline some basic elements of the respondents, such as their age and socioeconomic profile, any violence or discrimination they experienced in their lives and in old age, and access to housing and healthcare after the age of 60.

The second phase of the research – which is the methodological epicenter – consisted of interviews using the life history methodology in an attempt to understand the biographical aspects of the interviewees and their current experiences as older LGBTQIA+ people in Belo Horizonte. Seventy-five interviews were conducted using this model and the data collected is enormously complex and rich. They largely exceed the specific scope of this chapter, covering a huge range of topics like subjectivities and aging; sexuality and gender

1 This is a project resulting from a partnership between *Diverso* UFMG and the Department of Policies for the LGBT Population (DLGBT), an agency dedicated to LGBTQIA+ issues in Belo Horizonte, the capital of Minas Gerais.

identity; violence and discrimination; health; culture, leisure, and political activism; access to income and employability; and public services.

The Violence Against LGBTQIA+ People Observatory, the second project that provided the data we analyzed, consists of a set of research initiatives that has produced primary data on LGBTphobic violence since 2016 using questionnaires administered during the Belo Horizonte LGBT+ Pride Parades. During the COVID-19 pandemic and its social distancing policies and lockdowns, the Observatory's research was adapted to investigate LGBTphobic violence via virtual environments. Thus, in 2021, 2022, and 2023 the Observatory team carried out a study in two phases, aiming to deepen the research into the experiences of violence against LGBTQIA+ people in the Metropolitan Region of Belo Horizonte.[2]

The Observatory's target audience was people residing in the city who were 18 years or older at the time of data collection and identified as LGBTQIA+ (lesbian, gay, bisexual, *travesti*,[3] transsexual, intersex, and other non-cis and/or non-heterosexual identities). The first phase of the research was quantitative and involved applying 511 virtual questionnaires. The second phase of the research, which offers the most relevant set of data analyzed on this occasion, involved 78 semi-structured interviews with selected participants from the first phase. Therefore, this research sampling is non-probabilistic, voluntary, and intentional. This approach is due to the difficult collection of reliable data on the LGBTQIA+ population of Minas Gerais, meaning the sampling has internal, not external, validity.

The semi-structured interview model was chosen because it allows information to emerge more freely, with answers that are not determined by standardized alternatives (Manzini, 1990/1991: 154). Furthermore, a script was used to allow the interviewer to understand the different particularities that the research aimed to analyze. The script was produced to understand in detail the LGBTphobic violence experienced by the interviewees, the personal and social

2 The research project conducted between 2021 and 2023 received financial support from the Embassy of the Kingdom of the Netherlands and the Mandate of the Councilor of Belo Horizonte, Pedro Patrus.

3 According to ANTRA (National Association of Travestis and Transexuals), *Travesti* is a term used to designate people who live by feminine gender constructions, in opposition to their designated sex at birth (ANTRA, 2024). In Brazil, the difference between *travestis* and transgender or transexual women is not related to their bodies or physical conditions– it is, rather, a historical and political distinction that makes people recognize themselves in each of these identities. In order to maintain the particularity of this identity, we chose to use the original term in Brazilian Portuguese throughout this chapter.

repercussions, and the social and institutional obstacles they encountered in confronting it.[4]

Against this background of two very broad universes of information, we propose an analysis that centralizes the perspective of care. This analytical approach is justified in many ways. First, because of the relevance of care-related subjects recounted in the stories of the LGBTQIA+ interviewees, and because these stories called into question preconceptions about the design of care. Second, because the empirical data point out and reinforce the importance of theoretically outlining the aforementioned gap between care and dissident genders and sexualities. LGBTQIA+ studies, in general, focus little on the topics of care and aging. Likewise, the field of care has not centrally considered gender identities and non-hegemonic sexualities in its formulations, whether sociological, ethical, empirical, or economic. It is precisely in this articulation between presences and absences, the legible and the illegible, that we see the reflective window to be explored here, of LGBTQIA+ care and its manifestation during the COVID-19 pandemic.

3 The Idea of LGBTQIA+ Care: a First Approach

What is LGBTQIA+ care? Here we propose an inversion, starting first with an analytical question. In order to navigate the extensive empirically collected data gathered from more than 150 LGBTQIA+ life stories, a theoretical articulator, even if provisional, seems necessary. It is what gives meaning to a set of practices, relationships, and experiences that can eventually be understood as care, even if they are not explicitly formulated in the interviews or theoretically expressed in literature as such.

The question of what is LGBTQIA+ care depends considerably on the concept of care itself, which can be elusive in many ways (Georges, 2019). Let us consider here, then, without fear of automatic repetition, what has seemingly become the most famous definition in the field of care studies worldwide. Joan Tronto and Berenice Fisher (1990: 113), define care as “a species activity that

4 Similar to the *Longeviver* LGBT+ Project, the Observatory reports go far beyond the scope proposed in this work. In addition to narratives about care and relationships experienced in the domestic environment, the stories deal with LGBTphobic violence linked to family, religion, school, work, public security, and many other spaces and structures where LGBT people circulate in Belo Horizonte. The reports deal with physical, psychological, sexual, and verbal violence, but also with the resistance and alliances established by these subjects throughout their lives.

includes everything we do to maintain, continue, and repair our 'world' so that we can live in it as well as possible. That world includes our bodies, ourselves, and our environment."

Care, then, is something related to our species, which produces, maintains, and repairs who we are, our bodies, and our surroundings. Even though this formulation, purposefully elastic in its limits, can allow many interpretative differences regarding what is or is not care, a certain point stands out. The concept of care is strongly associated with our position as persons in the world – something that specifies us, and with how everything is built, maintained, and repaired based on that.

Along these lines, Patricia Paperman and Pascale Molinier (2015: 53) understand care as "what connects us and holds us to several others, whether individuals, groups or larger or smaller communities," in careful consideration of concrete and localized social relations, not to be disregarded in the name of structural analytical canons. Relationships that, to the authors, "can be asymmetric, unequal, unfair, conflicting with each other, that can engage different types and degrees of responsibilities, obligations of different strength and intensity for the parties" (Paperman and Molinier, 2015: 53).

If Angela and Paulo, our fictional characters, could look us in the eye for one minute, after years of a pandemic, perhaps they would tell us, even if indirectly, something about care. They would certainly talk about how their "world" was affected by it. How the most essential things could not be experienced, maintained, or repaired. How the process of producing and affirming their material and subjective existences – which has always been associated to being LGBTQIA+ – needed to be restructured during the pandemic.

Developing the conceptual potential of care is not, however, something easy to do. In fact, when it comes to the LGBT+ perspective, it is something that has not yet been done properly. Some initiatives in this direction fall within our scope of analysis, as, for example, what American trans theorist and activist Hil Malatino points out regarding transgender care:

> What happens if we … begin … by investigating networks of mutual aid and emotional support developed by trans femme communities …? The terrain of what constitutes care shifts radically once such decentering occurs. For queer and trans subjects, this is often less about exporting the feminized values of care associated with the White, bourgeois home to the public sphere than it is about seeking ways to make the multivalent and necessary care hustle that structures so many of our lives more sustainable, especially as we're often actively engaged in inventing or piecing

> together the units – domestic, familial, intimate – that are just assumed a priori in much literature on care labor and care ethics.
>
> MALATINO, 2020: 42–43

This is what we feel when investigating LGBTQIA+ people in Belo Horizonte. Their care relationships are not at the center. They access and fail to access care in ways that are closely linked to their expressions of gender and sexuality. Much of what is true for the general description of care does not necessarily apply to them. They do things that are vital for who they are, for the constitution of their bodies and subjectivities, which cisgender and heterosexual people do not even know about. And they do it in spaces that are considered clandestine, dirty, abject, or promiscuous. They imagine and recompose ties based on the rejection they experience from the world. They also experience isolation and loneliness in a particular way. Emerging literature is beginning to address these dimensions, investigating queer meanings in general care experiences (Malatino, 2020), family relationships (Park, 2013 Souza, 2022, aging (Araújo and Silva, 2020), and health (Mendes, Jorge and Pilecco, 2019).

All of this seems to indicate an important, albeit incipient, process of expanding the intelligibility of care designs. This idea is yet to unfold and give theoretical meaning to the many dimensions that the plural trajectories of LGBTQIA+ people can illuminate. These are not, by far, homogeneous experiences, also being intersected by both race and class. A poor, marginalized, black *travesti* certainly has a very different experience with care than an upper-class white gay man. And conceptually, all of this matters significantly. Nevertheless, what appears prominently in the analysis of empirical data carried out here is that, throughout their lives, LGBTQIA+ people are urged to negotiate their own care precisely because they are LGBTQIA+. Their identity expression can define whether or not they access care, how they access care, whether or not they will be asked to provide care, and if they will have to invent or recreate their own practices of care.

Thus, LGBTQIA+ care is the complex result of intersected LGBTQIA+ trajectories in the spheres of care. It encompasses experiences of deprivation and violence in family, social, and public processes, as well as in care, within the matrices of LGBTphobia. This results in rearrangements for producing LGBTQIA+ life in specific practices in non-hegemonic spaces through flows, positions, and relationships intersected by gender and sexuality dissent. Therefore, LGBTQIA+ care is everything that lesbian women, gay men, bisexuals, *travestis*, transsexuals, and intersex people do to produce their existence as LGBTQIA+, based on their bodies, alliances, and intersubjective exchanges that result in their experiences of the world. Hence, let us think from this perspective how the COVID-19 pandemic affected these arrangements by listening to young and old LGBTQIA+ people in Belo Horizonte.

4 The Nuances of "Stay Home" as a Form of Care: LGBTQIA+ People, the Pandemic, and Domestic Space

The imperative in facing the COVID-19 pandemic in its most acute moments was strong: "Stay at home". Social isolation and quarantines became public care strategies in the face of the disease, encouraged and demanded widely across the social fabric. And lived in multiple ways. Let us, then, enter into the debate on the daily effects of the pandemic on the lives of LGBTQIA+ people through this call for a domestic retreat to take care of oneself in the face of the pandemic: What did this "stay-at-home" mandate mean for LGBTQIA+ people? What house was this they had to return to? What street was that which they had to leave? In approaching the collected life histories, we are interested in understanding the relationship between dissident gender identities and sexualities, self-constitution practices, and the containment of spaces – the outcomes of being inside or outside the domestic environment.

It is necessary to remember that, from the start, the gesture of leaving, of being outside, is central to the lives of people of dissident genders and sexualities. Outside the compulsory standards of a socially produced normality, which generally incurred intense violence, many experience the process of coming out of the closet as best they can, when they can, and if they can, to affirm themselves in multiple ways. There is an issue in this process that is quite recurring. Coming out of the closet involves conquering new spaces that go beyond what is traditionally contained in a house or home. It is simultaneously a political and intimate reconstruction of the meanings of public spaces, and the physical and subjective occupation of new places in one gesture. This does not mean that the other spaces come with any guarantee. Work, school, the street, and university are also frequently places of confinement and violence. But they present new openings and possibilities for identification, experiencing, being, and resisting.

The importance of space in care relationships, however, is not exactly new (Gelsthorpe, Mody and Sloan, 2020). All that gives shape to what is understood as care unfolds in an intimate relationship with space, both physical and symbolic. The centrality of the home, of domestic space, of the private domain in the universe of care has long been discussed in the literature (Lerussi, 2014; Boris, 2014; Guimarães, 2016). Likewise, non-domestic care places such as daycare centers, nursery schools, hospitals, and long-term care institutions for older adults are the concrete arenas of debate. In fact, there is a hegemonic spatial catalog from which care unfolds.

During the COVID-19 pandemic, measures to control the movement of people restricted the daily lives of most of the population to domestic spaces. Even though Brazil was governed by a president who denied the need for social distancing and underestimated the effects of the virus, isolation measures were adopted by 98.6% of municipal governments in 2020 (IBGE, 2020). In this sense, it is reasonable to assume that care gained prominence during that period, highlighting the relationships, practices, and needs of private spaces, considered the *locus* of care *par excellence*.

However, the idea of LGBTQIA+ care, as we have seen, calls for new ways of interpreting spaces. First, it is necessary to recognize that LGBTQIA+ people circulate in all the classic spaces of care, so to speak. In all of them, their relationships are affected by the fact that they are LGBTQIA+. There seems to be a spatially localized affectation of gender and sexuality dissidence in care, which coexists with processes of deprivation, violence, and rejection that LGBTQIA+ people experience, for example, in their family relationships and domestic environments.

But beyond the limits of these spaces, there is a process of producing alternative practices and other relationships that are also located in different spaces. Much of this developed set of LGBTQIA+ care practices, in the sense of taking care of themselves *in order to be* LGBTQIA+ both materially and subjectively, takes place in spaces not immediately assimilated into reflections on care. In other words, there is a process of spatial displacement that locates these non-hegemonic practices in equally non-hegemonic physical spaces.

The centrality of spaces in affirming LGBTQIA+ identities is already widely assimilated and discussed in literature (Levine, 1979; Bell and Binnie, 2004; Macrae, 2018). From the debate about LGBTQIA+ "ghettos" to the affirmation of historical struggles for rights in self-proclaimed LGBTQIA+ spaces, everything is guided by the perception that gender and sexuality identities are spatially lived. There is an issue, however, that has not yet been debated to the same extent, which is the fact that care practices and relationships also unfold in these spaces. Locations that, at first glance, are seen as places for leisure, pleasure, sexual practices, distraction, and nightlife can also be fundamental arenas for understanding LGBTQIA+ care. Bars, nightclubs, bathhouses, porn cinemas, cruising grounds, prostitution zones, and the street itself can count.

The data collected by our team showed a consistency between the reports of older LGBTQIA+ people interviewed in the *Longeviver* project and the predominantly young population heard in the Observatory project, namely the importance of LGBTQIA+-friendly spaces for the self-discovery of gender or sexuality dissidence. The life stories narrated in both projects have a recurring "beginning of life" memory, a period considered a milestone of self-knowledge and self-experimentation in spaces such as LGBTQIA+ bars and nightclubs. As stated by an older lesbian woman recalling her self-discovery, "There was a gay bar, and that was where it all started."

The narratives show how places such as bars, in contrast to homes, are central in the constitution of an identity. An older gay man, when describing the relationship between freedom, discovery, and identity in nightlife, said, "What happened to me there was a kind of liberation. … And there were also the bars, right? So, I went to bars, I discovered things, right? Then you know what I saw? This thing of freedom."

This feeling of freedom is also seen when a 21-year-old gay man mentions the happiness he experienced when he discovered an LGBTQIA+ nightclub in his hometown. He emphasizes the importance of that space for him to envision his own future happiness and the possibility of being a successful gay man someday:

> I ended up meeting other people, expanding my horizons even more … it was great to know, like, dude, oh my god, I think everyone is gay. There are a lot of people at these parties, … so many people in this city that are LGBT, I'm not the only one … my experience is not … you know, I'm not the only one in the universe who's gay … And it was interesting to observe people who were gay in there, but who were very different from each other … some were company managers, some were … lawyers and everything. So, it was … a snap like that, to know that being gay is not just what was on TV … dead people who get shot in the street or who spend their whole lives, you know, dying, suffering, because society won't accept them. These people have their own lives … they're independent, they do what they want. They travel, they have partners, they have their own house, they have a salary, they … go to restaurants, … they go to concerts. You know, there are a lot of things you can do like this … being gay, it's not an obstacle. And then once it hit me, like … I embraced everything I was without any fear.

These narratives suggest that the meanings attributed to these spaces by LGBTQIA+ people do not correlate in the world of cisgender heterosexuality. Although heterosexual and cisgender men and women can and do widely frequent establishments of this type (bars and nightclubs), what happens there does not seem largely constitutive of what they are. Heterosexual socialization processes further integrate these spaces into a broad reiteration of gender and sexuality norms. For LGBTQIA+ people, in turn, the possibility for the opposite to happen is concentrated precisely these places. They serve as spaces for experimentation, knowledge, and recognition of oneself and others, in addition to enabling affection and sex. When LGBTQIA+ people meet, exchange experiences, and form a bond, they see themselves as LGBTQIA+ at night.

This broad understanding of night also integrates spaces that are even more specific to the LGBTQIA+ universe. This is the case for gay bathhouses as places of socialization and sex that carry a particular trait of secrecy, experimentation, stigma, and liberation. An older gay man describes discovering bathhouses in his youth: "I didn't even know where to go. The day I heard someone comment about … what happened in a sauna, I said, 'That's where I want to go,' you know? Then I discovered saunas." Another interviewee highlights: "My homosexual life revealed a new scenario, a new form of pleasure. And I started to live that in the dark, in the shadows… yeah… hidden. But I've allowed myself to… go to a movie, go to a sauna, take risks in some anonymous situations, but still hidden, right?"

Other spaces, however, have a particular function for *travestis* and trans women. For most of them, prostitution is a reality,[5] meaning wherever the sexual market is structured becomes central spaces. An older *travesti* interviewed in *Longeviver* says:

> At night I went for a walk in the red-light district ["*zona*"] and I saw *travestis* for the first time in my life. I said, 'This is what I want to be. That's what belongs to me.' I went back to the company, got my things, and went to the *zona*. … Everything for me was very new, but everything was very liberating, it was what I wanted. At the same time it was difficult, it was also very pleasant coming to [City], the beach, the sea, a lot of *travestis*, a lot of history, a lot of *Candomblé*, a lot of *Umbanda*, a lot of prostitution, a lot of glamour, a lot of parties, all that for me… It was the best phase of my life, it was in my transition. Even though I suffered a lot, having to work a lot to earn a plate of food, to earn an overnight stay, it was the best phase of my life.

Thus, for *travestis*, prostitution zones are workspaces as well as spaces in which they affirm their gender identity. There they meet other *travestis* and transgender women, get close, create bonds, and establish material and affective

5 Cf. https://antrabrasil.org/2019/11/21/antra-representa-o-brasil-em-audiencia-na-cidh/.

exchanges. And yet, there too, in the prostitution zones, they experience transphobic violence and protect themselves from it.

In this context, reflections on the impacts of the COVID-19 pandemic on this population must also consider sexual and gender dissidences as analytical issues. Just as care takes place in non-hegemonic spaces for queer people, the social isolation imposed by the pandemic and the resulting centrality of domestic spaces also have different meanings for LGBTQIA+ people. This is because restricting life to private environments excludes the non-hegemonic experience of care in everyday life, which for LGBTQIA+ people takes place in spaces of circulation, coexistence, and pleasure that are not usually included in reflections on care.

The data collected by the *Longeviver* and Observatory teams note that the circulation limitations imposed by the pandemic produced particularly negative results for LGBTQIA+ people. One of the observations was how the narratives frequently mention the deterioration of their mental health. These findings align with data showing that, in the first year of the pandemic, the global prevalence of anxiety and depression increased by 25% (WHO, 2022). Economic vulnerability, the absence of social protection networks, and health uncertainties are some of the reasons for exacerbating mental suffering. An older gay man stated, "I needed a psychiatrist in the pandemic. I went crazy. I freaked out, you know? I freaked out, alright. … I was very anxious about this pandemic thing, because I had to continue working while being scared to death."

For LGBTQIA+ people, the losses caused by the pandemic were also determined by their gender and sexuality. For young college students interviewed at the Observatory, a commonly reported issue was the increase in domestic violence perpetrated by various family members, due to the return of these young people to their family homes during the pandemic. Vulnerability and exposure to violence can be amplified for individuals who occupy the dependent pole in a care relationship reshaped by the pandemic. When asked about returning to his family home, a gay man said:

> It was hell. … There was a specific moment when, towards the end of the pandemic, … we were very stressed by the whole situation. I was having a close relationship with her [his mother] when we had a very ugly argument. And during this argument, she made a gesture that made me feel really bad, she imitated a woman, you know? To … imitate the way I was talking to her. … so directed at me like that. I ended up exploding and almost lost my temper with her. But my brothers separated us and I told her, "Look, I'm not coming home again … I'm going to cut this bond with

> you". And... that's what I did, I took my bags and left, kind of forced, to [City], because the situation became unbearable.

References to LGBTphobic domestic violence are not rare, unfortunately. The domestic environment for LGBTQIA+ people seems to be a place of intimidation and repression rather than a space where care can circulate. Although domestic and life-sustaining tasks do take place in the homes of gender and sexuality dissidents, the narratives we collected emphasized conflicts, disagreements, and the invisibility of LGBTQIA+ identities. A young bisexual highlighted the escalation of violence due to the expanded family life during the period of social isolation:

> Then family problems and abuse begin. These episodes of violence do not always happen outside our home. My father is a very violent guy. Most of the things that hurt me during my life came out of his mouth. Things like "this race has to die", "I hate faggots," "faggot I-don't-know-what." Everything I usually hear, most of these things came from my family. I cried many times, and my mother had to intervene in this relationship.

Increasing domestic violence was documented more broadly among, for instance, heterosexual couples. Violence against women escalated as a result of having to spend more time at home with abusive male partners (Vieira, Garcia and Maciel, 2020). However, to us there is a qualitative aspect to LGBTphobic violence in care relationships at home that was brought to the forefront in the stories we heard. It was not more intense or less threatening. Only different. A way of experiencing violence that is connected almost ontologically to the possibilities and impossibilities of existing in the world for LGBTQIA+ young people.

Sometimes, to avoid conflicts at home, our interviewees claimed to have experienced a kind of pause in their sexual dissidence, of being silenced in the family. A survival strategy that erases desire and an honest experience of subjectivity. A bisexual non-binary person stated:

> When I was living here, I was really at peace with my sexuality, but when I went back to live there [at their parents' house], I felt uncomfortable ... just not being able to, for example, make a connection with my friends or comment about a girl I had a crush on. ... I didn't feel like I had freedom.

In this aspect, differences can be observed between the experiences of older *Longeviver* interviewees and the younger Observatory interviewees. While young people's complaints about the pandemic centered around the difficulties of living with family members who do not know or do not accept their sexual and gender identities, the older adults often referred to how the loneliness they felt had been aggravated by the pandemic. The intersections between generation and sexual or gender dissidence, therefore, seem to influence each other by producing specific issues for different age groups. Asked about his interpersonal relationships, an older gay man said:

> the pandemic, it really inhibited any expansion of this horizon of relationships, right? The intimate relationships remained. Yeah, you had a lot of acquaintances, you went out to parties, met a lot of people, and so on, [but] today the relationships, the ones that remain, are few and very faithful. And... my relationship with family members is practically nil, you know? Because I don't visit them anymore, and they don't visit me.

Another older gay interviewee mentioned the loneliness he experienced due to the absence of his children:

> I see them once a year, they come here either at Christmas or on my birthday. But I haven't seen them in two years, you know? [because of the pandemic] So we talk on the phone, online. But it is not the same. I really miss them. We were very good friends, you know? I talked a lot with these kids, I miss all four of them.

From these LGBTQIA+ narratives, it is possible to think about how care is experienced differently by gender and sexuality dissidents, and how the spaces where this care occurs play a role in this diversity. Care, for LGBTQIA+ people, is not limited to the domestic sphere, although it also occurs there. There is a plurality of spaces in which LGBTQIA+ people engender fundamental processes for their self-constitution that tend to be bypassed by traditional reflections on care. Processes that involve their bodies in different ways, engage their subjectivities with proximity and complicity and transform them as people. Processes that are an expanded lens of care. What we see is that people largely understand themselves as LGBTQIA+ in these spaces that include relationships and care practices. The nightlife, the streets, the bars, the nightclubs, the saunas, the porn cinemas, the prostitution zones are much more than physical places for them. These are the places where, in one way or another, they become who they are.

Therefore, when we propose that LGBTQIA+ care occurs in other spaces beyond the traditional domestic sphere, we are not only suggesting a combination of private and public places, but a qualitatively different examination of the role played by space in the care relationships and practices experienced by LGBTQIA+ people.

This means that the pandemic-related social distancing measures produced different types of losses in the care of subjects considered outsiders to gender and sexuality norms. On one hand, there was a ban placed on care networks in places of LGBTQIA+ coexistence where sexuality and gender identity could be experienced more freely and collectively, where identity itself was constituted and lived collaboratively. On the other hand, tensions in domestic environments caused family relationships to weaken due to loneliness exacerbated by social isolation, or to LGBTphobic domestic violence that was revived upon having to return to the family home.

What we see here is that spaces and relationships that are fundamentally linked to the hegemonic concept of care, such as the home and the family, can be sources of direct violence against LGBTQIA+ lives and produce a sense of invisibility in their material and symbolic senses. Many LGBTQIA+ young people that returned to their family context are no longer able to be who they want to be. In a certain way, they cease to exist in the life they had hoped to produce for themselves, since the spaces, relationships, and experiences this other life requires are no longer there. Considering the specific role these dimensions play in the production of a queer self, the general effects of isolation on this population differ in substance from the effects on the general population. For older LGBTQIA+ that experience both ageist and LGBTphobic discrimination, the home can mean a space of extreme loneliness and of relationship dissolutions. Thus, a broader understanding of care can begin to incorporate spaces, relationships, and practices that are vital for LGBTQIA+, even though socially these same spaces, relationships, and practices are of lesser value. The life stories we collected indicate that the pandemic clearly exposed the fragility of the arrangements around LGBTQIA+ care.

5 Conclusion: Care and the Production of LGBTQIA+ Lives

This chapter tried to see care through the situated experiences of LGBTQIA+ people in a large Brazilian city. To see it through their eyes, even if at a quick glance, and in the obstacles caused by the pandemic. This is a population, in fact, that historically knows very well how unequal and cruel the effects of a pandemic can be. They know what it means to be stigmatized by a disease, to have their ways of life, their relationships, their identities, and their possibilities in the world all violently defined by certain moral and political standards reinforced in critical moments such as a pandemic. This was the case with HIV/AIDS, in an obvious and direct way. The same occurred with COVID-19 in ways that were certainly less explicit and harmful. When listening to our interviewees in Belo Horizonte, we discovered that the effects of public care strategies during the new pandemic, especially the isolation requirement and returning to family home environments, were unequally felt by LGBTQIA+ people. Many of them found themselves deprived of possibilities, which were already weak, illegible, threatened, or repudiated, to constitute who they are in their spaces, practices, relationships, and especially LGBTQIA+ care.

There is a certain widespread understanding that the pandemic made care more visible (Nicoli and Vieira, 2020), more palpable in the daily domestic work done in the home, now conducted more intensively before the eyes of those who had not necessarily done it or seen it. The chaos caused by the disease also made care more visible in the health field, in hospital environments and care institutions. The pandemic brought to light the centrality of care, its processes, and its unfair distribution. However, years later, it can be concluded that none of this meant structural changes or fairer designs in the arrangements that organize the social systems related to care.

In the life stories narrated by the LGBTQIA+ people, we heard how this pandemic-related emergence of care, this greater visibility of practices that produce and maintain life in general, also included a process of obscuring and hiding. To take care of themselves during the pandemic, many of our interviewees were forced to leave their LGBTQIA+ ways of caring. Young people in Belo Horizonte told us that being confined to their family homes meant experiencing discrimination on an intense daily basis. And they experienced it without the possibilities of repair, reconstitution, and re-creation granted by other practices and spaces that they had progressively conquered in their lives before the pandemic. They were far from friends, lovers, and connections, and far from any social, material, and subjective support for their existence as LGBTQIA+ people. Many told us about going back into the closet, a hidden cost of home care during the pandemic. They mentioned how re-hiding who they are was a strategy to keep themselves "safe" and "cared for" at home.

Older LGBTQIA+ people, in turn, who were already experiencing loss of vitality in their affective, family, and social ties in the aging process point to a specific relationship between isolation, loneliness, age, and sexual and gender identities. In addition to their fear of the disease, the pandemic was brutal for their subjectivities. The deprivation of all interactions, affective relationships, and social exchanges appeared in extreme forms in the data we collected. They described how they co-existed with a general feeling of involuntary isolation that was not limited to COVID-19 lockdowns. The isolation they felt had more or less already been there, precisely because they are older LGBTQIA+.

If we understand care as the material and symbolic process of producing life within spatially located relationships, perhaps there was an interruption of these vital flows for LGBTQIA+ people. Even if the body's basic operations were guaranteed, the production of an LGBTQIA+ life was suspended due to the high costs of isolation, violence, and deprivation. This is essential in the context of the subjective perceptions of some of our interviewees, who in their memories associate the beginning of their lives with the beginning of their experiences as LGBTQIA+.

Perhaps all of this is stretching too far a conceptual reflection that is still based on limited empirical findings. But the fact is, we cannot help but see what our interviewees showed us, even if at a glance. And the attempt to place it under the umbrella of LGBTQIA+ care is almost an involuntary preservation strategy, almost wishing it into existence and to be preserved, especially in the face of systematic threats to interrupt what happens in these spaces, relationships, and practices.

Perhaps this chapter, based on fragments, is just that. An attempt to see and name, with the hope of preserving. As if we could now look our opening protagonists of this chapter in the eyes and tell them that we see them. To understand where the violence that an older LGBTQIA+ person suffers in their profound isolation, based on discrimination, comes from. And understand how a young LGBTQIA+ person, who is denied the possibility of being, can recreate care. In clandestine spaces. In very sensitive and fragile operations of self-constitution. In fleeting communities, fragments, episodes that perhaps effectively assume the ethical dimension of care. From a dimension of care that has been seen and, as so, cannot be unseen.

References

ANTRA – Associação Nacional de Travestis e Transexuais [*National Association of Travestis and Transexuals*]. *Conceitos que trabalhamos*. 2024. Available at: https://antrabrasil.org/sobre/#:~:text=Conceitos%20que%20trabalhamos%3A,e%20interpessoal%2C%20atrav%C3%A9s%20dessa%20identidade. Accessed in February 20th, 2024.

Araújo, Ludgleydson Fernandes; Silva, Henrique Salmazo da (org.). (2020) *Envelhecimento e velhice LGBT*: práticas e perspectivas biopsicossociais. Campinas, SP: Alínea, 2020.

Bell, David, & Binnie, Jon. (2004). Authenticating Queer Space: Citizenship, Urbanism and Governance. *Urban Studies*, 41 (9): 1807–1820. https://doi.org/10.1080/00420980 42000243165.

Boris, Eileen. (2014) Produção e reprodução, casa e trabalho. *Tempo Social*, 26 (1): 01–122.

Fisher, Berenice; Tronto, Joan. (1990) Toward a feminist theory of caring. *In*: Abel, Emily; Nelson, Margaret. *Circles of care*: work and identity in women's lives. Albany, NY: Suny Press.

Gelsthorpe, Loraine; Mody, Perveez; Sloan, Brian (eds.). (2020) *Spaces of care*. Oxford/ New York: Hart.

Georges, Isabel. (2019) O "cuidado" como "quase-conceito": por que está pegando? Notas sobre a resiliência de uma categoria emergente. *In*: Debert, Guta Grin; Pulhez, Mariana Marques. *Desafios do cuidado*: gênero, velhice e deficiência. 2nd ed. Campinas, SP: UNICAMP/IFCH.

Guimarães, Nadya Araujo. (2016) Casa e mercado, amor e trabalho, natureza e profissão: controvérsias sobre o processo de mercantilização do trabalho de cuidado. *Cadernos Pagu*, 46: 59–77.

IBGE – Instituto Brasileiro de Geografia e Estatística. (2020) *Pesquisa de Informações Básicas Municipais 2020* (Munic 2020). Available at: https://cidades.ibge.gov.br/brasil/pesquisa/1/74454?ano=2020. Accessed in October 2023.

Lerussi, Romina. (2014) *La retórica de la domesticidad:* Política feminista, derecho y empleo doméstico en la Argentina. Buenos Aires: Universidad Nacional de La Plata.

Levine, Martin P. (1979). Gay ghetto. *Journal of homosexuality*, 4 (4): 363–377. https://doi.org/10.1300/J082v04n04_04.

MacRae, Edward. (2018). *A construção da igualdade-política e identidade homossexual no Brasil da "abertura"*. Salvador: Edufba.

Malatino, Hil. (2020) *Trans Care*. Minnesota: University of Minnesota Press.

Manzini, E. J. (1990/1991) A entrevista na pesquisa social. *Didática*, 26/27: 149–158.

Mendes, Lindalva Guimarães; Jorge, Alzira Oliveira; Pilecco, Flávia Bulegon. (2019) Proteção social e produção do cuidado a travestis e a mulheres trans em situação de rua no município de Belo Horizonte (MG). *Saúde em Debate*, 43 (8): 107–119.

Molinier, Pascale; Paperman, Patricia. (2015) Descompartimentar a noção de cuidado? *Revista Brasileira de Ciência Política*, 18: 43–57.

Nicoli, Pedro Augusto Gravatá; Vieira, Regina Stela. (2020) Cuidado em surto: da crise à ética. *Revista Cult*. Available at: https://revistacult.uol.com.br/home/cuidado-em-surto/. Accessed in October 2023.

Park, Shelley. (2013) *Mothering Queerly, Queering Motherhood*. New York: State University of New York Press.

Silva, Samuel Araujo Gomes da; Lena, Fernanda Fortes de; Miranda-Ribeiro, Paula de. (2018) Demografia e diversidade sexual: uma análise da produção acadêmica sobre gênero e identidade sexual na demografia entre 2000 e 2017. *XXI Encontro Nacional de Estudos Populacionais*, Poços de Caldas.

Souza, Érica Renata. (2022) Parentalidades LGBT+. In: Ramos, Marcelo M.; Valentin, Márcia F. R. C.; Nicoli, Pedro A. G. (Org.). *Dicionário Jurídico do Gênero e da Sexualidade*. Salvador, BA: Devires.

Vieira, Pâmela Rocha; Garcia, Leila Posenato; Maciel, Ethel Leonor Noia. (2020) Isolamento social e o aumento da violência doméstica: o que isso nos revela? *Revista Brasileira de Epidemiologia*, 23: 1–5.

WHO (2022). *World Health Organization. Mental Health and COVID-19: Early evidence of the pandemic's impact*: Scientific brief, 2 March 2022. Available at: https://www.who.int/publications/i/item/WHO-2019-nCoV-Sci_Brief-Mental_health-2022.1. Accessed in October 2023.

CHAPTER 12

Eldercare, COVID-19, and the Clash between State and Civil Society in Brazil

Guita Grin Debert and Jorge Felix

1 Introduction

One of the most important impacts of the COVID-19 pandemic has been the focus on care issues. Following the declaration of emergency by the World Health Organization (WHO) on March 11, 2020, the topic gained ground and provoked a broad debate about the lack of social protection networks, especially for older people, in several countries, regardless of the degree of economic development. In the words of Woodward (2012), care is no longer a "public secret," or something society chooses and/or agrees to leave in the shadows reserved for inconvenient matters. Until the pandemic, the scandalous denial of the centrality of our dependence on care had been a public secret which we hid from ourselves.

Choirs and orchestras, social networks, television stations, and newspapers opened exclusive spaces to honor professionals who, despite the dangers of contagion, continued to carry out their activities. They were healthcare professionals, caregivers for the older people, supermarket workers, and security officers. Even garbage collectors found thank you notes in the bins they collected during the pandemic. This was an unprecedented recognition of care work.

The attention being given to people whose previous existence was dedicated to serving us, but who today are seen as central to the functioning of society, mainly to guarantee a minimum of economic activity, is something extremely new. The context of the pandemic forced governments in several countries to adopt measures to valorize care professionals, expand public services, and supervise the private sector more consistently. In short, a new meaning for care was placed on political agendas (Legros, 2020).

In Brazil, the legacy of the pandemic was the politicization of care from 2023 onwards. A few days after the WHO declared the end of the pandemic on May 5, the Brazilian government officially announced the creation of an interministerial working group (IWG) to develop a National Care Policy and a National Care Plan. The group, coordinated by two Brazilian federal ministries (Ministry of Social Development, Family, and Fight Against Hunger,

 | DOI:10.1163/9789004707009_013

and Ministry of Women) was given the mission of formulating a diagnosis of the social organization of care in Brazil, and of identifying policies, existing programs, and services (Brazil, 2023). In October 2023, the IWG opened its first public consultation where society could participate in drafting the new legislation.

The urgency with which a National Care Policy was established can only be understood if we consider how the previous administration had handled the COVID-19 pandemic.

In this chapter, we first present some data about Brazil in the context of the pandemic, particularly in terms of the older population. To portray how the central government dealt with the worst moment of the crisis, we describe the denial of the pandemic that marked President Jair Bolsonaro's administration (2019–2022) and data on COVID-related infections and mortality rates. We discuss how the COVID-19 crisis was accompanied by a lack of interest in policies aimed at the older population, and in the section "Civil Society Takes Charge," we explore actions taken by society to mitigate the effects of the pandemic. In the section "The Pandemic: a Setback in Eldercare Policies", we show how issues related to old age took on new meanings before and after pandemic. Finally, we address the challenges involved in defining a National Care Policy.

2 COVID and the Brazilian Older Population

Brazil was one of the three countries in the world most affected by the COVID-19 pandemic. According to the Johns Hopkins Coronavirus Resource Center (CRC, 2021), the country was third in number of infections on May 3, 2021, with a total of 14,725,975. This was only surpassed by India with 19,557,457 and the United States with 32,392,274. Brazil was second in terms of total deaths, with 406,437 lives lost, while the United States led with 576,722 and India was third, with 215,542.

Relative analysis shows that the effect on the country appears even more severe, since its total population is 212 million (IBGE, 2021)[1] against 327 million in the United States and 1.3 billion in India (OECD, 2021). This means that,

1 IBGE, the Brazilian Institute of Geography and Statistics (Instituto Brasileiro de Geografia e Estatística) is responsible for the official collection of statistical, geographic, cartographic, and geodetic information in Brazil. The last census was carried out in 2021.

comparatively, the impact of the disease in Brazil was half of that in the United States but almost five times higher than in India (CRC, 2021).[2]

The first case of COVID-19 was confirmed in Brazil on February 26, 2020, and the first death on March 17, 2020. Just 10 months later, the pandemic in Brazil had spun out of control. Brazil has had an increasingly aging population since the late 1970s, making the older population a target of growing concern for healthcare professionals. This is relevant since statistical data coming from the first countries affected by the pandemic (especially China) and the alerts released by the World Health Organization (WHO) showed a higher incidence of serious and deadly cases among the older population.

Currently, 16% of the Brazilian population is above 60—the age used by the United Nations for classifying older people in developing countries, and which is also used Brazilian legislation. That translates into a total of 33.9 million people (IBGE, 2021). According to official projections, 19.9 million people are 65 or more, which is 9.5% of the total population. The age category showing the highest growth rate, however, is that of 80 or more years of age, currently estimated at 4.1 million people, or 2% of the total population. This category is expected to double in size over the next 15 years, as life expectancy at birth continues to rise, reaching an average age of 76.6 in 2019 according to official data.

This demographic change is happening in a socioeconomic environment of extreme social inequality. Brazil is the ninth most unequal country on the planet, and had a Gini index of 0.543 in 2019 (IBGE, 2021). Approximately 80% of the older population has access to social security (pensions) or social assistance (non-contributory benefits). However, about 70% of these policyholders receive only a minimum wage, which is about 157.14 euros (207.93 US dollars or 1,100 Brazilian reals, in the updated amount of 2021).[3]

According to Rogério Barbosa et al. (2020), there were significant drops in social inequality levels between 2000 and 2010, mainly due to wage increases for laborers (a policy that increased the minimum wage to above the inflation rate between 2003 and 2015), as well as a direct cash transfer program for the poorest in society. However, Barbosa et al. also state that since 2015, all gains for the poorest have been turned into gains for the wealthiest, seeing as over

2 Based on the number of deaths per 100,000 people, Brazil is in 6th place with 19,258 deaths. The United States is 19,119, and India is 1,577. Data from May 3, 2021. On May 10, 2021, Brazil reached 3rd place, behind only Hungary and Italy, according to the CRC.

3 In 2024, the minimum wage is equivalent to 262.45 euros or 284.67 US dollars. Regarding the income situation of the Brazilian retired population, see Felix, 2023.

80% of the observed financial growth was in the hands of the latter. For this reason, Barbosa et al. call the 2010–2020 period "the lost decade."

This situation was aggravated by the biggest economic recession in the country's history in 2015, when GDP dropped -3.55% and then -3.31% in 2016. In 2017, 2018, and 2019, the growth average was 1.4% p.a. With the country unable to combat the 2020 unemployment rate of 14.6%, informality reached 41.65% of the workforce. Furthermore, unemployment mainly affects young people and the older, as shown by Ana Amélia Camarano (2020).

Most Brazilian families faced the COVID-19 pandemic from this socioeconomic scenario. The country's older population, which have an average of 7 years of formal study[4] per individual, work mainly in the service sector and/or are self-employed. While older Brazilians are above the extreme poverty line (less than 1.90 US dollars a day), COVID-19 was still a threat, not only because of the higher rates of infection and death, but also because of the increased risk of falling into poverty due to illness, prejudice (ageism), unemployment, or government neglect.

3 "It's Not Going to Be a Little Cold That's Going to Bring Me Down"

According to the Human Rights Watch (HRW), President Jair Bolsonaro "tried to sabotage measures against the spread of COVID-19 in Brazil and promoted policies that compromise human rights" (HRW, 2021, p. 105). One of the groups most affected by this stance was the older population, because unlike other groups identified by HRW (Black, indigenous, women, people with disabilities), the older could not rely on democratic institutions to defend them from the inefficiency of the Brazilian government.

Jair Bolsonaro came to power in 2019 after a highly polarized election between what was considered the extreme right—represented by himself—and the center-left. His political ideology is characterized by antiglobalism and neoliberal approaches combined with a so-called moral agenda that pushes nationalism, family values, and the work ethic.

The COVID-19 pandemic was interpreted by Bolsonaro as a threat, a "plot" to prevent his administration from implementing policies like the privatization

4 The illiteracy rate of people aged 65 and over is 37.1% in the lowest income quintile (IBGE, 2021).

of state-owned companies, tax cuts, subsidies, environmental and labor deregulation, and increasing the defense budget.[5]

In January 2020, when news first arrived about the spread of COVID-19 through China and Europe, Bolsonaro aligned his position to that of Donald Trump, then president of the United States (2017–2021). One of the narratives he most endorsed was that the virus was only dangerous to the older and he advocated for the so-called "vertical isolation" (Maia and Leandro, 2020).

As COVID-19 spread across Brazil, Bolsonaro held press conferences several times a day, creating his own narrative of the crisis by inciting his 57.8 million constituents to disregard instructions about masks, social distancing, and hand washing. His first public statement on COVID-19, on January 26, 2020, included the words, "We are obviously concerned, but this is not an alarming situation" (Beraldo, 2020). Every morning as he left the official residence, the President stopped his car in front of a crowd of supporters to shake hands, take selfies, and sometimes even kiss them.

His statements began including words such as "exaggerated" (Gomes, 2020a), "fantasy" (G1, 2020), "neurosis" (Folha de S. Paulo, 2021), and "hysteria" (ibid.). He insisted that the disease "is not all that, as is being propagated by the media," the "media has no moral character" (G1, 2020). Shortly after, on March 11, 2020, after the WHO had declared a pandemic, Bolsonaro repeatedly stated that the disease would kill "only the elderly" and that the rest of the population could "go on with normal life" (Weterman, 2020). On March 16, 2020, a day before the country witnessed its first death from the virus, he said: "There will be problems, there are the elderly, those who are in trouble, those who have a disability, but it is not all they say it is" (Uribe, 2020).

Bolsonaro asserted that his biggest concern was the economy, because "if the economy ends, the government ends" (Folha de S. Paulo, 2021). When news of COVID-19 deaths came from Italy, the President's reaction was: "It's a country similar to the Copacabana neighborhood, where every apartment has a *little old man* or a *little old couple*. So, they are much more sensitive, more likely to die" (O Globo, 2020). Copacabana, in Rio de Janeiro, is a place known for its large number of older residents.

The day after the first COVID-19 death in Brazil, the President issued a statement that widely circulated throughout the country: "It's not going to be a little cold that's going to bring me down, okay?" (ibid.). He gave this statement when asked about his own age of 65. He said that his "athletic background" (UOL,

5 In 2020, the government spent 0.5% less on civil servants' salaries, and increased spending on military salaries by 12%. The military went through a career restructuring to make up for losses from the 2019 pension reform. Official inflation for the year was 4.52%.

2021a) would protect him from the most serious symptoms of the virus. One week after the country's first death, he once again compared Brazil to Europe as a way of rebuffing the possibility of a crisis: "The European population is extremely elderly" (Valfré, 2020). On March 24, 2020, he argued during a radio and television broadcast, "What is happening in the world has shown that the group at risk is people over 60. So why close schools?" (Planalto, 2020).

These statements by the President helped steer public opinion against the older person and to labelling them as a "risk group." This classification stopped other population groups, especially young people, from carrying out preventive measures. There were older people who experienced physical violence in supermarkets and pharmacies by people who said they should be socially isolating so young people and non-older adults could be free to move about, an idea reinforced by the President (Record TV Goiás, 2021). Bolsonaro's speeches in front of the cameras had a derisive, "anti-life" tone. For example, once, when questioned by reporters about the high number of deaths, he replied, "So what? I am not a gravedigger... All of us are going to die one day. There's no point running away from it, from reality. We have to stop being a country of sissies." (Gomes, 2020b).

The President's attitude was extremely harmful to the older population, as we will discuss below. Its consequences affected crisis management and resulted in the abandonment of precautionary measures and a lack of protective measures and care policies. Furthermore, it should be noted that Bolsonaro criticized local governments for adopting measures recommended by scientists and the WHO and publicly promoted the use of drugs that had no proof of effectively fighting the virus. This made thousands of older people take these non-prescription drugs, such as Reuquinol, Ivermectin, and especially hydroxychloroquine.[6]

Today, the amount of hydroxychloroquine Brazil has in stock could last the country a century. At the time, Bolsonaro encouraged the Army Chemical and Pharmaceutical Laboratory (*Laboratório Químico Farmacêutico do Exército*), run by the armed forces, to multiply the production of the medicine tenfold. From 265,000 pills a year, production jumped to 3.2 million. These drugs were recommended in the President's daily social media posts for consumption by the older population. In addition to the President himself, several television

6 In January 2021, when the city of Manaus experienced days of terror due to oxygen shortages, the head of the ICU service at Hospital Getúlio Vargas—the main hospital in the state of Amazonas—recorded a video that went viral on social networks, testifying that many of the dead had aggravated health conditions caused by medications they took upon Bolsonaro's recommendation (UOL, 2021b).

stations, journalists, and government supporters also recommended the drugs in their broadcasts or digital networks. On January 16, 2021, Twitter blocked a post on the Ministry of Health's official account for spreading fake news about the efficiency of preventive treatments against COVID-19. The older population was the main victim of this bombardment of disinformation, especially seeing as a large number of these drugs was distributed to this age group by mayors politically aligned to Bolsonaro.[7]

In the midst of the pandemic, the President fired two health ministers for refusing to follow his orders of recommending these drugs to the population. The first health minister strictly followed WHO recommendations and respected the public health system. The second (who remained in office only from April 17, 2020, to May 15, 2020) prioritized his commitment as a doctor above obedience to Bolsonaro. The third was an army general with no experience in the health field, but who faithfully followed all orders.[8] He later resigned, and on March 23, 2021, Bolsonaro gave in to pressure and replaced him with a physician, Brazil's fourth health minister since the beginning of the pandemic.

Failing to control the pandemic, the President deliberately started promoting public gatherings to demonstrate that he had the population's support. He attended these events without a mask and hugged many people. His attitude contaminated several government agencies, including the Ministry of Health, thus preventing any national action to adopt measures that could mitigate the effects of the pandemic for the most vulnerable groups like indigenous people, the poor, and the older population.

Brazil also lagged in purchasing respirators, PPEs, vaccines, syringes, and needles, which in early 2021, jeopardized the agility of vaccination campaigns for priority groups. In January, while vaccinations had already started in many countries, the Minister of Health stated that vaccinations in Brazil would be happen "on D-day and H-hour." This brought even more insecurity to the

7 The number of mayors who adopted the so-called "COVID kit" for early treatment of the virus, containing drugs with no proven efficacy, is unknown. The only official number is found in the state of Rio Grande do Sul where the press registered 159 municipalities that distributed these drugs (including hydroxychloroquine and ivermectin) provided by the Ministry of Health. In April 2021, Bolsonaro visited the municipality of Chapecó (in the state of Santa Catarina) to support the mayor, encourage the use of the drugs, and post photos on social media.

8 The minister explained his subservient relationship to Bolsonaro's orders in front of the cameras with a phrase that became symbolic of this relationship: "It's as simple as that: one commands and the other obeys" (Mazui, 2020).

general population, including, of course, the older people who were anxious for a vaccine, along with the rest of the world.

4 COVID-19 Infection and Morbidity Rates

The first point to be highlighted is the state's negligence of official data, along with the fact that there was no monitoring of lethality of the virus by age group. When the pandemic began on March 11, 2020, the federal government had a centralized data dissemination system at the Ministry of Health. In June 2020, however, when infection and death rates began reaching very high levels, the government decided to delay the release of statistics to the press. On the Ministry's official website, the focus was on the number of recoveries, not the number of deaths. The press reacted by carrying out its own analysis, based on data provided by the individual states.

The government's refusal to produce accurate and up-to-date statistics on COVID-19 hindered actions that could have helped the older person, especially those living in long-term care facilities (LTCFs).[9] Furthermore data on nursing homes and assisted living facilities has always been insufficient and incomplete in Brazil, and the government has no data on the number of institutes. Many institutes still operate covertly without official registration, although the sector has developed and become more professional in the last two decades, especially in private for-profit ventures.

In 2010, a survey by IPEA, (Institute for Applied Economic Research) estimated that there are 3,548 LTCFs in the country, 65.2% of which are philanthropic (Camarano and Barbosa, 2016). However, because these establishments are linked to the social sector and not the health sector, less than 50% receive regular medical visits from government programs focused on preventive care. These establishments generally lack PPEs and other health materials that were fundamental to combating COVID-19. In private enterprises, regular medical care reaches 86.3%.

The same survey estimates that only 1% of the country's older population lives in LTCFs. Although regulations for these establishments forbids the permanent residence of older adults with illnesses that require medical or chronic assistance, more than 63.2% of the institutions registered by the government do, in fact, house people in such situations. Therefore, the COVID-19 pandemic

9 There is no legal difference between assisted living facilities and nursing homes in Brazil.

TABLE 12.1 COVID-19 deaths by age in Brazil (2020)

Age (Years)	Deaths	% of total
60–64	10.649	10.4
65–69	12.914	12.6
70–74	13.526	13.2
75–79	12.727	12.4
80–84	12.060	11.8
85–89	8.495	8.3
90+	6.587	6.4
60+	76.958	75.1

SOURCE: INFOGRIPE/FIOCRUZ – REFERRING TO AUGUST 29TH, 2020, OR THE END OF THE 35TH EPIDEMIOLOGICAL WEEK

only worsened the situation of LTCFs, which were unable to rely on any federal government support.

Independent researchers at universities had predicted that older person mortality rates in LTCFs would make up 44.7% of Brazil's COVID-19 deaths when the total number of deaths reached 240,000, meaning that 107,548 older people would have died (Machado et al., 2020). The state of São Paulo would be worst affected with 24,500 deaths. These studies, however, were interrupted either because of a lack of resources, or unfavorable conditions due to the need for social isolation. This data blackout hindered making informed decisions about protecting the older population from the virus.

Regarding official data, the InfoGripe service provided by the Oswaldo Cruz Foundation (*Fiocruz, Fundação Oswaldo Cruz, 2021*) estimates that, up until the end of the 35th epidemiological week (August 29, 2020), people over the age of 60 made up 75.1% of total deaths (see Table 12.1), 14% of total infections, and 52.2% of total severe cases. Fiocruz is a scientific institution for research and development in biological sciences, dedicated to improving health of the general population by supporting the Brazil's public health system called SUS, the Unfied Health System (*Sistema Único da Saúde*).

Four months after the start of Brazil's vaccination campaign, which prioritized the older people, the COVID-19 death rate for this age group fell from 75.1% to 18.1% of total deaths. Data taken from the 14th epidemiological week of 2021, shows the proportion of older persons deaths because of COVID-19 by age group.[10]

In a country of deeply rooted inequality, some demographic groups have been hit harder by the COVID-19 pandemic than others. According to a recent IBGE survey, Black people were twice as likely to experience COVID-19 symptoms as white people. The study also found that Black people were more likely to lose their jobs or encounter pay cuts during the pandemic. The death rate in poorer cities was also substantially higher than in affluent ones.

The President's denialist attitude toward the effects of COVID-19 has been pointed out by several authors (Castro et al., 2021) and in scientific publications (*The Lancet*, 2020) as one of the most significant reasons for the tragic events in Brazil, mainly how he delegitimized scientists and science itself. The Health Law Research Center at the University of São Paulo's School of Public Health analyzed 3,049 laws and regulations related to COVID-19 issued by the federal government between January and November 2020. The study "revealed the existence of an institutional strategy for the spread of the virus, promoted by the Brazilian government under the leadership of the Presidency of the Republic" (CEPEDISA, 2021).

5 Civil Society Takes Charge

Since is impossible to think of the state as a homogeneous being, it should be noted that the federal government's performance encountered resistance from local governments. The governors of the 27 federation units (26 states and the capital, Brasília) took over pandemic management and adopted sanitary measures. In many cases, the inspections at LTCFs were carried out by the Health Surveillance agencies, since the ones responsible for those establishments overrun by death had been arrested. Many lives were saved in this way. Additionally, local governments offset up field hospitals in record time, which allowed the health service network to expand.

10 The average age of hospitalized patients has been progressively decreasing. In epidemiological week 1 of 2021, the average age for COVID-19 infection cases was 62, and 71 for deaths. The data show that in epidemiological week 10, the average age was 58 for new cases and 66 for deaths. According to Fiocruz, although recent consolidated data is still emerging, the behavior of the indicators for infections and deaths in the short future can verify whether the rejuvenation of the pandemic in Brazil will be sustained over time (Fiocruz, 2021a).

Although SUS is the largest public health system in the world (Castro et al., 2021),[11] the implementation of structured healthcare is extremely uneven across the country. The shortage of professionals, beds, and ICUs is most serious in northern, northeastern, and midwestern states. In the case of LTCFs, the situation is even worse. In the beginning of the pandemic, when research warned of chaos in residential homes for the older, civil society assumed its constitutional responsibility. Health professionals and researchers created the FN-ILPI, a National Front for Strengthening LTCFs (*Frente Nacional de Fortalecimento às Instituições de Longa Permanência para Idosos*)[12] to address the urgent need for emergency supplies to fight COVID-19, and to ask public authorities for effective actions to help older people living in these facilities.

The FN-ILPI works with the Brazilian Parliament. One of its main objectives is to support the Committee for the Defense of Older People Rights (part of the Chamber of Deputies) in tackling the COVID-19 pandemic with a specific focus on LTCFs. It also contributes to the development of a National Policy for Continuing Care—an old claim in the Brazilian field of gerontology.

During the pandemic, FN-ILPI worked alongside other non-governmental organizations such as the Brazilian Association of Collective Health (*Associação Brasileira de Saúde Coletiva*)[13] and the Human Longevity and Aging Observatory (*Observatório da Longevidade Humana e Envelhecimento, 2021*),[14] as well as initiatives such as All For Health (*Todos pela Saúde, 2021*),[15] a group of doctors and volunteer specialists funded by private sector actors including major banks and companies. Initiatives such as these received millions in donations and quickly came to the aid of LTCFs, health services, and the needy, most significantly by offering COVID-19 testing.

In the poorest neighborhoods of the larger cities—13.6 million people live in slums in Brazil (Agência Brasil, 2020)—residents created their own community organizations to raise awareness about preventing COVID-19 infection to counteract the lack of specific government advice. In these neighborhoods, conditions are unfavorable for controlling a virus. Houses are often overpopulated and flimsy, lacking basic sanitation and clean water, which makes doctor-recommended hand-washing impossible.

---

11 Brazil is the only country with a population larger than 100 million that has a free, universal, and comprehensive health care system (Castro et al., 2021).

12 See "Frente-Ilpi." Accessed 4 October 2021. https://frente-ilpi.com.br/.

13 See "ABRASCO (2021): Associação Brasileira de Saúde Coletiva." Accessed 4 October 2021. https://www.abrasco.org.br/site/.

14 See "Home – Olhe." Accessed 4 October 2021. http://www.olhe.org.br/.

15 See "Todos pela Saúde." Accessed 4 October 2021. https://www.todospelasaude.org/.

Another civil society initiative created during the pandemic was the National Front for the Councils of Older Population Rights. Thematic rights councils are provided for in the Constitution with the objective of building a decentralized and participatory democracy. So many councils were created from 2003 to 2010, that Carla Almeida and Luciana Tatagiba (2012) define this period as the time when an "army of councilors" emerged. This evolution was interrupted in 2019 by a decree signed by President Bolsonaro.

Brazil had 2,593 thematic councils across the country, of which only 32 (1.2%) survived. The councils had equal representation from civil society and the government, with around 24 to 30 councilors in each. The National Council for the Rights of the Older People (*Conselho Nacional dos Direitos da Pessoa Idosa*) was shut down by Bolsonaro in 2019, but after civil protests it was recreated with only 6 councilors, all appointed by the government and thus limiting its power to influence government actions related to the older people.

Created in 2020, the first move made by the National Front for the Councils of Older People Rights was to prepare the first national diagnosis of the Councils for the Rights of the Older People (FFC, 2020), which continued through the pandemic. The diagnosis survey recorded the perspectives of councilors regarding the main deficiencies in public policies for the older person in 1,645 cities. This civil reorganization, motivated by the pandemic, gave visibility to the issue of aging that went beyond the health crisis, awakening public opinion to the fast-moving demographic transition occurring in the country.

Never before had the aging been discussed so extensively in the media. Opinions differed immensely, ranging from increasing the scope of social assistance and meeting the needs of the homeless, to endorsements of the silver economy (Felix, 2019) as a strategy to deal with deindustrialization dependence on inputs, health equipment, and technology.

The federal administration's irresponsible behavior uncovered the urgent need for civil society to be more active on issues such as poverty and destitution, previously seen as the exclusive responsibility of the State.

At the end of April 2021, a parliamentary inquiry committee of 11 members was approved by the Senate to investigate the federal administration's negligence in combating the pandemic.[16] This shows the clash between the federal government, civil society, and other political institutions where doctors and scientists joined municipal and state governments and private companies to call for and implement endeavors to manage the health crisis. The media has

16 According to the press, the parliamentary inquiry committee created a document collating more than 200 of Bolsonaro's denialist phrases. This will be used by senators as evidence of the government's negligence. See Chaib and Machado, 2021.

listened to these dissenting voices and supported scientific measures. And yet it also left ample space for the President, even when he criticizes the attitudes of the federal government.

6 The Pandemic: a Setback in Older Population Care Policies

The past few decades have been marked by a heightened sensitivity to the rights of the older population in Brazil. The 1988 Constitution, the National Policy for the Older People (Act 8.842/1994), and the Statute for the Older People (Act 10.741/2003) are certainly among the most advanced legal stances regarding the older population in the world. These laws and proposed measures, developed by government institutions in collaboration with civil society organizations (Debert, 1999), establish rights for the older population according to concepts that are undeniably integrated with the country's social sector. The 1988 Constitution was the first to recognize the older people as having specific rights of their own (Graeff, 2019).

Several Brazilian states have police stations that specialize in protecting older adults and public attorney groups focused on defending older population rights. Likewise, municipal and state councils, that bring together civil society and state representatives, are actively and ceaselessly working to improve the living conditions of older people.

In the area of social assistance, the Continuous Cash Benefit Program, or BPC (*Benefício de Prestação Continuada*), initiated by Act 8.742/1993, is a non-contributory cash provision that guarantees a pension for those aged 65 and over equal to a monthly minimum wage, or a grant for people with disabilities. Beneficiaries must prove that they have no means to support their own or their family's needs. In the case of the BPC acting as a pension, the beneficiary must prove that the income of each individual living in the same household is not more than 25% over the minimum wage.

In some municipalities, BPC ensures family income to the point that Camarano (2020) hypothesized, based on official data, that the risk of entire families being without income increased during the pandemic if an older person in that family died. Therefore, this type of situation could contribute to exacerbating Brazil's poverty and inequality rates.

In short, the older adults have enjoyed specific rights in addition to their general citizen rights, such as priority service at public and private agencies or institutions, priority in processing judicial and administrative proceedings, half-price tickets and entry fees to cultural and leisure activities, BPC, a quota of 3% of public housing units, free municipal public transport in reserved seats, exclusive parking spaces, protective measures for older adults at risk, and free geriatric and gerontological care. Furthermore, these policies advocate for the participation of older people and civil society in defining public policies.

Federal government actions had progressively ensured democratic achievements in the rights of the older population. By 2015, the public debate on these rights had evolved in the direction of expanding the coverage of long-term state care. The inclusion of "dependency" in the Constitution was discussed as a fourth pillar of social security (Camarano, 2010) alongside free healthcare, social security, and social assistance, which were already guaranteed since 1988. However, the COVID-19 pandemic led to a setback. It started with some medical actors publicly advocating for the selective treatment of COVID-19 patients depending on age, in order to save the health system from collapsing. This pushed the country into an ethical dilemma that was unfavorable to the older person. The debate was then taken over by an economic view of productivity, where those deemed most "useful" to society should be the ones to survive the pandemic (Debert and Felix, 2020). On April 27, 2021, the Minister of Economy himself publicly voiced this view: "Everyone wants to live for 100 years, 120, 130… there is no investment capacity for the State to keep up with that" (Naldis, 2021).

7 Final Considerations: the Embarrassment of Exposing Public Secrets

The pandemic scenario has drawn attention to the issue of care and to caregiver rights. A National Care Plan was proposed by the government administration that come to power in 2023, as we showed at the beginning of this chapter. Sensitivity towards old age and its problems and challenges have gained new dimensions and meanings. Previously, Brazilian public policies for the older population were almost exclusively focused on encouraging community spirit: dances, tourism, participation in cultural events, universities, physical activities, and sports for the older were all promoted. The motivation behind these activities, of perceiving the older as people with functional autonomy and of enhancing their quality of life, seems to have taken a back seat during the pandemic (Debert, 1999). The pandemic forced people to consider issues related to dependency and care, thus exposing the public secret that had been so closely guarded.

A National Care Plan must also take into account the physical and mental loss that can mark old age, although these kinds of policies can be costly, since they include, for example, training professionals to care for citizens with lower levels of functional autonomy. Furthermore, it is important that the National Care Plan not fall into familism, because we know that making the family responsible for caring for its older members is, above all, a euphemism for attributing care work exclusively to women.

Yet, these changes have not necessarily been a step backward in gerontology. First, the pandemic was important for civil society to recognize the heterogeneity of the older people category and how it includes an inevitable dependence on other human beings for care, however much the State's or the economy's craving for productivity might wish to erase this category from society and relieve itself of its responsibilities.

The WGI, recognizing the importance of civil society, asked different actors such as researchers, human rights activists, care workers associations, domestic workers associations, and nurses associations for advice on drafting a preliminary version of the National Care Plan.

These actions, while relevant to mitigating the effects of the pandemic and inspiring "new" perspectives of old age, still require time to be able to measure their long-term and quantitative effectiveness. Care studies must consider how far society can go without State participation. What we saw was a tragedy that was perpetrated when eldercare had only civil society to rely on.

References

Agência Brasil (2020) Moradores de favelas movimentam R$ 119,8 bilhões por ano. Agência Brasil, January 27. Retrieved from: https://bit.ly/3aY22Ms Accessed May 3, 2021.

Almeida, Carla and Tatagiba, Luciana (2012) Os conselhos gestores sob o crivo da política: balanços e perspectivas. Serviço Social & Sociedade,109. https://doi.org/10.1590/S0101-66282012000100005 Accessed January 11, 2021.

Associação Brasileira de Saúde Coletiva, ABRASCO (2021) Accessed 4 October 2021. https://www.abrasco.org.br/site/.

Barbosa, Rogério Jerônimo; Ferreira de Souza, Pedro Herculano Guimarães and Soares, Sergei (2020) Distribuição de renda nos anos 2010: Uma década perdida para a desigualdade social e pobreza, Texto para discussão nº 2610. Rio de Janeiro, Brazil: Instituto de Pesquisa Econômica Aplicada.

Beraldo, Paulo (2020) "Não é uma situação alarmante", diz Bolsonaro sobre coronavírus. Estadão de S. Paulo. Retrieved from: https://saude.estadao.com.br/noticias/geral,nao-e-uma-situa-cao-alarmante-diz-bolsonaro-sobre-coronavirus,70003173424 Accessed 4 October, 2021.

BRASIL (2023) Decreto Presidencial nº 11.460 Retrieved from: https://www.in.gov.br/en/web/dou/-/decreto-n-11.460-de-30-de-marco-de-2023-474117782 Accessed February 05, 2024.

Camarano, Ana Amélia (2010) Cuidados de longa duração para os idosa: Um novo risco a ser assumido? Rio de Janeiro, Brazil: Editora Ipea.

Camarano, Ana Amélia (2020) Depending on the income of older adults and the coronavirus: orphans or newly poor? Ciência & Saúde Coletiva, 25(suppl. 2), 4169–4176. https://doi.org/10.1590/1413-812320202510.2.30042020 Accessed October 14, 2021.

Camarano, Ana Amélia and Barbosa, Pamela (2016) Instituições de longa permanência para idosos no Brasil: do que se está falando? In: Alexandre de Oliveira Alcântara, Ana Amélia Camarano and Karla Cristina Giacomin (eds.), Política Nacional do Idoso: velhas e novas questões (pp. 479–514). Rio de Janeiro, Brazil: Editora Ipea.

Castro, Marcia; Kim, Sun; Barberia, Lorena; Freitas Ribeiro, Ana; Gurzenda, Susie; Braga Ribeiro, Karina; Abbott, Erin; Blossom, Jeffrey; Rach, Beatriz Singer; Burton H. (2021) Spatiotemporal pattern of COVID-19 spread in Brazil. Science, 372(6544), 821–826. https://doi.org/10.1126/science.abh1558 Accessed October 14, 2023.

CEPEDISA (2021) Direitos na pandemia: Mapeamento e análise das normas jurídicas de resposta à COVID-19 no Brasil. Bulletin no. 10. São Paulo: Centro de Pesquisas e Estudos do Direito Sanitária; Universidade de São Paulo; Conectas. Retried From: https://cepe-disa.org.br/publicacoes/ Accessed May 3, 2021.

Chaib, Julia and Machado, Renato (2021) CPI mira discursos do governo e levanta 200 falas negacionistas de Bolsonaro. Folha de S. Paulo. Retrieved from: https://www1.folha.uol.com.br/poder/2021/04/cpi-mira-discursos-do-governo-e-levanta-200-falas-negacionistas-de-bolsonaro.shtml Acessed June 10, 2024.

Coronavirus Resource Center, CRC (2021) "Coronavirus Resource Center Online – Johns Hopkins University and Medicine." Retrieved from: https://coronavirus.jhu.edu/ Accessed January 11, 2021.

Debert, Guita Grin (2012 [1999]) A Reinvenção da Velhice: Socialização e reprivatização do envelhecimento. São Paulo, Brazil: EDUSP.

Debert, Guita Grin and Felix, Jorge (2020) Pandemia, idosos e os aspectos socioeconômicos do cuidado: reflexões para o « Pós-COVID ». In: Perspectivas Econômicas para o Pós-pandemia, Boletim Finde – Financialization and Development Research Group, (pp. 83–90). Niterói, Brazil: Federal Fluminense University. Doi: 10.13140/RG.2.2.35677.23526

Felix, Jorge (2019) Economia da Longevidade, o envelhecimento populacional muito além da previdência. São Paulo, Brazil: Editora 106 Ideias.

Felix, Jorge (2023) População brasileira envelhece endividada. Como a reforma tributária mexe com essa dinâmica, The Conversation Brasil. Retrieved from: https://theconversation.com/populacao-brasileira-envelhece-endividada-como-a-reforma-tributaria-mexe-com-essa-dinamica-212840 Accessed January, 30, 2024.

Folha de S. Paulo (2021) "Relembre o que Bolsonaro já disse sobre a pandemia, de gripezinha e país de maricas a frescura e mimimi." Folha de S. Paulo. Retrieved from: https://www1.folha.uol.com.br/poder/2021/03/relembre-o-que-bolsonaro-ja-disse-sobre-a-pandemia-de-gripezinha-e-pais-de-maricas-a-frescura-e-mimimi.shtml Accessed 4 October, 2021.

Frente Nacional de Fortalecimento dos Conselhos dos Direitos da Pessoa Idosa, Belo Horizonte, FFC (2020) I Diagnóstico Nacional dos Conselhos de Direitos da Pessoa Idosa. Retrieved from: https://www.mpma.mp.br/arquivos/CAOPID/I-Diagn%C3%B3stico-Nacional-dos-Conselhos-de-Direitos-da-Pessoa-Idosa.pdf Accessed January 11, 2021.

Fundação Oswaldo Cruz, Fiocruz (2021) Monitoramento de casos de síndrome respiratória aguda grave (SRAG) notificados no SIVEP-Gripe. Rio de Janeiro, Brazil: Oswaldo Cruz Foundation. Retrieved from: http://info.gripe.fiocruz.br/ Accessed: January 11, 2021.

Fundação Oswaldo Cruz, Fiocruz (2021a) Boletim InfoGripe -- Semana Epidemiológica (SE) 14 2021 Retrieved from: https://portal.fiocruz.br/documento/boletim-infogripe-semana-epidemiologica-se-14-2021 Accessed June 10, 2024.

G1 (2020) Bolsonaro diz que 'pequena crise' do coronavírus é 'mais fantasia' e não 'isso tudo' que mídia propaga. G1. Retrieved from: https://g1.globo.com/politica/noti-cia/2020/03/10/bolsonaro-diz-que-questao-do-coronavirus-e-muito-mais-fantasia.ghtml Accessed: 4 October, 2021.

Gomes, Pedro Henrique (2020a) Bolsonaro vê 'exagero' em ações contra coronavírus e faz apelo por reabertura do comércio. G1. Retrieved from: https://g1.globo.com/politica/noti-cia/2020/06/22/bolsonaro-defende-reabertura-do-comercio-e-fala-em-pouco-de-exa-gero-no-trato-da-pandemia.ghtml Accessed 4 October, 2021.

Gomes, Pedro Henrique (2020b) 'Não sou coveiro, tá?', diz Bolsonaro ao responder sobre mortos por coronavírus. G1. Retrieved from: https://g1.globo.com/politica/noticia/2020/04/20/nao-sou-coveiro-ta-diz-bolsonaro-ao-responder-sobre-mortos-por-coronavirus.ghtml Accessed 4 October, 2021.

Graeff, Bibiana (2019) Foundations and Evolution of the Rights of Older Persons in Brazil: A Brief Panorama. Macau Journal of Brazilian Studies, 2(1). Retrieved from: http://aebm.mo/en/2019Vol2Issue1/68 Accessed October 18, 2021.

Human Rights Watch, HRW (2021) World Report 2021: Events of 2020. New York, NY: Human Rights Watch. Retrieved from: https://www.hrw.org/sites/default/files/media_2021/01/2021_hrw_world_report.pdf Accessed 4 October 2021.

Instituto Brasileiro de Geografia e Estatística, IBGE (2021) Projeção da População Brasileira e das Unidades da Federação, National Household Sample Survey for the 4th quar-ter of 2019. Rio de Janeiro, Brazil: Brazilian Institute of Geography and Statistics. Retrieved from: https://www.ibge.gov.br/apps/populacao/projecao/index.html Accessed January 11, 2021.

Legros, Claire (2020) Le souci de L'autre, um retour a l'étique du care, Le Monde, Paris. Retrieved from: https://www.lemonde.fr/idees/article/2020/05/01/le-souci-de-l-autre-un-retour-de-l-ethique-du-care_6038332_3232.html#:~:text=Pour%20une%20%C3%A9thique%20du%20care,hommes%20dans%20de%20nombreux%20m%C3%A9tiers. Accessed February 09, 2024.

Machado, Carla Jorge; Pereira, Claudia Cristina de Aguiar; Viana, Bernardo de Mattos; Oliveira, Graziella Lage; Melo, Daniel Carvalho; Carvalho, Jader Freitas Maciel Garcia; Moraes, Flávia Lanna de; Moraes, Edgar Nunes de (2020) "Estimates of the impact of COVID-19 on morta-lity of institutionalized elderly in Brazil." Ciência & Saúde Coletiva, 25(9), Rio de Janeiro. https://doi.org/10.1590/1413-81232020259.14552020 Accessed October 18, 2021.

Maia, Gustavo and Prazeres, Leandro (2020) Bolsonaro compara Itália a Copacabana e coronavírus a gravidez: 'vai passar.' O Globo. Retrieved from: https://oglobo.globo.com/brasil/bolso-naro-compara-italia-copacabana-coronavirus-gravidez-vai-passar-1-24311233 Accessed 4 October, 2021.

Mazui, Guilherme (2020) 'É simples assim: um manda e o outro obedece', diz Pazuello ao lado de Bolsonaro. G1. Retrieved from: https://g1.globo.com/politica/noticia/2020/10/22/e-simples-assim-um-manda-e-o-outro-obedece-diz-pazuello-ao-lado-de-bolsonaro.ghtml Accessed 4 October 2021.

Naldis, Guilherme (2021) Guedes critica aumento da expectativa de vida: 'Todo mundo quer viver 100 anos'. IG. Retrieved from: https://economia.ig.com.br/2021-04-27/paulo-guedes-aumento-expectativa-de-vida.html

Observatório da Longevidade Humana e Envelhecimento (2021) "Home – OLHE." Accessed 4 October 2021. http://www.olhe.org.br/

O Globo (2020) "Bolsonaro volta a minimizar pandemia e chama COVID-19 de 'gripezinha.'" O Globo. News clip. Retrieved from: https://oglobo.globo.com/brasil/bolso-naro-volta-minimizar-pandemia-chama-COVID-19-de-gripezinha-1-24319177 Accessed 4 October, 2021.

Organisation for Economic Co-operation and Development, OECD (2021) "Population Data Online." Retrieved from: https://data.oecd.org/ Accessed January 11, 2021.

Planalto (2020) Pronunciamento do presidente da República, Jair Bolsonaro (24/03/2020). Video, 4:58. Retrieved from: https://www.youtube.com/watch?v=Vl_DYb-XaAE Accessed 4 October 2021.

Record TV Goiás (2021) Absurdo: idosa é agredida por ter saído de casa. Video, 3:00. Retrieved From: https://www.youtube.com/watch?v=7bNwpybq3Jw Accessed 4 October 2021.

The Lancet (2020) COVID-19 in Brazil: 'So What?'. Editorial. *The Lancet*, 395(10235), 1461. https://doi.org/10.1016/S0140-6736(20)31095-3 Accessed October 18, 2021.

Todos pela Saúde, TPS (2021) Accessed 4 October 2021. https://www.todospelasaude.org/.

UOL (2021a) Bolsonaro volta a falar em 'histórico de atleta' e pesquisador rebate. UOL. Retrieved from: https://noticias.uol.com.br/saude/ultimas-noticias/redacao/2021/03/22/bolsonaro-volta-a-falar-em-historico-de-atleta-e-pesquisador-rebate.htm Accessed 4 October, 2021.

UOL (2021b) Manaus: Coordenador de UTI desabafa sobre ineficácia do tratamento precoce. UOL. Retrieved from: https://noticias.uol.com.br/saude/ultimas-noticias/redacao/2021/01/15/manaus-coordenador-de-uti-desabafa-sobre-ineficacia-do-tratamento-precoce.htm Accessed 4 October, 2021.

Uribe, Gustavo (2020) Mesmo após 6.513 mortes, Bolsonaro diz que crise do coronavírus 'não é isso tudo que dizem. Folha de S. Paulo. Retrieved from: https://www1.folha.uol.com.br/poder/2020/03/mesmo-apos-6513-mortes-bolsonaro-diz-que-crise-do-coronavirus-nao-e-isso-tudo-que-dizem.shtml Accessed 4 October 2021.

Valfré, Vinícios (2020) Bolsonaro volta a criticar 'alarmismo' e diz que Brasil não pode ser comparado à Itália. Estadão de S. Paulo. Retrieved from: https://saude.estadao.com.br/noticias/geral,bolsonaro-e-mandetta-fazem-reuniao-com-prefeitos-para-falar-sobre-coronavi-rus,70003243457 Accessed 4 October, 2021.

Weterman, Daniel (2020) Bolsonaro diz que vai pedir ao Ministério da Saúde isolamento só para idosos e pessoas com doenças. Estadão de S. Paulo. Retrieved from: https://saude.estadao.com.br/noticias/geral,bolsonaro-diz-que-vai-pedir-ao-ministerio-da-saude-isolamento-so-para-idosos-e-pessoas-com-doencas,70003247093 Accessed 4 October, 2021.

Woodward, Kathleen. A public secret: assisted living, caregivers, globalization. *International Journal of Ageing and Later Life*, 2012 7(2), pp.17–51.

Index

Printed in the United States
by Baker & Taylor Publisher Services